A Concise Dictionary of Philosophy

A Concise Dictionary of Philosophy

K. Srinivas
Vempaty Kutumba Sastry

D.K. Printworld (P) Ltd.
New Delhi

Cataloging in Publication Data — DK
[Courtesy: D.K. Agencies (P) Ltd. <docinfo@dkagencies.com>]

Srinivas, K. (Kunchapudi), 1955-
A concise dictionary of philosophy / by
K. Srinivas, V. Kutumba Sastry.
xi, 426 p.; 23 cm.
ISBN 8124604002

1. Philosophy — Dictionaries. I. Kutumba Sastry, V. (Vempaty), 1950-, joint author. II. Title.

DDC 103 22

ISBN 81-246-0400-2 (Hardbound)
ISBN 81-246-0401-0 (Paperback)
First published in India in 2007

Published and printed by:
D.K. Printworld (P) Ltd.
Regd. Office: 'Sri Kunj', F-52, Bali Nagar
Ramesh Nagar Metro Station
New Delhi-110 015
Phones: (011) 2545-3975; 2546-6019; *Fax*: (011) 2546-5926
E-mail: dkprintworld@vsnl.net
Website: www.dkprintworld.com

Dedicated to

Prof. R. Balasubramanian

Foreword

It gives me deep pleasure to write these lines as Foreword to *A Concise Dictionary of Philosophy* which has been co-authored by Professor V. Kutumba Sastry and Professor K. Srinivas. Both are very distinguished scholars and quite familiar with the philosophy as developed in India and Europe. The subjects covered in this well-researched volume contain many entries which are central to the discipline of philosophy but, strictly speaking, not parts of it in the received sense. Some entries from the disciplines very close to philosophy have been thoughtfully included in this dictionary. I can well imagine the pains that the authors of this admirable volume have taken to produce it.

I am not aware of any other dictionary in India which is comparable in quality and scope to this really comprehensive work. I have the pleasure of knowing both the authors of this dictionary and am aware of their acuity of intellect and dedication to the subject. I am also very happy to note that this dictionary has been dedicated to Professor R. Balasubramanian who is an outstanding philosopher of our country and well known for his many-sided scholarship and familiarity with the current philosophical systems of the East and the West.

This book, I am sure, will be received well by the academia and prove very useful to the scholars, students and the reading public interested in knowing about the disciplines of philosophy in its broad and modern sense.

I take this opportunity to thank heartily the authors of this well-researched and valuable reference book.

April 15, 2006

D.P. Chattopadhyaya
Chairman
Indian Philosophical Congress

Preface

THE preparation of a dictionary like this would amount to performing an *yajña*. Just as the performance of an *yajña* is intended to do good to everyone (*lokakalyāṇa*), the preparation of a dictionary is intended to promote conceptual clarity. In the absence of conceptual clarity our understanding of the subject-matter in question remains opaque and blurred. The concepts of philosophy in general have many connotations. For instance, the concept of *dharma* is understood as ethical merit, as duty, as principle of motion, as *karma* and so on. Therefore, the sense in which a concept is used, by and large, is context-dependent. Yet, we assign primary or general meaning to the concepts, for otherwise they look empty. The purpose of this dictionary is to highlight the general as well as the intended meaning of a concept in a definite context. This is the reason why lexicography has been treated as an empirical science by W.V. Quine. Normally the intended meaning of a concept is highlighted through the philosophy of a thinker or through the philosophy of a particular school of thought. Keeping this in mind we have given equal importance to the concepts, to the various schools of thought, and to the philosophies of the most prominent thinkers of the Orient as well as the Occident. In the process of preparing a glossary to this work we might have missed some of the most important concepts, philosophies, and philosophers. Such omissions are purely the result of an oversight but not of deliberate choice.

The entries in this work are basically arranged in an alphabetical order. The use of diacritical marks to Sanskrit expressions does not make any difference to the original order, but it makes all the difference to the way in which an expression is pronounced. With the exception of expressions rooted in the English language, for all other expressions their root language is given within brackets. For instance, the letter 'S' represents the Sanskrit root of an expression, the letters 'Gk' represent the Greek root of an expression. The details of these abbreviations are separately given. At the end a glossary of frequently used foreign expressions with meanings is given for the benefit of the reader(s).

KS & VKS

November, 2006.

How to Use

THE present work consists of several entries. Some of the entries are derived from their etymological roots. Against such entries, excepting English, the language from which the entry is derived is indicated with the help of alphabets. The following alphabets signify the respective languages:

C	Chinese
F	French
Gk	Greek
Gr	German
H	Hebrew
L	Latin
Pl	Pāli
Pr	Prākṛt
S	Sanskrit
T	Tamil

Key to Transliteration

अ *a* (but)	ङ *ṅa* (sing)[1]	न *na* (numb)[4]
आ *ā* (mom)	च *ca* (chunk)[2]	प *pa* (spin)[5]
इ *i* (it)	छ* *cha* (catch him)[2]	फ* *pha* (loophole)[5]
ई *ī* (beet)	ज *ja* (john)[2]	ब *ba* (bin)[5]
उ *u* (put)	झ *jha* (hedgehog)[2]	भ *bha* (abhor)[5]
ऊ *ū* (pool)	ञ *ña* (bunch)[2]	म *ma* (much)[5]
ऋ *ṛ* (rhythm)	ट *ṭa* (start)[3]	य *ya* (young)
ए *e* (play)	ठ* *ṭha* (anthill)[3]	र *ra* (drama)
ऐ *ai* (high)	ड *ḍa* (dart)[3]	ल *la* (luck)
ओ *o* (toe)	ढ* *ḍha* (godhead)[3]	व *va* (vile)
औ *au* (loud)	ण *ṇa* (under)[3]	श *śa* (shove)
क *ka* (skate)[1]	त *ta* (path)[4]	ष *ṣa* (bushel)
ख* *kha* (blokhead)[1]	थ *tha* (thunder)[4]	स *sa* (so)
ग *ga* (gate)[1]	द *da* (that)[4]	ह *ha* (hum)
घ *gha* (loghut)[1]	ध* *dha* (breathe)[4]	

° *ṁ anusvāra* (nasalisation of preceding vowel)

: *ḥ visarga* (aspiration of preceding vowel)

* No exact English equivalents for these letters.

[1] guttural [2] palatal [3] lingual [4] dental
[5] labial

A

A fortiori (L) : This expression stands for "stronger reason." Any idea or opinion that is arrived at with stronger reason is said to be a fortiori.

A posteriori (L) : It is the knowledge that is derived from experience. According to Kant, mere a posteriori knowledge is not universal and necessary, although it provides us with new information about reality. Similarly, Neo-Positivists hold the view that propositions of natural sciences are a posteriori in nature. They do not make any distinction, unlike Kant, between synthetic and a posteriori.

A priori (L) : It is knowledge obtained prior to experience (sense-experience). In Kant's philosophy, a priori is the hallmark of necessity. Such necessity can never be explained in terms of experience. Both rationalists and empiricists are unanimous in claiming that analytical propositions are a priori. Thus the propositions of logic and mathematics are claimed to be a priori by Neo-Positivists.

Abādhita (S) : It is a state of experience wherein the object of experience cannot be contradicted by subsequent experience. According to Advaita, the valid knowledge (*pramā*) can never be contradicted. The world of objects may appear to be real, but it may render to be illusory when it is contradicted by the knowledge of *Brahman*, which is *abādhita*.

Abandonment : This expression is used by atheistic existentialists to explain the existential situation of a human individual. According to them, a human individual is thrown into this world. This state of human individual is called "abandonment." Since there is no God to interfere in the day-to-day affairs of humankind, every human individual has to take his/her own decisions, and should be in a position to distinguish right from wrong.

Abdera, School of : It was an ancient Greek school started by Democritus. The other members of the school were Metrodorus of Chios and Anaxarcus of Abdera, the teacher of Pyrrho the sceptic. Later on the school leadership fell into the hands of Pyrrho.

Abduction : It is a syllogism in Aristotle's logic in which the major premise is certain, but the minor premise is only probable. According to C.S. Pierce, it is a type of inference that yields an explanatory hypothesis rather than a result of deductive application of a "rule" or a "case." In philosophy of science, abduction signifies the canons of reason for the discovery of scientific theories or hypotheses as opposed to justification of theories. Contrary to this view, Hans Reichenbach made a distinction between "the context of discovery" and "the context of justification." According to him, philosophy as such is concerned with the latter, but not with the former.

Abelard, Peter or Abailard, Pierre (1079 – 1144) : He was a medieval French theologian who made use of logical techniques in his famous work *Theologia Christiana* (1124) to explain Christian dogmas. In his other logical works such as *Logica Ingredientibus*, and *Dilectica*, Abelard developed a novel theory of signification of words and sentences by making use of Aristotle's views on interpretation and the commentaries of Boethius on it. Abelard's theory distinguishes the signification of an expression from what the expression means and the idea in the mind of the speaker that is associated with the expression. According to him, propositions are sentences that are either true or false.

Ābhāsavāda (S) : It is known as the "theory of appearance." This theory is advocated by the Advaitins, according to which the individual soul (*jīva*) is an illusory appearance of *Brahman*.

Ābhāsvaras (S) : It means "the lustrous ones." They are the gods of higher spiritual realm. In Śiva's retinue, there are sixty-four deities.

Abhāva (S) : It means "non-existence." It is one of the independent categories recognized by the schools like Nyāya, Vaiśeṣika, Bhāṭṭa Mīmāṁsā, and Dvaita. But, Buddhism, Prābhākara Mīmāṁsā, and Viśiṣṭādvaita schools do not accept the view that *abhāva* is an independent category. The following are the types of *abhāva*.

(a) *Prāg-abhāva* or prior non-existence is a view, according to which a thing before coming into existence was non-existent. For example, a pot was non-existent before it came into existence.

(b) *Pradhvaṁsa-abhāva* or annihilative non-existence is a view, according to which a thing is non-existing after its destruction, for example, a pot cannot exist as pot after its destruction.

(c) *Atyanta-abhāva* or absolute non-existence is a view, according to which a thing is absolutely non-existing. For example, absence of pot on the floor or ground.

(d) *Anyonya-abhāva* or one object not being another is a view, according to which the distinction or difference between one object and the other is possible because no object is identical with the other. For example, a chair is not a table. Thus "chair-ness" is not found in a table, likewise "table-ness" is not found in a chair.

Abheda (S) : It means "non-distinction or non-difference." According to Advaita Vedānta, there is no distinction between *Brahman* and *ātman*.

Abhidhamma (Pl) : They are the part of the Buddhist Pāli scriptures that deal with the various doctrines of Buddhism like *sutta* in a scholastic or technical manner. They are known for their systematic presentation of the major conceptual categories of Buddhism. They are catechetical in form.

Abhihitānvayavāda (S) : It is also known as "the theory of restructuring of the spoken." According to Bhāṭṭa Mīmāṁsā, words have their independent meanings. When the words are properly arranged in a sentence their meaning is restructured in a way that it expresses one single connected idea.

Abhinava-anyathā-khyāti (S) : It is also known as "the neo-theory of apprehension otherwise." This theory of error was advocated by Dvaita Vedānta. According to this theory, the error is the resultant effect of *asat-khyāti* and *anyathā-khyāti.* In *asat-khyāti,* the object of erroneous cognition is considered to be unreal and in *anyathā-khyāti,* the object of error appears to be something other than what it is. In this way, what is seen in erroneous cognition is unreal, but the substance in which it occurs is real.

Abhinavagupta (c. 975 – 1025) : He was a philosopher and an aesthetician. He represents Kāśmīrī school of Śaivism. Abhinavagupta shows indifference to the reality of *māyā,* although he did not reject its reality. There are parallels between Kāśmīrī Śaivism and Advaita Vedānta. But the former is sectarian in its origin, for it holds that Śiva is the ultimate reality and *māyā* is his power. Abhinavagupta has more than forty works to his credit. The most important of those are *Abhinavabhāratī; Dhvanyāloka; Paramārthasāra; Pratyabhijñāvimarśinī.*

Abhiniveśa (S) : It means "self-love or will to love." According to Sāṁkhya, *abhiniveśa* is a form of *avidyā* or ignorance. The other forms of *avidyā* are fear, attachment and aversion.

Abhyāsa (S) : It is a practice of repeating either words or an idea to get it fixed in the mind. It is one of the signs (*ṣaḍvidhaliṅga*) that determine the purport of a Vedāntic text.

Ability : In its general sense, ability is psychic capacity of an individual that regulates his/her behaviour and serves as the best condition for his/her actions. Senses are regarded as the most important ontogenetic abilities of human beings.

Absolute : The term "Absolute" is often ascribed to various categories of existence (physical as well as metaphysical) such as certainty, knowledge, truth, space & time, God, to denote the final and immutable status of anything in question. In other words, Absolute is something that defies the conditions, qualifications, and relations. For example, in the system of Vedānta, *Brahman* is considered to be the Absolute. It is one, single reality. It cannot be compared with anything external to it. Thus the term "Absolute" signifies perfection, completeness, universality, non-relativity. Absolute is that which is ineffable, unthinkable, and indeterminable. For further details, see Śaṅkara's Advaita, Parmenides' doctrine of monism, Spinoza's pantheism, and Hegel's Absolute Idealism.

Absolute ego : In Fichte's philosophy, the term "absolute ego" refers to that ego or Subject that exists prior to its differentiation into an empirical or historical self and non-self.

Absolutism : It is a philosophical doctrine that is opposed to any form of relativism. In epistemology, it proclaims that knowledge is absolute and objective. For example, in Cartesian philosophy, the knowledge of innate ideas is universal, necessary, and indubitable. Hence such knowledge is absolute. In metaphysics/ ontology, this doctrine claims that reality is one and immutable. In Hegel's idealism, reality is the Absolute Spirit or Idea. In ethics, this doctrine insists that values are objectively real and absolute.

Absolute Personalism : It is nothing but the ascription of personality to the Absolute. For example, the ultimate reality *Brahman* is personified as the Lord Śrī Viṣṇu in Viśiṣṭādvaita.

Absorption : It is one of the rules of equivalence. This rule takes the following argument form.

$$\frac{p \supset q}{p \supset (p \,\&\, q)}$$

Abstract : It is an expression used by Hegel to designate a relation, a condition or a state of knowledge that is one-sided, partial, and separate from the total context of relations that essentially define (determine) it. This expression is opposed to the expression "concrete."

Abstract Labour Time : It is a concept used by Karl Marx to denote the basic measure of commodity's exchange value. It refers to the amount of time invested in the production of the commodity including the amount of basic labour that is required to sustain and produce skilled labour.

Abstracta : They are neutral and purely denotative entities such as qualities, numbers, relations, logical concepts that do not appear directly or literally in space and time.

Abstraction : It is one of the powers of the human mind through which the mind tries to isolate or separate one particular quality from other qualities for a special attention. In other words, it is a process that ideally separates a partial aspect or quality from a total object. John Locke recognized the importance of abstract general ideas (concepts) in the use of language. The essential features of various particulars or individuals are grouped together under one class to form a concept. This is possible only through the method of abstraction. For example, the concept "man" is an abstract general idea. It encompasses the entire human race irrespective of the differences in the accidental features among the humans.

Abstractionism : It is nothing but an illegitimate use of abstraction wherein abstractions are mistaken for concrete realities. For details see Whitehead's "the fallacy of misplaced concreteness."

Absurdity : In its general sense, absurdity is nothing but a palpable falsity that stands in contrast to common sense or reason. For example, it is absurd to conceive a "round-square," for an entity cannot be both round and square. It is a logical absurdity.

Academy of Plato : It was an ancient philosophical school started by Plato near Athens. The Pythagorean influence was so conspicuous on Plato's Academy from its condition that those who do not know mathematics should not enter the Academy. The Academy was started between 387 – 385 BCE.

Accent : It is a verbal fallacy resulting from wrong emphasis on some part of a sentence. For example, in the sentence "Sruti thinks that Sriram will win the race," if emphasis is laid on "Sruti," then it amounts to saying that no one except "Sruti" thinks so; if emphasis is laid on "thinks," then it amounts to saying that the opinion is not held with much conviction.

Accident : In Aristotle's logic, accident denotes any attribute that is predicated of a subject. For example, in the sentence "Socrates is wise," the term "wise" is attributed to Socrates, the subject of the sentence. An accident is something that is not universal, necessary, and essential.

Accidentalism : It is a doctrine according to which some events are undetermined, or that the incidence of a series of determined events is unpredictable. It is a form of indeterminism wherein chance or contingency has its role to play.

Acervus Argument : It is a form of sophistical argument that tries to establish the view that given any number of stones which cannot make a heap, one does not obtain a heap by adding one more to it. Yet, eventually, if this process is continued one has a heap.

Achilles Argument : It is one of the arguments advanced by Zeno against the possibility of motion. According to him, Achilles, the fastest runner in Greece, could not catch the proverbially slow tortoise. The alleged grounds for this are that during time $t_1 \ldots t_2$, which it takes Achilles to traverse the distance between his position and that of the tortoise at time t_1, the latter even with its slow pace would have moved on a finite distance farther. See Zeno's paradoxes.

Acintya Bhedābheda (S) : It is one of the schools of Vedānta according to which the *jīva* is both different and non-different from *Brahman* or God (Īśvara). But this conception is rationally inexplicable. However, it can be realized by practising *bhakti.* Although there is a difference between *jīva* and *Brahman* or God, the difference is highly indiscernible. Caitanya is one of the exponents of this theory. Nimbārka advocated *svabhāva bhedābheda.*

Acosmism : It is a theory according to which there is no external or physical world. Acosmism is a form of subjective idealism. The champions of such a view are Vijñānavāda school of Buddhism and George Berkeley.

Acquaintance, Knowledge by : Bertrand Russell in his *The Problems of Philosophy* (1912) made a distinction between knowledge by acquaintance and knowledge by description. According to him, the immediate data of our experience (hard-data) provide us with the knowledge of acquaintance.

Acrasia or Akrasia (Gk) : This expression stands for "weakness of the will." Aristotle distinguished a man who is morally weak (*akrates*) from a man who can resist the temptation of sensuous pleasures (*enkrates*).

Acroamatic : They are the teachings communicated to the students orally. This expression was applied to the private teachings of Aristotle to his select advanced students.

Act : In Scholasticism, it is something that perfects or determines the character of a thing. For instance, rationality perfects animality. In ethics, an act is a result of moral will of the agent.

Action at a Distance : It is an idea that explains how certain physical objects affect or influence other physical objects without having any mechanical contact between them. Gravitational pull is the best example for an action at a distance.

Activism : According to this doctrine, reality (natural as well as social) can be explained in terms of action or *praxis.* In opposition to intellectualism, activism emphasizes that action precedes intellect. For example, Pūrva Mīmāṁsā, the orthodox school of Indian philosophy, and Marxism advocate the philosophy of activism.

Actuality : In Aristotle's metaphysics, actuality is a concept that denotes change in being. Actuality tries to explain the concept of motion from the state of potentiality to actuality. According to Husserl, it is an effective individual existence in space and time as contrasted with mere possibility.

Acyutaprekṣa (c. twelfth century CE) : He was the teacher of Madhvācārya. Acyutaprekṣa, during the last phase of his life, got convinced by the doctrines advocated by Madhvācārya, namely, Dvaita Vedānta.

Adaptation : It is a process of quick adjustment to the conditions of external or internal environment. Both the scientists and sociologists use this concept. In science, a rational interpretation of adaptation as the outcome of the struggle for existence was first explained by Darwin in his *The Origin of Species* (1859).

Addition : It is one of the rules of inference. This rule takes the following argument form.

$$\frac{P}{pVq}$$

Additive and Non-additive : They are the concepts that reflect the types of relationship between a whole and its parts. Additivity is the relation according to which a whole is nothing but a sum total of its parts; whereas non-additivity is the relation according to which a whole is more than the sum total of its parts. By and large, it is admitted that mechanical wholes are the result of the process of additivity, and organic wholes are of non-additivity.

Ad hoc hypothesis : It is a hypothesis that serves as an explanation for one event or one set of events. In other words, it is a dubious assumption or argument or theory arbitrarily introduced as an explanation after the fact.

Adeism : Max Müller coined this term. Adeism does not accept the existence of *deva*s or gods of ancient India. It is similar to atheism, which denies the existence of God in any form.

Adequate evidence : In epistemology, every claim to knowledge has to be supported by adequate evidence. For example, there is adequate evidence to say that the planet Earth is round.

Adequation : According to Husserl, it is nothing but verification or fulfilment.

Adharma (S) : It means "vice" or "sin." It is opposite of the term *dharma*. In Jainism, *adharma* is used in a technical sense. It represents the principle of non-motion. But in its general sense, *adharma* is that which goes against the accepted norms of moral virtue and duty. This is how it is interpreted by the orthodox systems of Indian philosophy.

Adhikārin (S) : This expression refers to any competent person who is eligible to take up the study of the Vedānta or any important text. Such a person should possess purity of mind through the performance of his ordained duties.

Adhiṣṭhāna (S) : It means "support" or "base." The ground or the base on which something else is falsely superimposed is called *adhiṣṭhāna*. For example, snake is at times superimposed on a rope which is termed as *adhiṣṭhāna*.

Adhyāsa (S) : It means "superimposition." It is an imposition of a quality or an attribute on a thing that does not belong to the thing. *Adhyāsa* is of two kinds: (1) *svarūpa-adhyāsa*, and (2) *saṁsarga-adhyāsa*. In the case of the former, something illusory is superimposed on something real. For example, the superimposition of illusory silver on a shell is known as *svarūpa-adhyāsa*. In the case of the latter, an attribute is superimposed on the object.

Adhyātma (S) : This term refers to the absolute in the *Bhagavad-Gītā*. Emerson equates this expression with "over soul." For details, see his essay "The Over Soul."

Adiaphora (Gk) : It is a Stoic term that refers to those entities that are morally indifferent.

Adicto secundum quid ad dictum simpliciter (L) : It is a formal fallacy that occurs when a rule that is formed under special circumstances is applied to general cases ignoring the fact that such a rule is framed under special circumstances. For instance, during the time of war soldiers can indulge in the destruction of life and property of the enemies. But it is not allowed during the time of peace.

Adicto simpliciter ad dictum secundum quid (L) : It is a non-verbal fallacy that occurs when a general rule is applied to a special case without taking special circumstances into consideration. For instance, it is a general rule that killing human beings is a crime. On this count, however, a soldier cannot be condemned to death because he killed his enemy in the war.

Ādigranth : It is also called *Granth Sāhib*. It is the sacred book of the Sikhs. It was installed in the Golden Temple at Amritsar in 1604.

Adler, Alfred (1870-1937) : He was a follower of the Austrian psychoanalyst Sigmund Freud. Adler started his own school in Vienna in the year 1912. Unlike Freud, Adler tried to minimise the role of sexuality to explain the human behaviour and emphasized more on the ego. He investigated into the feelings of inferiority resulting from organic abnormality and deficiency and described the unconscious attempt of the ego to compensate such defects. Adler extended the concept of "inferiority complex" to include psychological and physical deficiencies and stressed the tendency of "compensation" to lead to over-correction. His important works are *Study of Organic Inferiority and Its Psychological Compensations* (1907); *The Neurotic Constitution* (1912); *Problems of Neurosis* (1930).

Adoptionism : It was a Christological doctrine prominent in Spain during the eighth century CE. According to this doctrine, Christ being a human was the son of God by adoption only. The Church condemned such teaching.

Advaita (S) : It means "non-dualism." The doctrine of Advaita does not distinguish between *Brahman* and the essential nature of the *jīva*, namely, *ātman*. Advaita is as old as the Upaniṣads. However, the philosophy of Advaita Vedānta became very popular because of Śaṅkara's *Brahmasūtra-Bhāṣya* on Bādarāyaṇa's *Brahmasūtra* or *Vedāntasūtra*. A few centuries before Śaṅkara, the Vijñānavādins and the Mādhyamika Buddhists called their reality non-dual (*advaya*). The Prajñāpāramitā literature that existed even before the birth of Christ, frequently used the expression "non-dual." Bhartṛhari (sixth century CE) developed the *sphoṭa* theory, as an independent thinker, in his famous work *Vākyapadīya* along the non-dualistic lines. Gauḍapāda, the grand teacher of Śaṅkara, in his *Māṇḍūkya-Kārikā* used the language similar to that of Vijñānavāda Buddhism, and even incorporated some of its ideas. The logical significance of *māyā* was already clarified by the Buddhists in terms of four-cornered negation (*catuśloki*). Gauḍapāda and after him the followers of Advaita tradition incorporated it. Nāgārjuna maintained that from the ultimate point of view, the world is neither born, nor exists nor disappears (*ajātivāda*). Gauḍapāda incorporated it in his Vedānta developed out of the *Māṇḍūkya Upaniṣad*. The forms of the world are illusory like hallucinations. They are the creation of *māyā-avidyā*. They are mere forms of flux appearing as Being. But, Gauḍapāda did not develop his ideas further. The task of developing the system was left to Śaṅkara, who is regarded as the greatest dialectician of the school. He heavily relied on the *prasthānatraya* (the Upaniṣads, the *Brahmasūtra*, and the *Bhagavad-Gītā*). According to Śaṅkara, *Brahman* is the one and only reality. It is *nirguṇa, niravayava,* and *nirviśeṣa*. The world of objects or forms is only a projection of *māyā*. Therefore it is *mithyā*. However, it is *bhāva-rūpa* for it is experienced. According to Advaita, there are three basic levels of reality. They are *prātibhāsika* or phenomenal, *vyāvahārika* or empirical and *pāramārthika* or absolute. The greatness of Śaṅkara lies in his attempt to resolve the problem of the One and many with the help of the explanatory concept of *māyā*. The essential nature of *jīva* is non-different from *Brahman*. Thus, there is no difference between *Brahman* and *ātman*.

Adventitious Ideas : In opposition to innate ideas, adventitious ideas come from without, from the objects outside the mind. In fact, Descartes' ontological argument for the existence of God is developed on the notion of adventitious ideas.

Aeon : According to Gnostics, it is a subordinate heavenly power derived from the Supreme Being by a process of emanation. The totality of *aeons* formed the spiritual world, which is regarded as intermediary between the Deity and the material world of sense objects, which is considered to be evil.

Aesthetics : It is a branch of philosophy that deals with the theories of beauty and appreciation. Aesthetics includes the study of art forms and the criticism of principles of art forms. The term "aesthetics" was first introduced by the German thinker Baumgarten around 1750 to imply the science of sensuous knowledge, whose aim is beauty. But the term "aesthetics" is not quite appropriate to the study of beauty as there are many forms of beauty that are more than sensual and appeal to imagination and feeling as well. In Kant's philosophy the expression "transcendental aesthetic" does not refer to aesthetic appreciation of beauty, but is concerned with space and time as forms of intuition.

Aetiology : It is an inquiry into causes of various phenomena.

Affect : It is an inner motive as distinguished from the intention or end of action.

Affective : It is the generic character supposedly shared by pleasure, pain and the emotions as distinguished from the ideational or volitional aspects of consciousness.

Affirmation : It is an act of asserting that something is the case or not the case.

Affirmation of the Consequent : It is a fallacious inference from B and $A \supset B$ to A. The law of the affirmation of the consequent is the theorem of the prepositional calculus. It has the following form.

$$q \supset (p \; \& \; q)$$

Affirmative : An affirmative sentence is a sentence in which there is no negative participle. For example, "All lions are carnivorous"; "All cows are herbivorous."

African Philosophy : It is the philosophy of Africa that represents the native cultures of Africa. In its traditional form it is unwritten, for there is no authoritative individual work, barring Ethiopian philosophy, on African philosophy representing the native cultures of Africa. This led to the widespread belief among the intellectuals that there is no philosophy called African philosophy. However, it is a mistake to think that a country or continent exists without any philosophy. It may not be in the limelight due to some obvious reasons. African philosophy is one such subject that is not properly dealt with by the writers on philosophy. Like any other philosophy, it has its own conception of nature, man's place in nature, and man's relation to nature. At times, African philosophy is characterized as ethno-philosophy or folk-philosophy. Such a label is attached to African philosophy for it is committed to a set of monolithic ideas or beliefs held by the whole community. Thus there is no scope for any individualistic elements in the traditional thought. The traditional philosophy of Africa finds its expression in literature, religion, rituals, beliefs, symbols, customs, folklore, and traditions.

Āgama (S) : Āgama literature is a part of Hinduism. Although the Āgamas do not belong to the Vedic tradition, they are treated as authoritative by their followers. There are Śaiva (*pāśupata*), Vaiṣṇava (*pāñcarātra*), and Śākta (*tantra*) Āgamas. It is believed that the Āgama literature belonged to the first century CE.

Agent : In moral philosophy, an agent is a person who is acting, or has acted, or is contemplating an action. A moral agent is one who is free and responsible. He must possess maturity, rationality, and sensitivity, which normal human beings are said to have. Moral philosophy's basic concern is to determine when such an agent is morally good or virtuous, when morally bad or vicious or alternatively, when he is acting rightly and when wrongly, when virtuously, when viciously.

Aggregate : In its general sense, it is a collection, a totality, a whole, a class, a group, a sum, an agglomeration, a cluster, a mass, an amount, or a quality of something with certain definite characteristics in each case. In logic, an aggregate refers to a collection, a manifold, a multiplicity, a set, satisfying a given condition. According to Cantor, an aggregate is any collection of separate objects of thought gathered into a whole.

Agnoiology (Gk) : The terms "agnoiology" and "epistemology" were coined by J.F. Ferrier (1854) as connoting distinctive areas of philosophical inquiry in support of ontology. Agnoiology is the doctrine of ignorance, which seeks to determine what we are necessarily ignorant of. It is a critique of agnosticism. Ignorance is defined in relation to knowledge since one cannot be ignorant of anything that cannot possibly be known.

Ahaṁkāra (S) : It refers to sense of "I" or "I-ness" or "mineness." According to Advaita, it is one of the functions of *antaḥkaraṇa* or internal organ that appropriates both objects and knowledge of objects.

Ahiṁsā (S) : It means "non-injury." It is one of the fundamental mottos of Jainism, Buddhism, and Hinduism. In Jaina ethics, avoidance of injury to life plays an important role. The Jaina attitude to *ahiṁsā* is the logical outcome of their metaphysical theory of the potential equality of all souls and recognition of the principle of reciprocity. *Ahiṁsā* is part of *yama*, which is one of the limbs of eightfold means of Yoga.

Aitareya Upaniṣad (S) : This Upaniṣad belongs to the *jñāna-kāṇḍa* of the *Ṛgveda*. It provides us with a semi-mythological account of creation. According to this interpretation, *ātman* correlates both with the microcosm and the macrocosm, and the gods are created as psycho-physical principles. This Upaniṣad holds that all our mental functions are only the names of our rational consciousness, which is none other than *Brahman* (*prajñānam brahma*).

Ajaḍa (S) : It means "non-static." There are two types of immaterial substances according to Viśiṣṭādvaita. They are: external (*parāk*), and internal (*pratyak*). The former is of two kinds, namely, eternal manifestation (*nitya-vibhūti*), and attributive consciousness (*dharma-bhūta-jñāna*). The internal is also classified into two types. They are: individual self (*jīva*) and god (*īśvara*).

Ajahal-lakṣaṇā (S) : It means "non-exclusive application." When a coherent idea is not conveyed by the primary meaning of a sentence, its secondary meaning is taken into consideration. However, primary meaning of a sentence is not totally rejected, but is retained, and something more is added to that by implied meaning. For example, the sentence "The white is beautiful" signifies the beauty of the white cow. The primary meaning of the word "white" is retained, and the implied meaning is added to that to refer to "white cow."

Ajātaśatru (S) : He was one of the Upaniṣadic personages. He taught his pupil Gārgya that *ātman* is experienced in the deep sleep (*suṣupti*), and the world comes out of *ātman* in deep sleep. Prior to this teaching, Gārgya was under the impression that *ātman* was an external object like the sun, moon, lightning, ether, space, fire, mirror, echo, shadow, and body.

Ajātivāda (S) : This theory is associated with Gauḍapāda. According to this theory, there is no causal change. In other words, anything that is non-existing in the beginning is non-existing in the middle, and even at the end. Therefore, it is totally non-existing.

Ajitakeśakambali (c. fifth century BC) : He was a non-believer or *nāstika* and a *lokāyata*, who held that every object is just a combination of the four material elements (earth, water, fire, and air). There is no rebirth of the individuals after death.

Ajīva (S) : In Jaina philosophy, *ajīva* refers to unconscious non-spirit. It includes not only matter (*pudgaḷa*), but also space (*ākāśa*), motion (*dharma*), rest or non-motion (*adharma*), and time (*kāla*). These unconscious non-spirits are without life. Matter is technically called *pudgaḷa*. It is liable to both integration and disintegration. Time is *anāstikāya* because it does not extend in space. It is infinite. Like time, space is also infinite, eternal, and imperceptible. *Dharma* and *adharma* are used in their technical sense representing the conditions of motion and non-motion respectively. Like space and time, they are also eternal and imperceptible.

Ākāṅkṣā (S) : It is one of the material conditions to bring about valid cognition from a given proposition. Words in a proposition must have expectancy with each other in order to fulfil this criterion. In other words, the meaning of every word of the sentence must be capable of anticipating the meanings of the other words. For example, when I say merely "eats" the hearer anticipates my answering the questions: "Who eats?" "When does he eat?" and so on. Thus each part of the sentence anticipates others and what is anticipated must be significant.

Ākāśa (S) : In Indian philosophical systems *ākāśa* is translated as "ether" or "space." Jainism treats *ākāśa* as one of the *ajīvas*. It is finite, eternal, and imperceptible. According to Vaiśeṣika, *ākāśa* is one among the nine substances (*dravyas*) infinite, eternal and one. It is viewed as a continuum, which is postulated in connection with *paramāṇus*.

Akhaṇḍākāra-vṛtti-jñāna (S) : It is known as modal cognition through which *Brahman* is apprehended. It leads to the direct knowledge of the Self (*ātman*), according to Advaita. This is the resultant effect of the mental mode, the object of which is bereft of attributes (*Brahman*). This modification (*vṛtti*) is known as *antya-vṛtti*.

Akhaṇḍārtha-vākya (S) : It is known as an identity statement. In this type of statement, both the subject and the object refer to the same entity. Though the subject-word and object-word have their own meanings, they refer to the same entity. For example, the words in the *mahāvākya*, "That thou art" (*tat tvam asi*) refer to the same entity.

Akṣara (S) : Anything that is imperishable is called *akṣara*. It is a descriptive synonym for *Brahman*, the Supreme Reality. It also means "syllable."

Alain's Formula : Sartre refers to this formula in his *Being and Nothingness*. According to this formula, "knowing is knowing that one knows." Epistemologists did not accept this as the right interpretation of knowledge on the ground that this formula could not distinguish knowledge from awareness.

Ālaya-vijñāna (S) : It is an expression used in Yogācāra school of Buddhism to refer to the storehouse consciousness. According to this school, reality is nothing but ideas located in the consciousness (*vijñāna*). This storehouse is the carrier of all the latent potentialities and the repository of accumulating tendencies. It is also known as absolute consciousness. This consciousness cannot be analysed, for it is always changing, dynamic, and continuous.

Alchemy : It is an ancient and medieval mystical art with quasi-scientific character practised with an aim to change base metals into gold, and also to develop the elixir of life for the purpose of being immortal. In a way, the science of metallurgy is the outcome of this effort in the West. Alchemy as a practice originated in Egypt around third century CE. It was believed that the purification of crude ores into gold requires a transmuting agent, the *philosopher's stone*, a mystical substance. It was a belief that if one swallows alcohol mixed with this substance, he will attain immortality or spiritual perfection.

Appayya Dīkṣita (c. sixteenth century CE) : He was an Advaitin and Mīmāṁsaka. He wrote *Kalpataruparimala,* a commentary on Amalānanda's *Kalapataru.* According to Appayya, the omniscience of *Brahman* consists in the fact that the pure consciousness, *Brahman,* manifests in all that exists either as actually transformed or as potentially transformed as future, or as latently transformed. It is the *parameśvara* who manifests Himself as the underlying consciousness (*śākṣin*) in individual persons. His major work is *Siddhāntaleśasaṁgraha.* He wrote nearly 100 books.

Appeal to Common Consensus : It is an appeal made to misplaced authority that tries to resolve the point at issue by bringing in an alleged general belief of humankind.

Appearance : Appearance is that which is given to consciousness through the medium of sensation or perception. It is often distinguished from reality. Appearance is what appears to be the case, whereas reality is what actually is the case. For example, in the process of perception one may be said to have perceived a round coin as elliptical. In this sense, the elliptical shape of the coin is appearance of the otherwise round coin. In its metaphysical realm, the distinction between appearance and reality is very vital and important. Behind the veil of appearances there is something real, which cannot be grasped by senses or intellect.

Apperception : This expression was introduced by Leibniz, according to which every perception is dependent upon the previous experience of man and on his psychic constitution at the moment of perception. In other words, "apperception" is designated as self-consciousness. According to Kant, the manifold of intuition has a necessary relation to the "I think" in the same subject in which this manifold is found. It is the self-consciousness that generates the representation "I think" which is capable of accompanying all other representations. Thus it is treated as the transcendental unity of self-consciousness.

Aprāpyakārin (S) : Excepting the visual sense, all other sense-organs remain in their respective places and perceive objects within their reach. The visual sense reaches out to the objects. Thus it is known as *prāpyakārin*.

Apṛthak-siddhi (S) : It is an internal relation of inseparability. It is one of the key concepts in Viśiṣṭādvaita literature. It is a relation obtained between *Brahman*, the souls (*cit*) and the matter (*acit*). This is also known as soul-body relationship.

Āpta-vacana (S) : According to Nyāya, *śabda* is the reliable statement. It is of two types, namely, *laukika* and *alaukika*. The former is the testimony of a trustworthy person (*āpta-vacana*). Since it is secular in character it is not infallible.

Āpta-vākya (S) : It is the statement of a trustworthy person and consists in understanding its meaning. A sentence is defined as a collection of words and a word is defined as that which is potent to convey something.

Apūrva-vidhi (S) : It is an injunction that enjoins something otherwise not known. According to Advaita, the realization of *Brahman* is the *apūrva-vidhi*.

Aquinas, St. Thomas (1225 – 74) : He was a great Scholastic Catholic theologian and disciple of Albert the Great. His philosophy is the outcome of Aristotle's philosophy and its adaptation to Christian theology. Thus he "Christianized" the philosophy of Aristotle. The fundamental principle of Aquinas" philosophy is the harmony of faith and reason. He firmly believed that reason is capable of providing the argument for the existence of God, and also capable of overruling the objections set against the truths of faith. Aquinas made a sincere attempt to delineate the boundaries between faith and reason, indicating what philosophy and theology respectively could and could not provide to the human mind. In fact, he attempted to combine the insights of these two disciplines for a better understanding of the knowledge of God. He found some specific differences between philosophy and theology, between reason and faith. He held that philosophy begins with the immediate objects of sense-experience and moves forward ending in the conception of God. Theology, on the other hand, begins with a faith in God and interprets all things as creatures of God. Thus there is a basic difference in their respective methods. The method of philosophy is such that it draws conclusions from the rational description of the essences of things, whereas theology rests the demonstration of its conclusions upon the authority of revealed knowledge. In spite of their divergent methods, philosophy and theology, according to Aquinas, do not contradict each other. Whatever is discussed by philosophy may not be significant for man's religious end. Theology is basically concerned with what man needs to know for his salvation. He put forward five important ways of proving the existence of God. They are as follows: (1) proof from motion, (2) proof from efficient cause, (3) proof from necessary versus possible being, (4) proof from the degrees of perfection, and (5) proof from the Order of the Universe. His chief works are *Summa contra Gentiles* (1256-59) and *Summa Theologica* (1269).

Ārambha-vāda (S) : It is also known as "the theory of origination." According to this theory, the effect does not pre-exist in the cause. It is totally a new production from the cause. This theory is also known as *asat-kārya-vāda*. This theory is advocated by Nyāya-Vaiśeṣika.

Āraṇyaka (S) : It is one of the portions of the Veda that consists of philosophical prose treatises. It interprets the ritual section by suggesting various modes of meditation. It is meant for ascetics. It belongs to the *jñānakāṇḍa* of the Veda.

Archetypes : In Plato's philosophy, Ideas or Forms are considered to be archetypes or prototypes. Such archetypes are original and immutable. They represent being, while all other objects or things are mere copies of those Ideas or Forms. These objects or things represent the state of "becoming." In Berkeley's philosophy, those ideas which potentially exist in the mind of God are called archetypes.

Argument : In formal logic, an argument is a statement or assertion put forward in confirmation of the truth of some other arguments. Sometimes the whole process of proof is called argument. In symbolic logic, an argument is an independent variable on which the value of any function or predicate is dependent.

Argument from Design : It is also known as teleological argument. It is one of the arguments advanced to prove the existence of God, according to which the order and purpose that is found in reality is the creation of God. It is humanly impossible for anyone to design this world excepting a supernatural designer. He is none other than God. But the objection raised against this argument is that who designed the designer?

Argumentum ad bacculum (L) : This is a form of *ignoratio elenchi.* This fallacy occurs when the arguments are proved invalid by using all force or by threatening the opponent with dire consequences. For example, Copernicus advocated the heliocentric theory according to which the Sun is the centre of the solar system. But the rulers of his time forced him to advocate the geocentric theory according to which the Earth is the centre of the solar system.

Argumentum ad hominem (L) : It is one of the forms of *ignoratio elenchi*. This fallacy consists in criticizing the opponent rather than arguing against his reasoning. For example, the statement of Berkeley "Reality is mind-dependent" can be disapproved by putting forward counter-arguments, but not by abusing him.

Argumentum ad ignoratiam (L) : This is a form of fallacy of *ignoratio elenchi.* This fallacy consists in exploiting the ignorance of people to prove the validity of one's arguments.

Argumentum ad populum (L) : This is another form of *ignoratio elenchi.* This fallacy occurs when an argument is proved valid by appealing to the passions and sentiments of the public instead of appealing to reason. Demagogues often follow this method to convince people.

Argumentum ad verecundium (L) : It is also a form of *ignoratio elenchi.* This is a fallacy that occurs when the arguments of the opponent are proved invalid by putting him to all sorts of shame.

Arhat (S) : It is one of the stages in Jaina ascetic order. An *arhat* is a spiritual person who spreads purity to all. In Hīnayāna Buddhism, an *arhat* is treated as an enlightened saint.

Aristotelian Logic : It is also known as traditional logic that makes use of a categorical syllogism in order to provide an analysis of arguments using two categorical statements as premises and a categorical statement as a conclusion. It is also referred to as syllogistic logic.

Aristotle (C. 384 – 322 BCE) : He is regarded as one of the celebrated ancient Greek philosophers and the most illustrious students of Plato. He is known as the fonder of the science of logic. He is also recognized as the encyclopedic scientist responsible for the classification of the various species. His philosophy can be classified under four subjects. They are as follows: (1) The theoretical aspect that deals with "Being" and its constituents, and their causes and origin, (2) the practical aspect that deals with human activity as such, (3) The beginning of motion, and (4) The aim of philosophy. In epistemology, Aristotle differentiated the *apodeictic* knowledge that which is proved beyond doubt from mere opinion. According to him, science cannot operate without logic. Aristotelian reasoning was particularly concerned with what we can state in precise language about reality, about what things exist and why they are as they are. According to Aristotle, categories are the starting point of any reasoning process. His doctrine of categories explains how we think about things. Whenever we think of a distinct subject matter we think of a subject and predicate or of some substance and its accidents. He recognized nine categories. They are as follows: (1) quantity, (2) quality, (3) relation, (4) place, (5) date, (6) posture, (7) possession, (8) modality, and (9) passivity. Aristotle made use of these categories for the classification of concepts that are used in scientific knowledge.

According to Aristotle, substance is the primary essence of all things. In metaphysics, Aristotle gave importance to causation, matter and form, potentiality and actuality, and so on. According to him, causation is invariably associated with change. Change is one of the basic facts of our experience. In his fourfold theory of causation Aristotle recognized four causes, namely, (1) *formal cause*, which determines what a thing is, (2) *material cause*, that out of which a thing is made, (3) *efficient cause*, by what a thing is made, and (4) *final cause*, the purpose for which it is made. As regards matter and form, Aristotle held that there cannot exist formless matter and matterless form. Coming to potentiality and actuality, he said that since all things are necessarily involved in motion, there is a dynamic power in all things that strives toward their end. An oak seed is potentially endowed with such a power to become an actual oak tree. Thus there is a fundamental mode of change from potentiality to actuality. The most significant aspect of this distinction is that Aristotle held that actuality is prior to that of potentiality. He argued that although something actually emerges from the potential, there cannot be any movement from potential to actual if there were no first of something actual. In ethics, he regarded man, as everything else in nature, has a distinctive "end" to achieve. For this reason, Aristotle's ethics is called teleological. In his very famous work *Nicomachean Ethics* he held that "every art and every inquiry, and similarly every action and pursuit, is thought to aim of some good." If this is so the question for ethics is "What is the goal at which human behaviour aims?" Aristotle believed that contemplation is the highest form of mental activity. In cosmology, Aristotle developed a geocentric theory of the Universe that was accepted as a Bible until Copernicus propounded the heliocentric theory. As regards motion, Aristotle held the view that the "Unmoved Mover" is the first principle of all motion. Aristotle found Plato's theory of Forms unacceptable. Like his teacher Plato, he wanted to discover universals, but he did not believe that they exist apart from particulars. The form of a table, for instance, can be thought of apart from the matter out of which the table is made, but the former does not subsist as a separate invisible entity. The universal "tableness" exists only in particular tables. There is no otherworldly "Form of tableness." Accordingly, Aristotle began his philosophy not with reflection on a dialogue about eternal Forms but with observations of particular objects. The "goal" or "end" (*telos*) of any given substance is key to understanding. This amounts to saying that everything in nature is understood in terms of final causes or purposes. Aristotle applied these insights to human beings. He asked: What would be the *telos* of a person? He held that by observing what is unique to persons and what they in fact do seek Aristotle arrived at the conclusion that the highest good or end for humans is *eudaimonia.* Although the word *eudaimonia* is translated as happiness, one must be circumspect enough to distinguish it from Aristotle's use of "happiness." According to him, it is not a feeling of *euphoria.* It is not a feeling at all. It is an activity in accordance with virtue. This is the central issue in his *Nicomachean Ethics*. Aristotle wrote on a wide range of topics. His writings include: *Categories; Prior Analytics; Posterior Analytics; Topics; On Interpretation; On Sophistical Refutations; Metaphysics; Nicomachean Ethics; Eudemian Ethics; Rhetoric; Poetics; On the Soul; On Dreams; On the Heavens,* and so on.

Artha (S) : It is one of the *puruṣārtha*s or goals of life recognized by the orthodox Indian philosophical systems. *Artha* is a secular value, which is desired and desirable. This value is intended to satisfy the acquisitive aspect in individuals. It has economic importance. But one has to pursue this value within the ambience of *dharma* or righteousness.

Artha-kriyā-jñāna (S) : It is the knowledge obtained by means of practical efficiency or pragmatic means.

Artha-kriyā-kāritva (S) : It is a criterion of right knowledge (*pramā)* according to Nyāya. For Buddhists, it is a criterion of existence. Advaitins call it pragmatic knowledge.

Arthāpatti (S) : It means "presupposition" or "presumption." Mīmāṁsā and Advaita consider *arthāpatti* as a valid means of knowledge. It is a process of knowledge that makes something intelligible by assuming something else. Nyāya does not admit *arthāpatti* as an independent *pramāṇa*. For example, we know that Devadatta is fat, but he does not eat during daytime. From this we have to presume that he eats during night.

Arthaśāstra (S) : It means the "science of polity and economy." It is a famous work of Kauṭilya, the minister of Candragupta Maurya (c. 323 – 297 BCE). In fact, Kauṭilya has been credited with being the founder of *arthaśāstra* tradition as distinguished from the *nītiśāstra* tradition. He was the first to make political economy an independent discipline. In his *Arthaśāstra* he propounded a theory of politics that deals with the immediate practical concerns of polity. He realized the dangers of anarchy as well as the absolute necessity to overcome it by establishing order in society. Therefore, he recommended that there must be a strong ruler capable of creating order.

Arthavāda (S) : According to Mīmāṁsakas, the sentences that occur in the Vedas in a particular context to describe existing things or praise or denounce some deed or injunction are only subordinate to injunctive sentences. These sentences are of three types. They are *guṇavāda* or figurative statements, *anuvāda* or statements that reiterate what is already known, and *bhūtārthavāda* or statements of a fact which is not yet known, and which is not contradictory to what is already known.

Artificial Intelligence : It is popularly known as AI. It is a scientific way of designing and building intelligent artefacts. This effort necessarily presupposes and tests the theories of intelligence. Thus it has a link with the philosophy of mind. In fact, of late, the domain of psychology has been influenced by the fundamental concepts of AI. As a science, AI came into prominence in 1950s and is basically associated with computer programming. In this field of study, intelligence is understood as a structural property or capacity of any active system. As such the research in the field of AI has been classified into language-oriented and pattern-oriented. Both these areas mainly focus on cognitive issues. Also they are concerned with perception and motor control. The psychologically prominent issues such as affect, personality development, aesthetic and moral judgement, conceptual change, mental illness do not form part of AI, for they cannot be brought under the purview of AI. The language-oriented research in AI conceives that thinking is like talking. It is like an inner discourse. Thus thoughts become sentences. The pattern-oriented approach is known as "connectionism" or "parallel distributed processing" and became popular in 1980s. Compared to language-oriented approach, the pattern-oriented approach is less developed. By and large, this approach relies on the microstructure of the brain. The main aspects of this approach are relatively simple active nodes and the interrelations among them. Each node is divided into layers, and each layer of a node is connected to the layer of another node. Every node has its own activation level.

Artificial Language : Any non-natural language such as Esperanto is called artificial language. Artificial languages are subject to the rules of formation and transformation. They are constructed for definite purposes. The natural languages are ordinary languages such as English, French, Chinese, Russian, Tamil, Telugu, etc.

Artificial Life : It is an interdisciplinary scientific study concerning the most fundamental aspects of the processes of life such as self-organization, self-reproduction, learning, adaptation, and evolution. Just as artificial intelligence is concerned with theoretical psychology, artificial life is concerned with theoretical biology. Artificial life science raises a few interesting philosophical questions. For instance, it is often questioned whether functionalism is the right approach towards life. When do systems exhibit the spontaneous emergence of properties?

Ārya-aṣṭāṅga-mārga (S) : It is known as "noble eightfold path." It is Buddha's fourth noble truth that leads to cessation of suffering. It is also the middle path that leads to *nirvāṇa*. The middle path consists of eight steps. They are as follows: right view (*samyag-dṛṣṭi*), right speech (*samyag-vāk*), right resolve (*samyag-saṅkalpa*), right conduct (*samyag-karmānta*), right livelihood (*samyag-jīva*), right effort (*samyag-vyāyāma*), right recollection (*samyag-smṛti*), right contemplation (*samyag-samādhi*).

Ārya Samāj (S) : It is a Hindu reform movement initiated by Swāmi Dayānanda Saraswatī (1824 – 83) in 1875. The chief motto of this movement is to revive the Vedic authority. Swāmi Dayānanda respected caste distinctions, but denied their religious status and introduced the "right of purification" (*śuddhi*) for readmission into Hinduism for converts. It is also the motto of the Ārya Samāj to give equal status to low-caste and outcaste communities with higher-caste Hindus.

Āryadeva (c. second century CE) : He was a Mādhyamika Buddhist and a disciple of Nāgārjuna, the great Śūnyavādin. He held that anything which does not depend on its own is only illusory. Since all our notions about external objects depend upon our senses they cannot be real. Apart from commenting on Nāgārjuna's *Kārikā*s, he wrote three important works. They are *Catuḥśataka*; *Hastabālaprakaraṇa-vṛtti*, and *Cittaviśuddhiprakaraṇa*.

Asādhāraṇa (S) : It is that which is free from the three faults of a definition. The three faults are over-applicability (*ati-vyāpti*), partial inapplicability (*avyāpti*), and total inapplicability (*asambhava*). It also refers to a kind of fallacious reasoning in which the reason is present only in the subject but not in any example. For example, "Ether is eternal, because it is ether."

Asādhāraṇa-kāraṇa (S) : It is the cause that produces its characteristics in the effect through the medium of the material cause (*upādāna*). For example, clay is not the cause of the colour of the pot, but the colour of the clay is the cause of the colour of the pot. In other words, it is not the inherent cause, but that which inheres in the inherent cause.

Āsana (S) : It means "posture." It is one of the eight limbs of Patañjali's *aṣṭāṅga yoga*. *Āsana* is required for practising meditation. It is a steady and comfortable posture. There are so many postures that are of physical help to meditation. *Āsana* is the part of the discipline of the body. Advaita accepts it as part of *nididhyāsana*.

Asaṅga (c. fifth century CE) : He was one of the prominent Mādhyamika philosophers. He advocated the view that *mahāyāna* cannot be realized by any rational means. Intellect (*tarka*) is only provisional, but not final. What is held as true today by the intellect may be found false on the very next day. His important work is *Mahāyānasūtrālaṁkāra*.

Asat (S) : According to Advaita, any entity that does not exist is called *asat*. For example, square-circle, gold-mountain, hare's horn, sky-lotus, barren woman's son, etc. do not have existence of any kind. On the contrary, *sat* is something that has permanent existence or being.

Asat-kārya-vāda (S) : It is known as the "theory of non-pre-existent effect." It is one of the theories of causation, according to which the effect does not pre-exist in its cause. Accordingly, the effect is viewed as something totally new. It is also known as *Ārambha-vāda*. For example, a pot is made out of clay. The pot as an effect, before its production, was not present in the clay. Thus the pot is something new. The chief exponents of this theory of causation are Nyāya-Vaiśeṣikas.

Asat-khyāti (S) : This theory of error was advocated by Mādhyamika school of Buddhism. This school holds that the object of error is totally non-existent. There is no object in reality (empirical word) which is absolute. Everything is relative. Since everything is relative the question of the existence of error does not arise.

Āsatti (S) : It is one of the formal conditions that words must possess to constitute a sentence. The words that go to form a sentence must be contiguous to each other in time when they are spoken or in space when they are written. It is also known as *sannidhi.*

Asceticism : It is a way of life, the basic features of which are extreme abstinence, mortification of one's own physical body, and rejection of all sensuous comforts to achieve a specific religious ideal. In ancient Greece, asceticism was practised in the moral realm. Ascetic practices are also common to the religious dogmas of Hinduism and Christianity. It ranges from restraint of the senses, celibacy, and general renunciation of worldly life to the extremes of self-torture. The ascetic practices are regarded as the means to liberation. It is believed that the self-torture will atone for past *kārmic* guilt resulting in liberation.

Ascriptivism : According to ascriptivism, to call an action voluntary is not to describe that action as caused in a certain manner by the agent who performed it, but only to highlight a commitment to hold the agent responsible for that action. Ascriptivism is a form of non-cognitivism applied to judgements about the voluntary actions. This theory was chiefly advocated by H.L.A. Hart in "Ascription of Rights and Responsibilities" (1949), and also by P.T. Geach in "Ascriptivism" (1960).

Asiddha (S) : It is one of the fallacious reasons. It is of three kinds. They are: (1) *āśraya-asiddha* or that which is not established in terms of abode; (2) *svarūpa-asiddha* or that which is not established in terms of itself; and (3) *vyāpyatva-asiddha* or that which is not established in terms of its concomitance.

Aśoka (*c.* third century BCE) : He was one of the greatest kings of Maurya dynasty, and the first Emperor of India. He is known for his rock edicts extolling charitable work, morality, and kindness in life. After the great Kaliṅga war, Aśoka realized the value of human life. It was the great turning point in his life. He embraced Buddhism and propagated its cardinal virtue *ahiṁsā.* However, he gave equal importance to all religions.

Āśrama (S) : It means "stage of life." There are four important *āśrama*s for the followers of Hinduism. They are: (1) *brahmacarya* or the student stage; (2) *gṛhastha* or the householder stage; (3) *vānaprastha* or the forest dweller stage; and (4) *saṁnyāsa* or the stage of renunciation. The first stage starts when the individual is about eight years old. As a student he goes to the teacher and lives with him until he completes his studies. The second sage starts when the individual completes his studies and is grown up to pay back his three debts as directed by his teacher. The first debt is to his forefathers and is paid back by marrying and having children, particularly male children. In a patriarchal society, only sons prevent the family line from becoming extinct. It was regarded as an important duty. The second debt is to the teachers and is paid back by educating the next generation and thereby transmitting the learning acquired from the teachers. The third debt is to the gods, who maintain and govern the universe, and is paid back by performing sacrifices. Here the expression "sacrifice" should not be understood as necessarily involving the killing of animals. A sacrifice may be of butter, cooked or uncooked rice, barley or wheat. In the third stage, after leading the life of a householder and paying back the three debts, and having one's own son married one retires to forest along with his wife and begins to reflect on the values of life. This stage is the stage of self-reflection and self-examination. The fourth stage is that of the renouncer of the world or that of the ascetic. If one finds that the worldly values have no attraction, one sends one's wife back to their son/s and renounces the world. He spends the rest of his life as a man of God, the holy man. He owns no property and lives by begging. He changes his name so that others do not know him. He may teach spiritual truths to men and women who are eager to know them.

Āśrava (S) : The human bondage is due to the inflow of the kārmic matter into the body of the individual soul. This process is known as *āśrava.* There are two types of *āśrava*: (1) *bhāvāśrava* and (2) *dravyāśrava.* There are five main channels, according to Jainism, through which the kārmic particles enter the soul. They are perversity in outlook (*mithyātva*), lack of self-control (*avirati*), dereliction of one's duties (*pramāda*), passion (*kaṣāya*), and actions of the body, mind and speech (*yoga*). The latter refers to the inflow of kārmic particles through material bondage. The only way to stop the inflow of kārmic particles, according to Jainism, is to practise right faith, right knowledge, and right conduct. This stage is called *saṁvara*.

Āśraya-anupapatti (S) : It is one of the great seven untenables advocated by Śrī Rāmānuja against the Advaita theory of *māyā-avidyā*. The objection is that *Brahman* being pure Consciousness cannot be the locus of *māyā-avidyā*, which is impure.

Āśraya-asiddha (S) : It is one of the fallacious reasons. For example, "A sky-flower is fragrant, because it is a flower in the garden." In this example, "the sky-flower" is the subject and as such it does not exist at all. So the question of its fragrance does not arise.

Assertion : An assertion is any declarative statement that is uttered and put forward as true.

Assertoric : It is a proposition which is an assertion of something to express whether that something is the case or not the case. Such propositions are contrasted with problematic or apodictic ones.

Associationism : It is a view in psychology, according to which associationism is the basic principle of any mental faculty. It is a supplement to sensationalism. According to Locke, mind has three important functions to perform. They are: (1) compounding; (2) comparison; and (3) abstraction. These three important functions are called the laws of association.

Aṣṭa-āvaraṇa (S) : According to Vīra Śaivism, there are eight important rules to be observed in order to protect the individual self from the three impurities (*mala*s). They are: (1) reverence to teacher (*guru*); (2) worship of the divine self (*liṅga*); (3)

reverence for a person who moves from place to place (*jaṅgama*); (4) sipping the water in which the feet of a *guru* or *jaṅgama* are washed (*pādodaka*); (5) offering food to a *guru, jaṅgama*, or *liṅga*, and then eating the left-over sacramentally (*prasāda*); (6) smearing of the sacred ash (*vibhūti* or *bhasma*); (7) wearing the sacred rosary beads (*rudrākṣa*); and (8) chanting the five syllables (*japa namaḥ śivāya*).

Asteya (S) : It is one of the moral precepts of Pātañjala Yoga. It means "non-stealing." It is treated under *yama*. According to this principle, one should not only abstain from taking anything that does not belong to him, but also not to entertain any thought to cover others' property. According to Jainism, it is one of the great vows leading to right conduct (*caritra*).

Āstika darśana (S) : All the orthodox schools of Indian philosophy that accept the authority of the Veda are known as *āstika darśana*s. The orthodox systems of Mīmāṁsā and Vedānta are directly based on the Vedas. The other orthodox systems such as Nyāya, Vaiśeṣika, Sāṁkhya and Yoga are indirectly related to the Vedas.

Astikāya (S) : According to Jainism, an *astikāya* is one that occupies space. It is a form of substance. Matter (*pudgala*), medium of motion (*dharma*), medium of no-motion (*adharma*), and space (*ākāśa*) are treated as *astikāya*s by Jainism.

Aśuddha-māyā (S) : Śaiva Siddhānta classified *māyā* into impure (*aśuddha*), and pure (*śuddha*). The impure *māyā* is mixed up with the impurities of ignorance (*āṇava*) and action (*karma*). The bodies, organs, worlds, and objects of enjoyment are evolved out of this *māyā*. It is like the *prakṛti* of Sāṁkhya.

Aśvaghoṣa (c. CE 80) : He was a Buddhist philosopher, who attributed "thusness" (*tathatā*) to the reality. The reality is only so-and-so or thus-and-thus. He held that there are two distinct aspects of soul, namely, the "thusness" (*bhūtatathatā*) and the cycle of birth and death (*saṁsāra*). His important work is *Buddhacarita*.

Asymptotic : A line or a series of lines that come close to a curve or a particular limit but can never merge or reach the curve or limit within a finite distance is known as asymptotic. For example, in Zeno's Achilles and tortoise paradox, Achilles can go closer and closer to the spot of tortoise but can never reach it.

Ataraxia (Gk) : It means "spiritual tranquillity and imperturbability." Ancient Greek philosophers believed that wise men attain *ataraxia* through cognition of the universe by overcoming fear and liberation from alarm. Greek skeptics believed that *ataraxia* can be attained by suspending all forms of judgement.

Atheist : One who does not believe in the existence of God or in any other supernatural power. A non-believer.

Ativyāpti (S) : It is a fallacy of definition that stretches the definition too much. In other words, it is the presence of the definition of something in other than what is to be defined.

Ātmakhyāti (S) : This theory of error is known as "the apprehension of the self." This theory of error is advocated by the Yogācāra School of Buddhism. According to this theory, the error consists in mistaking what is internal to be external. In this sense, all the determinate cognition of the objects is treated erroneous since there are no external objects. Everything that exists is only a mental projection. Thus the object of error is real, but not as an external object existing in space.

Ātman (S) : The reality that is the substance of the individual self is called *ātman*. It is in no way different from *Brahman*, according to Advaita. Its existence cannot be doubted, because it is the basis for all experience. It cannot be known by thought. According to Nyāya-Vaiśeṣika, it is the substratum in which cognitions inhere.

Atomic Proposition : It is a proposition in which there is no logical operator. Hence it is simple and further unanalysable. Wittgenstein called them "elementary propositions" in his

Tractatus Logico-Philosophicus. For example, the proposition "Red is a colour" is an atomic proposition.

Atomism : It is a philosophical standpoint that explains reality in terms of discrete, unconnected, and irreducible entities or elements. In other words, atomism is pluralistic in character. For example, in Leibniz's philosophy, monads are the ultimate constituents of reality. Similarly, in the philosophy of Hume, the ultimate constituents of reality are sense-impressions. They are discrete, unconnected neutral entities. In modern logic, Russell introduced a peculiar type of propositions called "atomic propositions."

Atonement : It is a religious act of experiencing consciousness of one's sins, penitence, and reconciliation. In theology, it is an attempt to reconciliation of God and man who had sinned against God.

Attribute : Any property, whether it is essential or accidental, that is affirmed or denied of a subject in question is called attribute. According to Spinoza, an attribute is something that is perceived by intellect or mind as constituting the essence of substance. For example, Spinoza's substance has two important attributes, namely, infinite thought and infinite extension.

Atyanta-abhāva (S) : It means "absolute non-existence." It is one of the four types of *abhāva*. If a thing is non-existent in the locus, then that thing is absolutely non-existent in that locus. For example, sky-flower, round-square, etc. do not have existence at all. "Absence of pot on the floor/ground" is also an example of *atyanta-abhāva*.

Augustine, Saint (c. CE 354 – 430) : He was a Bishop of Hippo (North Africa) and a great Christian theologian. He was the propagator of feideism. In fact, a series of personal experiences made him to arrive at a unique philosophical approach. His passion for learning was kindled by the writings of Cicero. St. Augustine was perplexed by the ever-present problem of moral-evil. The problem for him was how to explain the existence of evil in human experience. According to the Christians, God is the creator of all things, and also God is good. But, how is that the world which is created by the perfectly good God consists of evil? Since Augustine could not find a satisfactory answer from the Christianity, he approached a group called the Manichaeans, who were sympathetic to Christianity, but rejected the monotheism of the *Old Testament.* By rejecting it, the Manichaeans also rejected the concept of creator God who is also the redeemer of humankind. Instead, they advanced a doctrine of dualism, according to which there were two basic principles in the universe, namely, the principle of light or goodness, and the principle of darkness or evil. These two principles are eternal and conflict with each other eternally. This conflict is reflected in human life. The soul, which is composed of light, and the body, which is composed of darkness, are the basic components of every human individual. This theory of dualism, at first sight, appeared to have provided a solution to the much-discussed problem of evil in the world by overcoming the contradiction as to the presence of evil in the world created by a good God. St. Augustine attributed sensuous desires to the external power of darkness. Although this dualism solved the problem of evil, it raised new problems. First of all, one has to account for the existence of two contradictory principles in nature. If one cannot advance a convincing reason, can one arrive at it by means of intellectual certitude? Somehow, St. Augustine was not satisfied with the explanation advanced by Manichaeans and therefore broke with Manichaeanism. Then he turned towards skepticism, although he did not doubt the existence of God. Because of its influence St. Augustine developed a materialistic attitude towards things and started doubting everything that is immaterial including the immortality of the soul. But, St. Augustine realized that true philosophy was inconceivable without a confluence of faith and reason. He found this clue in neo-Platonism, although it could not solve his moral dilemma. According to him, refutation of faith leads to no knowledge and no truth. In his work *De Civitate Dei,* St. Augustine advocated a Christian conception of world history in the lines of fatalism. He believed that every process that takes place in this world is preordained by God. Consequently, to understand the concrete condition of man, one must look at it from the point of view of Christian faith. Thus the whole world has to be looked at from the vantage point of view of faith. For St. Augustine, there is no distinction between philosophy and theology. One cannot properly philosophize until one's will is transformed. His important works include: *Confessions* (397-400); *Literal Commentary on Genesis* (401-15); *On the Trinity* (399-412); and *City of God* (413-26).

Aurelius, Marcus (121 – 180) : He was an important emperor of Rome. He advocated stoicism, according to which acceptance of nature and self-control must be cultivated in the face of diversity. As a practical Roman he was not interested in the metaphysical materialism of the early stoa. Instead he stressed the need for active benevolence and the acceptance of the divine providence or fate. He held that apparent evil is the part of the overall good of the universe. Even today many adore his image.

Aurobindo, Sri (1872 – 1950) : He was one of the legendary figures of Indian nationalist movement, who in the later years became a great philosopher saint. Sri Aurobindo's philosophy is known as "Integral Yoga." He reinterpreted the sacred Hindu Upaniṣadic texts to put forward the view that there is a transition from "sub-conscious state" to "super-conscious state." His theory of evolution takes the notion of "involution" into consideration. The ultimate reality, according to Sri Aurobindo is *sat-cit-ānanda*. He was well-acquainted with the evolutionist philosophies of the West, but was totally dissatisfied with their explanation as regards the origin of the matter, life and the mind. He held that the evolution from matter to life to spirit can be explained only if there is in the very beginning of matter something to which the nisus belongs as its very nature. Then the original nature must be spirit. If so, why does it hide in matter at first? Why has it become, and why does it appear as matter? To become matter there must be something natural to it. The movement from spirit to matter and matter to spirit belongs to the very nature of the absolute (*sat-cit-ānanda*). If spirit is conscious and matter is unconscious, then both the conscious and unconscious are not separate from each other, but belong to each other. The movements of descent and ascent constitute a circular movement as in the philosophy of Plotinus. Man belongs to a stage in this circular movement. According to Sri Aurobindo, there are nine stages of descent of the Absolute into matter, which are also nine stages of ascent in the reverse direction. They are: Existence, Consciousness, Bliss, Supermind, Overmind, mind, psyche, life and matter. The stages from mind to matter belong to the empirical world. The stages from Supermind and above are supernal and divine. The Overmind is mediator between mind and Supermind. The aim of man's life, held by Sri Aurobindo, is to follow the path of the ascent and rise to the levels of the supernals one after another. At the highest level of experience there are no differences. Such an experience provides one with integral knowledge. His important works include: *The Life Divine* (1955); *The Human Cycle* (1949); *Savitri* (1951); and The *Foundations of Indian Culture* (1953).

Austic Thinking : It is a process of absorbing fanciful or wishful thinking without the support of any factual material. It is a kind of imagination.

Austin, John Longshaw (1911 – 60) : He is a well-known twentieth-century British philosopher who attempted application of methods of the standards of a scholar of classical texts to ordinary language. Unlike later Wittgenstein and Gilbert Ryle, Austin did not conceive of philosophical analysis as merely puzzle-solving activity. For Austin, the study, analysis, and cataloguing of the tremendous variety of language, as it is ordinarily used, is an end in itself. It is a kind of knowledge that may be sought for its own sake rather than for the sake of ridding ourselves of conceptual muddles. Austin felt that the real job is to indicate the precise way in which various formulations and meanings are related to different concepts, and not merely different ways of talking about the same concepts. Thus ordinary language analysis is one of the ways of doing philosophy among others, but not the only way of doing it. Austin's article on "Other Minds" (1946) received an unqualified acclaim for his meticulous and incisive analysis of the term "know." His main concern is with what people ordinarily say. His important works include: *Philosophical Papers* (1961); *Sense and Sensibilia* (1962); *How to do Things with Words* (1962).

Authoritarianism : It is a theory of knowledge that maintains that the truth of any proposition is determined by the fact of its having been advocated by an individual or a group of individuals considered to be an authority in their field.

Autological : A term is called autological when it is applied to itself. For example, the term "English" is applied to itself.

Automatism : It is a metaphysical theory according to which animal and human organisms are automata. In other words, they are machines controlled and regulated by the laws of physics and mechanics.

Autonomous and Heteronomous Ethics : They are two diametrically opposite views concerning morality. Autonomous ethics maintains that moral principles are the outcome of certain idealistic notions of the internally inherent a priori moral obligations. The heteronomous ethics tries to deduce the fundamental moral principles from the causes independent of the will of the acting agent. These external causes are considered to be the laws of states, religious commandments, and also such motives as personal interest, etc.

Autonomy : Rudolf Carnap introduced this term to philosophy. According to him, a word is autonomous if it is used as a name for itself. For example, the geometric shape, the sound, etc.

Autonomy of Ethics : According to intuitionists, moral philosophy cannot be deduced either from metaphysics or any other natural or social sciences.

Autonomy of the Will : According to Immanuel Kant, the autonomy of moral law consists in the freedom of the rational will to legislate to itself.

Avaccheda-vāda (S) : It is known as the "theory of limitation." According to Advaita Vedānta, an individual (*jīva*) in his essential nature is none other than *Brahman*. The infinite Self (*ātman*) is limited by body-sense-mind complex (*anātman*). When this adjunct is removed, one realizes the non-duality between them.

Avadhi (S) : It means "supernatural cognition." Jainism holds that an individual can perceive things that have shape, size and form without the aid of senses. Such an act of supernatural cognition is of three types, namely, *deśa-avadhi*, which is limited to space and time, *sarva-avadhi*, which is a cognition of apprehension of all modes of physical objects, and *parama-avadhi*, which is not limited by space and time.

Avasthā-traya-vicāra (S) : It is also known as the "inquiry into triple stream of experience." According to Advaita, individual or *jīva* undergoes three kinds of experience in its empirical existence. They are the waking experience (*jāgrat*), the dream experience (*svapna*), and the deep sleep experience (*suṣupti*). The Self is involved in all the three states of experience due to its association with material adjuncts (*upādhi*s). In the waking state of experience, the Self in its individual aspect is called *vaiśvānara*, and in the state of dream experience is called *taijasa*. In the state of deep sleep experience the Self is called *prājña*. *Turīya* or *caturtha* is the state of the pure Self. As a matter of fact, the Self is not affected by anyone of these three states of experience as it transcends every state of experience. It means that the Self is immutable (*kūṭastha*). Its involvement in the three states of experience is purely accidental (*aupādhika*).

Avatāra (S) : It means "divine incarnation." According to the Hindu tradition, there are ten *avatāras* of Lord Viṣṇu. They are: Matsya, Kūrma, Varāha, Narasiṁha, Vāmana, Paraśurāma, Rāma, Balarāma, Kṛṣṇa, and Kalki. Sometimes the Balarāmāvatāra is replaced by the Buddhāvatāra.

Avenarius, Richard (1843 – 96) : He was a German philosopher and a chief advocate of empirio-criticism. According to Avenarius, experience is the bridge between psychic and physical phenomena. Thus he proposed the idea of the absolute independence of the subject and object. In his post-Kantian critique, Avenarius advocated a radical positivist position that grounds all philosophy in basic scientific principles. He rejected all metaphysical claims that transcended the limits of experience. He treated them as mere imaginations of mind. One of his major works is: *Critique of Pure Existence* (1888 – 90).

Avesta : It is the sacred scripture of Zarathustra. It is preserved in the old Iranian language, which is akin to the Vedic Sanskrit. Avesta contains many parallels to the Vedic procedures and ideas.

Avicenna (Ibn Sina) (980 – 1037) : He was an Islamic philosopher. Avicenna's Supreme Being is attributed with both necessary and complete unity from which all other beings evolved. Avicenna was chiefly responsible in spreading the ancient philosophical and scientific heritage among Arabs and Europeans. His basic contribution to philosophy is in the field of metaphysics. His originality lies in his attempt to synthesize Aristotelian and neo-Platonic approaches with the help of Islamic dialectical theology (*kalām*).

Avidyā (S) : It means "ignorance." It is also known as individual illusion. It is a key concept in Advaita. It is due to *avidyā*, which is none other than *māyā*, that reality is projected as the world of objects. And this world of objects is regarded as real. Thus *avidyā* has both the power of concealment (*āvaraṇa śakti*) and the power of projection (*vikṣepa śakti*).

Avowals : Gilbert Ryle used this expression to denote first person utterances like "I am in pain" to distinguish them from their third person counterparts like "He is in pain." Ryle felt that the third person statements are open to doubt for one cannot introspect into the feelings of others, while the fist person statements (avowals) are infallible.

Awareness : It is an act of consciousness such as seeing a colour or the feeling of pain, which is distinguished from the content attended on the sensed colour patch or the felt pain. Awareness is distinguished from knowledge by epistemologists.

Axiology : It is a branch of philosophy that deals with the issues related to values. For example, there are material and non-material values. Economic value is considered to be material value. Moral, religious, aesthetic values are considered to be non-material values. Further, there are extrinsic values and intrinsic values. The former are means to certain ends; while the latter are ends in themselves.

Axiom : Any proposition that is considered to be self-evidently true is called an axiom. It does not require any proof to prove its validity.

Axiomatic Method : Axiomatic method is popular in symbolic/ mathematical logic. Unlike the decision procedures that are used in prepositional and predicate calculi to test the validity of a given argument, an axiom system generates tautologies called theorems. They are provable, since they are deduced from certain axioms. The three basic features of an axiom are: (1) independence; (2) consistency; and (3) completeness.

Ayam Ātma Brahman (S) : It is one of the *mahāvākyas* or logia. It means "This self is Brahman." This is a very famous statement from the *Māṇḍūkya Upaniṣad* (1.2).

Ayer, Alfred Jules (1910 – 89) : He was a famous British exponent of logical positivism through his matured work *Language, Truth, and Logic* (1936). In his later years, Ayer deviated from the orthodox form of logical positivism and came under the influence of linguistic philosophy. One of the chief mottoes of logical positivists is to get rid of metaphysics from the sphere of philosophy in order to make philosophy as scientific as possible. According to Ayer, logical positivists followed the legacy of Hume by accepting his empiricism. However, the empiricism of Hume has been given a new linguistic garb by adding some logical rigour to it. In epistemology, Ayer advocated phenomenalism as a theory of perception. However, he had to abandon that thesis as it came under severe attack from Isaiah Berlin. His sense-datum theory is akin to that of Russell and H.H. Price. Like Russell, Ayer held the view that all physical objects are the logical constructs out of actual and possible sense-contents. According to Ayer, the function of philosophy is the logical clarification of everyday language and science. Therefore, a philosopher must serve as an intellectual policeman to prevent others from trespassing into the domain of metaphysics. His principle of verification, which is aimed at distinguishing empirical statements from those of metaphysics, could not serve the purpose as the principle itself is involved in internal contradictions. In ethics, Ayer advocated emotivism, according to which all ethical pronouncements are mere emotions or sentiments expressed by the speakers. Thus they are exhortations to moral virtue. His other important works include: *The Foundations of Our Empirical Knowledge* (1940); *The Problem of Knowledge* (1956); *The Concept of a Person and other Essays* (1963); *The Humanistic Outlook* (1968); *Metaphysics and Commonsense* (1969); *The Central Questions of Philosophy* (1971); Russell (1972); *Probability and Evidence* (1973); *The Origins of Pragmatism* (1974); *Wittgenstein* (1975); *Hume* (1980); and *Philosophy in the Twentieth Century* (1984);

Āyurveda (S) : According to Śuśruta, it is a science of life, and is part (*upāṅga*) and parcel of the *Atharvaveda*. It is supposed to have been written by Brahmā, the creator God, before he created all beings.

Ayuta-siddha (S) : It is a kind of relation in which two entities are inseparably related to each other. Nyāya-Vaiśeṣika recognized five types of *ayuta-siddha* objects. They are: the relation between substance (*dravya*) and quality (*guṇa*), the relation between substance (*dravya*) and activity (*karma*), the relation between particular (*vyakti*) and universal (*jāti*), the relation between ultimate things (*nityadravya*) and particularity (*viśeṣa*), and the relation between whole (*aṁśin*) and parts (*aṁśa*).

B

Babism : This religious sect came into existence in Persia in the middle of the nineteenth century against orthodox Mohammedanism. Babism as a religious sect has a number of followers in America. As a religious sect Babism denies the finality of any revelation.

Bacon, Francis (1561 – 1626) : He was a British philosopher, and is regarded as the pioneer of the empiricist movement. Although a systematic account of empiricism was first given by John Locke in his *An Essay Concerning Human Understanding,* the seeds of empiricism are found in the writings of Bacon. He opposed all forms of scholasticism and dogmatism (Aristotleanism and Scholastic logic). According to him, truth can be obtained by the method of induction, which is dependent upon observation. Certain preconceptions and prejudices are the real impediments in using this method. These preconceptions and prejudices are classified into four important heads called "idols" by Bacon. They are as follows: (1) The Idols of the tribe or racially wishful anthropocentric ways of thinking. In other words, it is the tendency to explain everything in terms of final causes; (2) The Idols of the cave or personal prejudices; (3) The Idols of the marketplace or the failure to define terms; and (4) The Idols of the theatre or blind acceptance of tradition and authority. His attitude towards ethics was utilitarian. One of the important works of Bacon is *Novum Organum* (1620), where he wrote that the first step to acquiring knowledge is to cleanse the mind from all sorts of preconceptions and prejudices (Idols). The use of the inductive method suggests the extraction of the essential from the non-essential and the discovery of the underlying structure or form of the phenomena under investigation. The other important work of Bacon is *The Advancement of Learning* (1605).

Bacon, Roger (1214 – 93) : He was a British philosopher of Middle Ages, who opposed Scholasticism. He was a precursor of experimental science. He upheld the method of cognition based on experiment and mathematics. The aim of learning, according to Bacon, is to have mastery over nature. His most celebrated work *Opus Maius* was a veritable encyclopedia of the science of his time. His other works include: *Opus Tertium* (1268); *Compendium of Philosophy*; and *Compendium of Theology* (1292).

Baconian Method : It is the inductive method advocated by Francis Bacon. The objective of this method is to enable humans to attain mastery over nature for their own survival benefits. It is a process wherein the mind passes from particular instances to more generalized knowledge. In fact, he recommended induction through exhaustive enumeration in which an event manifests itself with greater or lesser intensity of instances.

Bad Faith : It is a popular notion in existentialist philosophy. According to Jean Paul Sartre, bad faith is a form of self-deception and also the deception of others. In the state of bad faith, an individual tries to shirk his responsibilities to become a passive subject of outside influences. Thus he cannot make any decision of his own.

Bādarāyaṇa (C. fourth or fifth century BC?) : He is also known as Vyāsa. He authored the *Brahma-Sūtra* or *Vedānta-Sūtra.* It is composed in an aphoristic style. The work is not all that easy to follow. Several commentaries were written on the *Brahma-Sūtra.* The three prominent commentators of the *Brahma-Sūtra* are by Śaṅkara (the Advaitin), Śrī Rāmānuja (the Viśiṣṭādvaitin), and Madhva (the Dvaitin).

Bādhita (S) : It means "contradicted" or "sublated." It is a logical fallacy that tries to validate a thesis contrary to direct experience.

For instance, when someone asserts "Ice is not cold, because it is a substance," it is logically fallacious. Not only that, any cognition that is contradicted by subsequent cognition is known as *bādhita jñāna.*

Bāhyānumeya-vāda (S) : It is a theory advocated by Vaibhāṣika school of Buddhism (a sect of Hīnayāna) that subscribes to realist epistemology. This theory assumes the reality and independence of both the mind and objects. The object is inferred (*anumeya*) as being outside (*bāhya*) consciousness and apprehended only when the sensory apparatus functions and certain physiological conditions are fulfilled.

Bāhyapratyakṣa-vāda (S) : This theory is advocated by Vaibhāṣika school of Buddhism (a sect of Hīnayāna), which subscribes to realism. According to Vaibhāṣika the objects exist outside (*bāhya*) the mind and consciousness. But the objects are known directly (*pratyakṣa*), but not inferentially.

Bain, Alexander (1818 – 1903) : He was a Scottish empiricist philosopher and psychologist. He was the founder of the famous philosophy journal *Mind*. Bain was a close friend of J.S. Mill and was influenced by his utilitarianism. He was chiefly interested in the philosophy of mind. His important works include: *Senses and the Intellect* (1855) and *Mental and Moral Science* (1868).

Banausic (Gr) : Anything that is vulgar or obscene, particularly in the fields of arts, science, or any other discipline, that leads to deformation of both mind and body is called *banausic.*

Bandha (S) : It means "bondage" or "attachment." According to Jainism, *karma* particles are responsible for bondage. It is caused by the activities of the mind-body complex. This bondage is of two types: (1) *bhāva-bandha,* which is a change in the individual consciousness due to passions (*kaṣāya*) and (2) *dravya-bandha,* which is the stage that brings the individual into that actual contact with the kārmic particles.

Baptism : It is a religious rite of dedication and induction of an individual into a circle of social and religious privilege. This rite is normally of a ceremonious nature with pledges given by proxy in the case of babes, and accompanied by prayers and other related rituals to seal the bond of fellowship. In Christian circles, this rite is treated as a sacrament, the supernatural rebirth into the Divine Kingdom.

Barber Paradox : It is a paradox that occurs in set theory. According to this paradox, the barber of Seville shaves all men, excepting those who shave themselves. Now the question is: does the barber shave himself? If he shaves himself, then he does not get shaved by the barber. This shows that he both shaves and does not shave himself. So the supposition that the barber of Seville shaves all those men, excepting those who shave themselves is false.

Baroque : It is a style of art produced especially in the seventeenth century. The Classicists regarded it as a kind of false art, and romanticists treated it as a product of magic imagination.

Barth, Karl (1886 – 1968) : He was a famous Swiss Protestant theologian, but widely influential among social pessimists of contemporary times. God, according to him, is wholly other than human. He is neither apprehensible by human reason nor by human endeavour. Christianity is a revealed and supernatural religion. Humans must have faith in God's plan of salvation or get ruined completely. God is the sole judge and His judgements are not attainable through human endeavour. Barth's theology is known as "crisis theology." The word "crisis" means "judgement" in Greek. Sometimes his theology is also known as "dialectical theology" because of his emphasis on the contradiction between God and the world. His important work is *The Knowledge of God and the Service of God* (1939).

Basic Propositions : They are also known as protocol propositions. Their truth can never be challenged since they are the translations of the data given in one's own sense-experience.

Ayer calls them basic propositions, whereas Neurath preferred to call them protocol propositions. In fact, the sense-datum statements are called basic propositions.

Basis and Superstructure : They are the two important philosophical categories of Marxism. In historical materialism, basis refers to economic base, while superstructure refers to various other social relations existing in a society. The change in base necessitates a change in the superstructure.

Bathmism : According to E.D. Cope, a Lamarckian, bathmism is a special force or growth force that exists and exhibits itself in the growth of organic bodies.

Baumgarten, Alexander Gottlieb (1714 – 62) : He was a pre-Kantian German philosopher and disciple of Christian Wolf. Baumgarten continued the encyclopedic work of Christian Wolf. In one of his major works entitled *Aesthetica* he analyses the problem of beauty. He regarded beauty as the recognition of perfection by means of the senses. The expression "aesthetics" for the study of beauty and art was first introduced by him.

Beasant, Annie Wood (1847 – 1933) : She was a freethinker, socialist, and a pacifist. She joined the Theosophical Society in England in 1889. She was influenced by H.P. Blavatsky's work *The Secret Doctrine.* In 1893 she came down to India and became the president of the Theosophical Society of India in 1907. She started a Central Hindu School in Banaras and it became a University in the year 1915. She promoted classical dance. In 1917 she became the Chairperson of Indian National Congress. She wrote several books on theosophical teachings.

Beauty : It is a category of aesthetics that reflects and assesses various phenomena of reality and works of art affording man to express an aesthetic sense of appreciation. Plato believed that beauty is an intrinsic property of the objects that can be measured in terms of purity, integrity, harmony, perfection and so on.

Becoming : In Plato's philosophy, the world of sensible things is known as becoming. According to him, the transient sensory world is subject to change. The classical representative of this view is Heraclitus who claimed that reality is under constant "flux." Contrary to this view, Parmenides held that reality is One and immutable. Such an immutable reality is referred to as Being.

Begging the Question : It is a logical fallacy of assuming the very conclusion in the premises of an argument which is either in dispute or yet to be proved.

Behaviourism : It is a well-known theory of psychology advocated by J.B. Watson. According to this theory, the psychical acts of any organism can be explained in terms of behavioural data obtained by observation. In other words, the behaviour of any sentient organism is defined in terms of stimulus and response. After Watson, it was B.F. Skinner who popularized behaviourism. There are three notable versions of behaviourism. They are as follows: (1) Metaphysical behaviourism which maintains that there is nothing like consciousness; (2) Methodological behaviourism views that a genuinely scientific psychology can only study the observable behaviour of the organism but cannot deal with the acts of introspection; and (3) Analytical behaviourism emphasizes that the terms of psychology can be analysed in terms of behaviour by means of which they can get their proper meanings.

Being : This expression is used by different philosophers to arrive at different philosophical doctrines. It is generally equated with the term "existence," since being is the essential property of all that exists. It is considered to be the defining subject of any metaphysical inquiry. In his metaphysics, Aristotle was basically concerned with the nature of "Being." This "Being" of Aristotle does not have any genus. The term "Being" is also used to refer to sentient finite existents. In Spinoza's sense, "being" is that which "is," pre-eminently without qualification and is the source and ultimate subject of all distinctions. In Meinong's system, being is equated with "subsistence" or "existence." According to him, objects have two types of existence, namely, physical (*sein*) and logical (*sosein*). Aristotle and Kant held the view that being cannot be attributed as a property to anything. Kant stated that "existence" is not a predicate. To say that something exists is not to describe it. In existentialism, especially Martin Heidegger recognizes two types of being, i.e. "Being" in its absolute sense and "being" in its relative or finite sense. Heidegger's whole metaphysical inquiry is directed towards the nature of "Being." Therefore his metaphysics is known as "fundamental ontology."

Belief : It is a kind of feeling that makes an individual accept something as true even when there is no conclusive evidence. In epistemology, belief is considered to be a claim to knowledge. However, it is not a mere opinion. Beliefs can be true and false. Epistemologists made a sharp distinction between belief and knowledge. The latter presupposes the former, but not vice versa. Belief is also defined by many epistemologists as a mental state or state of mind. Gilbert Ryle tried to explain belief in terms of dispositions in his *The Concept of Mind*. According to Gattier, a justified true belief can be treated as knowledge. C.S. Peirce, the pioneer of pragmatism, held that the best way to fix or unfix a belief is to put it for a pragmatic test. The theories of belief can be classified into the following heads: namely, (1) affective; (2) intellectual; and (3) volitional. Hume's theory of belief represents the affective theory of belief. According to him, belief is a feeling of vividness attaching to a perception or memory but not to a fiction of the imagination. Bain and James Mill advocated intellectual theory of belief, while William James advocated volitional theory of belief. According to scholastics, belief is nothing but faith or opinion lacking evidence.

Beneke, Friedrich Eduard (1798 – 1854) : He was a German philosopher who followed Kantian tradition modified by empiricism. He wrote a critical work on Kant's *Critique of Pure*

Reason and another on his moral theory. He was chiefly influenced by Herbart and British empiricism. He attacked rationalist metaphysics. Beneke's doctrines influenced psychology and educational theories of the nineteenth century. His psychology held that the hypostatization of faculties lead to a mythical psychology. He advanced a method that would make natural science of the soul or associationist psychology possible. Influenced by empiricism he held that the elements of mental life are dynamic, active processes or impulses (*trieben*). His important works include: *Psychologie Skizzen* (1825); *Lehrbuch der Psychologie als Naturewissenschaft* (1833); and *Metaphysik und Religionphilosophie* (1840).

Bentham, Jeremy (1748 – 1832) : He was a well-known British moral philosopher who advocated the famous doctrine of utilitarianism. He reduced all the motives of human conduct to either pleasure or pain. According to him, pleasure or happiness is the highest good desirable by any individual. He preferred quantitative pleasure to qualitative pleasure. Although J.S. Mill advocated utilitarianism, he attacked Bentham's views on utilitarianism. In law, Bentham is remembered for his criticism of Blackstone's views on the English Constitution, for his examination of the legal fiction and for his treatment of the subject of evidence. In politics, Bentham is known for his principles of legislation. His important works include: *An Introduction to the Principles of Morals and Legislation* (1789) and *Deontology* (1813 – 15).

Berdyaev, Nicolai Alexanderovitch (1874 – 1948) : He was a Russian religious philosopher who held that the Christian Common Wealth could be realized on the earth. He made a sharp distinction between material and spiritual world. Man being spiritual, according to Berdyaev, seeks freedom. His thought resembles that of the Christian Gnostics, and it owes a good deal to German idealism and mysticism (Boehme). He was an ardent critic of systems as diverse as communism,

Thomistic Scholasticism, etc. His important works include: *Smysl Istorii* (*The Meaning of History*), *Berlin* (1923); and *The Freedom and the Spirit* (1935).

Bergmann, Gustuv (1906 – 87) : He was an Austrian philosopher, mathematician, and the youngest member of the Vienna Circle. He advocated phenomenalism, although he disowned it in his later stages. However, his ontology of material objects remained phenomenalistic in its structure. Bergmann's world consists of bare momentary particulars exemplifying simple universals. He viewed that the world is independent of both our experience of it, and our thought and discourse about it. His important works include: *The Metaphysics of Logical Positivism* (1954); *Meaning and Existence* (1959); *Logic and Reality* (1964); and *Realism: A Critique of Brentano and Meinong* (1967).

Bergson, Henri (1859 – 1941) : He was a French evolutionist and a metaphysical philosopher. He advocated anti-mechanistic and spiritualistic metaphysics. According to Bergson, there are two ways of approaching an object. One approach is to observe the object in question from a vantage point of view to analyse the nature of the object, and the second is to be one with the object in question (intellectual sympathy). This is what is known as intuitive approach. Bergson held that intuition is the method followed by the philosophers. This method provides us with the complete knowledge of the reality. Analysis is the method followed by scientists, which provides us with the superficial knowledge of the reality. As an evolutionist, Bergson propounded that *elan vital* is the fundamental principle behind all biological processes. It takes every organism from its simplest form to the complex. The vital concept of his philosophy is "duration" rather than intuition. Duration is the original thing in itself. For Bergson, it is a specific experience revealed to the individual in immediate experience. All objects, consciousness, matter, time, evolution, motion, and the absolute are the specialized tensional forms of duration. His important works include: *Time and Free will* (1890); *An Introduction to Metaphysics*

(1903); *Creative Evolution* (1907); and *The Two Sources of Morality and Religion* (1932).

Berkeleianism : It is the subjective idealistic doctrine of Berkeley. He held that by admitting an extra-mental world would lead to materialism and atheism. Therefore, he denied the existence of any external world independent of human mind. The cause of the ideas in our mind is not the material substance, but a spiritual being, God, who communicates them to us in a certain order, which we call the laws of nature.

Berkeley, George (1685 – 1753) : He was a British empiricist, subjective idealist, and Bishop of Clione, who held the view that "to be is to be perceived" (*esse est percipi* or *percepere*). In other words, objects exist in so far as they are perceived. If no one is perceiving, yet they exist because the ever vigilant God constantly perceives them. Berkeley was an immaterialist. According to him, there are only spiritual substances in the form of infinite and finite spirits. The infinite spirit is the mind of the God, while the finite spirits are human minds. Ideas potentially exist in God's mind, but actually in human minds. According to Berkeley, there is no reality external to human mind. Reality is mind-dependent. Berkeley criticized Locke's notion of abstract ideas. He argued that abstract ideas are even inconceivable. Matter is an abstract idea. Therefore, the idea of matter is a misnomer. His important works include: *An Essay Towards a New Theory of Vision* (1709); *A Treatise Concerning the Principles of Human Knowledge* (1710); *Three Dialogues Between Hylas and Philonous* (1713); *Critique of Newtonian Mechanics* (1720); *Alciphron or Minute Philosopher* (1733); and *Siris* (1744).

Berlin, (Sir), Isaiah (1909 – 97) : He is regarded as one of the most influential contemporary British moral and political philosophers, who argued against the determinist philosophy of history. He stressed the importance of moral values only in the light of human responsibility and freedom. Berlin attacked the linguistic phenomenalism advocated by analytical philosophers in his well-acclaimed paper "Empirical Propositions and Hypothetical Statements," wherein he held that the propositions of categorical type can never be reduced to the statements of hypothetical type. If the statements about material objects are categorical, then the statements about sense-data are hypothetical. The former cannot be reduced to the latter. His important works are *Karl Marx* (1939); *Historical Inevitability* (1954); and *Two Concepts of Liberty* (1959).

Bernard of Chartres (c. twelfth century CE) : He was known as the most perfect Platonist of his time by John of Salisbury. According to him, Bernard was an extreme realist in his theory of universals, but he taught that the forms of things are distinct from the exemplary Ideas in the Divine Mind.

Best : It is the principle of the best of all possible worlds. Leibniz held the view that God created the best world out of the possible worlds because of His wisdom. His (God's) goodness makes Him choose, and His power always makes Him produce the best possible entity.

Bhagavad-Gītā (S) : It means "the song of the Lord." It is one of the most sacred books of the Hindus. It is a popular philosophic epic poem representing Lord Kṛṣṇa embodied as a charioteer giving a message to the prince Arjuna. As the story of the *Bhagavad-Gītā* goes, when Arjuna saw his own kith and kin on the other side, ready to exchange blows with him and kill, and when he realized that he had to destroy them, felt so dejected that he wanted to retreat from the war field to become a recluse. Kṛṣṇa saw Arjuna's mental and moral condition, taught him the truth about the world, man and ethics, and finally persuaded him to fight. The ethical question is not whether the men on the other side are kinsmen, but whether we are doing our duty. But why should we do our duty, if it requires killing of our own kinsmen? For duty is not based on our sentiments, likes and dislikes, but upon the nature of reality. By not performing our duty, we cut ourselves off from reality and become unreal or untrue to ourselves. We will become strangers to our own being. We surrender ourselves to our likes and dislikes, but not to our real being. The *Bhagavad-Gītā*, often called simply *Gītā*, is essentially theistic in its teachings, although Śaṅkara held that it taught supra-personal non-dualism. The *Brahman* is personal and Kṛṣṇa calls himself both the *Brahman* and God. The world including the *ātman* is only a part of Him, for He transcends the world. This position is often called panentheism advocated by K.C.F. Krause in German theology, which is different from pantheism. According to panentheism, *Brahman* or God is not to be found in the objects of the world, but they are the objects of the world in Him. The *Gītā* intends to say that God is not only transcendent, but also immanent. There is nothing other than God. The *Gītā* represents a unique synthesis of action, devotion and knowledge. The quintessence of the *Gītā* is that the Self is indestructible (*avināśī*), eternal (*nitya*), unborn (*aja*), undiminishing (*avyaya*), all-pervasive (*sarvagata*), immovable (*acala*), ancient (*sanātana*), unmanifest (*avyakta*), unthinkable (*acintya*), and immutable (*avikārya*). Only bodies are destroyed, but not the Self.

Bhakti (S) : It means "devotion." It is nothing but fervent loving devotion towards the object of contemplation or divine being itself. It is recognized as a way of salvation or *mukti* by the theistic schools of Vedānta like Viśiṣṭādvaita and Dvaita in opposition to *jñāna* or *karma*. The way of devotion was advocated by the saints like Rāmānanda, Vallabha, Nānak, Caitanya, and Tulsī Dās. *Bhakti* is classified as lower (*apara*) and higher (*para*) *bhakti*. The former is known as theistic piety, and the latter philosophical meditation on the Supreme Reality (*Brahman*), which is *avyakta*.

Bhāmati (S) : It is a commentary written on Śaṅkara's *Brahma-Sūtra-Bhāṣya* by Vācaspati Miśra. It is believed that Bhāmati was the name of Vācaspati's wife. He named his treatise after her for the support and encouragement given by her.

Bhartṛhari (c. sixth century CE) : He was an independent thinker and a well-known philosopher of language. He studied under Vasurāta. Bhartṛhari advocated a theory of meaning called *sphoṭa* in his *magnum opus Vākyapadīya*. According to him, all our knowledge is interwoven with words. In other words, whatever is known is known through words. The word is only a means of knowing even that which is absolutely unreal. Bhrtṛhari held that there is one eternal principle, namely, *śabda Brahman*, which has neither beginning nor end. It manifests itself in the form of the phenomenal reality. However, the ultimate principle is beyond space and time. Many believe that he is an Advaitin. According to Bhartṛhari *dhvanis* are the *vivarta* of *sphoṭa*. The words and phonemes that are abstracted by grammarians from the sentences are merely unreal.

Bhartṛprapañca (sixth century CE) : He was a pre-Śaṅkara philosopher who introduced the notion of identity-cum-difference (*bhedābheda*). According to this view, the relation between *Brahman* and the *jīva*, and *Brahman* and the world is one of identity in difference. The doctrine of Bhartṛprapañca is monism, and is of the *bhedābheda* type.

Bhāskara (c. ninth or tenth century CE) : He is known for his *bhedābheda* Vedānta. He opposed Śaṅkara's interpretation of the doctrines of *māyā* and *nirguṇa Brahman*. Bhāskara held that *prakṛti*, being the power of God, is as real as God. However, *ātman* is *Brahman* as limited by *prakṛti*. According to him, the world is a transformation (*pariṇāma*) of *prakṛti*. The transformation belongs to *Brahman*. Hence this doctrine may be described as *Brhma-pariṇāma-vāda*.

Bhāṣyakāra (S) : It means "a commentator." The most prominent commentators on the *Brahma-Sūtra* are Śaṅkara, the propagator of Advaita, Rāmānuja, the propagator of Viśiṣṭādvaita, and Madhva, the propagator of Dvaita. Of all the three Rāmānuja is known as *bhāṣyakāra*.

Bhattacharya, Krishna Chand (1875 – 1949) : He was a contemporary Indian philosopher who held that Vedāntic position can be understood by studying the philosophy of Immanuel Kant. He examined the Kantian problem of the impossibility of metaphysics. It is evident from the analysis of Kant in his *Critique of Pure Reason* that reason cannot go beyond certain limits. If it ventures to go beyond its limits, the result is that it will end up in antinomies. Therefore, the transcendental can be approached by something that is not an ordinary reason. Vedāntins call this extraordinary reason intuition. Bhattacharya follows Kant up to an extent and goes beyond him on the negative side to ring out the true implications of Kant's unknowable. According to him, the unknowable cannot be treated as reality, for it is unthinkable. Thought of the absolute unknown is not at all a thought. The unknown in the form of indefinite hovers around all our definite experiences creating the most fundamental dualism between the definite and indefinite, between what we know and what we do not. Every definite content of awareness implies an outlaying indefinite out of which it has been carved. In this sense the indefinite is "immanent". It is as much immanent in the definite as transcendent. His important works include: *Studies in Vedantism* (1903); *The Subject as Freedom* (1930); and *Studies in Philosophy* (1956 & 1958).

Bheda (S) : It means "difference." It is an important concept for Dvaita Vedāntins. The *bheda* is of five types. They are as follows: (1) the difference between the God and individuals, (2) between two individuals, (3) between the God and matter, (4) between the individuals and matter, and (5) between matter and matter itself.

Bhūta (S) : It means "element." According to Indian philosophers, there are *pañca bhūta*s or five elements. They are earth (*pṛthvī*), water (*ap*), fire (*agni*), air (*vāyu*), ether (*ākāśa*). It is also believed that the earth is the cause of sense of smell; water, the sense of taste; fire, visual sense; air, the sense of touch; and ether, the sense of hearing.

Biconditional : In propositional logic, a biconditional statement is expressed in the following manner:

Mr Sriram will be the President of the Students Union *iff* he wins the election (if and only if is abbreviated as *iff*). To put it in other words, in a biconditional statement the possession of one property is "necessary and sufficient condition" for possessing another property. The following is the truth-table for a biconditional statement.

p	*q*	*p iff q*
T	*T*	*T*
T	*F*	*F*
T	*T*	*F*
F	*F*	*T*

Bimba-pratibimba-vāda (S) : It is known as "the reflection theory." According to Vivaraṇa School of Advaita, an individual is a reflection of consciousness in egoity. Since there is no distinction between a reflection and the original, the *jīva* is non-different from the Supreme Reality, *Brahman*.

Biologism : It is the view according to which all behaviour can be explained in terms of fixed biological drives.

Biometry : It is a scientific application of mathematical analysis to the field of biology. It is also known as "mathematical biophysics."

Black Box : In behaviourism, it is considered as a hypothetical unit specified only by functional role in order to explain some effect or behaviour. This term is applied to a single entity with an unknown structure, which is intended to realize some known function. In behaviourism the basic functions of an organism are taken to be generalized mechanisms that govern the relationship of stimulus to response. Such a relationship includes reinforcement, inhibition, extinction, and arousal. The organism in question is treated as a black box realizing these functions.

Black, Max (1909 – 88) : He is a well-known American philosopher of mathematics, logic, and language who followed the lines of Wittgensteinian approach towards language. His training in mathematics at Cambridge made Black write on *The Nature of Mathematics* (1933). His other important works include: *The Importance of Language* (1962) and *A Companion to Wittgenstein's Tractatus* (1964).

Blanshard, Brand (1892 – 1987) : He is regarded as one of the influential American rationalist philosophers who claimed that his entire work consists in the vindication of reason against any philosophical argument. His main works include: *The Nature of Thought* (1939); *The Importance* of *Language* (1962); *Reason and Goodness* (1962); *Reason and Analysis* (1962); and *Reason and Belief* (1962).

Blavatsky, Helena Petrovna (1831 – 91) : She founded the Theosophical Society in 1875 along with Colonel Olcott. She wrote voluminous works based on the Hindu and the Buddhist teachings. Her works influenced the neo-Hindu reform movements in India.

Block, Ernst (1885 – 1977) : He was a German philosopher influenced by Marxist philosophy. However, he went beyond the limits of Marxism by advocating unorthodox ideas, which were not relished by the communist authorities in East Germany. The he was forced to move to West Germany in 1960s. His major work, The *Principle of Hope* (1954-59), is a product of many influences such as German idealism, Jewish mysticism, neo-Platonism, Utopianism, and Marxism. According to Block, humans are essentially unfinished, moved by cosmic impulse called "hope." There is a tendency in them to strive for the as-yet-unrealized vision of future possibilities. His views influenced both philosophers and theologians of his time.

Blondel, Maurice (1861 – 1949) : He was a French philosopher trained in the spiritualistic tradition of Maine de Biran and Boutroux. According to Blondel, the philosophy of action tries to establish the relation between thought and action. It attempts to compromise between the extremes of intellectualism and pragmatism. His important works include: *L' Action* (1893) and *La Pensee* (1934).

Bodhāyana (S) : He was a pre-Śaṅkara philosopher. According to Rāmānuja, it is Bodhāyana who propagated Viśiṣṭādvaita in its true spirit. Some identified him with Upavarṣa.

Bodhisattva (Pl) : It means "existence (*sattva*) in a state of wisdom (*bodhi*)." In other words, he is one who is enlightened. Gautama Buddha is known as *bodhisattva*.

Body : In its material sense, it is an object with spatio-temporal dimensions. It is often contrasted with mind, soul or self or spirit. This view lead to the much discussed mind-body problem in the history of philosophy. Both idealism and materialism are considered to be the offshoots of this distinction. The former rejects the material forms of existence, and the latter spiritual forms of existence. According to Descartes, mind and body are two independent substances. The former has thought as its attribute, and the latter extension. Although they are functionally independent from each other, they interact with each other in the pineal gland of the human soul. Two most important theories concerning mind-body problem are interactionism and parallelism. See mind-body problem.

Boehme, Jacob (1575 – 1624) : He was a German Protestant speculative mystic born to poor parents. He studied Bible and the works of Pastor Valentine Weigel. He became a noted mystic and theosophist of his time. According to him, all reality contains, including God, duality in the form of good and evil. The universe and human soul cannot exist without God. The world is good, as God is, but withers away, and is restored at the end of history, though not entirely, for some souls are damned forever. Human beings enjoy free will and create themselves through rebirth in faith. His important works include: *Mysterium Magnum* and *Vierzig Fragen von der Seele.*

Boethius, Anicius Manlius Severinus (c. 480 – 524) : He was a Roman philosopher. He was known for his translation of works of Aristotle. He believed that faith and reason are two distinct approaches by means of which a valid interpretation of the universe can be given. Between the two he preferred the latter to the former to arrive at a rational approach to the universe. It is believed that his *magnum opus Consolation of Philosophy* is widely read after the Bible.

Bohr, Niels (1885 – 1962) : He was a famous Danish quantum physicist who won the Nobel Prize for his contribution to physics. In order to overcome methodological difficulties in quantum theory and its interpretation, Bohr put forward and substantiated the principle of complimentarity, which is a method of description that can be applied to various fields of knowledge.

Boltzmann, Ludwig (1844 – 1906) : He was an Austrian physicist who advocated the atomic theory. He was chiefly responsible in propagating the kinetic theory of gases and statistical mechanics. His transport equation, H-theorem, and the probabilistic interpretations of entropy made him a popular physicist of his time. His important works include: *Lectures on the Theory of Gases* (1896-98) and *Popular Writings* (1905).

Bolzano, Bernard (1781 – 1848) : He was an Austrian philosopher who established himself in the disciplines such as philosophy, mathematics, physics, and theology. In fact, Husserl, Lukasiewicz, Tarski, and the logicians of the Warsaw school were influenced by his ontology and logical semantics. His views on ethics and social philosophy influenced the cultural life of Bohemia and Austrian form of education. Bolzano made distinction between actual thoughts and judgements of humans, their linguistic expressions, and the abstract propositions, which exist independent of thoughts, judgements, and expressions. According to Bolzano, a proposition is a pre-existent sequence of ideas-as-such. Similarly, Bolzano distinguished religion from its objective and subjective senses. Religion in its objective sense is a set of propositions, whereas in its subjective sense it is a set of religious judgements. His important works include: *Wissenschaftslehre* (1837) and *Paradoxien des Unendlichen* (1851), a posthumous publication.

Bonaventura, Giovanni di Fidanze (1221 – 74) : He was an Italian Catholic scholastic philosopher and a mystic, who held the view that the pious way of life and prayer are the indispensable conditions of learning the truth and the supernatural ecstasy that is experienced by a person who receives God's blessings. He joined Franciscans in 1248. He taught theology in Paris for seven years and received his doctoral degree in 1257. His philosophy is Augustinian with some Aristotelian modifications in his theory of intellection and matter of form. His important works include: *Comentaria in IV L Sententiaarum, Itenerarium mentis in Deum* and *Quaestiones Disputate.*

Boo-hooray Theory : It is a nickname given to the emotive theory of ethics advocated by Alfred Ayer in his *Language, Truth and Logic*. According to this theory, all utterances concerning morals are simply the emotions of the speaker. They do not state anything more than what is uttered by the speaker. Thus moral statements are mere pseudo-statements. They cannot be brought under the purview of the principle of verification.

Boole, George (1815 – 64) : He was a well-known British logician and mathematician who invented algebra and also modern symbolic logic. He was a Professor of mathematics in Queen's College, Cork (1849-64). His important works include: *Mathematical Analysis of Logic* (1847) and *Laws of Thought* (1854).

Borderline Case : In logic it is a case, which falls within a grey area or twilight zone because of the usage of a vague concept. In its pragmatic sense, it is a case, which is doubtful, disputable, or arguable. For instance, a borderline case of day and night is the moment of time near sunrise or sunset.

Bosanquet, Bernard (1848 – 1923) : He was a famous British philosopher who came under the influence of Hegelian thought. According to him, an idea of the individual is regarded as a concrete universal or unity of opposites, which is capable of independence. Such individuality finds its expression not in the religion, art, and society. His important works include: *Knowledge and Reality* (1885); *History of Aesthetics* (1892) and *The Principles of Individuality and Value* (1912).

Bourbaki, Nicolas : It is a collective pseudonym given to a group of French mathematicians who have been working on a definitive survey of mathematical structures since 1939. According to them, mathematics can be developed from a few basic axioms with the help of strict logical arrangements. They do not compartmentalize mathematics as algebra, geometry, etc. Instead they classify mathematics into various parts on the basis of algebraic structures.

Bourgeoisie (F) : In the historical materialism of Karl Marx, bourgeoisie refers to the class of urban, commercial, banking, manufacturing, and shipping entrepreneurs. This is diametrically opposed to the expression "proletariat."

Boutroux, E (1845 – 1921) : He was a teacher of Henri Bergson. He became very popular for his defense of radical contingency and indeterminacy in metaphysics. He was influenced by French "spiritualism" of Maine de Biran. Boutroux was critical of psychological and sociological treatment of religious experience. His important works are *Science et Religion* (1908); *Philosophy and War* (1916); and *Contingency of the Laws of Nature* (1920).

Bouwsma, O(ets) K(olk) (1898 – 1978) : He was an American philosopher who practised ordinary language philosophy. Bouwsma is best known among the philosophical circles for his understanding of Wittgenstein's technique of philosophical analysis. Bouwsma did not advocate any philosophical theory. He was interested in highlighting the significance of any argument by exposing a central sentence as nonsense. His important papers were published under the following titles. They are: *Philosophical Essays; Toward a New Sensibility; Without Proof or Evidence;* and *Wittgenstein Conversations* (1949-51).

Boyle, Robert (1627 – 92) : He was a well-known British physicist and chemist of Irish descent. He became very popular by promoting the corpuscular or atomistic view of matter. He experimented on gases. He tried to show in his work *The Skeptical Chemist* (1661) that chemistry is different from alchemy. He insisted that the nature of material substance must be detected from experimental evidence. Thus he opposed the Greek view of substance (*ousia*).

Bradley, Francis Herbert (1846 – 1924) : He was a British idealist philosopher who was chiefly influenced by Immanuel Kant and Hegel. According to Bradley, no particular thing can be viewed as a collection of properties attributed to it. The particularity and the individuality of anything is imparted by the relatedness of its properties. What is called "Absolute" is not a mere system of appearances, but a container of that system. All relations, held Bradley, are internal. His main aim was to purge contemporary thought of the extremely sensationalistic and utilitarian elements embodied in the tradition of empiricism. The important works of Bradley include: *Ethical Studies* (1876); *Principles of Logic* (1883); and *Appearance and Reality* (1893).

Brahmā (S) : He is one of the Gods of Hindu trinity, *trimūrti* Gods, who is responsible for creation. According to the Hindu belief, Brahmā writes on the forehead of each individual what is destined to him. He is supposed to have four faces.

Brahma satyam jagat-mithyā jīvo brahmaiva nāparaḥ (S) : This is the central teaching of Advaita Vedānta, according to which *Brahman* is the only reality, the world is illusory, and the individual soul is none other than *Brahman*.

Brahmacarya (S) : This means "celibacy." This is the first stage in the *āśrama-dharmas*, wherein an individual leads his life as a student. In this stage a student has to lead a life of austerity.

When the boy is eight years of age, he goes to his teacher's house and lives there until he finishes his studies.

Brahman (S) : According to Advaita, *Brahman* is the Supreme Reality. It is *nirguṇa, niravayava,* and *akṣara*. It is *satcidānanda*. It cannot be described in terms of language as it transcends all the concepts and relations. *Brahman* in association with *māyā* is known as *saguṇa Brahman* or *īśvara* or God. It is responsible for the creation of the world in the sense that it is both the material and efficient cause. However, *Brahman* does not transform (*pariṇāma*) itself into the world. The world of objects is the transfigurative (*vivarta*) aspect of *Brahman*. According to Viśiṣṭādvaita, *Brahman* is the only reality, but is qualified by consciousness (*cit*), and material world (*acit*). This is what is called qualified monism. *Brahman* is equated with Viṣṇu. According to Dvaita, both *Brahman* and the world of objects are real. Both Viśiṣṭādvaita and Dvaita do not admit the concept of *nirguṇa Brahman*.

Brāhmaṇa (S) : They belong to the *karma-kāṇḍa* of the Veda. They are the Vedic dictums or treatises of a ritualistic and sacrificial character. The word *brāhmaṇa* is that which relates to *Brahman*. They basically deal with the ritualistic aspect of the original texts and it is this aspect that has come to be technically called *Brāhmaṇa*s.

Brahma-sūtra (S) : It is the work compiled by Bādarāyaṇa to make the teachings of the Upaniṣads more intelligible. Also, the purpose of this work is to present the cardinal doctrines of the Vedānta in a systematic manner. However, it is believed that the work is more complicated and difficult to follow. It is regarded as one of the important components of *Prasthānatraya*.

Brahmo Samāj (S) : It is a Hindu social reform movement started in 1828 by Raja Rammohun Roy. This movement stressed on the unity of God. It rejected all forms of sacrifices, priesthood, representations of God, the caste system, and the teaching of reincarnation. The members of this movement are called "Brahmos."

Brain : It is a central part of the nervous system that consists of the cerebrum and the spinal cord. The uppermost parts of the cerebrum are directly connected with the mental and psychic life of humans and animals. They are the organs of control through which various activities of the individual are regulated. According to Aristotle, brain is the cooling organ of the body. In the history of philosophy, brain is often regarded as closely connected with consciousness and the activities of the soul. Descartes conceived that mind-body interaction takes place in the pineal gland located between the two hemispheres of the brain. Cabana, a famous sensationalist, held that brain produces consciousness in a manner similar to the liver, which produces bile. According to modern scientists, the talk about the identity of mind and brain is almost outdated, since apparently there is no distinction between mind and brain. The identity theorists have attempted to provide a respectable basis for the equation of mind and brain by maintaining that mind is just a term for the group of activities and dispositions, which are in turn to be identified with brain processes.

Brentano, Franz (1838 – 1917) : He was a German-Austrian philosopher and psychologist who introduced the notion of "intentionality." According to him, mental events can be classified under three important heads. They are (1) perception; (2) judgement of belief; and (3) approval or disapproval. In any mental experience the content is merely a physical phenomenon intended to be referred to. What is psychic is merely an "act" of representing, judging, and valuing. Brentano considered himself an Aristotelian. His influence on later German thinkers is remarkable. The philosophers such as Alexius Meinong, Edmund Husserl were chiefly influenced by him. The former made use of Brentano's notion of "intentionality" in the field of analytic philosophy, and the latter to phenomenology. Brentano's important work is *Psychology from an Empirical Standpoint* (1874).

Bṛhadāraṇyaka Upaniṣad (S) : It is the largest of all the Upaniṣads. It consists of the information regarding meditations, and the various philosophical doctrines. According to this Upaniṣad, in the beginning there was only *ātman*. It did not know anything else and asserted "I am" and became the "I." This one becomes into two, namely, man and woman. The entire human race came out of them. The state of love and embrace is unmanifest (*avyakta*). Thus unmanifest becomes manifest world. The *ātman* is the same as *Brahman*. One who realizes "I am *Brahman*" becomes one with *Brahman*. In this Upaniṣad, there is a story that the king Ajātaśatru tells Bālāki that the *ātman* is found in the deep sleep (*suṣupti*). Yājñavalkya teaches his wife Maitreyī that no one wants an object of pleasure for the sake of object, but for the sake of *ātman*. We should therefore, know what *ātman* is. This self is *Brahman* (*ahaṁ brahmāsmi*). Yājñavalkya teaches the king Janaka that *ātman* is the guiding principle of man. It is the light of the *ātman* that guides us in dream. This light is imperishable.

Bṛhad-devatā (S) : It is a summary of the deities and myths found in *Ṛgveda* ascribed to Śaunaka. It was probably composed in the fifth century BCE.

Bṛhaspati (fifth century BCE?) : He is believed to be the heretical teacher and the founder of the Cārvāka School of materialism. Sometimes he is identified with the teacher of the *deva*s, who is also Bṛhaspati. It appears that the teacher of *deva*s propagated materialism among the *asura*s mainly to ruin that race. Cārvāka is believed to be the ideal disciple of Bṛhaspati.

Broad, Charlie Dumbar (1887 – 1971) : He is a well-known British philosopher who distinguished critical from speculative philosophy. According to him, critical philosophy analyses the basic concepts and propositions of everyday life and science. By going beyond science, Broad tried to reach the total view of the world by bringing in the facts and principles of aesthetics, religious, ethical and political experience. The speculative philosophy is concerned with correlating the findings of natural sciences with religion, art and society. Broad showed interest in parapsychology too. As an emergent evolutionist he held the view that everything happens by the blind combination of the elements of matter or energy, without any guidance, excluding the assumption of a non-material component. He considered primary qualities as physical emergents, and the secondary qualities trans-physical emergents. His important works include: *Scientific Thought* (1923); *The Mind and its Place in Nature* (1925); *Five Types of Ethical Theory* (1925); and *Examination of McTaggart's Philosophy* (1933 and 1938).

Bruno, Giordano (1548 – 1600) : He was a famous Italian philosopher and astronomer who was burnt to death for his radical views on reality. He promoted an extreme form of pantheism by holding the view that God is the unifying substance from which everything has evolved. He supported Copernicus' heliocentric theory. His well-known works include: *The Italian Dialogues; The Ash Wednesday Supper; On Cause; Principle and Unity; The Expulsion of the Triumphant Beast;* and *On the Infinite Universe and Worlds*. All these works were published in 1584.

Büber, Martin (1878 – 1965) : He was an Austrian born Jewish philosopher of religion. He was an active member of Zionist movement and a Professor of Jewish philosophy at Frankfurt. Büber made a distinction between viewing things from without as objects on the one hand, and entering into a full two-way relationship on the other. Thus we silently observe things, but normally enter into discourse with fellow human beings. This is the famous distinction between the "I-It" and the "I-Thou" relation. In a way, it is the second type of relation that involves our full being and establishes a personal relation. It is in this relation that we stand to God, for example, in prayer, and to other people when we acknowledge the divine spark in them. The "I-Thou" relation is open-ended and risky. It cannot be rationally predictable. This view of Büber is akin to Kierkegaard's "leap of faith." His important works include: *I* *and Thou* (1923); *Moses* (1946); *Between Man and Man* (1947); and *Eclipse of God* (1957).

Buddha (C. 560 – 480 BCE) : His original name was Siddhārtha. He belonged to the ancient family of Gautama or Gotama. Buddha means "the awakened" or "the enlightened one." Siddhārtha became Buddha, the enlightened, by recognizing the difference between a sense of fact and the dream of life. He believed that human life is full of suffering and misery. *Nirvāṇa* is the only way out of this misery. He preached the four noble truths. He attacked the Vedic-Brāhmanical tradition. He rejected all sorts of sacrifices and idol-worship to make Buddhism a progressive religion.

Buddhaghoṣa (fourth century CE) : He was a Buddhist philosopher belonging to Theravāda order. Theravādins belong to the Hīnayāna sect of Buddhism.

Buddhi (S) : It means "intellect." It is the first evolute from *prakṛti*. It is the basis for all the intelligence of the individual. According to Nyāya-Vaiśeṣika, it is of two types, namely, *smṛti* or recollection, and *anubhava* or experience.

Buddhism : It is one of the heterodox schools of Indian philosophy named after the teachings of the Buddha. It defied the Vedic authority, and is treated as one of the most progressive philosophies of its time. Buddhism as a way of wisdom taught and practised for the sake of improving the quality of life by removing the causes of suffering is a complicated phenomenon incorporating a great many historical changes, but in its essence, as taught by the Buddha, it is a relatively simple teaching to grasp. The basic message of Buddhism constitutes its four Noble Truths and the Eight-Fold Path advocated by the Buddha. These truths are: (1) there is suffering; (2) suffering is caused; (3) suffering can be eradicated by eliminating the causes of suffering; and (4) the way to put an end to the causes of suffering. This fourth Noble Truth is called Middle Path. This Middle Path, which sums up the way of life that characterizes

Buddhism as a practical philosophy, is built upon the eight principles constituting the fourth Noble Truth. These principles are: (1) Right views (*samma ditthi*); (2) Right resolution (*samma sankappa*); (3) Right speech (*samma vaca*); (4) Right action (*samma kammanta*); (5) Right livelihood (*samma ajiva*); (6) Right effort (*samma vayama*); (7) Right mindfulness (*Samma sati*); and (8) Right concentration (*samma samādhi*). There are two important sects of Buddhism, namely, Mahāyāna and Hīnayāna. The Theravāda schools of Buddhism belong to the latter. They are Sautrāntika and Vaibhāṣika. The former advocates representative realism and the latter direct realism.

Bultman, Rudolf (1888 – 1976) : He was a German theologian and a *New Testament* scholar. He was skeptical about the validity of the narratives of the Gospel. However, as a follower of Barth, he believed that Christian faith does not require any support either from natural theology or historical evidence. Later on Bultman came under the influence of his Marburg associate Martin Heidegger, and claimed that modern Christianity must involve itself in the process of "demythologizing." The critics pointed out that Bultman reduced the doctrine of God and man to man alone. His important work is *New Testament and Mythology* (1953).

Bundle Theory of Self : It is a conception of the self according to which self is nothing but an aggregate of mental states. This view of self is attributed to David Hume, who held that "self is a bundle or collection of different perceptions, which succeed each other with an inconceivable rapidity and are in a perpetual flux and movement." For details see his *A Treatise on Human Nature*.

Bureaucratic Socialism : It is a system in which economic and political life is centrally administered by the state. In the communist regimes patterned after Marxist-Leninist ideology, the state is controlled by bureaucratic elite drawn exclusively from the party.

Buridan, Jean (1300 – 58) : He was a French philosopher who wrote extensively on logic and natural philosophy. His most important works on logic are *Summulae de dialectica* (*Sum of Dialectic*) and *Tractatus de consequentiis.* The former provides a revised introduction to logic and the latter a treatise on modes of inference. Like other medieval nominalists, Buridan held that universals are not real. They are only concepts that help mind to conceive of many things in different ways. In his ontology he accepted only particular substances and qualities.

Buridan's Ass : It is a story of an ass attributed to Jean Buridan, a fourteenth century nominalist, who supported the doctrine of freedom of will (indeterminism). According to this story an ass died of hunger and thirst because it was incapable of deciding between food and water that were placed at equal distances from him. But, it is argued that a human being if confronted with a similar situation would exercise his freedom of will. Thus he would certainly be able to resolve the equilibrium between two opposing forces.

Burke, Edmund (1729 – 97) : He was a British statesman and a philosopher who argued that our enjoyment of beauty consists in the way in which our imagination is engaged by obscurity and suggestiveness rather than by intellectual clarity. As a political philosopher, Burke supported the Irish cause and American independence. His important works include: *Philosophical Inquiry into the Origin of Our Ideas of the Sublime and the Beautiful* (1756) and *Reflections on the Revolution in France* (1790).

Burley, Walter (1275 – 1344) : He was a British philosopher who taught philosophy at Oxford and theology at Paris. He was an orthodox Aristotelian and a realist. He criticized Ockham's logic and his interpretations of the categories of Aristotle. Most of his work is confined to natural philosophy. His important works include: *On the Intension and Remission of Forms;* and *On the Faculties of the Soul; On First and Last Instants.*

Butler, Joseph (1692 – 1752) : He was a British theologian and Anglican Bishop known for his contributions to moral philosophy, especially to deontological ethics. He defended religion against deist criticism on the basis of empiricism. He employed analytic method to arrive at influential arguments in support of virtue and personal identity. These arguments appeared in a collection called *Sermons* (1725). Butler refuted psychological hedonism. He opposed all moves to reduce virtue to benevolence. His other important work is *The Analogy of Religion* (1736).

C

Cabala (qabbala) : It was a Jewish tradition and a system of mysticism and theosophy practised during thirteenth to eighteenth century. It was believed by followers of the Cabala tradition that it was communicated to Moses at Sinai. The main portion of Cabala, the *Zohar*, is believed to be the work of Moses de Leon of Guadalajara in the thirteenth century. *Zohar* consists of a number of references to gnostic and neo-Platonic themes. It narrates the mysteries of God's being, human destiny, and the meaning of the commandments. The Rabbanic Judaism believes in transcendent and strictly unitary God. The real divine powers of God are called *sefirot*.

Caird, Edward (1835 – 1908) : He was a Scottish philosopher and an absolute idealist. In his major work entitled *The Critical Philosophy of Kant* (1877), Caird held that Kant made use of reason to reconcile rationalism and empiricism. According to Caird, Kant's treatment of reason as subjective principle is something unfortunate. This view of Kant lead to the opposition between the self and the world. As an absolute idealist Caird held that objective reason or the Absolute is a larger whole in which both the self and the world are mere fragments. In religion, Caird was of the opinion that Christianity is the highest evolutionary stage of religion. His other important work is *Evolution of Religion* (1893).

Caitanya (S) : It means "consciousness." It is a quality near the in-itself aspect of the Absolute spirit. Therefore, it is used as a synonym for the Absolute. In fact, it represents the *cit* aspect of *sat-cit-ānanda*.

Caitanya, Śrī Kṛṣṇa (1486 – 1533) : He was a Bengali representative of Bhakti Vedānta Vaiṣṇava cult coupled with *sahajīva* elements. He was a great devotee of Lord Kṛṣṇa. He was touring from place to place and mostly lived in Purī (Orissa) where he used to lead singers and dancers accompanying the Jagannātha processions. According to him, *Brahman* (God) is different from the *jīva* and the world, but at the same time *Brahman* is not different from the *jīva* and the world in so far as the latter is dependent on the former for their existence. However, the distinction between *Brahman* and the *jīva* and the world is indiscernible. This position is called *acintya bhedābheda.*

Cajetan (Tommaso de Vio) (1469 – 1534) : He was an Italian prelate and theologian, who entered Dominican order. He became cardinal in 1517. In Germany he entered into a theological controversy with Luther. Cajetan's major work is his commentary on St. Thomas Aquinas' *Summa Theology* (1508), which aroused interest in Scholastic and Thomistic philosophy during the sixteenth century. Like St. Aquinas, Cajetan held that all human knowledge is possible through sense-experience. His work on logic resembles the traditional Aristotelian logic, but its originality lies in its discussion on the notion of analogy. According to Cajetan, there are three types of analogy. They are — analogy of inequality, analogy of attribution, and analogy of proportion. However, he rejected the first two types as they are logically ill-founded. Cajetan recognized the importance of the last type as it helps us in knowing how humans come to know about God. Thus analogical reasoning can be applied to God.

Calculus : It is a set of rules to manipulate symbols. Calculus extends thought in solving problems and providing statements expressed by means of the given calculus. The important feature of calculus is that the figures, the letters, and the other symbols dealt with in it do not practically change when the rules of calculus are applied to them. In logic, there are two types of calculus. They are propositional or sentential calculus and predicate calculus.

Cāḷukya : It is a dynasty in the Deccan, India (550 – 753), whose capital was Bādāmī. The fame of these rulers reached as far as Persia. They were great builders of the Hindu temples. In Bādāmī they dedicated the rock-carved shrines to Śiva and Viṣṇu.

Calvin, John (1509 – 64) : He was a French theologian and a popular figure in the Protestant Reformation. He was chiefly responsible for the reformed churches in Germany, France, Switzerland, Netherlands, Scotland, and England. His theology is blended with humanism. He always held that philosophy is a noble gift of God. However, he rejected philosophical speculation about "higher things."

Calvinism : This term refers to the theological doctrines of John Calvin (1509 – 64). It is a theological discipline in which God is made the centre of all that is and all that happens. God's will pervades human and cosmic events, and upon whom man is utterly and cheerfully dependent.

Cambridge Platonists : They were a small group of Cambridge philosophers whose views represented a kind of revival of Platonism. They believed that ethics rests on certain absolute and self-evident truths. The prominent seventeenth-century Cambridge Platonists were Ralf Cudworth and Henry More.

Campanella, Tommaso (1568 – 1639) : He was a Dominican monk who revolted against Aristotleanism. Campanella was influenced by the naturalism of Telesio. His philosophical conclusions are akin to those of Descartes in many respects. He distrusted the information obtained about the reality by means of sense-experience and reason. The only trustworthy fact is one's own existence, and the inferences drawn from that fact. Even the existence of God is inferred from one's own existence. As a political philosopher, Campanella developed utopia on the lines of Plato. He believed that temporal power of the papacy in its political and religious sovereignty must control the world. His important work is *City of the Sun*.

Camus, Albert (1913 – 60) : He was a French existentialist philosopher, novelist, who won Nobel Prize for his literature. Camus was born and brought up in Algeria. As a young journalist and playwright he established himself in Algeria. He was influenced by Kierkegaard, Nietzsche, and Dostoevsky. He was an atheist. His philosophy was concerned with the meaning of human existence. According to him, man's existence is "absurd." Thus he made the category of absurdity as the basis of his philosophy. He defined the notion of "absurd" as a confrontation between ourselves, i.e. with our rationality and justice, and an indifferent universe. In his famous work *The Myth of Sisyphus* (1943), Camus tried to show how Sisyphus, who was cursed by the Gods throughout, makes a futile attempt to roll a rock uphill without realizing the fact that it may roll down without any effort because of its own weight. This is the condition of the human existence. We constantly struggle hopelessly and pointlessly to achieve some goal in our life. His other important works include: *The Plague* (1947) and *The Rebel* (1951).

Candrakīrti (c. sixth century CE) : He was a Mādhyamika Buddhist who wrote a commentary on Nāgārjuna's *Mūlamādhyama Kārika*. He is known for his destructive dialectics (*vitaṇḍa*). His chief aim was to show the unreality of the phenomenal world.

Canon : Epicurus replaced the ancient dialectics by canonics. It represents any norm or rule obeyed by a logical process. J.S. Mill puts forth five experimental methods that are regulated by certain canons. According to Kant, a canon is a sum total of all principles a priori of the correct use of our powers of knowledge.

Cantor, Georg (1845 – 1918) : He was a German mathematician who is regarded as a father of set theory. Cantor transformed the mathematics and its philosophical foundations like Frege,

Dedekind, Peano, Russell, and Hilbert. Cantor turned arbitrary collections into objects of mathematical study. He created a coherent mathematical theory of the infinite, especially the theory of transfinite numbers. Also, he was the first to indicate that it is possible to present mathematics in the form of sets. He is widely known for his paradox, according to which the whole universe of sets is considered to be a set, thus engendering contradiction. He also held that a set of all natural numbers is not equivalent to the set of real numbers. Thus, there are more than one infinite number.

Capacity : It is nothing but power, potency, ability and talent possessed by a thing, either to act or to suffer. Capacity may be innate, acquired or dormant.

Capitalism : It is a form of economic production wherein the instruments of production such as land, factories, raw materials, etc. belong to private individuals. In other words, the production process and production relations are controlled by an individual or a group of individuals for his or their own interests. Thus it encourages private property and profit-oriented economy for the benefit of a section of people in the society. According to Karl Marx, capitalism is a state in which an individual is exploited in ever so many ways. This results in alienation or estrangement of the individual. For instance, the individual is alienated from the product that he produces, and form the fellow workers, and from his own self.

Caraka (c. CE 78) : He was an ancient Indian physician. In his medical treatise *Caraka Saṁhita* he recognized some important categories. They are: *dr̥ṣṭānta, prayojana, pratijñā,* and *vitaṇḍa.* These categories resemble those found in the *Nyāya-Sūtra* of Gotama. It appears that Caraka developed them independently. His treatment of Sāṁkhya system is different from that of Kapila, the founder of Sāṁkhya system.

Cardinal Number : Two classes are said to be equivalent if there is a one-to-one correspondence between them. Cardinal numbers are obtained by means of abstraction with respect to equivalence, so that two classes have the same cardinal number if and only if they are equivalent. According to Frege, the cardinal number of a class is the sum of all classes equivalent to it. If two classes *X* and *Y* have no members in common, the cardinal number of the logical sum of *X* and *Y* is uniquely determined by the cardinal numbers of *X* and *Y*, and is called the sum of the cardinal number of *X* and the cardinal number of *Y*. For example, 0 is the cardinal number of a null set. 1 is the cardinal number of a unit set. All unit classes have the same cardinal number.

Cardinal Virtues : The cardinal virtues are those virtues, which a culture or society regards as primary and all other virtues are derived from those virtues. According to the ancient Greeks, the cardinal virtues are wisdom, courage, temperance, and justice to which Christians added three more, faith, hope, and love or charity.

Carnap, Rudolf (1892 – 1970) : He was one of the most distinguished members of the "Vienna Circle" who led the radical wing of the circle. Like any other logical positivist, Carnap held the view, in his *Philosophy and Logical Syntax* (1935), that the sole function of philosophy is the "logical analysis of the language of science." The purpose of logical analysis is to discover how we can become certain of truth or falsity of a given proposition. In his first major work, *Die Logische Aufbau der Welt* (*The Logical Structure of the World*), which appeared in 1928, he tried to apply the logic developed by Frege, Russell, and Whitehead to the problem of the philosophy of science. In his *The Logical Syntax of Language* (1937), Carnap gave importance to syntax rather than to semantics. According to him, the very syntax of a sentence discloses its metaphysical nature. In this work Carnap made a distinction between material and formal modes of speech. It was his intention that the material mode, commonly used in philosophy, often leads to ambiguities and errors of metaphysicians and in general is the source of meaningless controversy in philosophy. To overcome these problems, Carnap felt that it is necessary to translate sentences from their material idiom to the more accurate formal idiom. For example, the sentence "The moon is a thing" is cast in the material mode. It can be translated into the formal mode by rewriting it as "The word 'moon' is a thing designation." Every sentence, which states "such and such is a thing" belongs to the material mode of speech. Carnap held that many other words, such as "quality," "relation," "number," and "event" also function the same way as the word "thing." Carnap realized the importance of semantics when he first read Alferd Tarski's writing on "The Semantic theory of Truth" that appeared in 1935. In 1941 he published *Introduction to Semantics.*

Carneades (c. 215 – 125 BC) : He was an opponent of Stoics. His important contribution to philosophy is his doctrine of logical probabilism as a basis of skepticism.

Cartesianism : It is another name for the philosophy of René Descartes (Cartesius). As a dualist, Descartes advocated the view that the mind and body are two independent substances. Mind has thought as its attribute, and body extension. However, they interact with each other in the pineal gland located in the human soul. The criticism levelled against Cartesianism is: how can a non-extended substance interact with a substance with extension? See Descartes.

Cārvāka (S) : It is the ancient Indian materialist school founded by Bṛhaspati. This school does not owe any allegiance to the Vedic authority. Another name for this school is Lokāyata, meaning worldly or mundane philosophy. Although there is no direct evidence of any writings of the founder of this school, it is mentioned in Jayarāśi's *Tattvopaplavasiṁha* (seventh century CE), which appears to be the summary of the *Bṛhaspati-Sūtras.* Also, in Madhava's *Sarvadarśanasaṁgraha* some references are made to this school. In epistemology, this school admitted sense-experience as the only legitimate source of knowledge. There is nothing beyond the purview of sense experience. *Anumāna* or inference, according to this school, is a leap in the dark. In metaphysics, this school held that ultimate reality is of physical nature. It is made up of four elements, namely, earth, water, fire, and air. Cārvāka did not accept *ātman*. Consciousness, which is the byproduct of these elements, disappears at death. In ethics, this school admitted pleasure as the sole ideal of life. The wealth and enjoyment alone bring pleasure. The pleasures are the pleasures of the sense and mind. Like Epicurus, Cārvāka taught controlled satisfaction of the desire for pleasure. The popular sayings of Cārvāka are summarized in the following way:

> Live happily so long as you live,
> Borrow money and drink ghee.
> When the body is turned to ashes,
> How can you to the world return.

Cassirer, Ernst (1874 – 1945) : He was a German philosopher and a member of Marburg School of Neo-Kantianism. Cassirer rejected the view that scientific abstractions are the reflection of the reality. The influence of Kantian philosophy on Cassirer is seen in his writings. His works are in the field of history, culture, and philosophy. According to Cassirer, all human knowledge depends on the power to form experience through some type of symbolism. The forms of human knowledge are co-extensive with forms of human culture. Myth, religion, art, history, language, and science are forms of human culture. These forms of symbolism constitute a total system of human knowledge and culture, which forms the subject matter of philosophy. Susanne Langer was influenced by Cassirer's philosophy. His important works include: *The Problem of Knowledge* (vols. 1-3, 1906-20, vol.4, 1950); *The Philosophy of Symbolic Forms* (1923-29); *An Essay on Man* (1944); and *The Myth of the State* (1946).

Casualism : It is a doctrine according to which all things and events came to existence by chance. This is basically the view of the Epicureans.

Casuistry : It is a case-analysis approach to interpret general moral rules. Casuistry starts by applying paradigm cases to any general moral rule. In the process it accommodates new ideas and that challenges the existing social order. Casuistry as a method was popular during the first half of the seventeenth century. However, casuistry was attacked by Pascal in his work *Provincial Letters* (1656). But the term "casuistry" did not lose its charm in the contemporary ethics.

Catechetic : It is a method or procedure of imparting religious instruction orally by means of questions and answers, mainly to children.

Categorematic : In traditional logic, a denoting term or word that can stand on its own apart from its usage in a sentence or statement is known as categorematic word. For example, the words such as "blue," "cat," "bird," etc.

Categorical Imperative : It is one of the prominent expressions that we come across in Kantian ethics. According to Kant, it is the supreme, absolute moral law of rational, self-determining beings. It is distinguished from hypothetical imperatives, which admit of exceptions. The essence of Kant's categorical imperative is "Act on maxims which can at the same time have for their object themselves as universal laws of nature." Therefore, a categorical imperative is an unconditional obedience to the moral laws for their own sake and not for the sake of any other higher kind. See Kant.

Categorical Judgement : According to Aristotle, any direct, explicit, affirmative judgement is called categorical judgement. Like modern logicians Aristotle too distinguished categorical judgements from conditional ones. For Kant it is a judgement which comprises of two concepts joined by a copula, typically an attribute asserted of a subject. He denied that hypothetical and disjunctive judgements can be reduced to categorical type.

Category : The most important concepts are called categories. All sciences (exact, natural, and social) are based on certain fundamental categories of their own subject matter. For example, physics is based on certain fundamental categories like matter, motion, change, space, time, acceleration, etc. Similarly, there are certain philosophical categories, which are very important for the better understanding of the subject matter of philosophy. For example, form and content, freedom and necessity, cause and effect, appearance and reality, determinism and indeterminism are very important categories of philosophy. However, in Aristotle's philosophy the term "category" covers all ten classes, which in turn explain all the modes of existence (being). Thus, a predicate belonging to one category may not be applicable to a subject belonging to another category. Aristotle recognized ten categories. They are: substance, quality, quantity, relation, place, time, position, state, action, and effection. In modern times, it was Kant who focused his attention on the categories of understanding. Unlike Aristotle, Kant did not restrict categories merely to "subject and predicate" of a statement but rather extended the categories of understanding to entire judgements. Kant recognized twelve categories of understanding, which can be reduced to four basic categories of understanding. They are: quantity, quality, relation, and modality.

Category Mistake : Gilbert Ryle introduced this term in his *The Concept of Mind* (1949). According to him, we often commit category mistake by attributing same qualities or properties to the entities belonging to different logical types. For example, Descartes advocated the view that mind can exist independent of body and body independent of mind. Here mind and body belong to two different logical types, yet the notion of existence is attributed to both. Ryle illustrates the origin of the category mistake by citing the following example. Suppose a person visited a university for the first time, and is shown the field house, the library, the dormitories, the administration and all the rest. After all this, if the person says "I have seen all the major buildings of the university, but I have not yet seen the university," this results in, what Ryle called, a category mistake. The person assumed that a university is a different sort of entity apart from all those buildings that he visited. The university does not belong to the same category as its buildings do. In a way, the university is a whole that comprises of all its buildings.

Catharsis (Gk) : It means "cleansing." Early Greek medical practitioners used this expression to explain the purging of body and soul. This concept describes the influence of aesthetics on man. The expression "catharsi" was used by Greek philosophers in many senses such as religious, ethical, physiological, and medical. In other words, catharsis is a synthesis of physiological and ethical elements that promote aesthetic sense of appreciation in man. In this sense it is nothing but purging of emotions.

Causa sui (L) : It means "cause of itself." According to Spinoza, Substance is *causa sui.* He identified Substance with God and Nature. Thus, God for Spinoza, exists in every object. Such a God is uncaused.

Causation or Causality : It is one of the most important philosophical categories of experience that attracted the attention of philosophers of all times. Causation has been conceived to prevail between processes, parts of a continuous process, changing parts of an unchanging whole, objects, events, ideas and so on. It was Aristotle who for the first time in the history of philosophy introduced the notion of causation by putting forward his fourfold theory of causation. According to him, there are four important causes. They are: (1) formal cause, (2) material cause, (3) efficient cause, and (4) final cause. For example, a sculptor wants to make a statue of Socrates. The idea that he forms in his mind becomes the formal cause. The material that he chooses to make a statue of Socrates becomes material cause. The paraphernalia that he uses to make the statue of Socrates becomes the efficient cause. And the purpose for which the statue of Socrates is made becomes the final cause. But, in modern times, it was Hume's theory of causation, which attracted the attention of many philosophers. According to Hume, a cause is an event that precedes another event called effect. Thus cause is antecedent and the effect is consequent. Hume held that the entire theory of causation is based on four important factors. They are contiguity, succession in time, co-existence, and necessary connection. He held that the first three factors are given in sense experience, while the fourth factor is inferred from the first three. Since the idea of necessary connection is not given in sense-experience, Hume denies any objective significance to causation. Unlike Hume, Kant held the view that the principle of causation is based on generality. Therefore, the idea of necessary connection is a priori. It cannot be proved by means of sense-experience.

Causes : Aristotle's theory of causation is based on formal, material, efficient, and final causes. In modern times it was J.S. Mill who advocated the doctrine of multiplicity of causes. According to him, many causes may produce one single effect. See causation or causality.

Cause-theory : It is a theory concerning mind-body problem. According to this theory, mind may influence body or vice versa or both influence each other.

Cave, Myth of the : In Plato's philosophy, the myth of the cave is a metaphor which intend to explain the nature of reality. According to Plato, the prisoners of the cave can only see the shadows of various objects on the walls of the cave, and believe that it is the only reality without realizing that there is something behind every shadow. The analogy of Plato goes like this. The shadows of the objects seen on the walls of the cave are nothing but the objects belonging to this transient phenomenal world. The objects that are responsible for such shadows are nothing but the eternal Forms.

Certainty : It is a quality of a proposition arrived at by means of logical demonstration or by a priori means. It represents an objective state of affairs rather than a subjective state of mind.

According to epistemologists, unlike belief, which may be true or false, knowledge is always certain.

Certitude : It commonly refers to the mental state of being sure or certain. In other words, it is a subjective state of mind. It is an unquestioned assurance. It is also described as psychological certitude as opposed to logical or rational certainty.

Chala (S) : It means "quibbling." It is one of the arguments found in Gautama's *Nyāya-Sūtra*. The argument consists in an unfair criticism of the opponent through a misleading interpretation of his statement. In this sense, the argument is always a kind of equivocation. There are three possibilities of *chala*. (1) If a word has two meanings, the opponent may criticize one's position by attacking the unintended meaning of the word. (2) When one makes a categorical statement like "This horse is white," the opponent may interpret it as a statement of necessity and ask; How can you infer from it being white its being a horse? Or how can you infer from it being horse its being white? (3) If a word has both literal and metaphorical meanings, the opponent may take advantage of playing with those meanings.

Ch'an wei (C) : It is a system represented by a group of prophetic writings called *ch'an* and a group of apocryphal "compliments" or "woofs" attributed to the "Confucian Classics" called *wei*. Their attempt is to interpret these "Classics" in terms of medieval Chinese theology, which highlights the correspondence between man and the Universe.

Chance : It is something undetermined. It is opposed to what is necessary or inevitable. Chance events, according to Aristotle, are occurrences purposive in appearance, but not actually the result of either conscious or unconscious teleology.

Chāndogya Upaniṣad (S) : This is the second largest Upaniṣad. According to this Upaniṣad, everything is *Brahman*. It is immanent in us. It is the smallest, yet it is the largest. The person seen in the eye is *ātman*. Aruṇi tells his son Śvetaketu that in deep sleep speech enters mind, mind the life principle (*prāṇa*), the life principle the psychic force (*tejas*), the psychic force enters the Supreme Deity. All these things belong to *ātman*. And "That art thou" (*tat tvam asi*). Ultimately, this Upaniṣad holds that "I am all this" (*ahameva idam sarvam*), and the "*ātman* is all this" (*ātma eva idam sarvam).*

Ch'ang (C) : It means "invariables." They are the universal or eternal laws or principles responsible for phenomenal change in the universe.

Chang Hsueh-ch'eng (1738 – 1801) : He was a Chinese philosopher and historian known for his dialectical theory of civilization. According to him, beliefs, practices, institutions and arts are developed due to natural needs. Such a process reached its culmination several centuries before Confucius. His view that "the Six Classics are all history" provides us with a clue that the Classics are not mere theoretical statements about the way of life (*tao*), but traces of it in operation. An ideal age is represented by the unity of government (*chih*) and teaching (*chiao*). There were no private institutions for learning and all writing was anonymous.

Ch'ang sheng (C) : It means "everlasting existence." The earth and heavens have everlasting existence for they do not exist for their own sake. According to Taoism, long life is the result of nourishment of the soul and rich accumulation of virtue.

Chang Tsai (1020 – 77) : He was a Chinese philosopher who followed the teachings of Confucius. As a Neo-Confucian he adopted and provided a metaphysical basis for Neo-Confucian ethics in his famous work *Western Inscription* (*Hsiming*). He argued that the entire cosmos came out of a single source, the Supreme Ultimate (*t'ai chi*). The undifferentiated ether (*ch'i*) took form out of an inchoate, primordial state called supremely tenuous (*t'ai-hsu*). Although the sage experiences his oneness with the universe, yet he knows his particular place and role in the greater scheme. The true nature of the world is not realized by many because of the impure endowments of ether (*ch'i*). This is the reason why they remain selfish. However, they can overcome this state by ritual practice and learning, which elevate him to sagehood.

Change, Philosophy of : This refers to any philosophical doctrine that is concerned with the principle of change. It is also applicable to any philosophy that makes change as an essential or pervasive aspect of reality.

Chaos (Gk) : Aristotle held that chaos is the pre-philosophical concept of space. Greek philosophy in general attempts to justify the origin of the world by means of imposition of order on pre-existing chaos. In fact, the term "chaos" was introduced by Hesoid in his *Theogony* to describe the gap between the heaven and the earth when the world came into existence.

Characterizing : This expression is used as an adjective or noun without supplying a principle for counting what falls under it. For example, "thing," "object," "place," "action," etc.

Characters : They are the statements or Ego-values or attitudes like pleasant, true, known, etc.

Charron, Pierre (1541 – 1603) : He was a French catholic theologian who presented the ideas of Montaigne in a didactic form. In his earlier work, *The Three Truths* (1595), Charron argued against atheism, non-Christian religions, and Calvinism. But his arguments had a negative impact on Catholicism. He held that we cannot understand or know God because of His infinitude. Human faculties are too finite to know anything about God. Therefore, one should accept Christianity on the basis of faith. In his later work, *On Wisdom* (1603), he systematically presented Pyrrhonic form of skepticism coupled with a fideistic defense of Catholicism.

Chatterji, Bankim Chandra (1838 – 94) : He was a great novelist who promoted religious and national feelings among the Indians during the freedom struggle. He was influenced by Sri Aurobindo in his early part of life. He is known to all the nationalist Indians for his poem "Bande Mataram," which is treated as a national anthem of India.

Cheng hsin (C) : It means "setting one's own heart right or rectifying it." It is a Confucian view that a person's heart loses its balance when he is upset by anger, disturbed by fear, blinded by love, or involved in worries and anxieties. It must be rectified before it loses its balance.

Cheng ming (C) : It is a doctrine of the "rectification of the names." According to this doctrine, names should correspond to the objects in reality to serve as standards for social organization and personal conduct. The actual must in each case be made to correspond to the name.

Chen jen (C) : It means "the true man." The expression refers to a person who is pure like gold, which has limitless inward resources. He is one who has transcended the self and non-self, and life and death, and who has reached a mystical union with the Universe.

Chi (C) : It means "the moving power." It is a great scheme from which everything comes and to which everything returns.

Chiliasm : It is a religious doctrine that believed in the thousand-year-old "kingdom of God" on earth, which is supposed to precede the end of everything in this world. Some Jews and Christians advocated this doctrine. It is also known as Millenarianism.

Chinese Philosophy : It covers a wide range of philosophical ideas developed by Confucianism, Taoism, and Buddhism. In fact, Confucianism and Taoism dominated the Chinese philosophy to a great extent, although it is not chronologically established which of them is prior to the other. Taoism (*tao chia*) viewed nature as opposed to man. It glorified Tao, or the way, which aims at long life and lasting vision for preserving the life and keeping the essence of our being intact. On the other hand, Confucianism (*ju chia*) advocated true manhood (*jen*) as the highest good, the superior man (*chun tz*) as an ideal being must feel that cultivation of life (*hsiu shen*) is the supreme duty of man. In fact, Confucius (551 – 479 BCE) taught the doctrines of *chung* or being true to the principles of one's nature, and *shu* or the application of these principles in relation to others to establish moralism and humanism. His concept of "golden mean (*chung yung*)" is intended to find out the clue to our moral being and to be harmonious with the Universe. The doctrines of humanism were further strengthened by Mencius (371 – 289 BCE) who held that man must develop his nature fully because benevolence (*jen*) and righteousness (*i*) are natural to his nature which is originally good. This view of Mencius was reinforced by Hsun Tzu (335 – 286 BCE) who held that human nature is evil; therefore it needs to be controlled. However, both Taoism and Confucianism shared the view that reality is an unceasing change. But, the critics held that Taoism has become too mystical and Confucianism too formal. Gradually Taoism was degenerated and identified itself with the lower forms of religious belief. Its naturalistic philosophy was reduced to mere fatalistic mechanism in *Lieh Tz* (CE 300). Medieval Chinese philosophy was essentially an amalgamation of indigenous philosophies and development of Buddhism. During the second century BC, the *Yin Yang* movement identified itself with the common and powerful movement under the names of the Yellow Emperor and *Lao Tz* (Huang Lao). This movement interfused with Confucianism to produce the Eclectic Sinisticism lasting until tenth century CE. In the meantime Buddhism was establishing its roots in the Chinese soil. Many Buddhist doctrines, which were latent in India, were developed in China. The *śūnyavāda* or nothingness of Mādhyamika became popular in China due to Fahsiang school (CE 563 – 1000). According to this school, reality is imaginary in the sense that it is devoid of any special character. This doctrine did not accommodate the Chinese ideal of "golden mean." Therefore, China had to develop its own Buddhist philosophy to be consistent with its general philosophical outlook.

Ching (C) : They are the Classics of Confucians or Taoists. They also mean cardinal standards or direction in Confucian ethics and government. *Ching* also means reverence, seriousness or inner state of respect or politeness.

Ching shen (C) : It is the spirit and soul of man, or the vital force (ch'I), which is endowed by Heaven as against the physical form which is endowed by earth.

Choice : According to Sartre, man is condemned to be free in the sense that he can make his own choices. In ethics, choice refers to an agent's act of volition in deciding between two or more alternatives. Sometimes a moral agent may choose between alternative courses of action or alternative ends of action. In either case choice is deliberate, wilful, and knowing as compared to preference, which may be spontaneous.

Chomsky, Avram Noam (1928 –) : He is a living leading American linguist and philosopher, whose grammar has revolutionized the scientific study of language. Chomsky held that the function of grammar is not to give order to the facts of language, but to discover an underlying rule-structure. Therefore, grammar is a procedure for rule-structure, which is independent. Further he held that grammar is independent of semantics. Thus he argued for the autonomy of grammar. According to Chomsky, the speakers of a language have innate ability to create infinite number of sentences that are intelligible. His important works include: *Syntactic Structures* (1957); *Aspects of the Theory of Syntax* (1965); *Cartesian Linguistic* (1966); *Language and Mind* (1968); and *The Logical Structure of Linguistic Theory* (1975).

Chrematistics : This term was introduced by Ingram (1823-1900) and followed by others in a restricted sense to that portion of political economy which deals with the management of wealth and property.

Christology : It is a totality of those doctrines, which deal with the nature and personality of Christ. First of all, Christology must concern itself with the promise of a saviour and redeemer of the human race. It includes the prophecies foretelling the

Messiah, as well as their fulfilment. Further it must inquire into the mystery of the incarnation, of the word made of flesh, and examine all the circumstances of the birth, passion, and resurrection of Christ. Since he acknowledged that he is and was God, the son of God, one with the Father, it becomes necessary to examine his credentials, his own prophecies, miracles, and saintly life, which were to serve as evidence that he was sent by God and really possessed all power in heaven and on earth. Christology deals with the human and the divine nature, their relation to each other, and the hypostatic union of both.

Chrysippus (280 – 209 BCE) : He was one of the leaders of the Stoic school. His writings are lost. It appears that he deviated from the central teachings of the Stoics. For instance, he combined the principle of natural necessity, or determinism, with the doctrine of providence.

Chu His (1130 – 1200) : He was a Neo-Confucian philosopher, who considered that ideal substance *li* is primary, while the material substance *ci* is secondary. The ideal or spiritual substance *li* is bereft of all qualities and form, and is inaccessible to sense-experience. Due to constant alteration of motion and rest five important elements came into existence. They are: water, fire, wood, metal, and earth.

Chuang Tzu (399 – 295 BCE) : He was a great Taoist philosopher, who was a petty officer in his native state. His love of nature, his vivid imagination, and subtle logic, made his works masterpieces of his time. He denied premiership in favour of freedom and peace.

Church's Thesis : Alanzo Church proposed this thesis according to which "the notion of an effectively calculable function of positive integers should be identified with that of a recursive function." This proposal is known as Church's thesis.

Cicero, Marcus Tullius (106 – 43 BCE) : He was a great Roman statesman, orator, and essayist. Cicero was not recognized for advancing any individual philosophical arguments, but for his attempt to unify philosophy with rhetoric. His trilogy, *On the Orator; On the Republic;* and *On the Laws,* depicts the vision of wise statesman-philosophers, who always managed their political affairs through rhetorical persuasion rather than violence. Philosophy, according to Cicero, needs the company of rhetoric to achieve its most important practical goals. At the same time rhetoric becomes helpless in the absence of psychological, moral, and logical justification provided by philosophy. The combination of rhetoric and philosophy constitutes what he called *humanitas.* In *Academics,* Cicero offered detailed accounts of Hellenistic epistemological debates by sticking to a middle position between dogmatism and radical skepticism. His important works, *On Divination*; *On Fate*; and *On the Nature of the Gods* provide us with a survey of Epicurean, Stoic, and Academic arguments about theology and natural philosophy.

Circulus in demonstrando (L) : This non-verbal fallacy is called "arguing in circle." This fallacy occurs when an unproved premise is used to derive a desired conclusion. For example, if a person tends to say that chinaware is better than earthernware, because it is made of superior quality of clay, and when asked why the clay is superior, he argues that it is superior because it is used to make chinaware. This is a circular argument.

Cit-śakti (S) : According to Śaiva Siddhānta, *ātma-cit-śakti* is the only valid source of knowledge. All other *pramāṇa*s serve as only auxiliary sources.

Citsukha (c. thirteenth century CE) : He was one of the post-Śaṅkara Advaitins known for his dialectics. Citsukha was commentator and follower of Śrīharṣa, who wrote *Khaṇḍanakhaṇḍakhādya*. Citsukha's important work is *Tattvapradīpikā.*

Citta (S) : According to Yoga, it is the phenomenal form of the mind as the first creation of *prakṛti,* which is differentiated into various mental states (*vṛtti*s) such as true and false knowledge, imagination, memory, sleep. According to Advaita Vedānta, *citta* is one of the functions of the internal organ (*antaḥkaraṇa*). The function of *citta* is recollection.

Class : It is a collection of entities or individuals of any type that share a definite common property that allows them to form into a class. For example, all the philosophers form a class. However, each class can be considered as a sub-class of a class provided a sub-class shares something in common with other sub-classes of the same class. For instance, all philosophers can form into a class by themselves, yet it is considered to be a sub-class of a class known as social scientists.

Class Consciousness : It is a form of awareness that a group has its own collective economic interests as against the interests of other economic classes.

Class Struggle : It is a very important expression in the philosophy of Karl Marx. In the historical materialism, it is held that the class struggle is considered basic to the dynamics of history in the sense that the widespread changes in the techniques or a fuller utilization of them necessitates changes in the economic relations, and in turn in the social superstructure. The economic aspects of the class struggle manifest directly in a capitalist society with regard to the amount of wages, rate of profit, rate of interest, amount of rent, length of a working day, and so on.

Classification : It is a process of grouping objects or entities into various classes on the basis of the discovery of common properties or the results of such grouping. It is also a process of grouping species into genera, genera into still larger genera, and so on.

Cleanthes (c. 320 – 230 BCE) : He was a disciple of Zeno and one of the most prominent thinkers of the Stoic school. Of all his writings, only his hymn on Zeus is extant.

Clement of Alexandria (150 – 217) : He was an early Christian thinker and theologian who attempted to raise the attitude of faith to the level of knowledge. Clement was influenced by the philosophers like Plato, Aristotle, the Stoics, and Philo Judaeus.

Clericalism : It is a socio-political approach that seeks to strengthen the role of religion and the Church in different spheres of social life.

Clocks, Image of the Two : In an attempt to explain the mind-body problem of Descartes, Leibniz made use of this example. When two clocks are functioning perfectly by showing accurate time, there is a possibility that, (1) they are mutually influenced, or (2) the mechanic constantly adjusts the needles of the two clocks so that they show the accurate time, or (3) they have in-built exactitude. If we substitute mind for one clock and body for the other, then we have three possibilities of relationship between the mind and the body. They are: (1) psycho-physical interactionism, (2) occasionalism, and (3) psycho-physical parallelism. Leibniz subscribed to psycho-physical parallelism.

Co-consciousness : It is the consciousness, which is disassociated from the central core of personality and of which that personality is unaware. According to Morton Prince, co-conscious and unconscious are the two species of the subconscious.

Coenaesthesis : It is an organic sensation that is responsible for circulatory and digestive functions as distinguished from external sensations such as visual, auditory, gustatory, tactile, etc.

Cogito ergo sum (L) : It means "I think, therefore I exist." It is the fundamental and indubitable foundation of Cartesian philosophy. Descartes claimed to have constructed a valid philosophical system from this "First Principle" of philosophy. He reached this principle by employing the "doubting method." His doubting method should not be confused with the usual skepticism employed in epistemology. According to Descartes, the doubting method can doubt anything that can be doubted, excepting the very substance of doubt called Mind, whose important attribute is consciousness or thinking. Thus Descartes is said to have arrived at this fundamental axiom of his philosophy, "I think, therefore I exist."

Cognition : In opposition to volitions and emotions, cognition is a mental process that is connected with the understanding, the formation of beliefs, and the acquisition of knowledge of the various phenomena. In its restricted sense, it is always identified with sensory cognition. In other words, it is an assimilation of the mind and object in question.

Cognitive Achievement Word : Any word in a proposition whose truth makes that proposition invariably true is called cognitive achievement word. For example, "Sriram knows that the milk is hot." It is true that Sriram knows, then it is also true that the milk is hot. Cognitive achievement words are often contrasted with the words like "believe," "think," "hope," etc.

Cognitive Science : It is an interdisciplinary enterprise that aims at establishing intelligent activity exhibited by a living organism like an adult human being or a machine. Both cognitive psychology and artificial intelligence are the important branches of cognitive science. However, there are other disciplines such as neuroscience, linguistics, philosophy, anthropology, which constitute cognitive science. In other words, it is a cross-disciplinary enterprise. Cognitive science as an important branch of human knowledge gained its momentum in 1970s. As a matter of fact, every discipline that became a part of cognitive science defied both positivistic and behaviouristic proscriptions that denied any systematic inquiry into the functions of mind. The pioneer of such an attempt was Noam Chomsky, whose generative grammar is an abstract theory of the structure of language, but also an account of language users' linguistic competence. The fundamental idea behind the cognitive science is to arrive at an abstract theory that could be applied to machines (computers) for manipulating information. Artificial intelligence is an important branch of cognitive science. If the entire human cognitive system is reduced to mere computational skills, then what is needed is to simulate its performance.

Cognitum (L) : It is a cognition in which the aspects, qualities, properties, attributes, and relations of objects are given in experience with a definite purpose.

Cognoscendum (L) : It refers to the object of cognition. The *cognoscendum* may be real, imaginary, ideal, etc.

Cohen, Herman (1842 – 1918) : He was one of the important figures of Marburg School, which developed Neo-Kantian philosophy. According to philosophers of Marburg School, all cognition is exclusively a priori. The Neo-Kantians rejected not only the "things-in-themselves," but also anything that is immediately given in sense-experience. There is no other reality excepting that which is projected by thought; and this holds good for object, subject and God. Unlike Kantian epistemology, they accepted Kantian ethics without any reservations. The sole objective of moral conduct is fulfilment of duty. Both Cohen and his illustrious colleague Paul Natorp (1854 – 1924) tried to reinterpret Plato and Kant.

Coherence Theory of Truth : It is one of the classical theories of truth. According to this theory, the truth of any given statement is dependent on the condition that it must cohere with the already accepted propositions in a definite system. In this sense, to be true is to be part of a non-contradictory system. Here the term "system" is understood as language structure that is deductively developed from a set of axioms. By and large all the rationalists and idealists subscribe to this theory of truth. The critics of this theory hold that the notion of "coherence" is very vague and not well defined by the advocates of this theory.

Coleridge, Samuel Taylor (1772 – 1834) : He was one of the leading British poets of his time. His writings vindicate his keen interest in spiritual affairs. It was Coleridge who introduced the writings of German Idealists to English reading public. The following works of his have philosophical significance. They are *Aids to Reflection* and *Confessions of an Inquiring Spirit*.

Collective and Distributive Properties : A general term is taken in its collective sense when what is predicated of it applies to the whole class. On the contrary, the distributive properties are those applicable only to that particular object or entity.

Colligation : J.S. Mill appropriated this term from Whewell. According to Mill, colligation is different from induction. The former is a simple description of observed facts, while the latter is an extension to the unknown and future.

Collingwood, Robin George (1889 – 1943) : He was a British philosopher who was chiefly interested in ancient history and archaeology. Though he attempted to show the relationship between history and philosophy, yet he viewed philosophy as a discipline distinct from history because of its unique and distinctive methods, the perennial polemics with regard to nature of reality, nature of knowledge, etc. His important works include: *Religion and Philosophy* (1916); *An Essay on Philosophical Method* (1933); *Principles of Art* (1938); *Essay on Metaphysics* (1940); *The New Leviathan* (1942); *The Idea of Nature* (1945, posthumously published); and *The Idea of History* (1946, posthumously published).

Colonization of the Life World : This expression was used by Habermas to refer to the way in which economic and administrative systems take over areas of familial and public life organized by communicative action. Because of colonization, interaction ceases to be regulated "democratically" by means of discussion regarding the validity of norms. Instead, it is regulated strategically by persons interested in maximizing their own personal gain *vis-à-vis* money and power. The net result is commodification (the reduction of persons and things to commodities or monetary exchange values) and bureaucratization (the subsumption of everyday life under grater administrative control).

Combination : It is a process by which a new whole is formed by the union of parts. It can also be the product of such a union. There are two types of combination. They are: (1) *composition* is such a union of parts that the component parts are discernible in the compound. (2) *fusion* is such a union of parts into a whole in which the identity of the parts is obliterated. Thus the amalgamation of two sense-images to form a new quality would, if this phenomenon were psychologically possible, be an instanance of psychic fusion.

Combination of Ideas : Locke held that mind with the help of its own operations combines simple ideas presented to it by means of sensation and reflection into complex ideas to form totally new ideas. See his *Essay Concerning Human Understanding*.

Combinatorial Logic : It is a branch in mathematical logic that is concerned with the analysis of various concepts that are accepted without further study within the framework of classical mathematical logic. Such concepts are those of variable and function.

Comedy : In Aristotle's *Poetics,* comedy is a play in which the chief characters behave worse than what men normally do in their daily life. On the contrary, in a tragedy, the main characters act more nobly. In Plato's dialogue *Symposium,* Socrates held that the writer with good comedies is able to write good tragedies.

Commodity Fetishism : This expression was used by Marx to describe the manner in which the products of labour under capitalism take on a life of their own. The deification of the laws of the market coincides with the dehumanization of the producers, who lose control over their lives.

Common Sense : It is a kind of general awareness of certain things and processes that take place in our day-to-day life, which is expected of in every normal human being. The common sense beliefs with regard to matters of everyday world are normally taken for granted. According to Aristotle, common sense is the sense that integrates the data of all the five senses in order to have a comprehensive perception of the object in question. The chief defender of the common sense viewpoint against philosophical skepticism in the twentieth century was G.E. Moore.

Common Sense Argument : This argument proceeds from a common acceptance of a belief to the truth of such a belief. This argument is chiefly interested in the belief that God exists.

Common Sense Realism : It is a philosophical standpoint advanced by the Scottish philosopher John Reid (1710 – 96). According to this doctrine, the objects exist independent of the perceiving mind. Later on Moore subscribed to common sense realism by accepting the independent existence of the physical objects in his realism and analysis.

Commonsensibles : In Aristotle's psychology, the qualities of a sensory object such as motion, rest, number, shape, size may be apprehended by several senses as against the qualities such as colour, taste, smell, etc.

Communication : This term is used to refer to a certain feature of sign-situations such as identity, similarity, or correspondence, of what is understood by the interpreter with what is expressed or intended to be expressed by the speaker. In its ordinary sense, communication is possible by means of speech, writing, gesture, facial expression, and bodily movements or by the direct contact between minds by mental telepathy and other occult means.

Communism : It is the highest stage of social development, according to Marx. It is a stage characterized by the disappearance of the state as an instrument of political domination, and the full emancipation and development of humanity. Marx believed that all the class distinctions will disappear in this stage. However, such a stage is yet to be realized on the earth by human beings.

Commutation : It is one of the rules of equivalence. It has the following form.

$$(p \;\&\; q) \equiv (q \;\&\; p)$$

$$(p \vee q) \equiv (q \vee p)$$

Comparison : It is a kind of juxtaposition of two or more entities or objects to find similarities or differences between them. The method of analogy is basically dependent on comparison. It is one of the sources of knowledge in Indian philosophy. See also Upamāna.

Compathy : Humans feel with each other the same sorrow, the same pain, etc. This feeling of with-each-other is called compathy. Only psychical suffering can thus be felt, but not physical pain.

Completeness : It is one of the important characteristics of an axiom system. The notion of completeness can be explained in the following manner. All the tautologies of a given system of logic must be provable from the accepted axiom set of the system in question, and if this is so, then that system is said to be complete.

Complex : A complex unit consists of distinguishable parts or a property of distinguishable parts. It can also be anything that possesses distinguishable parts, which are related in such a way as to give unity to the whole.

Composition : It is a verbal fallacy. This fallacy occurs when a particular term is used collectively instead of using it distributively. For example, the sentence "Philosophers are little interested in politics," may be true of some cases, but if it is understood in collective sense, then it is a fallacy because it is not true that all philosophers are not interested in politics. In another sense, it is the form of valid inference of the propositional calculus. It has the following form.

$$A \supset B \text{ and } A \supset C \text{ to } A \supset BC.$$

Compossibility : According to Leibniz, the things, which are literally co-possible, belong to the same possible world. For Leibniz, the metaphysical possibility means absence of contradiction. Two or more things are compossible, if, and only if, their joint ascription to a single world involves no contradiction.

Comte, Auguste (1798 – 1857) : He was a well-known French sociologist and philosopher who revolted against speculative or transcendental metaphysics which dominated the scene during his time. Comte's major philosophical contribution centred around his conception of the positive sciences and the positivistic theory of knowledge. It was also his concern that his new philosophy would provide the basis for a true religion. His chief objective was the total reorganization of society by means of his positivist philosophy. He defined positivism as a general attitude of mind, a spirit of inquiry, and an approach to the facts of human existence. Its central feature is to oppose that nature has some ultimate purpose or end. Thus he opposed teleology. Positivism, according to Comte, does not aim at discovering either the "essence" or internal causes of things. On the positive side, it aims at studying the facts by observing the constant relations between things and formulating the laws of science. According to Comte, there are three important stages of development of human thought. These stages are the *theological,* in which phenomena are explained as being caused by divine powers; the *metaphysical,* in which anthropocentric concepts of divinity are replaced by impersonal and abstract forces; and *positive* or *scientific,* in which only the constant relations between phenomena are considered and all attempts to explain things by references to beings beyond our experience are given up. His important works are *Le systeme de politique positive* (1851-54); *Catechisme positiviste* (1852); and *Synthese subjective* (1856).

Concept : The most general terms are called concepts. A concept is formed by observing the essential features of particular entities belonging to the same class. But certain concepts are also formed by mere a priori reasoning. For example, the concept "man" subsumes all particular men under this name irrespective of the accidental features. But, "truth" as a concept is attributed to certain characteristics, which are a priori. In Kant's philosophy, a concept is considered to be the product of understanding that stands in contrast to a percept, which is obtained through sense-experience. According to Kant, "concepts without percepts are empty and percepts without concepts are blind."

Conceptual Realism : This doctrine is akin to Platonic realism in many respects. It ascribes objectivity to conceptual cognition.

Conceptualism : In opposition to realism and nominalism, conceptualism holds that universals are mental concepts. Conceptualists share the view with nominalists that universals cannot exist apart from particulars. But, unlike nominalists, they recognize the existence of general a priori concepts as a special form of knowledge of reality.

Concomitance : This expression became popular in philosophy due to J.S. Mill, who advocated the method of concomitant variations. According to this method, appearance or disappearance of certain characters, which under certain circumstances admit, but do not necessarily postulate casual interrelatedness.

Concrete : This term is used in opposition to the term "general" or "abstract." In other words, it refers to anything that is specific or individual.

Concrete Universal : In Hegel's Absolute Idealism, a category is concrete when it possesses the basic character of the real, i.e. dialectical opposition. Such a Universal comprises a synthesis of two opposite abstractions. The Absolute Idea of Hegel can be characterized as a concrete universal.

Concurrence : According to St. Augustine, before the *Fall* it was possible for man not to sin, but he needed God's help. After the fall man needs God's grace or concurrence that acts with him. This term also signifies the general co-operation of God.

Condillac, Etienne (1715 – 80) : Voltaire regarded Condillac as one of the greatest philosophers of France. He was a sensationalist. He elaborated on the epistemology of John

Locke. According to Condillac, mind is passive and all its experiences are derived from the outside. He was a skeptic. He held that we can never know the real nature of the physical world. He assumed that self exists, and believed in its immateriality. The truths of religion, held Condillac, are known through revelation. His important work is *Traité des sensations*.

Condition : It is a conditional statement in formal logic that takes the form of "if *p* then *q*." It is also called hypothetical statement. For example, the statement "If today is Friday, then tomorrow is Saturday" is a hypothetical or conditional statement. In a conditional statement, the truth of the antecedent is dependent upon the consequent, but the truth of the consequent is not necessarily dependent upon the antecedent.

Configurationism : This is an English equivalent to Gestalt psychology. See Gestalt Psychology.

Confirmation : The verification of any given statement leads to the test of confirmation or confirmability. The criterion of such a test is experience. However, some philosophers of science like Karl Popper deny the view that experience can confirm the hypotheses of a scientific theory. Paul Feyerabend, another noted philosopher of science, claims that there is no established method or criterion to confirm any scientific theory.

Confucianism : It is the philosophy advocated by Confucius (551 – 479 BCE). According to Confucianism, the fate and destiny of man are determined by the "Heaven." Basically all human beings are either noble or base. Confucianism teaches that younger must obey the elders, and subordinates their bosses.

Confucius (551 – 479 BCE) : He was born in the state of Lu (Shangtung) in China. He lived in the time when the moral and cultural traditions of Chou were in decline. To salvage the lost culture, he taught poetry, history, ceremonies, and music to many of his students. He taught literature, human conduct. He wrote chronicles called *Spring* and *Autumn*. His tacit judgements on social and political events were such that "unruly ministers and villainous sons" were afraid to repeat their evils. His most important teachings are found in *Lun Yu* (Analects).

Conjunct : It is a term in conjunction. For example, *p* is a conjunct in "*p* and *q*."

Connotation : This term is often used as a synonym for intention or comprehension. J.S. Mill identified connotation with signification and meaning. The connotation of a general term (singular terms excepting descriptions are non-connotative) is the aggregate of all the other general terms necessarily implied by it as an abstract possibility and apart from exemplification in the actual world. It cannot be determined by denotation because necessity does not always refer to singular facts. Logicians who adopt this view distinguish connotation from comprehension by including in the latter contingent characters, which do not enter in the former. Thus, comprehension is the intentional reference of the concept, or the reference to universals of both general and singular terms. In short, the connotation of a concept is its intentional reference determined intentionally; while its comprehension is its intentional reference extensionally determined.

Conscience : It is an ethical category that describes the highest form of a person's ability to moral self-control. Conscience prevents man from any act that brings dishonour to the personal dignity. Conscience makes an individual to be self-critical and also critical of others' opinions when they go against the objective needs of a society.

Consciousness : It is the highest form of reflection of various aspects concerning reality intrinsic in man. Consciousness is the sum total of mental processes that actively participate in man's understanding of reality and of his own personal being. According to existentialists, man is a conscious subject who takes part in various aspects of life. His existence is far superior to the existence of any other being in this world. For Husserl, consciousness is the starting point of any phenomenological analysis, and is always intentional. According to Advaita, *Brahman/ātman* is pure Consciousness (*cit*). In psychology, a conscious act is distinguished from a mere instinctual act. Epiphenomenalists believe that consciousness is the epiphenomenon of the molecular changes that take place in the human body.

Consequent : It is a non-verbal fallacy. This fallacy occurs when the proposition of the following form is assumed. For example, "if *p* then *q* implies if *not-q* then *not-p*." Although it is true that *p* is true only when *q* is true, the converse of it may not be true, as *q* may be true without *p*. This fallacy is also called illicit conversion.

Consistency and Inconsistency : In logic, a set of statements is considered to be consistent if it entails a non-contradiction, and is inconsistent if it entails a contradiction. Consistency is one of the properties of an axiom system. The notion of consistency accounts for the derivability of formulae in the sense that if *S* is derivable then ~ *S* should not be a derivable formula. If both are derivable then such a system must be inconsistent.

Constants : Logical constants are nothing but a set of symbols whose value structures remain constant irrespective of their occurrence in any logical system. There are two types of constants, namely, logical and descriptive. Logical constants are the symbols such as "⊃ (implication)," "& (conjunction)," "*V* (disjunction)," "~ (negation)," etc. Descriptive constants function as names that stand for a particular entity, or a person, or a quality, a relation, etc.

Constative : This expression was first introduced by J.L. Austin to denote an utterance or an assertion with which one makes a true or a false claim.

Constructivism : It is a view according to which mathematical entities exist in so far as they are constructed by means of intuition or by any other way, and then mathematical propositions are true only when there is a constructive proof in support of them.

Contemplation : In its epistemological sense, contemplation is knowledge of an object in contrast to enjoyment, which is the mind's direct awareness.

Content of Consciousness : It is the totality of the qualitative data presented to consciousness in contrast to the act of apprehending such data.

Content and Form : They are two important philosophical categories that reflect the interrelation between two sides of reality. Content represents the very essence of object in question, while the form represents the mode of existence of a particular object. In Aristotle's philosophy, content is nothing but matter. He asserted that there cannot be formless matter inasmuch as there cannot be matterless form.

Contextual Dependent : The referent of an expression is dependent on the context of utterance. The expression, "The present Prime Minister of India is principled" refers to Dr. Manmohan Singh.

Contextualism : It is a way of aesthetic interpretation of art that insists on the view that any form of art is to be understood in its cultural context as every form of art is historically conditioned. Contextualism also plays an important role in understanding the nuances of our everyday language.

Contingency : It is a philosophical notion often contrasted with necessity. Leibniz classified truths into contingent and necessary truths. Contingent truths are those truths, whose truth is dependent on the law of sufficient reason alone. In short, such truth does not have universal validity since its truth-value is subject to change.

Contradiction : A proposition that involves in asserting something and denial of the same assertion is called a contradiction. In other words, it is a proposition, which is both true and false.

Contradiction, Law of : It is one of the laws of traditional logic, according to which a proposition cannot be both true and false simultaneously. Aristotle formulated this law for the first time.

Contraposition : It is an immediate form of inference in which a universal or conditional statement occurs as a premise and its conclusion as contra-positive. For example, the contra-positive of conditional statement "if *p* then *q*" is "if *not-q* then *not-p*." For a universal statement "All *X*s are *Y*," the contra-positive is "All *non-Y*s are *non-X*."

Contrary : It is a logical relation between two statements that cannot be true at a time, but can be false at a time.

Conventionalism : It is a philosophical conception, according to which all the scientific concepts and the theoretical conventions are mere agreements among scientists. For example, the value structures of mathematical symbols are mere conventions accepted by all without any kind of proof. Similarly, language is purely conventional.

Conversion : It is a form of immediate inference in which the order of the terms is reversed. For example, the converse of the statement "No *S* are *P*" is "No *P* are *S*." Similarly, the converse of "Some *P* are *S*" is "Some *S* are *P*."

Copernicus, Nicholas (1473 – 1543) : He was a Polish founder of astronomy who held the view that Sun is the centre of the solar system. His theory of heliocentrism is considered a revolution in astronomy. Prior to Copernicus, it was believed that Earth was the centre of the solar system. Such a theory is known as geocentrism.

Corpuscular Theory : According to this theory, reality is an aggregated product of minute particles called corpuscles. This is akin to atomism. Corpuscular theory emphasizes that there is one substance. Change is possible because this substance is divided into units, which are capable of motion. The arrangement of these units called corpuscles is the real essence of the bodies. These essences are called primary qualities. The secondary qualities are the resultant changes in the arrangement and the state of motion of constituent corpuscles. Gassendi, Boyle, and Locke were the chief advocates of this theory.

Correspondence Theory of Truth : It is one of the most popular traditional theories of truth, according to which truth consists in correspondence between a proposition and a fact. Accordingly, a proposition is said to be true if and only if it corresponds with a fact. Here the term "fact" denotes any aspect of objective reality. Plato advocated a form of correspondence theory of truth. Modern empiricists subscribe to this theory of truth. According to William James, correspondence theory of truth is nothing but a copy view of truth. It does not take functional aspect of an object into consideration. Moreover, it is not exactly defined what does "correspondence" mean. The critics of the theory question, how can there be correspondence between two different categories? Propositions and facts belong to two different categories. See picture theory of meaning, verification theory of meaning.

Corroboration : Karl Popper uses this term in his *The Logic of Scientific Discovery* as a substitute for confirmation. According to Popper, a scientific hypothesis is valid if there is sufficient corroboration in support of it. However much corroboration is found in favour of a scientific theory, yet it is not conclusively proved.

Cosmogony : It is a branch of astronomy that deals with the origin and the development of the heavenly bodies and their systems. Scientific cosmogony goes back to some 200 years when Kant advanced the hypotheses of the development of the planets from nebula, which at one time surrounded the Sun. The ancient Greek philosophers based their cosmogony on what they understood to be the qualities and the properties of the four elements (earth, water, air and fire).

Cosmological Argument : It is one of the popular proofs for the existence of God. It is also known as the argument from the

First Cause. The processes that take place in nature require an explanation. Such processes include the social, the physical, the biological, and the psychological events. We cannot explain the processes of nature by employing the concept of "nature" alone, just as we cannot explain why earth is moving by referring to earth alone. Hence, we can explain the processes of nature by appealing to the concept of something supernatural. Nature could not have brought itself into existence without a cause. That cause is God. Such a cause is an uncaused cause or the First Cause.

Cosmology : It is a branch of astronomy that views Universe as an integral whole, and part of the Universe which is under astronomical observation as a part of that whole. According to Kant, the problems of cosmology are of different kinds that they could never be solved.

Cosmos : It is the Universe as a whole, including the earth, the solar system, and all other galaxies. According to Pythagoreans, the world is a rationally ordered whole.

Count Noun : It is a term that stands for an individual entity or an item in a countable class. Thus, boys being countable, "boy" is a count noun.

Cratylus of Athens (*c.* third century BCE) : He was the first teacher of Plato who held the doctrine of irreconcilability of opposites so far that he renounced the use of spoken language. Plato in his dialogue *Cratylus* criticized the Heraclitean theory of language.

Creationism : It is a view that the world and the nature, the animate and inanimate were brought into existence with a single act of creation.

Creative Theory of Perception : As against selective theory of perception, creative theory advocates that the data of sense are created or constituted by the act of perception and do not exist independent of actual perceptual process. The theories of perception advocated by Descartes, Leibniz, Locke, and Berkeley are the examples for creative theory.

Credo quia impossible (L) : It means "I believe because it is impossible." This expression is derived from the statement made by Latin Father Tertullian that "It is certain because it is impossible."

Critical Idealism : It is another name for Kant's transcendental idealism. According to this doctrine, we arrive at certain judgements a priori (without having any recourse to experience). These judgements in principle can never be refuted by experience. Therefore, we are certain about their validity. Among such judgements, held Kant, are the judgements of geometry. Kant also tried to justify his idealistic doctrine in another way. He analysed the nature of human mind to show how our minds arrive at judgements. This analysis provides us with the view that the spatial form and the concepts (categories of understanding) participate in the constitution of the objects of perception. This is the reason why Kant held that "concepts without percepts are empty, and percepts without concepts are blind."

Critical Realism : It is a doctrine according to which objects are identified neither with the complexes of sensations nor with the impressions, nor with the constructions of our minds, but are recognized as trans-subjective existents. Ordinary sense-experience gives us a picture of the world that is not totally free from the subjective constituents and it attempts to rectify this picture and free it from these subjective constituents. Generally critical realists believe that the picture of reality as presented immediately to the senses does not correspond to reality as there are no colours, sounds, and scents in reality as otherwise conceived by our senses. All these qualities are the products of physical organization of our mental faculty.

Criticism : It is an investigation of the nature and limits of reason and knowledge, conducted in a manner to avoid both dogmatism and skepticism. For example, Kant in his *Critique of Pure Reason* (1781) undertook a critical examination of pure reason, it nature, and limits with a view to exhibiting a criterion for judging the validity of propositions of metaphysics.

Croce, Benedetto (1866 – 1952) : He was an Italian philosopher who is well known for his contribution to aesthetics and cultural history. His philosophy of spirit distinguishes spirit of thought from spirit of action. The former is classified into poetry (art) and logic, and the latter into economics and ethics. His important works include: *Logica* (1905); *Filosofia della practica* (1909); and *Teoria e storia della storiografia* (1917).

Cross-roads Hypothesis : It is a theory of relation between mental and physical which holds that an identical item (e.g., a green colour patch) may in one relational context be considered physical and in another context mental. The neutral entity may accordingly be represented as the point of intersection of the physical and mental cross-roads.

Cudworth, Ralph (1617 – 88) : He was a leading Cambridge Platonist, who attacked Hobbesean materialism calling it atheistic. He advocated rationalism of Cartesian type. He found clear and distinct fundamental notions or categories reflecting universal reason, God's mind, the nature and essence of things, and the moral laws, which he held to be binding on God as axioms of mathematics. His important works are *The True, Intellectual System of Universe*; and *A Treatise Concerning Eternal and Immutable Morality*.

Culture : It represents the intrinsic worth or value of a given society. Culture in general represents the customs, the habits, and the institutions of social groups. In psychology, culture represents the enlightenment or education of the individual. Culture is often distinguished from civilization on the ground that the former is the effect on personal development and expression (art, science, religion) of the institutions, and social organization identified with the latter. According to

Wittgenstein, it is a collective creation of the individuals living in a society.

Cultural Impoverishment : It is the inability of the cultural traditions to provide meaningful values. Such impoverishment has several causes. They are the colonization of the life-world and the splitting of elite sub-cultures, which prevent persons from developing the sorts of critical aptitudes required for analysing and synthesizing tradition, and the ideological manipulation and devaluation of tradition to the status of meaningless habit and slogan.

Cultural Value Spheres : This expression is used by Weber to refer to those spheres of activity such as law, science, ethics, and art/erotic life, which involve three principal loci of value, namely, the true (knowledge), the good (just norms), and the beautiful (aesthetic values).

Cusa, Nicholas of (1401 – 64) : He was a German philosopher who was interested in mathematics, astronomy, philosophy and ecclesiastical policy. His thought was Neo-Platonic and mystical. He was a critique of Aristotelian scholasticism. He believed that all opposites such as finite and infinite, the smallest and the greatest, single and multiple, etc. find their place in God.

Customs : They are the social behaviour patterns in which persons participate as members of a social group. Customs are differentiated from personal or random group behaviour patterns.

Cybernetics : It is a branch of science that deals with the common features of processes and control systems in technological devices. The emergence of cybernetics as a science was first noticed by a number of technological and scientific achievements in the theory of automatic control, the radio electronic systems, etc.

Cynics : It was a Greek school of thought that followed the teachings of Antisthenes of Athens, who was a friend of

Socrates. But the school was named after Gymnacium Cynosarges. The prominent representative of this school of thought was Diogenes. According to Cynics, happiness means living according to nature. Any desire that is not necessary for the minimal bodily satisfaction should be condemned as unnatural. According to them, right and virtuous life consists in a course of conduct, which is as much as possible independent of all events and factors external to man.

Cyrenaics : It was a Greek school of thought founded by Aristippus and Cyrene. This school advocated the philosophy of hedonism or the doctrine of enjoyment for its own sake. According to Cyrenaics, the virtuous or the good life is that which yields the greatest enjoyment. Such an enjoyment makes an individual master of pleasure rather than its slave.

D

D'Ailly, Pierre (1350 – 1420) : He was a French philosopher, prelate, and writer. D'Ailly was influenced by William of Ockham. He tried to show the relation between astrology and history and theology. In his major work *Tractatus de Concordia astronomicae* (1414) he predicted the 1789 French Revolution. He wrote a commentary on Boethius' *Consolation of Philosophy*, and another on Peter Lombard's *Sentences.* In his epistemology, D'Ailly distinguished indubitable knowledge or natural light from relative knowledge or reason. He claimed that experimental knowledge is uncertain and the classical proofs for the existence of God are mere probabilities. He distinguished the absolute power of God or *potentia absoluta* from God's ordained power or *potentia ordinata.* In his theology there are elements of fideism and the spirit of Protestantism and Lutheranism.

Dakṣiṇa (S) : It is one of the Śaiva schools. The cult of Śakti is called Vāma or Left. Sometimes these two can be considered as one school.

D'Alembart, Jean Le Rond (1717 – 83) : He was a French mathematician, philosopher and encyclopaedist. In philosophy, he was basically concerned with man, pneumatology, logic, and ethics. His pneumatology was only an investigation of the human soul. He held that philosophy is a comparative examination of physical phenomena. His epistemology associates Cartesian psychology with the sensory origin of ideas. He was influenced by Bacon, Locke, and Newton. D'Alembart held that the substance of the soul and matter is unknowable. His important works are *Treatise of Dynamics* (1753); *Discourse préliminaire* (1751); and *Elements of Philosophy* (1759).

Dalton, John (1766 – 1844) : He was a British physicist who held the view that the atoms are indivisible. His discoveries helped to convert philosophical brand of atomism advocated by ancient Greeks into a scientific one.

Damascius (*c.* 462 – *c.* 550) : He was a Greek Neo-Platonist philosopher and the last head of the Plato's Academy and a commentator on the works of Plato. He composed many works, including that of his teacher Isidorus. His philosophical system is a further elaboration of the scholastic Neo-Platonism of Proclus.

Dance : It is one of the art forms that is accompanied by musical rhythm with the movement of the human body. There are a variety of dance forms such as Kathak, Bharatanāṭyam, Kucipuḍī, Maṇipurī, Yakṣagāna, Mohiniaṭṭam.

Daṇḍanīti (S) : It is one of the aspects of political science that deals with the types of punishment. Kauṭilya in his famous work *Arthaśāstra* recognized *daṇḍanīti* as an important aspect of polity.

Darśana (S) : It can mean "perception," "view," "vision," "philosophy," "system." The Indian systems of philosophy are known as *darśana*s. They are the philosophies of life. There are six orthodox and three heterodox *darśana*s. The orthodox ones accept the authority of the Veda. They are Nyāya, Vaiśeṣika, Sāṁkhya, Yoga, Pūrva-Mīmāṁsā and Vedānta or Uttara-Mīmāṁsā. The heterodox *darśana*s are Cārvāka (the ancient Indian materialist school), Buddhism and Jainism.

Darwin, Charles Robert (1809 – 82) : He was a very famous British evolutionist whose theories of evolution revolutionized the entire natural science. Darwin explained the nature of evolution by means of natural selection, and the survival of the fittest. According to him, biological species evolve primarily by means of chance variation and natural selection. The significance of

Darwinism in philosophy lies in its opposition to Aristotleanism. There is also ample empirical evidence in support of Darwin's theories. However, there are many missing links in his theory of evolution. Darwin was not the first scientist to advance the idea of kinship of all life, but is memorable as the expositor of a provocative and simple explanation in his theory of natural selection. His *magnum opus* is *The Origin of Species by Means of Natural Selection* (1859).

Dasein (Gr) : It means "being there." Dasein in Heidegger's philosophy is basically concerned with the investigation of human existence. Man's existence is characterized by his relation with his surroundings and the members of his community. According to Heidegger, there are three distinctive features of Dasein. They are: (1) Factuality; (2) Existentiality or the apprehension of his purposive being and potential; and (3) Fallenness or man's tendency to get lost in the course of his very many preoccupations. Thus fallenness leads to "unauthentic existence."

Datum : The datum is anything that is given in sense-experience or in sensation.

Davidson, Donald (1917 – 2003) : He is regarded as one of the influential American philosophers whose chief interest lies in the philosophy of language, in the philosophy of action, and in the philosophy of mind. His theory of meaning has two aspects. They are: (1) the theory of truth and (2) a theory of radical interpretation. Davidson makes use of Tarski's theory of truth in order to provide a meaning for a sentence. He distinguishes causal relations from law like sentences on the ground that the former merely relates events, while the latter link the descriptions of events. His important works include: *Essays on Actions and Events* (1980 & 1982) and *Inquiries into Truth and Interpretation* (1984); One of the most important articles of Davidson is "Truth and Meaning."

Dayānanda, Swāmī (1824 – 83) : He was the founder of Ārya Samāj. He advocated the Vedic revivalism by clearing Hinduism of Purāṇic and Epic ballast. He was also influenced by the Western ideas and inventions. According to him, the Vedic interpretation should be based on *ādhyātmika*, *ādhidaivika*, and *ādhibhautika* levels expounded by Yāska in *Nirukta*. He opposed all forms of animal sacrifices, though he did not oppose the caste system. He worked for the social upliftment of the lower and outcastes.

Deanthropomorphism : It is a philosophical tendency first cynically applied by Xenophanes. He felt that it would have been something different had the cattle and lions have hands to paint. Later on it was followed by rationalists and addicts of Enlightenment to get rid of an understandable, if primitive, desire to endow phenomena and the hypostatized objects of man's thoughts and aspirations with human characteristics.

Death : In existentialist philosophy, death is a very important concept. Man's anxiety and anguish are the outcome of the imagination of death, which cannot be avoided. Heidegger's important slogan on death is that "None can die on my death by proxy." According to early Wittgenstein "Death is not an achievement in one's own life."

Death of God : Nietzsche in his *The Gay Science* used this expression. In the passage called "The Madman," the madman claims that the greatest deed of mankind is it killed God. He even talks about the decomposition of God. According to Nietzsche, for all practical purposes the God is dead on the earth.

Death Instinct (thanatos) : This expression is used by Freud to refer to the natural tendency of complex unities to dissolve into their original atomic elements. Ultimately, it seeks release from tension (pain).

Decadence : It is referred to a period of art that is often considered to be destructive of aesthetic values that were perfect at one time.

Decision Theory : It is a rational theory, which is probably the idea of Pascal. This theory was published in Arnaud's *Port-Royal Logic* (1662). To quote it: "To judge what one must do to obtain a good or avoid an evil one must consider not only the good and the evil in itself but also the probability of its happening or not happening, and view geometrically the proportion that all these things have together."

Deconstruction : It is a way of demonstrating the incompleteness or incoherence of a given philosophical position by means of concepts and principles of argument whose meaning and use is legitimated only by that philosophical position. In a way deconstruction can be viewed as internal conceptual critique in which the critic implicitly and provisionally adheres to the position criticized. Deconstruction as a method was popularized by Jacques Derrida through his writings. His earlier works on deconstruction argue against the possibility of an interior "language" of thought and intention in such a way that the senses and referents of terms are determined by their very nature. Such terms are "meanings" or *logoi*. According to Derrida, the concepts of Western metaphysics are based on such conception of *logoi*. Thus, metaphysics is fundamental to our cultural practices and languages. In this sense there is no "ordinary" language which is uncontaminated by philosophy. All our accounts of intention, meaning, truth, and logical connection are rooted in these *logoi*. According to Derrida the accounts of *logoi* are present throughout the history of philosophy starting from Plato through empiricists to Husserl.

Dedekind (Julius Wilhelm), Richard (1831 – 1916) : He was a noted German mathematician whose foundations of arithmetic and analysis are contained in his *Stetigkeit und Irrationale Zahlem* (1872). His philosophical contribution is based on the following three aspects: (1) the fundamental numerical systems of mathematics must be developed independently of spatio-temporal or geometrical notions; (2) the number systems rely on certain mental capacities fundamental to thought; and (3) to recognize this mental creation as "creation" according to certain key properties, properties that certain careful mathematical analysis reveals as essential to the subject matter.

De dicto (L) : This expression refers to the necessity that is attached to the whole assertion or substance. Modal logic is basically concerned with logical modalities whose formal properties are well known, but their interpretation gives rise to some logical and metaphysical difficulties. The distinction between *de dicto* and *de re* modalities is at times ambiguous. In the former case, it is often the case that necessity is attributed to the entire assertion. In the *de re* claim the necessity is attributed to the thing's possession of a particular property.

Deduction : It is one of the processes of logical thinking, according to which a valid conclusion can be arrived at by proceeding from generalizations or universals to particulars. If the premise that consists of generalization is true, then the conclusion deduced from that premise must also be true. See the following example:

All men are mortal.
Socrates is a man.
Therefore, Socrates is mortal.

Deduction of the Categories : According to Kant, transcendental deduction is an exposition of the nature and possibility of a priori forms and the explanation and justification of their use as necessary conditions of experience. For details see his *Critique of Pure Reason.*

Default Logic : It is a formal system of reasoning that makes use of certain defaults as its axioms. Default logic was developed by Raymond Reiter in 1980. According to this logic, whether a proposition is consistent with one's beliefs is dependent on what defaults have already been accepted as axioms and their application.

Definiendum (L) : A definition consists of two parts, namely, *definiendum* and *definiens*. The *definiendum* is the term that is going to be defined. For example, in the statement "A triangle is a three-sided closed geometrical figure," the term "triangle" is the *definiendum*.

Definiens (L) : The defining feature of the *definiendum* is called the *definiens*. For example, in the statement "A triangle is a three-sided closed geometrical figure," the expression "three-sided closed geometrical figure" is the *definiens*.

Definist Fallacy : It is an aspect of the "naturalistic fallacy" advocated by G.E. Moore in his *Principia Ethica*. It is a confusion that arises by defining a term in terms of the other. For instance, "good" is defined as "that which produces pleasure." However, "good" and "pleasure" are two distinct terms.

Definite Description : Russell introduced a kind of a singular term called "definite description" in his theory of descriptions. A definite description like "The present Prime Minister of India" does not only serve as a denoting phrase, but also picks up a unique individual referent. However, it is an incomplete symbol as it remains meaningless out of the context.

Definition : It is a process of logical description through which a precise meaning of a word is formulated. The definition of any work or a phrase constitutes the essential distinctive properties of the expression which in turn determine the content and the boundaries of such an expression. Every definition consists of two parts, namely, *definiendum* (the word or the phrase that is going to be defined) and *definiens* (the logical equivalent of the word or the phrase in question). One of the important features of a definition is that whatever appears in *definiendum* should not appear in *definiens*. Take the statement "A triangle is a three-sided closed geometrical figure," here the term "triangle" is the *definiendum* and the description "three-sided closed geometrical figure" is the *definiens*. There are many types of definition. The two important varieties of definition are: (1) explicit definition, and (2) definition in use. A lexical or a reportive definition is called explicit definition (e.g. "occulist"), whereas the definition in use is "eye doctor" which is popularly used in our day-to-day language. Thus every explicit definition can be translated into a definition in use. It is one of the activities of the philosophical analysis.

Deism : It is a popular view in theology. According to deism, God transcends the world of phenomena. Though the world is his creation, he has no intimate relation to it.

Delusion : According to J.L. Austin, a delusive experience is one where something is conjured up from nothing. In the case of illusion, something else is created out of something. In epistemology, delusion is considered to be an erroneous or non-veridical cognition. The term is properly restricted to perception, memory, and other non-inferential forms of knowledge.

Demiurge (Gk) : It means "designer," or "craftsman." In Plato's philosophy, *demiurge* represents the God who is responsible for this world of things.

Democracy : It is a form of government that is elected "by the people" and stands "for the people," and consists "of the people." Plato believed that democracy would be the worst form of Government. According to J.L. Austin, democracy is a "notoriously useless term."

Democritus of Abdera (c. 460 – 370 BCE) : He was one of the ancient Greek atomists and a young contemporary of Leucippus. He was nicknamed "the laughing philosopher." Democritus was known for his atomic theory. According to him, atoms, being indivisible particles of matter, are immutable, eternal, and continuous in motion. His influence was carried on by Lucratius' poem until Renaissance when scholars' attention turned towards the study of nature. The variety of atomic forms corresponds to, and accounts for, the variety of material qualities; the finest, smoothest, and the most agile atoms constitute the substance of mind. He explained human perception as an emanation of tiny copies of sensible things (*eidola*) that influence the atoms of mind and leave impressions responsible for facts of memory.

Demonology : It is a study of the widespread religious ideas of hostile forces or superhuman beings called demons. These creatures are thought of as inhabiting a super or under-world and playing havoc with the fortunes of humans by bringing diseases, mental twists, and natural calamities in general. Demonology as a theory of demonic behaviour was popular among the Egyptians, the Babylonians, the Assyrians, the Persians, the post-exilic Hebrews, the Jews, the Greeks, and many scattered people including the ancients.

Demonstration : The proof of any given proposition is disclosed by means of deductive process by which it can be inferred. John Locke held that demonstrative knowledge occurs when our minds engage in trying to discover the agreement and disagreement of ideas by calling attention to still other ideas. Ideally, each step of demonstration must have intuitive certainty. This is particularly the case in mathematics.

De Morgan, Augustus (1806 – 71) : He was a British mathematician and logician. His work *Formal Logic* (1847) contains some points of algebra of logic that are similar to those of Boole. His contribution to mathematical logic is that he introduced the following rules of equivalence that can be applied to propositional calculus.

$$\sim(p \ V \ q) \equiv (\sim p \ \& \sim q)$$

$$\sim(p \ \& \ q) \equiv (\sim p \ V \sim q)$$

Denial of the Antecedent : The fallacy of the denial of the antecedent is a fallacious inference from $\sim A$ and $A > B$ to $\sim B$. the law of the denial of the antecedent is the theorem of propositional calculus, $\sim p \supset \{p > q\}$.

Denomination : In its literal sense denomination is naming of something from some other thing. In Scholastic logic, it is the operation of applying a term to a subject, when the term is derived from something to which the subject is related. Thus a substance may be denominated by deriving a name from its accidents. Extrinsic denomination is dependent on external relationship.

Denotation : The meaning of a word is ascertained by means of denotation. When one is not clear about the characteristics of an object, it is possible to give the meaning of that word by referring to various particulars to which the word is properly applicable. Thus the denotation of the word "man" is all the particular existing individuals such as Socrates, Plato, Aristotle, etc. J.S. Mill replaces the term "denotation" with the term "extension." The extension of a word is made up of all those entities to which that word correctly applies. In common usage, "denotation" does not carry any special meaning. In fact, "to denote" means "to designate." Thus denotation is a synonym for designation.

Deontology : It is a theory of ethics that considers duty as the basis of all morality. According to this theory, some actions are morally obligatory irrespective of their consequences. It was Immanuel Kant who advocated this theory of ethics, according to which "duty is for duty's sake." Deontological ethics does not make a theory of obligation totally dependent on the theory of value. It is opposed to axiological ethics.

Depersonalization : It is a kind of personality disorder in which the subject's own actions and words assume his or her character as strangeness or unreality. In its extreme form the subject is obsessed with the fear of complete dissolution of personality.

Deproblematization : It is the gradual cessation of the former problematical tone of any object or idea.

De re (L) : This expression refers to the necessity that is attached only to a specific or a particular quality of a whole or a substance. See *de dicto*.

Derrida, Jaques (1930 – 2004) : He was an Algerian-born French Philosopher and well-known for his method of deconstruction.

His views on language and meaning, and his complex style of writing are exciting, challenging and at times highly controversial. Being a second generation French phenomenologist, Derrida understood philosophy in terms of the contributions made by Hegel, Nietzsche, Husserl, Heidegger, and Levinas. His method of deconstruction is dubbed by his critics as a form of moral skepticism or moral relativism which denies all absolute values and fixed meanings. Thus it ends up in moral paralysis. Derrida often found it difficult to come out of this charge against him. As an attempt to respond to his critics, Derrida claims that deconstruction never proposes an endless *deferral* of meaning, rather it is precisely because a final decision cannot be made the issues appear to be undecidable. Undecidability for Derrida does not mean that nothing can be done, but rather something must be done and that we cannot be certain what to do. In fact, Derrida used deconstruction as a strategy to overcome the *logocentrism,* which is nothing but the traditional prioritization of reason, and the *metaphysics of presence* which dominated the Western philosophical thought ever since the time of the ancient Greeks. According to him, deconstruction is the process of unravelling of meaning of a given text. In the process the supposed argument or thesis actually turns against itself owing to the impossibility of meaning present in its essence. Thus every speech act contains the seed of its own negation. Derrida's important works include: *Of Grammatology* (1967); *Dissemination and the Margins of Philosophy* (1972); *Positions* (1981); *The Post Card: From Socrates to Freud and Beyond* (1987); *Spectres of Marx* (1994); and *Rogues: Two Essays on Reason* (2004).

Descartes, René (1569 – 1650) : He was a French philosopher, mathematician, and physicist, who is regarded as the father of modern Western philosophy. Descartes was chiefly interested in intellectual certainty. He broke with the past to give philosophy a new impetus. Neither the authority of Aristotle's great reputation nor the authority of the Church could suffice to produce the kind of certainty he sought. His ideal was to arrive at a system of thought whose various principles were true and were related to each other in such a clear way that the mind could move easily from one true principle to another. Descartes' method consists in harnessing the powers of the mind with special set of rules. He insisted upon the necessity of method, upon systematic and orderly thinking. Descartes looked to mathematics for the best example of clear and precise thinking. In fact, he wanted to make all knowledge "universal mathematics." Mathematics itself is not the method but merely exhibits the method Descartes is searching for: geometry and arithmetic. Descartes places the entire edifice of knowledge upon the foundation of intuition and deduction. According to him, these two methods are certain routes to knowledge. Descartes insisted that a rule must provide a clear and orderly procedure for the operation of the mind. The mind must start with simple and absolutely clear truth and must move step by step without losing clarity and certainty. In epistemology, Descartes assumed certain innate ideas, in the sense that we are born with some inborn qualities. Because we know these innate ideas to be indubitable, they are the most reliable foundation for our deductions. Thus the idea of God and the ideas of mathematics are innate. For Descartes, the criterion of truth is "clarity and distinctness." Descartes tried to establish his First Principle of philosophy by employing the method of doubt. He doubted everything that could be doubted, but not the very doubting substance, which is none other than the mind. Thus he arrived at the fundamental axiom of his philosophy called "*Cogito ergo sum* (I think, therefore I exist)." As a dualist Descartes accepted the independent existence of two substances, namely, mind and body. According to him, the mind can exist independent of the body, and the body can exist independent of the mind. The most important attribute of the former is thinking, and the latter is extension. He also conceived that mind and body are relative substances, whereas God is the only absolute substance on which these two relative substances are dependent for their existence. Although mind and body are functionally independent from each other, held Descartes, they interact with each other in the pineal gland of the human body. Thus, he subscribed to the doctrine of interactionism. As regards the existence of God, Descartes could not accept the proofs for the existence of God advanced by Aquinas as those proofs were based upon the facts, which were doubted by him. Instead he advanced the ontological proof that was advocated by St. Anselm. Through this argument Descartes sought to demonstrate the existence of God by exploring what the very idea of God implies. God being perfect he possesses every quality. Therefore, the quality of existence cannot be taken away from him, which may lead to his imperfection. His important works are *Discourse on Method* (1637); *Meditations on First Philosophy* (1641); *Principles of Philosophy* (1644); and *The Passions of the Soul* (1649).

Descending Induction : It is an alternative name suggested for the method of infinite descent.

Description, Knowledge of : Bertrand Russell in his *The Problems of Philosophy* (1912) recognized two forms of knowledge, namely, knowledge by acquaintance and knowledge by description. The latter is the knowledge of objects, which is inferred from the sense-data, which are possible through direct acquaintance.

Descriptions, Theory of : It is a theory advocated by Bertrand Russell to differentiate the grammatical structure of a sentence from its logical structure. The problem arises when certain denoting phrases, though they do not refer to anything, make the sentence in which they appear meaningful. For example, the sentence "The present King of France is bald" is meaningful irrespective of whether its denoting phrase, "The present King of France" refers to some unique individual or not. To avoid this difficulty Russell introduced the theory of descriptions. The logical meaning of a sentence can be obtained by analysing a sentence into its conjunctions. If one of the statements of a conjunction is false, then the whole conjunction turns out to be false. Russell analyses the sentence "The Present king of France is bald" in the following way:

1. There exists at least one person who ruled over France.
2. There exists at most one person who ruled over France.
3. Whosoever reigned over France is bald.

The above conjunction is false because France is not a monarchy. Therefore, the question of ruling it by any king does not arise.

Descriptivism : It is an ethical view, according to which the moral judgements have mere descriptive value as against the prescriptive value. The descriptive meaning of a moral judgement is derived from a factual statement. According to R.M. Hare, it is a form of ethical naturalism. The weakness of this theory, holds Hare, is that to admit a moral judgement does not necessarily lead us to act on it.

Designator : It is a term that is used to refer to an individual. For example, the terms like "Socrates," "table," "red," etc. are designators.

Deśikārādhya (S) : He is one among the *gurus*, according to the Vīra-Śaiva-*parampara.*

Determinism : It is a view that opposes the freedom of will. In other words, determinism opposes all forms of contingency, and claims that everything that happens is necessarily determined by a particular pattern or a law. For instance, David Hume advocated the causal indeterminism. According to him, there is no necessary causal connection between one event and another because such a connection is not given in sense-experience. Kant advocated the causal determinism by holding the view that "every effect has a cause." The necessary connection between the cause and the effect, held Kant, is not given in sense-experience, but is known a priori.

Deva Sūri (1088 – 1172) : He was a Jaina thinker and the author of *Pramāṇanyāyatattvālokālaṁkāra.*

Dewey, John (1859 – 1952) : He is regarded as one of the most outstanding and influential pragmatic philosophers of America. Dewey's pragmatism is a synthesis of the logical and the ethical considerations. He contributed a lot to metaphysics, epistemology, logic, psychology, aesthetics, religion, ethics, politics, and education. In his writings one can witness the spirit of democracy, and an abiding faith in the efficacy of human intelligence. Dewey attacked the earlier philosophy on the ground that it confused true nature and function of knowledge. For the most part, it was empiricists who held that thinking refers to fixed things and that for each idea there is corresponding something in reality. This conception of empiricists supposes that knowing is modelled after what is supposed to happen when we look at something. This is what is called "a spectator theory of knowledge." In other words, to see something means to have an idea of it. Dewey held that man being a biological organism is best understood only in his relation to his environment. If both man and his environment are dynamic, then the simple spectator theory of knowledge advocated by empiricists does not work. The mind, according to Dewey, is not a fixed substance, and knowledge is not a set of static points. Intelligence is the power of man, which can cope up with man's environment. Thinking is not an individual art carried on in private, in isolation from practical problems. Thinking as an active intelligence arises in problem situations. Thus, for Dewey, thinking and doing are intimately related. Although Dewey recognized the influence of environment on human beings, yet every individual inherits certain structures. These structures are nothing but certain basic human instincts. These instincts, as Dewey put it, are fixed by highly flexible in their nature. As regards values, Dewey held that the mind discovers values in the way in which it discovers facts, namely, in experience. Values do not exist as eternal entities. They are created for the welfare of human beings. The modern education system in America owes a lot to Dewey. His philosophy is popularly known as instrumentalism. His important works are *Psychology* (1886); *Outline of Ethics* (1891); *Studies in Logical Theory* (1903); *How We Think* (1910); *Influence of Darwin on German Philosophy* (1910); *Democracy and Education* (1916); *Reconstruction in Philosophy* (1920); *Human Nature and Conduct* (1922); *Experience and Nature* (1925); *The Quest for Certainty* (1929); *Art as Experience* (1933); and *Logic: The Theory of Inquiry* (1939).

Dhāraṇā (S) : It is one of the eight limbs of Yoga. *Dhāraṇa* is concentration or fixation of the mind on some object, especially a desired object. It is the activity or the process of centering the mind. The object upon which the mind is fixed may be an external object, an idol or image of God, or any part of one's own body, or the inner sense itself.

Dharma (S) : It means "duty," "righteousness," "virtue," and "right." In fact, the word *dharma* has many connotations in the context of Indian philosophy. It is derived from the etymological root *dhr̥* which means "to bind" or "to hold together." *Dharma* is one of the four *puruṣārtha*s or goals of human life, according to Hindu ethics. The Hindu philosophy is basically concerned with two higher values, namely, *dharma*, and *mokṣa.* As an overarching or regulative principle, *dharma* regulates our actions concerning the pursuit of *artha* and *kāma.* According to Mīmāṁsā, *dharma* is *karma.* There are *varṇa-dharma*s and *āśrama-dharma*s. The former represent the duties of the various classes, namely, brāhmaṇa, kṣatriyas, vaiśyas, and śūdras; and the latter represent the duties of the individuals in the various stages of life, namely, *brahmacarya, gr̥hastha, vānaprastha,* and *saṁnyāsa.* The *varṇa-dharma*s are intended to maintain the division of labour in the society and for social progress; while the *āśrama-dharma*s are meant for self-discipline and individual progress. In the *Bhagavad-Gītā* one comes across the notion of *svadharma,* according to which one's own duty is superior to another's.

Dharma-bhūta-jñāna (S) : It is known as attributive consciousness. It is one of the most important concepts in Viśiṣṭādvaita. In this system, knowledge is attributed to God and individuals. Such knowledge is non-material, self-conscious, and unconscious substance. In one sense it is both a substance and attribute. It is substance because it is subjected to the changing states of expansion and contraction. Also, it is an attribute because it inheres in the substances like *īśvara* and individuals. It is considered to be eternal and all-pervasive when it is in eternals like *īśvara*, *nitya-sūri*s, *mukta*s. But its eternality is obscured when it is associated with the bound individuals. All objective knowledge is the result of its modifications. It operates through the mind in all knowing processes.

Dharma-jijñāsā (S) : It was a desire to inquire into *dharma.* In Jaimini's *Mīmāṁsā-Sūtra*, the first *sūtra* talks about it. *Dharma* is *karma* or duty according to Mīmāṁsā.

Dharmakāya (S) : It is known as the sheath of law. According to Buddhism, it is the reality of all beings and appearances whether they are immanent or transcendent. It is both the essence of worldly beings and the Buddhas. As the essence of worldly beings it is called "suchness" or "emptiness."

Dharmakīrti (C. CE 635) : He was a Sautrāntika Buddhist philosopher and the author of *Pramāṇavārttika* and *Nyāyabindu*. It is basically concerned with logic and epistemology. According to Dharmakīrti, right knowledge (*samyag-jñāna*) is the pre-condition for the accomplishment of any desire of man.

Dhātu (S) : According to Buddhism, *dhātu*s are the subtle elements whose combinations gave rise to knowledge. In Sāṁkhya, earth, air, fire, water, ether, and *cetanā* are treated as the elements.

Dhūrtta Cārvākas : It was one of the pre-Buddhist schools of ancient Indian materialism of the Upaniṣad type. The exact date of its existence is not known.

Dialectical Materialism : It is the philosophy advocated by Karl Marx, according to which matter is fundamental. In opposition to idealism, dialectical materialists hold that the matter is not the product of mind, but the mind is the highest product of matter. Marxist's view is that the laws that govern the matter are not mechanical but are dialectical. In other words, dialectics is a method applied to materialism. The method of dialects is borrowed from Hegel. Dialectical materialists rejected both mechanism and idealism as forms of metaphysics. According to dialectical materialists, all things must be investigated in terms of their histories. The important consideration is not the state in which a thing is presented at that moment but the direction and the probable outcome of the changes which are taking place as a result of the conflict of both internal and external forces. Dialectical materialists reject all forms of a priorism. They held that nature is the test of dialectics. Historical materialism as a social theory represents the application of general principles of dialectics to human society. The fundamental changes and stages of development of human society in the course of its complex evolution are traced primarily to the influence of changes taking place in its economic base. See historical materialism.

Dialectics : This term was introduced by Socrates for the first time to philosophy. According to him, the dialectics is a method of argumentation. Later dialectics was held by Plato as a science of the first principles. In Kant's critical philosophy, dialectics is restricted to thesis and antithesis. The most lucid analysis of dialectics was given by Hegel in modern times. According to him, dialectics involves the following laws: (1) the law of identity; (2) the unity and struggle of opposite forces; (3) the transformation of quantitative changes into qualitative changes; and (4) the law of negation of negation.

Dialogism : It is an inference from one premise to the disjunction of the conclusion, and the negation of the other premise is dialogism. If the inference from A to B to C is a valid inference, then from A to $C \vee \sim B$ may be called a dialogism.

Dianoetic Virtues : In Aristotle's ethics, the virtues or excellences of *Dianoia* are called *dianoetic* virtues. They are often distinguished from moral virtues as they have as their end the explicit apprehension of rational principles. Moral virtues are basically concerned with the rational control of the sensitive and appetitive life.

Diaspora (Gk) : It means "scattering or dispersion." This is the name given to those countries through which the Jews were dispersed after being exiled or deported from their homeland. It also applies to those converts from Judaism to Christianity.

Dichotomy : It literally means "a division into two parts." For instance, the dichotomy between mind and body is one of the major issues of Cartesian philosophy. In Sartre's existentialism there is a dichotomy between "thing-in-itself" and "thing-for-itself."

Didactics : It is the branch of education concerned with methods of teaching and instruction. In theology and religion, didactics is viewed as an instruction in fundamentals of religious doctrine.

Diderot, Denis (1713 – 84) : He was a French philosopher, essayist, and editor of *Encyclopedia*. Diderot quickly passed from deism and ethical idealism to materialism. According to him, experiment is possible because there is one single principle, which is operating in nature. Substance is neither unitary nor uniform but composed of different elements divisible into molecules. He showed keen interest in science and may be viewed as a forerunner of positivism. He entered into polemics with Christianity. His important works are *Dela suffisance de la religion naturelle* (1747); *Letter sur les aveugles* (1749); and *La religieuse* (1760).

Differentia (L) : It is the part of the essence of a particular thing that distinguishes its species from other species belonging to the same genus.

Dilemma : It is a form of inference that contains two premises, namely, conjunctive affirmation of two hypothetical propositions, and a disjunctive premise containing the grounds for the hypothetical propositions. It also describes a situation involving a choice between equivalent alternatives. A dilemma consists of (1) a compound hypothetical major premise; (2) a disjunctive minor premise; and (3) a disjunctive or categorical conclusion. A dilemma can be presented in the following way:

1. If an elected member acts in accordance with his own judgement he will be criticized; if he acts in accordance with the views of his constituents he will be criticized.
2. He acts either in accordance with his own judgement or in accordance with the views of his constituents.
3. Therefore, he will be criticized.

Dilthey, Wilhelm (1833 – 1911) : He was a German philosopher, who was acclaimed as a devoted student of biography. Dilthey developed a new methodology and interpretation of the study of society and culture. He formulated the doctrine of *Verstehungs-psychologie,* which is basic to the study of social ends and values. He was the founder of *Lebesphilosophie.* Being the first humanist philosopher historian of his age, he led in the comprehensive research in the history of intellectual development. According to Dilthey, the distinction between the natural sciences and the human sciences is also related to the methodological difference between explanation and understanding. Dilthey recognized value, purpose and meaning as the three important categories of human sciences. He distinguished the categories of human sciences from those of natural sciences. His important works are *Introduction to the Human Sciences* (1883); and *Formation of the Historical world in the Human Sciences* (1910).

Ding an sich (G) : This expression was used by Kant in his *Critique of Pure Reason* that refers to what lies beyond human experience and observation. "Things-in-themselves" are transcendent, not transcendental. They exist independent and apart from all knowledge. They have an independent reality apart from the subjectivity of human knowledge.

Diṅnāga (c. sixth century CE) : He was a disciple of Vasubandhu, the Buddhist logician. Diṅnāga was supposed to be the founder of the school of medieval Indian logic. He criticized the *Nyāya-Sūtra* of Gotama and *Nyāyabhāṣya* of Vātsyāyana. His important work is *Pramāṇasamuccaya.*

Diogenes Laertius (second century CE) : He was a great Greek doxographer and commentator. The most accessible doxographical material about the ancient Greek philosophers is available in his compilation entitled *Lives and Opinions of Eminent Philosophers.* He arranged philosophers by schools and treated each school in a chronological order.

Dionysian : It is an art impulse in which life is re-lived, in which life's joys and pains are re-experienced. It is the dynamic and passionate aspect of the will and power. See Nietzsche.

Direct and Indirect Perception : According to Russell, the "knowledge by acquaintance" is possible through direct perception, whereas the indirect perception of an object in question is possible through the "knowledge by description." For example, the sense-data are directly given in sense-experience, while the knowledge of material objects is inferred from the sense-data. Thus the knowledge of material objects is possible through indirect perception.

Disconfirmation : It is the term that is opposed to confirmation. In other words, it is called information.

Discourse : It is a technical term used by Habermas to refer to pure communication freed from pressures, constraints, and inequalities in power and ability that normally accompany any communicative action.

Discursive : It is one of the processes of thinking in which the conclusions are reached systematically with the help of a series of intermediary operations.

Disjunct : It is a term in a disjunction. For example, "*p*" is a disjunct in "*p* or *q*."

Distribution : In logic, a particular term is said to be distributed when that term is attributed to all the members of the class.

For example, in the statement "All men are mortal," the subject term "men" is distributed to mortality. This is a universal affirmative proposition (*A*). In a universal negative proposition (*E*), "No men are mothers" both subject and predicate terms are distributed. In a particular affirmative proposition (*I*), "Some cats are black beings" both subject and predicate terms are not distributed. In a particular negative proposition (*O*), "Some metals are not white things" the predicate term alone is distributed.

Proposition	*Subject*	*Predicate*
A	Distributed	Undistributed
E	Distributed	Distributed
I	Undistributed	Undistributed
O	Undistributed	Distributed

Distributive Justice : It is justice as exhibited in the distribution of honour, money, rights, and privileges among the members of a community. According to Aristotle, distributive justice is characterized by equality of proportion between persons and rewards.

Division : It is one of the formal fallacies that occurs when a particular term is used distributively instead of collectively. For example, the sentence, "Indians are fond of cricket" may be true if it is understood in a collective sense. But, if it is understood in a distributive sense, then it is false because every Indian is not fond of cricket.

Doctor Angelicus (L) : It is a Latin expression for "Angelic Doctor." St. Thomas Aquinas was known as Angelic Doctor.

Doctor Mirabilis (L) : It is a Latin expression for "Miraculous Doctor." Roger Bacon was known as a Miraculous Doctor. He was a scholastic philosopher and a scientist.

Doctor Subtilis (L) : It is a Latin expression for "Subtle Doctor." John Duns Scotus was known as Subtle Doctor.

Doctor Universalis (L) : It is a Latin expression for "Universal Doctor." Albertus Magnus was known as Universal Doctor.

Dogmatism : This term indicates a way of thinking that does not change according to circumstances. Dogmatism, in other words, is an unalterable way of thinking that rests on the traditional conceptions without any rational explanation.

Double-aspect Theory : According to this theory mind and body are two distinguishable but inseparable aspects of a single underlying substance or a process. Spinoza in his metaphysical doctrine advocated that "thinking substance and extended substance are one and the same thing." Thus he is committed to the double aspect theory of the mind-body relation. For further details see his *Ethics*.

Double Negation : It is the principle according to which a proposition implies and is also implied by the negation. For example, if *p*, then *not-p* or if *not-not-p* then *p*.

Double Truth : It is a view that some notion or an idea may be philosophically false, yet it may be true from the standpoint of religion.

Doubt : In a sense it is a denial or withdrawal of a belief in a proposition that is formerly held to be true. In psychology, doubt is nothing but a suspended judgement. Philosophical doubt is different from definitive or provisional doubt. Definitive doubt leads to skepticism, while the provisional doubt is the rule proposed by the Cartesian method of voluntary suspension of judgement in order to arrive at certainty.

Doxa : It is the positional character that is common to all modes of believing. Doxa in Husserl's sense includes *epistemé*. It is not only present in syntactical-categorical judging, but in simple pre-categorical perceiving.

Doxastic : It is something pertaining to belief. A doxastic mental state presupposes a belief. Doxastic mental states are distinguished from non-doxastic states as desires, sensations and emotions. A doxastic principle might set out certain conditions under which an agent is said to be forming or abandoning a belief.

Doxographer : A doxographer is a compiler of and commentator on the opinions of ancient Greek philosophers. This expression is an English translation of a Latin term coined by Hermann Diels for the title of his work *Doxography Graeci* (1879). Most of the available works of the ancient Greek philosophers are the outcome of doxography. For instance, Diogenes Laertius (second century CE) was a famous Greek doxographer.

Dravidians : It is the name given to the non-Āryan population, which has ancient Mediterranean origin. Before the Āryan invasion, it formed the bulk of Harappan population. The Dravidians are now in the southern part of India. There are some Dravidians in Baluchistan who speak Brahui. The four major Dravidian nationalities and language in south India are Tamil, Kannada, Telugu, and Malayalam.

Dravya (S) : It is one of the categories of Vaiśeṣika. It consists of both living and the non-living things. It is a substratum wherein qualities subsist. Such a substance manifests in the form of earth, water, fire, air, ether, time, space, individuals, and mind.

Dṛṣṭisṛṣṭivāda (S) : It is one of the theories of perception advocated by Prakāśānanda (sixteenth century CE), according to which in the process of perception an object comes into existence only when it is perceived. This theory is akin to George Berkeley's "to be is to be perceived." See Berkeley.

Dualism : Irrespective of any field of inquiry this theory reduces the variety of its subject matter to two irreducible principles. For example, *noumena* and *phenomena*, good and evil, determinism and indeterminism, appearance and reality, form and content, cause and effect, subject and object, etc. Renè Descartes is known for his dualistic approach towards metaphysics. According to him, the mind, whose important attribute is thought, can exist independent of the body or the matter, whose important attribute is extension. Thus he is known as a dualist.

Ducasse, Curt John (1881 – 1969) : He was a French-born American philosopher of mind and aesthetics. His most important work is *Nature, Mind and Death* (1951). He advocated a non-Humean theory of causation. According to him, the relation of causing is triadic. It comprises the following three aspects: (1) an initial event; (2) the set of conditions under which it occurs; and (3) a resulting event. The initial event is the cause, and the resultant one is the effect. On the basis of this view he constructed a theory of categories, which explains the concepts such as substance, property, mind, matter, and body. According to him, the minds are substances, which causally interact with bodies. In epistemology, Ducasse advocated a realist theory of perception. He held the view that Berkeley is right and realists are wrong in so far as the nature of sensible qualities is concerned, but the realists are right and Berkeley is wrong when it comes to the nature of material things. Sensible qualities are not objects of experience, but ways of experiencing. His other works are *A Critical Examination of the Belief in a Life After Death* (1961) and *Truth, Knowledge, and Causation* (1968).

Duhem, Pierre-Maurice-Marie (1861 – 1916) : He was a French physicist who was chiefly interested in history and philosophy of science. Like other leading physicists such as George Helm, Wilhelm Oswald, Duhem held that thermodynamics is the foundation of all physical and chemical sciences. His work in the field of history and philosophy of science can be viewed as a defence of the aims and methods of energetics. Duhem opposed atomism (anti-Cartesian). According to Duhem, the atomists resolve the bodies perceived by the senses into smaller, imperceptible bodies. The explanation of observable phenomena is then referred to these imperceptible bodies and their motions, suitably combined. Duhem's philosophical works were discussed by the founders of the twentieth-century philosophy of science such as Mach and Poincarè, the members of Vienna Circle, Karl

Popper and others. A renewed interest in Duhem's philosophy took place in early fifties due to W.V. Quine. In fact, it was known as Duhem-Quine thesis. His important works are *The Aim and Structure of Physical Theory* (1954) and *To Save the Phenomena* (1969).

Duns Scotus, John (1266 – 1308) : He was a Scottish Fransciscan philosopher and theologian. He was popularly known as *Doctor Subtilis* (the subtle doctor). Duns Scotus altered Avicenna's metaphysics as the science of being *qua* being. The goal of metaphysics, according to him, is to demonstrate God as the Infinite Being as revealed to Moses as the "I am who I am." God's creative will is the source of the world's contingency. Out of love God created each creature with a unique "haecceity" or particularity formally distinct from its individual nature. Duns Scotus highlighted the insights of St. Augustine when the Aristotlenism was a dominant philosophy of his time. He held that intellectual intuition is not the basis of epistemology. In fact, intellect in association with sensory imagination becomes the starting point of epistemology.

Duration : The term "duration" was introduced by Henry Bergson to denote the essence of any living organism, which is continuous. The analytic method practised by science virtually destroys the duration of the object under study. The duration is the essence of an object, which is dynamic, thriving, pulsing, living, continuous existence. See Bergson.

Durkheim, Emile (1858 – 1917) : He was a well-known French sociologist who advocated positivism. According to Durkheim, the point of reference for all human knowledge is the group mind. The group mind has an impersonal, non-subjective character that is superior to the individual mind and acts as a directive force for the individual agents that comprise society. He approached both religion and ethics from the point of view of positivism. His important works include: *De la division du travail sociale* (1893); *Les régles de la méthode socilogique*; and *Les formes: elemementairs de la vie religieuse* (1912).

Duty : It is an ethical category denoting a special form of moral obligation. It is a kind of moral obligation applied to every individual. According to Kant, "duty is for duty's sake." It is an a priori moral law. The *Bhagavad-Gītā* also mentions about the duty as an obligation by introducing the notion of *niṣkāma-karma*, according to which every individual must resort to renunciation in action.

Dvaita (S) : It means "dual." It is the name given to Madhva Vedānta. Madhva's original names were Nārāyaṇa and Vāsudeva. Later on he assumed two other names, Pūrṇaprajña and Ānandatīrtha. Madhva is the last name that he accepted. Madhva received his philosophical training from Acyutaprekṣa. Like Rāmānuja, Madhva followed Vaiṣṇavism. According to Dvaita Vedānta, there are two important types of categories. They are independent (*svatantra*), and dependent (*paratantra*). The only independent reality is God (*Brahman*). The dependent categories are further classified into two types, namely, conscious and unconscious. The conscious are the individual souls (*ātmans*), and some supernal beings like the consort of Viṣṇu, Śrī Lakṣmī. The supernals are eternally liberated and perform certain cosmic and divine functions. The unconscious categories are of three kinds, namely, *prakṛti*, space and time. Like Rāmānuja's Viśiṣṭādvaita, Dvaita follows certain mythological epics and *pāñcarātrāgamas*. The philosophical foundation of Dvaita Vedānta is rooted in its theory of perception and knowledge. According to this school, to perceive is to become aware of something as being unique and different from other things as well as from the perceiving self. It accepted three sources of knowledge, namely, *pratyakṣa* or perception, *anumāna* or inference, and *śabda* or verbal testimony. Genuine knowledge is the articulation of perceived differences between things as well as between things and the perceiving self. Consequently, to deny perception is to deny the very possibility of knowledge. Therefore, one who accepts identity, but denies difference is in an absurd position of claiming knowledge by rejecting its very foundation. Dvaita Vedānta is a philosophy of difference. It recognizes five fundamental and absolute distinctions. They are: (1) between *Brahman* and individual souls; (2) between *Brahman* and matter; (3) between matter and individual souls; (4) Between one individual self and another; and (5) between one material object and another. The pluralistic system of Dvaita Vedānta recognizes three important realities, namely, *Brahman*, individual souls, and matter, although the last two are absolutely dependent on the first. According to this school *bhakti* or devotion is the only path of liberation from bondage.

Dyadic : According to Russell, a fact is called dyadic when it requires the addition of two singular entities. Thus a dyadic fact is represented by a proposition that consists of two singular terms. For example, Ram is taller than Krishan.

Dynamism : This term is applied to any philosophical system that accepts force as its explanatory concept rather than mass or motion as adopted by the philosophy of mechanism. Leibniz's philosophy can be termed as the philosophy of dynamism in contrast to Descartes' philosophy of mechanism.

Dyophysites : This term is applied to those followers of Catholic sect of Christianity who believed that there are two natures in Jesus Christ. They are the Divine and human. The followers of Eutyches held that this duality ceases in Christ after the union. The followers of Eutyches are called Monophysites.

Dysteleology : This particular doctrine indicates the presence of the factors that defy the adaptation of the good or the desirable ends. In other words, they are called non-teleological factors. For example, agony, disease, death, etc. These unfavourbale environmental factors make life difficult if not impossible.

E

Eckhart (Johannes), Meister (1260 – 1327) : He was a German mystic, theologian and preacher. He entered the Dominican order and taught theology. In theology, Eckhart was influenced by Albertus Magnus and St. Thomas Aquinas. When he was in Paris he wrote a commentary on Lombard's *Sentences*. His thought, although mystical and at times difficult in terminology, appears to contain elements of Aristotleanism, Agustinism, neo-Platonism, and Avicennism. In the early 1320s, there were doubts about the nature of Eckhart's orthodoxy. People were concerned about the characteristic of his teaching. Eckhart held that the "soul" attains "emptiness" to give "birth to God." Accused of pantheism and other theological errors he stood trial in 1326. His important works include: *Book of Divine Consolation* (1313/22); *Opus Tripartium;* and *Questiones Parrisiences.*

Eclecticism : It is a practice of constructing a theory or a school of thought by freely borrowing ideas from various philosophical and other sources. The chief defect of eclecticism is that it fails to connect the views that are borrowed from various sources to make a harmonious system.

Economic Determinism : It is a notion according to which all social, political, and cultural changes are caused by economic changes. Economic determinism is often understood to imply an irreversible, law-like succession of modes of production, culminating in the inevitable downfall of capitalism and ascension of socialism. According to this view, the role of free, enlightened political action in determining the course of history is minimized.

Economy, the Principle of : It is another name for "Ockham's razor." According to this principle, one must not multiply the entities beyond necessity.

Ecstasis (Gk) : It means "enlightenment" or "ecstasy." In fact, the word "ecstasy" is derived from *ecstasis.*

Eduction : The expression "eduction" is derived from Latin. To educe means "to draw out." It is a form of immediate inference. This term was introduced by E.E. Constance Jones as a substitute for immediate inference. Eduction is a process of inferring of drawing out directly the implications of a given proposition. There are two primary forms of eduction. They are: (1) *obversion;* and (2) *conversion.* The former is the process of changing the quality of a given proposition without changing the meaning. The given proposition is called the *obvertend* and the inferred proposition is called the obverse and the process itself is called *obversion.* The latter is a process of transposing the subject and the predicate of a given proposition without changing the quality. The given proposition is called the *convertend,* the inferred proposition is called the converse and the process itself is called *conversion.*

Edwards, Jonathan (1703 – 58) : He was a well-known American theologian and a hardcore Calvinist. He is regarded by many as the first theologian to be produced by the New World. Although his system appears to be formalistic in many respects, there is visible aesthetic foundation in his emphasis on "divine and supernatural light" as the basis for illumination and for a detailed exposition on the topics such as freedom and original sin. Edwards was influenced by the Continental rationalists like Malebranche and Cambridge Platonists. His doctrine of absolute sovereignty of God's is explained by occasionalists and phenomenalists. According to him, what are "vulgarly" called causal relations are mere constant conjunctions. True causes necessitate their effects. Since God's will alone meets this condition, God alone is the true cause of everything that happens in this world. His important works include: *A Treatise Concerning Religious Affections* (1746); *Freedom of the Will* (1754); *Original Sin* (1758); and *On the Nature of the True Virtue* (1765).

Effect : It is an event that succeeds its cause. Every effect has its cause. According to Hume, there is no necessary relation between cause (antecedent) and effect (consequent). The so-called causation is based on mere habit and custom. See Causation.

Ego : It is a spiritual centre of human personality, which is not co-extensive with either the body or the mind. Every human individual who is capable of displaying initiative possesses ego.

Ego-centric Predicament : It is a form of epistemological predicament of a knowing mind which, by confining to its own circle of ideas, finds it difficult, if not impossible, to escape to a knowledge of external world. This form of epistemological predicament became very popular due to Descartes.

Ego, Empirical : The individual self that is conceived as a series of conscious acts and contents is called empirical ego. Mind is capable of cognizing those acts by direct introspection.

Ego, Pure : The self that is conceived as a non-empirical principle is called pure ego. It is ordinarily inaccessible to direct introspection, but inferred from introspective evidence. The principal theories associated with the notion of "pure ego" are: (1) the soul theory that regards the pure ego as a permanent, spiritual substance underlying the fleeting succession of conscious experience; and (2) the transcendental theory of Kant, which considers the self as an inscrutable subject presupposed by the unity of empirical self-consciousness.

Egoism : It is a particular principle of life, and a moral quality according to which an individual is guided only by his self-interests ignoring the larger interests of the society. It is one of the forms of individualism.

Egoism, Ethical : It is a view according to which each individual should seek as an end only his own good. Sometimes it is also viewed that individual's own good is the sole thing that is ultimately valuable for him/her.

Egoism, Psychological : According to this doctrine, the determining motive, although concealed, of every voluntary action is a desire for one's own good. It is often combined with psychological hedonism.

Eidetic : In Husserl's phenomenology, anything that pertains to *edios* or *eide* is called *editic*. For instance, an *eidetic* judgement does not posit individual existence, even though it is something about an individual. Similarly, *eidetic* necessity is concerned with actual state of affairs in so far as it is a singularization of an *eidetic* universality.

Eidos (Gk) : This term was used by Plato to refer to "the Forms or the Ideas or the Concepts" that exist in the eternal world (Being).

Einstein, Albert (1879 – 1955) : He was a German physicist, and a founder of the theory of relativity. His philosophical thinking was influenced by the philosophies of Kant, Hume, and Mach. Einstein argued against Kant's a priorism and the views of Poincaré, who claimed that the scientific truth is only conditional. Einstein rejected Poincaré's geometrical conventionalism. He supported causal determinism in quantum physics against Heisenberg's theory of indeterminacy. Einstein's understanding of relativity stressed the invariance of the space-time interval and promoted realism as regards the very structure of space-time. According to him, every object has four dimensions. They are breadth, length, depth and space-time. He opposed Newtonian conception of space-time. Einstein held that the motion of the bodies is not caused by the force external to them, but it is part and parcel of the bodies.

Eka (S) : It means "one." According to Advaita, *Brahman* is *eka*.

Élan vital (L) : It is the principle of life process in Bergson's philosophy. According to Bergson, evolution of the world cannot be explained in terms of accidental collection of dead circumstances, as supposed by mechanism. Also, evolution cannot be explained by reference to a perfect, pre-arranged plan. The only way to explain evolution is to accept a common living force that strives to express itself along divergent paths and striving constantly for balance and harmony. Such a force is nothing but *élan vital.* It is identical with the basic reality underlying all manifestation. It is the essential interior element of all living beings; and is the creative power that moves in unbroken continuity through all things. The intellect can only grasp static things, but not the *élan vital,* the moving force and essence of duration.

Eleatics, the : It was a Greek philosophical school that comprises the philosophies of Parminides, and his followers like Zeno of Elea, and Melissus of Samos. Their approach was monistic, and they vehemently attacked Heraclitus' notion of "flux." Plato was greatly impressed by Parmenides' thought and acknowledged his debt to the Eleatic philosopher.

Elective Affinity : It is an expression used by Weber to refer to correspondence or psychological affinity. Elective affinity links ideas with material interests.

Emanationism : It is a view that is chiefly associated with Neo-Platonic school pertaining to the origin and the structure of reality. Emanationism tries to explain the nature of reality, especially its origin and structure, in terms of a spontaneous flowing out from a supernatural or transcendental principle. Modern theories of evolution do not subscribe to this view. Emanation is opposed to creation.

Emergent Evolution : It is a theory of evolution expounded by Samuel Alexander (1859 – 1938), according to which the world is set in space and time, and all other evolutes have their base in this space-time matrix. His realism tries to combine absolute law in physics with absolute unpredictability of emergent features. Nature, according to him, starts as a four-dimensional matrix in which it is the moving principle. Materiality, secondary qualities, life, and mind are all emergent modifications of proto-space-time. Alexander held that Deity is the highest level to be emerged out of any given level.

Emergent Mentalism : It is a theory of emergent evolutionism considered as an explanation of the genesis of mind or consciousness in the world. Mind is a novel quality emerging from the non-mental when the latter attains a certain complexity of organization.

Emerson, Ralph Waldo (1803 – 82) : He was a renowned American poet-philosopher and essayist. He is ranked as a leading transcendentalist. According to Emerson, every human individual by nature is a poet. He championed the cause of freedom, individualism, and democracy. His most important essays include: "The American Scholar," "The Over-Soul," "Self-Reliance," and "Compensation." His lectures delivered at the Divinity school earned him wide publicity as a leading figure. He was the editor of *The Dial*, an official journal of the transcendental movement. His association with the great poets like Coleridge and Wordsworth made all the difference to his transcendental and romantic idealism.

Emotion : In its widest sense emotion is applicable to all affective phenomena including the familiar "passions" of love, anger, fear, hatred, etc. as well as pain and pleasure.

Emotivism : It is a theory of ethics according to which ethical pronouncements are merely exhortations to moral virtue. In that sense, they are mere sentiments of the speaker. Emotivists hold that the moral assertions are pseudo-propositions as they cannot be verified. The chief exponents of this theory are A.J. Ayer who advocated emotivism in his *Language, Truth and Logic*, and C.L. Stevenson who modified Ayer's version of emotivism in his *Ethics and Language*. Emotivism is also known as "Boo-hoorey theory."

Empathy : It is the projection by the mind into an object of the subjective feeling of bodily posture and attitude that result from the tendency of the body to conform to the spatial organization of the object. This phenomenon is of specific significance in aesthetics.

Empedocles (c. 490 – 433 BC) : He was an ancient Greek philosopher who reduced the whole diversity of things in this world to four important elements: earth, water, air, and fire. His doctrine was accepted by many ancient and medieval philosophers. The union and division of elements were explained by him in terms of two opposing forces, namely, attraction and repulsion.

Empirical : Philosophically speaking any knowledge that is based on sense-experience is empirical. However, the expression "empirical" is also used for any information or process that relies on observable data. All natural sciences are called empirical sciences for their knowledge is derived from empirical means.

Empiricism : It is a theory of knowledge that claims that all genuine knowledge is possible through sense-experience alone. As opposed to rationalism, empiricism maintains that there are no preconceived ideas (innate ideas) in the mind. Thus it rejects a priorism. Ideas are channelled either through sensation or reflection. While receiving these ideas the mind is a mere passive unit. Once the mind is furnished with various simple ideas, it becomes active to produce various complex ideas with the help of certain operations like compounding, comparison and abstraction. These complex ideas represent objects of reality. Locke, the pioneer of empiricist movement, is the chief advocate of such a theory. However, his successors, Berkeley and Hume, differ with him by advocating presentative theory of perception. In other words, they advocated phenomenalism. According to Berkeley, reality is mind-dependent, whereas Hume reduces reality to sense-impressions. These discrete, unconnected, and vivid sense-impressions are supposed to be the ultimate constituents of reality. These impressions are neither mental nor material, but regarded as neutral stuff. Unlike Locke and Berkeley, Hume admits a priori forms of knowledge. He classifies knowledge into relations of ideas and matters of fact. All the propositions of mathematics and logic come under "relations of ideas"; while all the propositions concerning natural sciences come under "matters of fact." Relations of ideas, according to Hume, are universal, necessary and certain. Their truth is indubitable. The truths of matters of fact are mere contingent truths in the sense that they are mere probabilities. The modern empiricists such as logical atomists and logical positivists accepted the same empiricist tenets.

Empiricism, Radical : It is William James in his *The Meaning of Truth,* who first adopted this philosophical position, according to which experience is the final criterion of reality in knowledge. James held that this philosophical position consists of a postulate, a statement of fact, and a generalized conclusion. (1) The postulate is that the only things that shall be debatable among philosophers shall be things definable in terms drawn from experience. (2) The statement of fact is that relations between things, conjunctive as well as disjunctive, are as such matters of direct experience. (3) The generalized conclusion is that the parts of experience hold together from next to next by relations that are themselves parts of experience. The directly apprehended universe needs no extraneous trans-empirical connective support, but possesses in its own right a concatenated or continuous structure.

Empirio-criticism : It is a theory that views economy of thought as the fundamental principle of knowledge. It extracts the understanding of experience from the concepts such as matter, necessity, causality, etc., by reducing them to a priori apperceptions. These concepts, maintains empirio-criticism, are wrongly introduced to experience. According to empirio-criticism, reality is made up of neutral elements called "sensations." The champions of this theory are Richard Avenarius and Ernst Mach.

Empty : According to Husserl, it is something that is bereft of intuitional fullness. In that sense it is obscure or materially indeterminate. Emptiness is compatible with distinctness. In logic, it is a class that does not consist of any members.

Ends : In Kantian ethics, humanity and every rational creature is an end in itself. The natural end that all men have is their own happiness. Kant's notion of the "kingdom of ends" is a systematic union of different rational beings by common laws.

Energy : It is the power by means of which things or objects act to change other things. It also represents the potentiality inherent in physical objects. In physics, energy is the capacity for performing work. In modern physics it is represented as $E = mc^2$ (Einstein's view).

Engels, Friedrich (1820 – 95) : He was a German materialist philosopher who collaborated with Karl Marx in writing several important works on politics, history, and philosophy. One of his very famous works is *Dialectics of Nature* in which Engels tries to explain the role of dialectics in science. Like Marx, Engels took interest in communism when he was young. His important works include: *Dialectics of Nature*; *Anti-D'hring*; *Ludwig Feuerbach and the Outcome of Classical German Philosophy*; *Origin of the Family*; and *Private Property and the State.*

Enlightenment : It is also known as "the age of reason." Kant explained "enlightenment" as man's coming of age from the state of childhood, which rendered him incapable of using reason without the aid of others. Thus Kant provided a subjective meaning of the term. Objectively speaking, it is a cultural period distinguished by the fervent efforts of the leading personalities to make reason the absolute ruler of human life, and to shed the light of knowledge upon the mind and conscience of any individual. The term "enlightenment" is generally applied to the European enlightenment stretching from the early seventeenth to the beginning of nineteenth century, especially fostered by English, Dutch, French, and German philosophers.

Enlightenment took its start in England from the empiricism of Francis Bacon, Thomas Hobbes, and John Locke. It found its religious version in the writings of Edw. H. Cherbury, J. Toland, M. Tindal, H. Bolingbroke and others. The powers of human reason are revealed in the writings of the French philosopher René Descartes and the German philosopher Leibniz. Thus both the rationalists and the empiricists contributed to the development of enlightenment in their own right, although it reached its heights in the writings of Kant, Hegel, Marx, Nietzsche and others.

Entelechy (Gk) : It is a term used by Aristotle to show that the purposefulness or the active principle converts a possibility into a reality. In other words, it is the realization of actuality in opposition to mere potentiality. In vitalism, enteclechy is considered to be the vital principle that is present in all living beings.

Enthymeme : It is a syllogism in which a premise is suppressed. For example, in the enthymeme, "All Indians are hardworking people, therefore, this man is hardworking," the minor premise "this man is an Indian" is left out. This is a syllogism: if the major premise is omitted then it is called first order enthymeme; in the second order enthymeme minor premise is omitted, and in the third order enthymeme conclusion is omitted. The following examples highlight the nature of each enthymeme.

Enthymeme of the first Order : *Example*: Ram is mortal because Ram is a man.

Enthymeme of the second order : *Example*: All Indians are hardworking, therefore this man is hardworking.

Enthymeme of the third order : Example: All men are mortal beings and all ministers are men.

This form of enthymeme is basically used in rhetoric and in law courts.

Entropy : It is a term often used by classical physicists to express the view that the greater the entropy the lesser is the energy that is to be converted. It is also called the law of the increase of entropy or the second principle of thermodynamics. The chief exponent of this principle is the physicist R. Clausius.

Enumerative Induction : It is a kind of inference, which proceeds from a number of instances to generalizations of a specific sort. For instance, the generalization, "Every *A* is *B*" should be understood with the qualification "Every observed *A* is *B*." This process is used specially in statistical methods, as a matter of fact, to enumerate means to count. In this method a generalization is reached by the process of counting the instances observed. Enumerative induction is of two types, namely, complete enumeration and incomplete enumeration. The former is called the perfect enumeration and the latter imperfect.

Epagoge (Gk) : In Aristotle's logic, it is a process of establishing a general proposition by inductive argument.

Epicheirama : It is a form of syllogistic conclusion whose premises are enthymemes. *Epicheiema* is a type of highly condensed reasoning. It is of two types. If it uses the enthymeme in the place of one of the premises it is known as the single *epicheirema.*

Example: All kings are mortal because they are men.

George is a king.

Therefore, George is mortal.

If the *epicheirema* uses two enthymemes in the place of the two premises, it is called double or complex *epicheirema.*

Example: The Sikhs are a minority; because they constitute a small section.

The Sikhs are entitled to freedom.

Epictetus (c. 50 – 130) : He was a famous Stoic philosopher and a moralist whose teachings have been classified into physics, logic, and ethics. Like Socrates, Epictetus never wrote anything, but one of his disciples by name Arrian composed eight *Discourses* based on Epictetus' lectures along with a summary of the great man's thought, the *Encheridion* or *Manual*. He argued that master can be a slave to his own passions, whereas a slave can experience freedom in his inner spiritual independence. Good and evil are not inherent in things but they lie in our attitude towards things. Education, held Epictatus, is necessary if we have to learn how to connect moral insights with life. We have to realize that we cannot change the events that happen to us, but we can very well change our attitude towards them. To realize this truth we have to go through three stages. (1) We must order our desires and overcome our fears. (2) We must perform our duties properly. (3) We must think and judge accurately. These three stages lead to inner tranquillity.

Epicurean School : It was a school founded by Epicurus in Athens in the year 306 BCE. According to Epicureans, every desire is a refined type of happiness, which is the reward of a cultured man. Epicurus adopted the atomism of Democritus but modified its determinism by admitting chance to cause a swerve (clinamen) in the fall of the atoms.

Epicurus (C. 341 – 270 BCE) : He was an ancient Greek materialist who advocated the view that God does not interfere in the worldly affairs of the humans. He revived the atomistic interpretation of the world advanced by Leucippus and Democritus. According to him, sensations are true by themselves, because they proceed from objective reality. All mistakes arise out of the misinterpretation of sensations. In ethics, Epicurus justified the joy of the mind based on certain pleasures. The most rational state of man is not the activity but absolute peace.

Epiphenomenalism : It is a view that describes consciousness as an epiphenomenon of certain molecular changes that take place in the brain. In opposition to interactionism advocated by Descartes and psychophysical parallelism of Spinoza, epiphenomenalism maintains that all the mental events are resultant effects of certain physical events but not vice versa. T.H. Huxley advocated this theory.

Epistemics : It is a branch of epistemology that is primarily concerned with the scientific approach to knowledge in opposition to philosophical one. This term was coined by some Edinburgh University scientists in 1969.

Epistemological Idealism : It is a form of epistemological monism that identifies the content and the object of knowledge by assimilating the object with the content. Berkeley's subjective idealism is an example for epistemological idealism.

Epistemological Monism : According to this theory, in the non-inferential knowledge such as perception, memory, etc. the object of knowledge is numerically identical with the data of knowledge. Thus everything is ultimately reduced to sense-data or sense-contents.

Epistemological Realism : It is a theory according to which the object of knowledge enjoys an independent status. It is not dependent upon the knowing subject or mind. It is one of the most popular theories of perception.

Epistemology : It is a branch of philosophy that is concerned with various theories of knowledge. The term is derived from the Greek root *epistemé*. Epistemologists are chiefly concerned with the aspects such as what is knowledge? the origin and the scope of knowledge, justification of knowledge, and limitations of knowledge. There are two major epistemological theories, namely, rationalism, and empiricism which are basically responsible for the other theories of knowledge. Rationalism maintains that all genuine knowledge is possible through reason alone, while empiricism sticks to the view that all genuine knowledge is derived from sense-experience. In opposition to these two views, Kant advocated transcendentalism, according to which neither reason nor sense-experience in isolation from each other can ever give us the genuine knowledge of reality (phenomenon). Thus he asserts that the pure concepts without the percepts are empty, inasmuch as the pure percepts without the concepts are sightless.

Episyllogism : It is a case where the conclusion of one categorical syllogism is used as one of the premises of another syllogism. The former is called prosyllogism and the latter episyllogism.

Epoché (Gk) : It means "suspension of judgement" or "bracketing out." Edmund Husserl used this expression to explain his philosophy of phenomenology as a rigorous science. According to him, one has to bracket out all the natural conceptions about any phenomenon before the phenomenological reduction. See Phenomenology.

Equivalence : The relation between p and q when p implies q, and q implies p is called equivalence. It is also known as bi-conditional statement. It is shown in the following manner.

p	q	$p \equiv q$
T	T	T
T	F	F
F	T	F
F	F	T

Equivocation: It is one of the verbal fallacies. It is the result of the ambiguous use of the words or the terms. For example, the arguments of a person are considered to be "impertinent" with regard to saying that they are not relevant in this context. However, it can also be interpreted that those arguments are "impudent." Similarly, the term "each" or "all" has an ambiguous meaning. Thus every word is an ambiguous one. It is only the context that makes their meanings clear.

Erastianism : It is a trend that believes in the authority of secularism rather than in the authority of the Church.

Eristic Reasoning : It is a way of reasoning that was prevalent among Sophists. The main purpose of any argument, according to eristic reasoning, is to win over others irrespective of the validity of their reasoning.

Eros (Gk) : It means "sexual attraction or physical love." In Greek mythology, it is believed that Eros is the first God to emerge from Chaos. In contrast to Eros, Agape was used to designate the highest form of love that exists between the God and the humans, or vice versa.

Erotetic Reasoning : It is a way of reasoning that is concerned with interrogations. It is often connected with logical nature of various interrogation statements. For example, the interrogation "When did you reach the railway station?" can be construed in such a way by using propositional function which is bound by a quantifier (*t*). To expand it, what time "*t*" was it such that you reached the railway station at "*t*"?

Error : It is nothing but a distorted form of truth or non-veridical apprehension. Normally error occurs in perception and memory. The propositions that represent error are false.

Eschatology : It is that aspect of systematic or dogmatic theology that deals with last things such as death, judgement, heaven and hell, and also with the end of the world. In a way it is concerned with the life after death.

Esoteric : Anything that belongs to the inner circle of initiates or experts to pursue an objective is called esoteric. In ancient Greece, the esoteric doctrines are attributed to the Stoics.

Esse est percipi (L) : It means "to be is to be perceived." It is a famous slogan of Berkeley, according to which objects exist in so far as they are perceived. Berkeley claims that the objects exist because the finite minds perceive them. Even if the finite minds do not perceive the objects still they exist because an ever-vigilant spectator is perceiving them all through. That ever-vigilant spectator is none other than God (Infinite Mind or Spirit). If this principle is applied to the existence of God, then God should not exist as He is not perceived by the finite minds. To this, Berkeley answers that we have a "direct notion" of God.

Essence : It is a salient characteristic or a property of a thing that makes what it is. In Aristotle's metaphysics, essence represents an immutable and timeless possibility of existence. Nevertheless, it was Aristotle who classified properties into essential and accidental. Essential properties are those properties that constitute the "thing-in-itself" (Kantian terminology). They are inseparable from the object itself. Accidental features or properties are those, whose absence does not change the very nature of things. John Locke made a sharp distinction between the real and the nominal essences. The real essence (nature of a substratum), according to Locke, is "unknown and unknowable," while the nominal essences are produced by the real essence. These nominal essences are none other than the primary qualities (solidity, figure, extension, motion or rest, and number), and the secondary qualities (colours, tastes, smells, etc.). For Kant, the apparatus of empirical or phenomenal knowledge (categories of understanding and sense-experience) do not provide any knowledge of a "thing-in-itself." American pragmatist John Dewey considers that whatever properties happen to interest us are called "essential." Hence the essence of a thing varies according to the context.

Essentialism : At least there are three varieties of essentialism. (1) In Plato's philosophy, essentialism is explained in terms of the existence of the World of Forms. Forms being eternal constitute the essence of reality. All the objects existing in the world of phenomena are mere carbon copies of those Forms. (2) An object or a thing can be defined or described because it possesses an essential property. (3) The objects or the things are grouped under various classes by virtue of their sharing certain essential properties with others. Without such properties (essential), objects cannot exist. Hence the existence of every object is subjected to having certain essential features that help us to classify things under various classes.

Eternal : In opposition to phenomenal or transient existence, eternal existence is considered to be trans-phenomenal or everlasting. For example, God being perfect is eternal. The Forms of Plato are eternal. The "Absolute" in Hegel's philosophy is eternal.

Ethics : It is a branch of knowledge that is concerned with the study of moral values. Ethical code is the part and parcel of human societies. Its main purpose is to regulate the behaviour of an individual or a group or a society. Moral obligations differ from society to society. Even professional societies such as medical societies, business organizations, etc. have their own code of conduct. Ethics has been chiefly classified into normative and descriptive ethics. Normative ethics is chiefly concerned with the standardization of moral principle, whereas descriptive ethics is concerned with the analysis of various concepts and their application to various situations. Descriptive ethics is a part of meta-ethics.

Ethics, Absolute : According to absolutists, the ethical standards are absolute in their nature. Therefore, they are permanent.

Ethics, Relative : The kind of ethical code that is operated in the human societies is relative to those societies. The ethical standards of a society keep changing according to the changing needs of the society.

Ethnocentrism : It is a tendency to view people of other ethnic (national, cultural, and racial) identities from the prejudiced perspective of one's own ethnic identity.

Ethos : It means "character," "moral purpose." Aristotle distinguished ethos from thought or intelligence.

Etiology : It is a science that studies the causes of some particular phenomena.

Euclid (300 – 400 BCE) : He was an ancient Greek mathematician who founded a school at Alexandria to teach Geometry. Until 1914 or so in most of the British Universities geometry was simply called Euclid.

Eudaemonism (Gk) : It is an ethical point of view advocated by Aristotle. According to this theory, the happiness and general human well-being of any individual is possible only when all the potentialities of that individual are actualized.

Euthanasia : Etymologically "euthanasia" means good dying. It is one of the concepts of ethics that has received considerable attention in the field of medical ethics. Euthanasia is administered when a patient is suffering from an incurable disease or pain that is intolerable.

Evambūtanaya (S) : It means "the such like point." According to Jainism, this theory of *naya* takes into consideration the functional aspect of the object suggested by the etymology of the word. For example, a cow can be called *gauḥ* only when it is moving not otherwise.

Evaluation : It is a process that involves both quantitative and qualitative comparison of values or worth.

Event : It is a happening that causes change, but does not endure over a long time. Therefore, it is opposed to an object or a thing.

Evil : It is the negation of the extrinsic elections of things. In practice, evil is the positive effect of such negation. Anything that is morally bad is also termed as evil.

Evolution : It is a natural process of development of living organisms through phylogenetic changes. Evolution is best explained and interpreted by Charles Darwin in his *Origin of Species* (1859). However, there are various theories of evolution such as philosophical theories, biogenetic theory, abiogenetic theory, biblical theory, Upaniṣadic theory, emergent theory, creative theory, and so on.

Evolution, Creative : Henri Bergson's theory of evolution is known as creative evolution. According to him, the conserved multi-dimensional life force (*élan vital*) diversifies the living organisms into various living forms by dividing itself more and more as it advances. Evolution is creative precisely because the future is open; and there is no "preordained" final goal. Duration constantly endures by producing always genuinely novel events like an artist who never knows precisely what he will create until he has created his work.

Evolutionary Ethics : Any ethical theory that is developed in accordance with the doctrine of evolution in explaining the origin of moral sense and the determination of moral standards is a part of evolutionary ethics. Spencer's social evolution is an example of evolutionary ethics. The moral standards set up by the evolutionists are adaptation, conduciveness to life, social health, etc.

Existential Proposition : In its general sense an existential proposition is that which asserts the existence of its subject. According to Brentano, an existential proposition is one that directly affirms or denies the existence. He held that all the four traditional kinds of categorical propositions are reducible to existential propositions. For example, the traditional universal affirmative proposition "All men are mortal" can be reduced to an existential proposition by rewriting it as "Immortal men do not exist."

Existential Psychology : It is a school of introspective psychology represented by American psychologist E.B. Titchener (1867-1927). According to existential psychology, the task of psychology is to be the description, analysis and classification of the experiences of an individual mind considered as existences. It denies imageless thought.

Exoteric : Anything that is meant for outsiders or non-initiators or experts.

Expectation : It is a state of mind wherein the individual concerned will look forward to an event that is going to take place. Expectation can be interpreted in terms of supposition, anticipation, reasonable hope, probable occurrence, or prediction.

Experience : It is a kind of personal involvement that guarantees a human individual that his belief in such and such a thing is true. Experience in its narrower sense is restricted to sensory experience. For example, empiricists claim that all genuine knowledge is possible through experience alone. In Kant's epistemology, experience means not only sense-experience but also the categories of understanding. The admixture of these two will give rise to knowledge. Experience in its broadest sense can include intuition, revelation, reason, and sense-experience. Intuition and revelation are considered to be mystic experiences in the sense that they do not involve any process. Thus they are direct experiences.

Exportation : In modern or symbolic logic, it is one of the rules of equivalence. It is stated in the following manner.

$$(p \,\&\, q\,) \supset r) \equiv (p \supset \{\, q \supset r\})$$

Expression : According to Husserl, a symbol embodies and signifies the *noematic* objective sense of an act of thinking. Thus the sense is expressed, and the act is manifested.

Extensive Quantity : By means of some physical process of addition the existing quantity can be increased or multiplied. This is opposed to the process of intensive quantity wherein the existing quantity is reduced to lesser quantity.

Extension and Intension : This distinction is first introduced by Port Royal logicians like that of denotation and connotation. According to J.S. Mill, extension can replace denotation, whereas intention replaces connotation. In the case of extension, a term can be extended to all the members belonging to a particular class. In the case of intention, a term can be attached to only a specified individual or a particular mainly to separate it from the other individuals or the particulars. Thus an extended meaning of a term is different from its intended meaning.

Exteriority : It is the character of externality ascribed to physical or material objects by common sense and by the realist epistemologists.

External Reference : It is the tendency of the mind to objectify sensory data and construe them as referring to a real external world.

External Relations : It is a theory according to which the relations are not dependent upon the nature of their terms. The relations of a thing are external to it and not constitutive of its nature. G.E. Moore is the chief advocate of this theory.

External Sense : In Kant's epistemology, external sense refers to the intuition of spatial properties, as contrasted with the internal sense which is that of the a priori form of the time.

External World : The reality that exists independent of human consciousness is called external world. Here the term "reality" designates the world in which all the material objects exist. For example, the objects like chairs, tables, mountains, trees, etc. have independent existence. Their existence is not dependent on the human consciousness. The world that consists of such material objects is external to us. Both Berkeley and Hume deny the existence of such an external world. According to Berkeley, reality (world of physical objects) is mind-dependent. This position is known as phenomenalism. Hume claims that reality is nothing but a stream of sense-impressions.

Externalization : It is a mental act by means of which sensory data, which are originally considered to be internal, are projected into the external world. The problem of externalization was first formulated by Candillac in the following manner. "If one admits that sensations are only modifications of the mind, how does it come about that the mind apprehends them as objects independent of and external to it?"

Extramental : It is a status external to and independent of knowing mind. This status is often attributed to physical/material objects by physical realists, and to universals by Platonic realists.

Extra-sensory Perception : It is a theory of perception in para-psychology. This sort of perception does not involve ordinary sense-organs. For instance, intuition can be called extra-sensory perception as it is not a mental process that involves any sense-organ. It is a direct experience of something. Similarly, telepathy and clairvoyance are considered to be extra-sensory perceptions (ESP).

Extraspective Situation : It is situation of the mind wherein we seem to be in direct cognitive contact with other minds and their states. It is almost like extra-sensory perception.

Extrinsic : The extrinsic value of a thing is decided by relating it to some other value. Thus it becomes an instrumental value.

Extrojection (L) : It literally means "to throw." It is a tendency of human mind to externalize sensuous qualities and affective states.

Ezra, Abraham Ibn (1093 – 1167) : He was a Jewish exegete and philosopher. His philosophy is known through his commentaries and short treatises like *Yesod Mora,* i.e. *Foundation of the Knowledge of God, Shaar ha-Shamayyim,* i.e. *The Gate to Heaven.* He was basically concerned with the right conception of the universe and its becoming and that of knowledge. He was influenced by Neo-Platonism, and Gabirol.

F

Fa (C) : It means "standard," "model," "paradigm." The behaviour, the institutions of the sage-kings are all *fa* to every good ruler. At the dawn of Buddhism in China, *fa* is translated as *dharma* or righteousness.

Fa chia (C) : It was an ancient Chinese school of legalists and philosophers of law, whose members had utmost faith in reward and punishment. As regards the implementation of the law, they did not show any discrimination between honourable and humble. They held that everyone is equal before the law, and the power is natural to the ruler. The supporters of such a law were Kuan Tzú (sixth century BCE), Shén Tao (350 – 257 BCE), Shén-Pu-hai (400 – 337 BCE).

Fact : A fact is an event or a phenomenon or a fragment of objective reality that is an object of man's experience. According to Wittgenstein, world consists of facts, but not of things. Anything that is simply is a fact. It is that which is contrasted with the possible. It is also viewed as an indubitable truth of actuality.

Fact-value Distinction : It is one of the most fundamental distinctions in moral philosophy. The distinction is based on the view how things are and how things should be, or how it is desirable for things to be. People obeying a particular law is one thing; that they ought to is obviously another. The former is a matter of fact, and the latter a matter of value. It was Hume who made a distinction between "is" (fact) and "ought"(value). According to him, "ought" cannot be deduced from "is" without any controversy. But, moral prescriptivists like R.H. Hare claimed that it is possible to derive a value from a fact.

Faculty : Medieval psychologists distinguished several faculties of the soul, which are said to be really distinct from each other and also from the substance of the soul. According to Aquinas, the distinction is based on objects and their operations. The faculties are considered to be the accidents of the soul's substance, but they pertain to its nature. The soul operates through faculties. Modern experimental psychologists and nominalists attacked this position.

Faculty Psychology : It is a branch of psychology according to which mind as the unit in a number of special faculties like sensibility, intelligence, volition by reference to which individual process of sensation, thought or will is explained. Faculty psychology is an outcome of Plato's tripartite division of soul into the appetitive, the spirited and rational faculties. Faculty psychology was revived by Christian Wolff (1679-1754) in his *Rational Psychology* (1734). Faculty psychology is basically associated with the soul-substance theory of mind.

Faith : It is a strong belief in something as true or genuine even without sufficient proof. In other words, it is the acceptance of the ideals, which cannot be theoretically demonstrable. According to Kierkegaard, it is the act of faith that leads one to religious level. Religious faith does not entertain reason at all. Kierkegaard felt that "faith is the shipwreck of reason."

Fallacy : Any logical inconsistency is called a fallacy. There are formal and material fallacies. For instance, it is fallacious to argue, given a generalization that "All politicians are social workers," "Mother Teresa is a social worker," therefore, it follows that "Mother Teresa is a politician." Here the fallacy is called the fallacy of "undistributed middle."

Fallibilism : It is a theory propounded by C.S. Peirce, according to which every inquiry is an activity resulting from the confused state of mind. To arrive at a state of calmness, the mind tries to find a right answer to the problem in question. However, such calmness is never assured as there may be an evidence to show that what is considered to be right is wrong. Thus, the mind is under constant pressure to find a right solution.

False Consciousness : According to Karl Marx, ideology is a form of false consciousness that lacks clear awareness of the source and significance of one's beliefs and attitudes concerning society, religion, or values. Collingwood interprets false consciousness as something self-corrupting untruthfulness in disowning one's emotions and ideas.

Falsidical : It is an opposite for the term "veridical." Anything that is false is called falsidical.

Falsification : In opposition to verification, falsification was first introduced by Karl Popper. According to this view, a theory is scientific in so far as it is falsifiable or refutable. This does not mean that a theory is considered to be scientific if it is refuted by experience. On the other hand, it should be understood in the sense that a theory is considered to be scientific if it leaves some scope for falsification. Thus the statement, "The combination of hydrogen and oxygen will give rise to water (H_2O)" is truly scientific as it gives chance for its refutation. Similarly, a generalization like "All crows are black" is false. The main purpose in introducing the principle of falsification is to demarcate science from pseudo-science, and also to reduce the number of contending observations.

Fantasy : It is an imaginary idea that is often contrasted with something real or objective, e.g. gold-mountain, sky-lotus, winged-horse, round-square, and so on.

Fascism : It is an expression used to refer to those modern political movements that seek to retain traditional forms of authority and class domination within the framework of a totalitarian state. Fascism found penultimate expression in Italy (1922 – 45) and in Germany (1933 – 45) where the racist and anti-Semitic ideologies colluded with a virulent nationalism in fuelling expansionist political aims.

Fatalism : It is a belief in the predetermination of every event that takes place in the world. Thus whatever has to happen will happen. This view rules out any possibility of freedom or creative endeavour. For example, Leibniz's notion of pre-established harmony of monads is a form of fatalism. In Hegel's philosophy, it is the "Absolute" which is ultimately responsible for every change that takes place in reality. This doctrine is theological, rather than philosophical. The advocates of determinism do not admit fatalism as a form of determinism.

Fate : It is a superstitious view that all events in one's life are pre-determined by some supernatural force. All modern religions consider fate as divine predestination.

Fechner, Gustuv Theodor (1801 – 87) : He was a German physicist who advocated pure Objective idealism although he believed in induction, analogy, history and pragmatic procedure. Like his mentors Oken and Shelling, he advocated that everything is in consciousness. There are no substances, no things-in-themselves. Everything including animals, plants, earth, and heaven, shares the life of the soul. According to Fechner, in God there is pure and infinite consciousness without an objective world. Evil arises from darker levels of consciousness. Obsessed with the mind-body problem, Fechner advanced an identity according to which every object is both mental and physical. He advanced a theory of psychophysics which deals with the exact functional relations between mind and body. Thus he is said to be the founder of the experimental psychology. His important works include: *Elemente der Psychophysik* (1860) and *Vorschule der Aesthetik* (1876).

Feeling : It is a state of non-perceptual awareness or a state of reflection, which is an outcome of an emotion or any other experience. Feeling being an internal experience is a form of psychical act that can be grasped by others by way of the individual's behaviour towards certain things. It can also be interpreted as a conscious, subjective impression, which does not involve cognition or representation of an object. Pleasure and pain are two types of feeling. Kant held that there are life promoting and life destroying forces in pleasure and pain respectively.

Feminist Philosophy : The major concerns of feminist philosophy are to challenge male-dominated philosophy. Feminism refuses to identify the human experience with mere male experience. It refutes traditional philosophy on the ground that it deliberately let down the interests, identities and issues of women in general. Also, the traditional philosophy ignored the women's ways of being and their thinking capability. Feminist philosophers in general do not admit ontological dualism as they hold that individuals interpenetrate each other's psyches through empathy. Feminist philosophers decried that the Western philosophy often equated rationality with "masculinity" and emotionality with "feminity." The traditional epistemologists underrated women by holding the view that women are less human than men as they lack sufficient reason to think. Feminist philosophers did not approve of traditional science as objective as it failed to listen to nature's revelations. Similarly, feminist philosophers attacked traditional ethics and socio-political philosophies as they are mainly male-dominated disciplines with rules and principles that normally take care of the interests of men rather than general humankind. The post-modern feminist philosophers dub the entire history of philosophy as a story of male heroes who were responsible for the dissemination of knowledge, truth, ethics, and socio-political principles.

Fetishism : It is a primitive view that attributes a few magical powers to the objects to influence the life of humans.

Feuerbach, Ludwig Andreas (1804 – 72) : He was a German materialist philosopher who asserted that religion is nothing but a dream (earthly dream) of human mind. He considered that the essence of man is the one and only subject matter of any philosophical discussion. Like his contemporaries, Feurbach was influenced by the objective idealism of Hegel. He openly opposed immortality. This resulted in the ire of the authorities, which eventually led to the termination of his academic career. His important works include: *Das Wesen des Christentums* (1840) and *Philosophie u. Christentum* (1859).

Fichte, Johann Gottleib (1762 – 1814) : He was a German philosopher who proclaimed that science of science is the prerequisite for practical philosophy. Fichte's thought centred around the passionate arousal of Kant's practical reason or the autonomy of goodwill is the legitimate creative source of all that is distinctive in personality. According to him, religion is a kind of belief in the divine moral law, whereas the practical reason is the foundation of epistemology that satisfies all its subjects. Fichte assumed that consciousness, including the representation of physical objects that make up the outer world, is the product of one ultimate cause in the Universe. The world in which each individual lives is his/her own world, brought into the being through the creative agency of the ultimate. For Fichte, thinking is purely a practical affair. It is a form of action. Since experience is presented in the form of consciousness, the origin and nature of consciousness is the key to all problems. The ego is the centre where the creative activity of the Absolute emerges in the individual consciousness. The world, held Fichte, does not have its independent existence. It exists for the sole purpose of enabling man the occasion of realizing the ends of his existence. It is merely material for his duty. His important works include: *Versuch einer Kritik aller Offenbarung* (1792); *Grundlage der gesamten Wissenschaftslehre* (1794); and *Grundlage des Naturreschts* (1798).

Ficino, Marsilio (1433 – 99) : He was a well-known Italian neo-Platonist and one of the leading members of Platonic Academy in Florence. He made use of Platonism to attract people to come closer to the teachings of Christ. The Latin-speaking West had access to Plato's works because of Ficino's translation of and commentaries on Plato's works. Ficino was influenced by Plato and Plotinus. His important work is *Three Books on Life* (1488).

Fiction : It is a logical or imaginative construction formed by the mind to which nothing corresponds in reality. Also, it is held that whenever a symbol, as part of an utterance, occurs in such a context that the truth of any utterance of the same form would normally guarantee the existence of an individual denoted by the symbol, whereas in the case considered no such implication holds, the symbol may be said to occur fictitiously in the context. For example, in the utterance "The average Indian is five-and-a-half feet tall" the phrase "average Indian" occurs fictitiously, since it does not denote any particular individual.

Fictionism : It is an extreme form of pragmatism or instrumentalism according to which the basic concepts and principles of natural science, mathematics, philosophy, ethics, religion, and jurisprudence are pure fictions, which though lacking objective truth, are useful instruments of action. This theory had the Kantian base.

Fideism : According to this view, no essential religious doctrine can ever be established by reason. An essential religious doctrine can be accepted by mere acts of faith. The extreme form of fideism is seen in the writings of Søıen Kierkegaard. Fideism in its moderate form is also found in the writings of St. Augustine. According to him, reason is not opposed to faith, but only helps us in deciding what must be accepted by faith.

Figure of Speech : This verbal fallacy should not be confused with "metaphor." This fallacy occurs when a particular term is misinterpreted assuming that its prefix or suffix has the same meaning as it has in other cases. For example, the terms "sufficiently," "accurately," etc. convey a positive meaning, but the term "hardly" does not mean it is "hard." It has a negative meaning.

Final Cause, the Doctrine of : It is a view according to which the things and events in the world can be explained by reference to some ultimate end or purpose or final cause to which they are conducive. The doctrine of final cause was advocated by Aristotle and Leibniz.

Finalism : It is a form of teleology, according to which purpose is present in all the events of the physical order.

Fine Arts : They are opposed to mechanical arts. The fine arts are poetry, painting, sculpture, architecture, music, and so on.

Finite : Anything that is limited as opposed to unlimited is called finite. In mathematical analysis, any fixed real number (or complex number) is called finite. Also, various physical and geometrical units measured by real numbers are called finite.

Finitism : It is a philosophical standpoint that denies the notion or the category of infinite. According to finitism, there is no infinity in the Universe. Since man's experience is the experience of finite things and their properties, man's thinking is also limited to finite things. In formal systems of mathematics, finitism is nothing but the application of those methods that are free from ambiguity.

First Cause : According to St. Thomas Aquinas, God is considered to be the first efficient cause of this world.

First Heaven : In Aristotle's cosmology, first heaven refers to the outermost sphere of the fixed stars.

First Mover : In Aristotle's metaphysics, it represents the origin of motion in the Universe. The "First Mover or Unmoved Mover" is responsible for all the motion in the Universe. However, the "First Mover" remains unmoved. According to St. Aquinas, there must be some "First Cause" that is responsible for all the motion in this Universe. This "First Cause" is none other than God.

Formal Language : It is an uninterpreted system of signs. Formal language is conditioned by formation and transformation rules. It is also called logically perfect or ideal language. Both Russell and early Wittgenstein developed formal language to uphold their logical atomist thesis.

Formal Logic : It is a science of reasoning that can be traced back to Aristotle's *Prior Analytics.* The reasoning in formal logic is based upon the premise that the validity of an argument is a function of its structure or logical form. The modern form of formal logic is called symbolic or mathematical logic. Modern logic is basically concerned with valid inference in artificial, but precisely formulated languages, the grammatical structure of whose sentences or well-formed formulae is intended to mirror the logical forms their natural language counterparts. These formal languages can be viewed as mathematical models of fragments of natural language.

Formal Mode of Speech : This expression was first introduced by Rudolf Carnap in order to distinguish it from material mode of speech. For example, "This apple is red" is a material mode of speech directly concerned with the object in question. "The apple is a thing word" is a formal mode of speech in which it is concerned with the formal structure of a word or a term that denotes an object or a thing.

Formal Reason : This expression is used by Weber to refer to very general procedures for reaching valid decisions. These procedures would include logical rules of deductive inference as well as scientific methods geared towards the calculation of consequences. In opposition to the contingent (situationally relative) calculation of formal rationality, which is situationally relative, substantive rationality primarily consists in unconditional commands whose validity is ostensibly rooted in some metaphysical absolute such as God or nature.

Formal Semantics : It is the study of the interpretation of formal languages. A formal language can be defined irrespective of any interpretation of it. This can be done by specifying a set of its symbols and a set of formation rules that determine which strings of symbols are grammatical or well-formed. Any formal language is interpreted by assigning meaning to its symbols and truth conditions to its sentences.

Formalism : It is a method of art based on abstraction, absolutizing, and aesthetizing of art forms. It represents various trends of art such as futurism, abstract art, surrealism, expressionism, etc. Formalism proceeds from an idea that artistic endeavour and creativity do not come into the fold of reason. In mathematics, formalism tries to solve problems concerning the foundations of mathematics by means of formal axiomatic rules. It was David Hilbert who introduced formalism in mathematics. In ethics, formalism aims to arrive at certain moral principles and solutions applicable to different social conditions by appealing to the abstract, absolute principle. In Kant's philosophy, such a principle is called "categorical imperative."

Foucault, Michel (1926 – 84) : He is regarded as one of the leading contemporary French philosophers and a great historian of thought. Foucault's earlier writings show that he was under the influence of Marxism and existential phenomenology. Later on he moved away from these positions and got attracted to two fundamental disciplines, namely, history and philosophy of science. Foucault developed a distinct approach to intellectual history, the archaeology of knowledge, which treated systems of thought as discursive formations independent of any personal beliefs. The distinguishing feature of Foucault's archaeology is that it displaced the human subject from its central place that it occupied in the humanism that dominated our culture since the time of Kant. According to Foucault, archaeology provided no account of transitions from one system to another. He introduced a genealogical approach, which does not negate archaeology, but goes beyond it to explain changes in systems of discourse by connecting them to changes in the non-discursive practices of social power structures. According to him the developments that take place in the new systems of thought are only the contingent products of many small, unrelated causes, but not the fulfilments of grand historical designs. Foucault felt that power is not always repressive, but sometimes creative too. His important works include: *The Birth* *of the Clinic* (1963); *The Order of Things* (1966); *The Archaeology of Knowledge* (1969); *Discipline and Punish* (1975); and *History of Sexuality* (1976).

Four Books : They are the Confucian texts that include: *Ta-hsüeh* (Great Learning); *Chung-Yung* (Doctrine of the Mean); *Lun Yü* (Analects); and *Meng Tzu* (Book of Mencius). The former two books are the chapters from *Li-Chi* (*Book of Rites*), and the latter two books contain the teachings of Confucius (sixth century BCE) and Mencius (fourth century BCE). Chu Hsi (1130 – 1200) considered these texts as basic for the Confucian form of education and also wrote commentaries on them.

Four Elements : According to ancient Greek philosophers, the Universe is composed of four basic elements, namely, earth, air, water, and fire. Every element possesses two important qualities. For example, earth (dry and cold), air (wet and hot), water (wet and cold), and fire (dry and hot).

Four Humours : To maintain proper physical and mental conditions, the body fluids such as blood, choler (yellow bile), phlegm and melancholy (black bile) must be in proper proportion. These body fluids are known as four humours. Galen felt that any excesses in their quantities may cause some physical or mental illness.

Four Terms : It is one of the formal fallacies. It occurs when an ambiguous middle term is used in the syllogism-like arguments. It only appears like three-termed syllogism, but it actually consists of four distinct terms. Hence it is a pseudo-syllogism. For example, No genuine academician makes impertinent criticisms. Mr 'X' made impertinent criticism; therefore, Mr 'X' is not an academician. If the term "impertinent" means "impudent" or "offensive" in the major premise, and "irrelevant" in the minor premise, then there are four distinct terms. There is no middle term. Hence it is a fallacy.

Frank, Phillip (1884 – 1966) : He was a member of the "Vienna Circle." He was influenced by Ernst Mach. As a physicist, Frank worked on the aspects related to both physics and philosophy. His important work is *Between Physics and Philosophy* (1941).

Frankfurt School : A group of like-minded philosophers, who are popularly known as Critical Theorists, established this school in 1929. The founder of this school was Max Horkheimer (1895 – 1973). The Frankfurt School philosophers are basically cultural critics and social scientists. Their basic aim is to resolve the theory-practice conflict existing since the time of Descartes. Most of the members were of Jewish dissent or the sympathizers of the Jews. Apart from Horkheimer, the other prominent members of the school were Theodor Adorno (1903-69), Herbert Marcuse (1898 – 1979), the famous psychoanalysts Erich Fromm (1900-80), and the literary critic Walter Benjamin (1892 – 1940). Jürgen Habermas is one of the leading second generation Critical Theorists. Their chief objective is Marx's transformation of moral philosophy into social and political critique. However, the Frankfurt School members opposed orthodox Marxism.

Freedom of Will : It is a view that is opposed to determinism. According to this view, an individual acts in certain circumstances as per the dictates of his will. Thus his actions are neither guided by any other force nor predetermined.

Frege, Gottlob (1848 – 1925) : He was a German logician and mathematician who is considered to be the father of modern mathematical logic. Frege constructed a formalized arithmetic with the intention to reduce all mathematics to logic. Frege was opposed to psychologism. According to Frege, the sense of an expression cannot be identified with its reference. To defend his thesis Frege cited one of the famous examples, namely, "The morning star is the evening star." Frege's work was unknown to many when he was alive, but his work became popular and important through the writings of Russell and Wittgenstein. In fact, he was recognized as one of the greatest logicians of the nineteenth century. After Boole, Frege is considered to be the second founder of the algebra of logic and his contribution to the field of symbolic logic is well acknowledged. The modern form of propositional calculus, the notion of propositional function, and the use of quantifiers are well defined in Frege's logical works. Frege contributed to the field of arithmetic as well. He made a distinction between using a formula to express something else and naming a formula in order to make a syntactical statement about it. His important works include: *Grundlagen der Arithmetic* (1884); *Grundgesetze der Arithmetik* (1893-1903).

Freud, Sigmund (1856 – 1939) : He was a well-known Austrian physician and a founder of psychophysical analysis. He regarded psychic activity as something independent, but existing along with the material process. Freud subjected all the psychic conditions, all the actions of man. And also all the historical events and the social phenomena to psychoanalysis. He tried to interpret them in terms of unconscious, above all sexual impulses. In his own practice, he employed hypnotic methods of treatment in combination with his own techniques of free association and dream interpretation. Freud not only developed a therapeutic technique for the treatment of hysteria and neurosis, but advanced an elaborate psychological theory of which the main tenets are the predominance of sex and the doctrine of the subconscious. Freud's psycho-analytic method was used by critical theorists (Frankfurt School Marxists) for the analysis of the life in the modern societies. His important works include: *The Interpretation of Dreams* (1900); *Psychology for Everyday Life* (1901); and *Eros and Civilization* (1920).

Fulguration : It is a lightning flash of the mind. According to Leibniz, the monads are God's perpetual fulguration.

Function : It is a kind of purpose explained in terms of outward manifestations of the properties of various objects in a given system of relations. It is one of the key concepts in mathematics.

Functional Psychology : This branch of psychology was developed by William James, G.T. Ladd, G.S. Hall, J. Dewey, and J.R. Angell. According to functional psychology, the mental processes of sense-perception, emotion, volition and thought are the functions of the biological organism in its adaptation to and control of its environment. Functionalism was developed as an alternative to structuralist psychology, according to which the task of psychology is to analyse and describe the nature of consciousness. Both pragmatism and instrumentalism advocate functional theory of mind.

Functor : In the terminology of Rudolf Carnap, a functor is a sign for a non-propositional function. In other words, it is synonymous with non-propositional function symbol.

Futurology : It is a branch of science that deals with the future of mankind and the prospects of social progress. The term "futurology" was first introduced by a German Sociologist O. Fledhtheim. In other words, it is a science of future, whose basic aim is to predict the nature and the utility of various scientific disciplines and various steps to be taken in maintaining a bright future of mankind.

Fuzzy Set : It was L.A. Zadeh, who developed the fuzzy set theory. In a fuzzy set membership is a matter of degree. In classical set theory, *X* may be or may not be a member of a particular set *S*. But in fuzzy set theory, things *X* may be members of sets *S* to any degree between 0 and 1, inclusive. Degree 1 denotes that *X* "is a member of," and 0 denotes that *X* "is not a member." The intermediary degrees are degrees of vagueness or uncertainty. For example, the set *S* has members who are men with grey hair at the age of thirty-five. But the degree of greyness differs from member to member.

G

Gadādhara (seventeenth century CE) : He was a Navya-Nyāya philosopher and wrote a commentary on Gaṅgeśa's *Tattvacintāmaṇi*. Gadādhara wrote independent treatises on *anumāna* and *śabda*. Gadādhara used the latest technique of Navya-Nyāya in his works.

Gadamer, Hans Georg (1900 – 2002) : He is a contemporary German philosopher who is known for his philosophical hermeneutics, and contemporary philosophy. Toeing the line of his teacher Heidegger, Gadamer in his philosophical hermeneutics holds that the ties to one's present *horizons*, one's knowledge and experience, serve as the real background for understanding. But, these limitations can also be transcended, argued Gadamer, by getting exposed to others' discourse and linguistically encoded cultural traditions for their *horizons* convey views and values that place one's own *horizons* in relief. A *horizon*, maintained Gadamer, is something into which we move and which moves with us. *A horizon* is not a closed framework of options or standpoints. Regarding tradition, Gadamer held that it is the locus and summation of human awareness of the most important truths and hence it has normative content. The progressive revelation of the meaning of the content of tradition in and through the concrete circumstances of history is possible. Hermeneutics is a method for making positive use of the distinctiveness of our own point in history in order to appreciate the meaning and value of the tradition. According to Gadamer, tradition is not a mere storehouse of materials depending entirely upon the inquirer, but its content of authentic wisdom plays a normative role for life in subsequent ages. This history is the playground for tradition. Classical tradition gives history an evaluative power. History, Gadamer felt, is only considered as the chronological record of events. Thus it has neither a reflective nor evaluative role to play. The contextual interpretation or the social relevance of the events was not properly highlighted by history. Classical tradition is the repository of historical events as well as human social experience. Thus it fuses both past and present to pave the way for the future. Thus understanding is inbuilt in history because understanding deploys the knower's *effective history*. Gadamer's important works include: *Truth and Method* (1960); *Philosophical Hermeneutics* (1967); *Dialogue and Dialectic* (1980); *Reason in the Age of Science* (1982); and *The Relevance of Beautiful and Other Essays* (1986).

Galen, Claudius (129 – 215) : He was a philosopher and a physician from the Greek Asia Minor who combined peripatetic and Stoic teachings. He was chiefly interested in philosophy of science, nature and logic. Galen advocated an extreme form of teleology based on the doctrines of Plato, Aristotle, the Stoics and the medical writers of his time. In his philosophical psychology, Galen is known for his materialist account of mind. Also, he held that proper mental and bodily health is invariably dependent upon the four basic bodily constituents (four humours). His views in this regard were akin to Hippocrates. Galen was regarded as the most influential doctor of his time. His important works include: *On the Therapeutic Method; On the Function of Parts; On the Passions and the Errors of the Soul;* and *On the Doctrines of Hippocrates and Plato.*

Galileo, Galilei (1564 – 1642) : He was a well-known Italian physicist and astronomer who attacked the dogmatic scholasticism and the blind worship of Aristotelian physics by advancing a scientific method, especially modelling of natural phenomena. One of his main contributions to mechanics is his discovery of the law of inertia. His astronomical discoveries were corroborated with the heliocentric theory of Copernicus as against the fundamental principles of Aristotelian cosmology. Galileo advocated hypothetico-deductive method in his scientific methodology. His important works include: *Dialogue Concerning the Two Chief World Systems* (1632) and *Discourse Concerning Two New Sciences* (1638).

Gambler's Fallacy : It is also known as Monte Carlo fallacy according to which in a sequence of independent events, the gambler is tempted to believe that the probabilities of latter outcomes may increase or decrease to compensate for earlier outcome. For example, the gambler may believe that a tossed coin has a memory, so that after a run of a particular kind of result its opposite becomes more probable.

Game Theory : It is a mathematical theory that deals with game-like situations wherein participants wish to maximize some property in an uncertain situation in respect to the actions of the others. It is a situation wherein a person predicts what others would do given such a situation so that he can act accordingly.

Gandhi, Mohandas Karamchand (1869 – 1948) : He is known throughout the world as the freedom fighter for an independent India and the father of the nation. Although Gandhi was not an academic philosopher, his practical aspects of philosophy influenced young and old alike. As a religious man, Gandhi was influenced by the great religions of the world. He advocated the gospel of peace and non-violence not only in his personal life but also in political action. The impact of the teachings of the *Bhagavad-Gītā* was quite evident in his actions. For Gandhi, non-violence, compassion, and love are the three great pillars of any human society. According to Gandhi, God is Truth. He arrived at this definition because no one would like to ignore truth as an important aspect of one's life. Gandhi strongly advocated self-rule (*svarājya*) as the precondition for any harmonious society. His philosophy is often characterized as the philosophy of *satyāgraha,* which means "passionate adherence to truth." Gandhi held that non-violence without love is only a body bereft of life. And love without non-violence is only a disembodied spirit. Therefore, his philosophy is a form of activism.

Gaṅgeśa (c. twelfth century CE) : He was a Navya-Nyāya philosopher. In his *Tattvacintāmaṇi*, Gaṇgeśa discussed at length about the nature of *anumāna* although he admitted the four *pramāṇa*s recognized by the Naiyāyikas. Several commentaries were written on his position on *anumāna* and *śabda*. Gaṅgeśa held that space, time, and *ākāśa* are not different from God.

Gassendi, Pierre (1592 – 1655) : He was a French philosopher who strongly opposed scholasticism. He questioned Descartes' claim that "clarity and distinctness" is the criterion of truth. According to Gassendi, how are we supposed to know that anything is "clear and distinct" to us? He also attacked the doctrine of innate ideas of Descartes. Although Gassendi accepted the dogmas of Catholicism, he was interested in science and mathematics. He was chiefly responsible in reviving the Epicureanism in the West. He held that the world is made up of atoms, but this concept cannot be applied to the existence of God. Gassendi, unlike Descartes, admitted sense-experience as a reliable source of knowledge. In ethics, Gassendi advocated a type of hedonism, according to which pleasure is the highest good. But his concept of pleasure is different from that of Thomas Hobbes. According to Hobbes, pleasure is derived from the egoistic impulse, while for Gassendi, pleasure produces social solidarity and indeed is one of the main sources of religion. His important works include: *Commentarius de vita; moribus etplacitis Epicuri* (1659); and *Syntagma philosophiae Epicuri* (1684).

Gauḍapāda (c. eighth century CE) : He is known as the "teacher's teacher (*parama guru*)" in the Advaita tradition. He is considered to be the first systematic exponent of Advaita Vedānta. He is the author of *Māṇḍūkya-Kārikā* or *Gauḍapāda-Kārikā*. Śaṅkara admires Gauḍapāda for the latter provided a non-sectarian interpretation of the Upaniṣads. It appears that Gauḍapāda himself was a Buddhist before he became an Advaitin.

Gautama or Gotama (C. fourth century BCE) : He was a great sage and seer, who founded the Nyāya school. He is also known as Akṣapāda. He is the author of *Nyāya-Sūtra*. Nyāya is a combination of pluralistic atomism and logical realism. Gautama's chief interest was to formulate the principles of logic and epistemology. He did not divorce logic from metaphysics as he believed that what we know depends on the form of knowledge. However, in his philosophy metaphysics did not receive much attention. Gautama developed his principles of logic with reference to the context of debate, in which two different schools advocate different doctrines as hypotheses and argue for establishing their doctrines. His *Nyāya-Sūtra* was chiefly intended to lay down the procedure for a proper debate. The most important commentator of his work is Vātsyāyana.

Gay, John (1699 – 1745) : He was a British moralist and clergyman. According to him, since people are destined to be happy the obligation of keeping them happy is founded on the will of God. As an advocate of associationist psychology, John Gay held that it is the general tendency of human beings to pursue those objects which ultimately promote happiness. Thus his moral philosophy is a mixture of divine command theory and utilitarianism.

Geist (G) : It means "spirit" or "mind." According to Kant, Geist refers to that quality in a beautiful object, which animates mind to give life to a work of art.

Generative Grammar : They are the rules of grammar that allow speakers to construct countless number of sentences in any natural language. In the initial stages language learners are exposed to finite number of sentences, later on they acquire the ability of constructing more and more sentences on the basis of the rules of grammar. Noam Chomsky's transformational grammar is often regarded as the generative grammar.

Generalization : It is a process of arriving at a general concept or principle by means of particular instances. For instance, the proposition "All men are mortal" is a universal generalization.

Genesis : It means "emergence," "coming into existence." According to the Biblical account of creation, the world is created by God in six days. For details see the *Book of Genesis*.

Genetic Fallacy : It is a belief that something is now such and such because it was such and such at an earlier stage. Or it is understood that something is such and such at an earlier stage, therefore it has to be such and such now. For example, all men are evolved out of apes. This means that all men are really higher apes.

Gentile, Giovanni (1875 – 1944) : He was a well-known Italian idealist philosopher and educationist. He encouraged fascism. As an orthodox Hegelian, Gentile held that art, religion, and science are the various phases of the Absolute Spirit. All these disciplines are superseded by philosophy in his system. He tried to interpret reality in terms of spirituality. Like Hegel, Gentile held that the real is rational, and the rational is real. Human beings can find themselves in this world as modes of this world process. According to him, the state is a complete expression of rationality. Ethical principles and truth are established by the authority of the state. Like Plato, Gentile held that democracy represents a degenerate form of liberalism. His important works include: *La filosofia di Marx* (1899) and *Sistema di logica come teoria del conoscere* (1917).

Genus : In Aristotle's classification, genus involves many classes called species. This classification of Aristotle is considered to be a significant contribution in the field of science, especially in the field of natural sciences.

Geometry : The famous Greek mathematician Euclid is the founder of this branch of mathematics. In his work on *Elements* (c. 300 BCE), Euclid puts forward the basic principles of geometrical science. It deals with the laws concerning lines, angles, planes, etc. For example, a triangle is a three-sided closed geometrical figure.

Gestalt Theory (G) : *Gestalt* means "shape" or "form." This school of psychology was founded in 1912 in Germany by M. Wertheimer, K. Kofka, and W. Köhler. This school of psychology emerged as a challenge against the psychic elements of analytic or associationist psychology. It is a theory of perception, according to which it is an organized systematic whole that is given in perception; but not discrete, unconnected parts of any whole. This view is popular in psychology. In opposition to empirical theory of perception, Gestalt theory puts forward the view that "organized wholes" form the basis for any mental activity rather than transient sensations.

Geulincx, Arnold (1624 – 69) : He was a reputed Dutch philosopher, who was chiefly influenced by the works of Descartes. However, Geulincx was not satisfied with the Cartesian solution to the mind-body problem. He advocated a theory of occasionalism, according to which since the interaction between mind and body is impossible God effects bodily motions "on occasion" for each mental process. His important works include: *De virtute et primis ejus proprietatibus* (1665); *Ethica* (1675); *Physica peripatetica* (1690); and *Metaphysica vera* (1691).

Ghost in the Machine : This phrase was introduced by Gilbert Ryle in his work *The Concept of Mind* (1949) to denote human mind. Descartes believed that the mind exists independent of body, and the body independent of the mind. The important attribute of the mind is consciousness, while the important attribute of the body is extension. Descartes claims that the mind is like a pilot in the ship. Reinterpreting Descartes' idea, Ryle held the view that the mind is like a ghost in the machine. Ryle calls the doctrine of Descartes an "official doctrine" and attacks Cartesian dualism.

Gīta-Govinda (S) : It is a poetical work by Jayadeva written in the twelfth century CE depicting the erotic moments of Kṛṣṇa with Rādhā and other *gopikā*s. It is often interpreted as a mystical allegory.

Gnosis (Gk) : It means knowledge. The term *gnosis* generally implies the knowledge of esoteric type dealing with religious and philosophical truths to be acquired by an elite group of intellectually developed believers. The forerunner of Jewish Gnosticism was Philo Judaeus (30 BCE – CE 50). He allegorically interpreted the *Old Testament* by using the Greek philosophical concepts, especially the doctrine of Logos.

Gnosticism : It is a religious belief that the knowledge of God is directly given or revealed to the followers in order to help them attain salvation. Gnostics strongly believe that there is a distinction between good spiritual world and an evil material world. The cause of such an evil material world is Demiurge.

Gobineau, Arthur de (1816 – 82) : He was a French nobleman who authored the *Essay on the Inequality of Human Races*. He advocated a doctrine of "nordic supremacy," according to which the white race originally possessed the monopoly of beauty, intelligence, and strength. But because of its mix-up with the other races new races came into existence. These races, held Gobineau, are beautiful but lacked strength, strong but lacked intelligence, and intelligent but lacked beauty and strength.

God : It is an intuitive conception of supernatural omnipotent, omnipresent, and benevolent Being, who is supposed to have created the world. Such a view of God is assumed by theology on the basis of revelation, authority, and faith. However, there are a number of philosophical systems such as idealism, monism, dualism, which held that the existence of God could be demonstrated. In fact, the proofs for the existence of God are based on facts of experience (need for perfection, dependence, love, salvation), facts of religious history (*consensus gentium*), postulates of morality (belief in ultimate Being, justice, conscience, sense of duty), postulates of reason (cosmological, teleological, causal, ontological), and the inconceivableness of the opposite. As regards the nature of God, there are a variety of views. Sometimes the characteristics of God assume non-personal attributes (pantheism) or personal attributes (theism). According to Aquinas, there are five ways to prove the existence of God. They are as follows: (1) proof from motion; (2) proof from efficient cause; (3) proof from Necessary versus Possible Being; (4) proof from the degrees of perfection; and (5) proof from the order of the Universe.

God of the Gaps : It is a derogatory usage applied to various theories appealing to the concept of God to explain certain things that cannot be explained by the scientific method. For example, the origin of life, consciousness, the world, etc.

Gödel, Kurt (1906 – 78) : He was an Austrian mathematician and logician who is known for his first incompleteness theorem. According to his theorem, in any formal system "S" of arithmetic, there will be a sentence P of the language of "S" such that if "S" is consistent, then neither *P* nor its negation can be proved in "S." In 1930s, Godel proved the completeness of the first-order predicate calculus that consists of a set of sentences that have "one-place" predicates such as "red," "yellow," "cold," and so on. Godel held that if mathematics can be reduced to logic, as claimed by Russell, then mathematics is undecidable since it contains propositions that are neither provable nor disprovable.

Godhead : In general, it is a state of being a God, Godhood, Godness, Divinity, Deity.

Goethe, Johann Wolfgang Von (1749 – 1832) : He was a German naturalist, philosopher, a poet and a lawyer by profession, who held the view that theory and experience are the two sides of the same coin. He recognized the objectiveness of the laws of nature. He considered that the motion is the basic form of the existence of matter. Otherwise, he advocated hylozoism. In his philosophy, Goethe highlighted the tension between individual and society, culture and nature. He felt that the best way to overcome social problems is to cultivate self-discipline. His important works include: *The Sorrows of Young Werther* (1774); *Wilhelm Meister's years of Apprenticeship* (1795-96); *Elective Affinities* (1809), and *Faust* (1808-32).

Golden Age : This expression has a metaphorical significance. The "golden age" refers to that period where there was harmonious relationship between man and nature, and between man and man.

Good : It is a moral concept, which is used in opposition to the concept "evil." In general anything that is praiseworthy is called good. In axiology, we come across two types of good, namely, extrinsic and intrinsic. The former for its existence is dependent upon some object, end purpose that it serves. It is also known as instrumental good since it derives its being from its service as an instrument in promoting or sustaining some ultimate good. On the contrary, intrinsic good is good in itself without depending upon anything else for its goodness.

Goodman, Nelson (1906 – 98) : He is regarded as one of the influential contemporary American philosophers who advocated an extreme form of nominalism. Although his work resembles that of Quine in many respects Goodman's work has a distinct style. According to Goodman, people objectify similarities since they tend to objectify the properties and the characteristics of various objects in space and time. He has reservations in admitting certain things such as powers or dispositions, counterfactual assertions, entities or experiences that are possible but not actual, neutrinos, angels, devils and classes without proper evidence. In fact, his rejection of classes substantiates his nominalist position that runs throughout his work. His important works include: *The Structure of Appearance* (1951); *Fact, Fiction and Forecast* (1966); *Problems and Projects* (1972); and *Ways of World making* (1978).

Goodman's Paradox : According to Nelson Goodman, there is a paradox in the theory of confirmation. Suppose we define "grue" to be applicable to all those objects which were examined before time t_1, just in case they are green but to other things in case they are blue. Then at t_1, for every evidence statement that a given stone is green there is a parallel statement that it is grue. Then it appears that the prediction that all the stones examined later will be green, and that they will be "grue" are equally confirmed by past evidence statements describing the same observation. However, if we later examine a stone and it is "grue," it is blue and therefore not green. Therefore, if confirmation is defined in terms of past success, by suitably contriving a strange predicate, anything can be made to confirm anything else.

Gorgias (*c.* 480 – 375 BCE) : He was an ancient Greek philosopher, who was known for his skills of oratory, rhetoric. He was one of the leading Sophists. One of the dialogues of Plato bears his name. According to Gorgias, nothing exists. If anything exists, it is comprehensible, then it is incommunicable. The things that exist are perceptible. Speech cannot give any information about perceptibles.

Govindabhagavatpāda (c. eighth century CE) : He was a disciple of Gauḍapāda and the teacher of Śaṅkara. Govindabhagavatpāda shot into limelight not because of his contribution to Advaita, but because he was the teacher of the gifted Advaitic dialectician Ādi Śaṅkara.

Greek Academy : This was the name given to the school of philosophy founded by Plato in 385 BCE. It appears that this school is named after a public park called Academia in Athens. The school's long history reveals that in the early stages the discussions in the Academy centred around the works of Plato. But in the Middle Ages it was dominated by the dogmatic skepticism of Arcesilaus of Pitane (c. 315 – 240 BCE). Later on it was dominated by the Pyrrhonian skepticism of Carneades of Cytrene (c. 213 – 129 BCE).

Green, Thomas Hill (1836 – 82) : He was an influential British philosopher who vehemently criticized Humean empiricism. According to Green, to be real is to be related to other things. The relations are necessarily the work of mind. He attacked the Humean conception of self. According to Hume, the self is a bundle of impressions. Green asks the question, in the absence of a continuous self who witnesses the series of impressions? Green was mainly responsible in introducing Kant and Hegel to the English-speaking world when empiricism, utilitarian and Spencer's positivism were dominating the philosophical scene in England. According to Green, all knowledge is invariably dependent upon self-awareness. His important works include: *Prolegomena to Ethics* (1883) and *Lectures on the Principles of Political Obligation* (1885).

Grotius, Hugo (1583 – 1645) : He was a Dutch humanist and a theoretician of natural law. Grotius developed a unique law of nature to oppose moral scepticism and to settle moral disputes on rational grounds in spite of religious differences. He made a sharp distinction between inviolable natural law and the ever-changing positive or civil law. According to him, humans are both competitive and sociable. The laws of nature help us to live in harmony despite the fact that we have a general propensity to conflict with each other. In other words, these laws remind us that each and every individual possesses certain natural rights which set the boundaries for social space within which we are free to pursue our own goals. His important work is *The Law of War and Peace* (1625).

Guhadeva (S) : He was a Viśiṣṭādvaitin. Rāmānuja refers to him in his *Vedārthasaṁgraha*.

Guilt : In ethics, it is the conduct that breaches the moral law. The commission of a moral offence is considered to be the failure of duty. Defection from obligation or responsibility is also treated as guilt. In the psychology of ethics, the sense of guilt is the awareness of having violated an ethical precept or law.

Guṇa (S) : It means "quality." There are three important *guṇa*s. They are *sattva* or light, knowledge and happiness, *rajas* or mobile, pain, action, and *tamas* or indifference, lazy, dark, dull. According to Sāṁkhya, *prakṛti* is *triguṇātmaka*.

Guru (S) : It means "teacher." A *guru* is one who initiates a student into a particular discipline. Without a *guru* one cannot pursue one's education. In the Indian tradition, *guru* is equated with Brahmā (the creator), Viṣṇu (the sustainer) and Maheśvara (the destroyer). In the order of venerable persons, *guru* stands next to mother and father.

H

Habermas, Jürgen (1929 –) : He is one of the leading second generation German Critical theorists and a well-known philosopher in the contemporary scene. He has inherited the philosophical lineage from the pioneers of the Frankfurt School like Max Horkheimer, Theodor Adorno, Herbert Marcuse, and Erich who were instrumental in bringing Critical Theory into prominence. Like his predecessors, Habermas attacked the reason that dominated Enlightenment for gifting its allegiance to technical interests intent on domination. Habermas does not belittle the role of science but denounces only the paradigmatic claim of science as the only means through which all matters pertaining to human understanding are to be viewed. He distinguished scientific temper from scientific method. He attacked capitalism for reducing everything to commercial exchange in which mutual benefits are the coveted motives. Politics becomes a pawn in the hands of the market, which is being manipulated by science and technology. This science and technology become "ideological" in the sense that they produce an image of society based on a technical model. The line that separates technical activity and human relationship has been deliberately obscured so that the transition is not difficult. Habermas argued that only a return to "praxis" could be the remedy and not a category controlling social phenomena. In his *The Theory of Communicative Action* (1981), Habermas dwelt upon the challenges to a theory based on understanding. He weighs the consequences and installs various safeguards like discursivity and hermeneutic approach to prevent reification and over- subjectivism, for which he borrowed much from Luckacs and Gadamer. Thus in his later work Habermas tried to ground the ideology critique in the discourse ethic. His important works include: *Knowledge and Human Interests* (1968) and *Moral Consciousness and Communicative Action* (1983).

Habits : They are certain actions of the individuals that become the characteristic of those individuals due to prolonged repetition. According to Hume, the belief in necessary causal relation is a kind of habit formed out of constant repetitions of certain phenomena.

Habit Memory : It is an act wherein what is learnt is retained and reproduced. This is the case with a poem, a geometrical demonstration, etc.

Hades : In Greek mythology, Hades is referred to as the god of underworld, the son of Cronos and Rhea and the brother of Zeus. Hades ruled over the kingdom, which is the abode of the dead.

Haecceity : This term originally introduced by Duns Scotus to denote a formal property of an object, or a person on the basis of which it is individuated. According to C.S. Peirce, it is a means through which a person is referred to without any description.

Haeckel, Ernst Heinrich (1834 – 1919) : He was a German biologist and interpreter of Darwinism. He advanced materialistic monism. Haeckel believed in the essential unity of organic and inorganic. As a materialist he opposed revealed religions and their ideals of God, freedom, and immortality. In their place he advocated a monistic religion of nature based on the true, the good and the beautiful. His popular work is *The Riddle of the Universe* (1899).

Ha-Levi, Judah (1080 – 1140) : He was a famous Arabic poet and philosopher. In his work *Kuzari*, which is written in a poetic style, Ha-Levi tried to extend proofs and arguments in support of the dignity and worth of Judaism. Also, he aimed at showing the inadequacy of philosophy and the superiority of the truths of revealed religion to those arrived at by logic. The admission of both Christianity and Islam that Judaism is their source proves its superiority as a revealed religion.

Hallucination : It is a state of experience in which something is always imagined when there is nothing. In a state of hallucination something is created or imagined out of nothing. It is something different from illusion, wherein something is perceived as something else.

Hamann, Johann Georg (1730 – 88) : He was a German philosopher and a close friend of Immanuel Kant. Hamann held that Kant's critical philosophy was an unsuccessful attempt to treat reason as independent of all tradition, belief, and experience.

Hamilton, (Sir) William (1788 – 1856) : He was a Scottish philosopher and logician who denied objectivity of truth in order to advocate agnosticism. He believed that reality is cognizable through supernatural revelation only. He followed Kantian line by admitting a priorism and moral postulates as the foundations of religious faith. According to Hamilton, perception is the direct source of the knowledge of the objects. But he held that this knowledge cannot be taken in its absolute sense as it is phenomenal. One of his major works is Lectures on *Metaphysics and Logic* (1859-60).

Hampshire, Stuart Newton (1914 – 2004) : He is regarded as one of the influential contemporary British philosophers who realized that the world or reality cannot be analysed in terms of sense-experience. Self-consciousness is a kind of awareness of one's own situation in this world. Personality, according to Hampshire, can be exhibited through action and will. Freedom is possible through the knowledge of the factors that are responsible for making intentions ineffective. Goodness is a means for any action. His important work is *Thought and Action* (1952).

Han Fei Tzú (third century BCE) : He was regarded as the greatest Chinese philosopher of law and a pupil of Hsön Tzú. He advocated the government by law and statecraft. He was asked by his native state to appeal to the king of Chin, Shi Huang-ti, not to invade his country. First he was invited cordially, but later on he was forced to commit suicide by the premier of Chin and incidentally the schoolmate of Han Fei Tzú, Li Ssú, as he was jealous of Han Fei Tzú's popularity.

Happiness : Kant in his ethics considered happiness as an ideal possibility rather than a realization in actual human experience. Justice, freedom and happiness are the three pillars of any ideal society. In the absence of happiness human life becomes miserable. Pleasure cannot be equated with happiness since the former is less enduring when compared to the latter.

Hare, Richard Mervyn (1919 –) : He is a famous British moral philosopher who attacked ethical naturalism. He claimed that the moral judgements are not mere descriptions of certain actions but imperative or prescriptive. As a champion of moral prescriptivism, Hare held that "ought" can be derived from "is." His important works include: *The Language of Morals* (1952); *Freedom and Reason* (1963); and *Moral Thinking* (1981, 4 vols.).

Harmony, Pre-established : According to Leibniz, monads have pre-established harmony as established by God in the beginning. The perfect functioning of mind and body is due to the pre-established harmony among monads. God had perfect knowledge of all bodies and minds. There is a perfect co-ordination between mind and body due to this pre-established harmony. Leibniz compares this co-ordination with that of two clocks, which are conditioned once for all by the clock maker. Thus they do not need any intervention from anybody.

Hartley, David (1705 – 57) : He was a British physician and the founder of associationist school of psychology. His theory of association of ideas was further developed by the work of John Gay, who provided this theory with a physiological interpretation. This school of psychology influenced the utilitarians such as Jeremy Bentam, James Mill, and his son John Stuart Mill.

Hedonism, Ethical : In its ethical form, hedonism as a doctrine is concerned with those entities that possess intrinsic value. According to ethical hedonism, pleasure or pleasurable consequences alone have positive and ultimate value. Such pleasure or pleasurable consequences alone are intrinsically good as they do not have any constituent parts, which are intrinsically good. Ethical hedonism is usually combined with the teleological view of the nature of the right action.

Hedonism, Psychological : According to this form of hedonism, psychological motivation is explained exclusively in terms of desire for pleasure and aversion from pain. As a theory of motivation, psychological hedonism is concerned with pleasure-pain consequences of an act.

Hedonistic Aesthetics : The theories of hedonistic aesthetics reduce beauty to the pleasure of seeing, hearing, and playing to the satisfaction of sensuous enjoyment.

Hedonistic Calculus : This theory is attributed to Jeremy Bentham, according to which the pleasurable ends of mankind may be calculated by determining the preponderance of the pleasurable over painful consequences.

Hedonistic Paradox : It is a paradox that arises out of hedonistic theory due to the following reasons: (1) the doctrine that since pleasure is the only good, everyone ought to seek pleasure; and (2) the fact that whenever pleasure itself is the object sought, it cannot be found. Pleasure normally arises as an accompaniment of satisfaction of a desire for any end except when that end is pleasure itself. The way to attain pleasure is not to seek for it, but for something else through which pleasure is derived. In the similar fashion, one should not seek to avoid pain, but only actions that produce pain.

Hegel, George Wilhelm Friedrich (1770 – 1831) : He was one of the most influential German idealist philosophers, whose philosophy is known as Absolute Idealism. According to Hegel, reality is "Absolute Idea." Thought can approach the reality with the help of triadic movement, namely, thesis, antithesis, and synthesis. Thus he employed dialectics to human thought in order to reach reality. He felt that "all real is rational and all rational is real." Hegel joined with Fichte and Schelling in the enterprise of transforming the philosophy of Kant into a metaphysical idealism. Hegel criticized Kant's unknowability of "thing-in-itself." For he considered that everything is knowable. Thus "thing-in-itself" is also knowable. According to Hegel, both the content and the forms of knowledge are the products of mind. Thus all objects of knowledge, including things, must be the products of mind. If all objects of our knowledge are products of mind, but not our minds, it must be assumed that they are the products of a higher intelligence other than that of a finite individual. For Hegel, the world is an organic process. The truly real for him is what he called the Absolute. In theological terms, Absolute is called God. But, Hegel was not talking about that being which is separated from the world of nature or even human individuals. Nothing is unrelated. Everything that is experienced by us, upon careful reflection, leads us to other things to which it is related. This process of dialectical thought ultimately leads to the knowledge of the Absolute. Yet, Hegel held that the Absolute is not the unity of separate things. As an anti-materialist, he conceived that the Absolute is a dynamic process. It should not be viewed as an entity separate from the world, but is the world when viewed in a special way. The inner essence of the Absolute could be approached by human reason by means of dialectical thought. What connects the Absolute with nature and human mind is thought process. An individual's way of thinking is fixed by Nature, by the way things actually behave. Things behave as they do, since the Absolute is expressing through the structure of Nature. According to Hegel, logic is virtually the same thing as metaphysics. Such a conception of logic becomes inevitable in Hegel's philosophy since knowing and being coincide. As Hegel puts it, Logic is the process by which we deduce, from pure experiences of the actual, the categories that describe the Absolute. His dialectical process exhibits a triadic movement. This dialectical movement proceeds from thesis to antithesis and finally to synthesis. What Hegel emphasized in his dialectical logic is that thought moves and that contradiction, rather than bringing knowledge to a standstill, acts as a positive moving force in human reasoning. Throughout his vast and intricate system, Hegel employed the same dialectical method of logic. The culmination of the Absolute is found in art, religion, and philosophy. His important works include: *The Phenomenology of Mind* (1807); *Encyclopedia of Philosophical Sciences* (1816); and *The Philosophy of Right* (1921).

Heidegger, Martin (1889 – 1976) : He was a German existentialist philosopher whose main concern was man's inner experience. Heidegger was a student of Edmund Husserl. He shared the phenomenological method of the former to analyse the human existence in respect to its temporal and historical character. His metaphysics is known as "fundamental ontology" as Heidegger's main objective was to explore the nature of Being. Such an exploration is possible through the analysis of and description of human "being" (*Dasein*), which is supposed to be the basic mode of being in this world. Heidegger started his inquiry into the notion of "Being" by taking the cue from the Greek tradition. Although he totally differed from the approach of the Greeks, he sought to find his way back to an inner independence of philosophy from the special sciences. He transformed the concept of "Being" from a highly abstract and remote concept into a subject of intense concern to every human being. In the process, he fashioned new vocabulary and gave old words new meanings to convey his philosophical thought. He aimed at reviving the genuine act of philosophizing, which has vanished in the Western world because of the excessive autonomy and importance given to science over philosophy. The human reality is structured in such a way that it discloses itself immediately. Heidegger endeavoured to explore the unexplored phenomena which ontology generally disregarded. *Sorge* (concern) being *par excellence* of consciousness, is elevated to the ultimate. *Angst* (dread), the feeling of being on the verge of nothing, represents an eminently transcendental instrument of knowledge. His important works include: *Being and Time* (1927); *An Introduction to Metaphysics* (1935); *Nietzsche* (1961); and *The Matter of Thinking* (1969).

Heliocentric Theory : It is a view of solar system propounded by Copernicus. According to him, sun is at the centre of the solar system. All other planets, including earth, revolve round the sun.

Henotheism : This term was first introduced by Max Müller, according to which each of many Gods, when praised, is extolled by the hymn as the supreme God.

Heraclitus (544 – 483 BCE) : An ancient Greek philosopher who held the view that everything in this world is under constant "flux." He believed that the fire is the archetypal form of matter and that for God all things are good, beautiful, and just, but men have supposed certain things as unjust. God is everything. He is the day, night, winter, summer, war, peace, hunger, etc. He undergoes alteration the way fire undergoes alteration when it is mixed with spices, it is named according to the scent of each spice.

Hermeneutics : It is originally a study concerning the interpretation of Biblical texts. Of late, hermeneutics as a method is employed in the investigation and interpretation of human behaviour. In Heidegger's existentialism, hermeneutics is considered to be an inquiry into the purpose of human existence.

Heterological : It is a term that is inapplicable to itself. For example, the term "Greek" is heterological, because it is not a Greek word.

Hetu (S) : It means "reason." It is one of the five limbs of syllogism or inference (*anumāna*). *Hetu* is the reason from which something is inferred.

Heuristic : In research methodology, heurism is considered to be a stimulating factor of investigation. An investigation in any field of research involves a trial and error method. It need not necessarily provide a satisfactory solution.

Historicism : It is a view that cognizes the things and phenomena in their historical perspective, namely, the process of their origin and development, and the factors responsible for their existence. It is considered to be a major principle of Darwin's theory of evolution. This thesis has been criticized by Karl Popper in his work *The Poverty of Historicism.*

Holism : According to this thesis, a whole can never be a mere sum total of its parts. A whole is more than the sum total of its parts. Reality is governed by holistic processes. This view rejects the idea that matter is preserved in the process. In social sciences, holism views that the fundamental data for analysing any social situation are not individual manifestations but the laws that govern the society.

Homological : Contrary to heterological, a homological term can be applied to itself. For instance, the word "Englis" is homological, because it is an English word. Homological is also interpreted as a similarity based on the structure, the origin, and the development of any phenomenon.

Homonyms : Words with the same form and sound but having different meanings are called homonyms. For example, enquiry and inquiry.

Humanism : It is a viewpoint that insists on the better dignity and rights of man. It is concerned with better social life and promotion of better human personality. Humanism opposes all forms of fanaticism, intolerance and disrespect for the views and knowledge of others. The term humanism is also used to denote the culture and ideology of the Renaissance. It is different from humanitarianism.

Humanitarianism : This expression is often confused with humanism. It is a view that regards human value as central. It is a moral or social programme that lessens the human suffering by aiming at the welfare of human beings. Humanitarianism is also extended to prevention of cruelty to animals. Philanthropy and altruism come under humanitarianism. As a theological doctrine, humanitarianism denies the divinity of Christ.

Hume, David (1711 – 76) : He was a Scottish empiricist philosopher who denied the existence of material as well as spiritual substances. According to him, reality is nothing but a stream of sense-impressions. These unconnected, discrete sensory units are neither mental nor material, but neutral entities. Hume's philosophy is also known as pure sensationalism, atomism, neutral monism. Hume conceived that what we suppose as cause and effect relation between two entities or events is purely psychological. It is based on "habit and custom." In his theory of knowledge, Hume classified knowledge into "relations of ideas, and "matters of fact." The former consists of the propositions of logic and mathematics, which are necessary, universal and certain. The latter consists of propositions of natural sciences, which are highly probable. He also held the view that there is no continuous self. What is called self is nothing but "a bundle of sense-impressions." In ethics, Hume made a distinction between "is" and "ought." According to him, "is" represents the fact, and the "ought" value. One cannot reduce "is" to "ought" or vice versa. Morality, according to him, is a human affair based on human circumstances. Futher, Hume made a distinction between natural virtues and artificial virtues. The former are generosity, benevolence and so on. The latter are justice, allegiance, and so on. His important works are *A Treatise of Human Nature* (1739-40); *Essays Moral, Political, and Literary* (1741 & 1752); *An Enquiry Concerning Human Understanding* (1748); *An Enquiry Concerning the Principles of Morals*

(1751); *The Natural History of Religion* (1757); *History of England* (1754-62, six volumes); *My Own Life* (1777); and *Dialogues Concerning Natural Religion* (1778).

Hume's Fork : Hume's classification of knowledge into "relations of ideas," and "matters of fact" is known as Hume's fork. According to Hume, relations of ideas are those truths that are obtained independent of experience. Their truths are universal, necessary, and certain. The propositions of mathematics and logic come under this class, while all the propositions of empirical sciences come under the category of matters of fact whose truths are highly probable. At the same time they are obtained through sense-experience.

Husserl, Edmund (1859 – 1938) : He was a German philosopher and mathematician who studied under Franz Brentano. Husserl is known for his phenomenology. There are various stages of philosophical development before phenomenology took a definite shape in Husserl's writings. The pre-phenomenological phase was between 1887-94. In his *Philosophy of Arithmetic* (1891), Husserl tried to derive the fundamental concepts of mathematics from psychological acts. This view was criticized by Gottlob Frege. Later on Husserl abandoned psychologism by attacking it in a series of lectures delivered by him in 1895. These lectures were incorporated in his *Logical Investigations* (1900). With the publication of this work the phenomenological movement of Husserl came into existence, although it did not take any definite shape. In the initial stage, Husserl introduced phenomenology as a descriptive analysis of subjective processes. In fact, philosophy as a rigorous science is identified with phenomenology by Husserl. According to him, the goal of philosophy is to describe the data of consciousness without any bias or prejudice, ignoring all metaphysical and scientific theories in order to accurately describe and analyse the data gathered by human senses and the mind. Husserl's philosophical ideas are the outcome of his reaction against naturalism and historicism. Naturalism, according to him, is an absurdity for it conceived the physical things as real and also the naturalistic standpoint cannot exemplify the foundation of science. Also, it cannot provide any answer to the questions concerning experience. During this stage Husserl intended to clarify certain fundamental notions of phenomenology such as "intentionality," "intuition," "essence," "meaning," and so on. The function of such science is to unravel the foundations of logic and epistemology on the basis of the phenomena given to consciousness. Such a descriptive study of consciousness is not an empirical study. Husserl distinguished "pure description" of phenomenology from "empirical description" of natural sciences. In its pure description phenomenology tries to present the very essences of phenomena. Husserl's phenomenological reduction is an attitude to exclude everything from the considerations of transcendent and scientific or logical inference. A phenomenologist would only consider those entities that are directly presented in consciousness. Prior to this reduction one has to suspend judgements about the object in question. This is what is technically called *epoch*? or bracketing. His other important works include: *Ideas* (vol. I, 1913; vols. II & III, 1952 posthumous publications); *Formal and Transcendental Logic* (1929); *Cartesian Meditations* (1931); *The Crisis of European Sciences and Transcendental Phenomenology* (Parts I & II 1936), and other parts were published in *Husserliana* (1954).

Hylomorphism : It is a metaphysical view, according to which every natural object is composed of matter and form. In opposition to Plato, Aristotle held the view that the matterless form and the formless matter cannot exist.

Hylozoism : It is a doctrine, according to which all matter is animate. This doctrine attributes sensations and mental acts to all forms of matter. This term was first introduced in seventeenth century. A well-known Greek hylozoist was Bruno.

Hypostasis : It is a Greek term that denotes a self-subsistent entity that can act as a basis for other things or objects. For example, a substratum acts as a base for all the qualities and the attributes. Thus all the qualities and the attributes are dependent upon a substratum for their existence, but it is not dependent upon them for its existence.

Hypothesis : It is a form of deduction based on a series of observations from which we infer the existence of an event or a fact. Science cannot operate without hypothesis. It is one of the scientific postulates. Scientists arrive at various theories by means of hypotheses. The validity or invalidity of a hypothesis is decided by subjecting it to the test of verification.

Hypothetical Statement : A conditional statement is known as hypothetical statement. For example, "if there is good rain, then there will not be water scarcity" is a conditional statement. In symbolic form, it is expressed in the following manner. If p then *q*. The truth table of a conditional or hypothetical statement is as follows:

p	q	$p \supset q$
T	*T*	*T*
T	*F*	*F*
F	*T*	*T*
F	*F*	*T*

Hypothetico-deductive Method : It is a method of arriving at a scientific theory by formulating a hypothesis from which new scientific predictions are deduced and put to the test of verification. One of the popular advocates of such a theory is Karl Popper.

I

I : It is an indexical sign used by an individual to refer to himself without any reference to any particular aspect of himself. Such a reference does not have any descriptive content. Some philosophers used "I" as a transcendental self or pure ego. In the philosophy of Descartes, the statement "I think, therefore I am" signifies that the thinking "I" is the pure ego which is different from the empirical "I" which exists. According to him, the latter is derived from the former. Kant called this "I" transcendental subject. This substantial "I" of Kant is known intuitively. According to Kant, the substantive "I" is not a substance, but the functional dynamic unity of consciousness which is a necessary condition for all experience and the ultimate subject for which everything is an object. Wittgenstein in his *Tractatus* held that "I" as a transcendental subject cannot exist in the world of facts. Therefore, he called "I" as an error in grammar. Wittgenstein refuted solipsism on the ground that if "I" has to exist, there must exist others for otherwise the talk about "I" becomes meaningless.

Icon : It is a sign or image that represents something. For instance, the third eye of Lord Śiva represents the destruction of the evil.

Iconoclasm : It is a religious struggle launched against images, and towards any form of symbolic art in eighth and ninth centuries.

Iconology : It is a discipline concerning the study of the history of art forms and the interpretations of art forms by the artists.

Idea : It is an object of thinking which is an exclusive property of the mind. Thus ideas are mental. Ideas may represent objects, properties, relations, and also imaginary objects. Epistemologists claim that the ideas constitute the very essence of knowledge. However, they may disagree with each other as regards the sources of such ideas. For instance, Descartes claimed that innate ideas constitute the indubitable foundations of knowledge. For empiricists, the ideas are necessarily obtained through sense-experience of sensation and of reflection. Locke defined an idea as "whatsoever is the object of understanding when a man thinks." He claimed that the ideas are the copies of objects external to us. Both rationalists and empiricists hold that the ideas are the bedrocks of human knowledge. However, rationalism and empiricism differ with each other with regard to the origin or source of these ideas.

Idea, Absolute : It is an expression used by Hegel to designate the fully realized and comprehended unity of the knowing subject and the known object (the totality of essential relations).

Idea, Abstract : It is an idea that is arrived at by means of abstracting the particular objects. The abstract idea of "horse" is arrived at by observing particular horses. According to Berkeley, there are no abstract ideas for it is impossible to imagine an idea without specific features.

Ideal : In social philosophy, an "ideal state" is one that is most perfect from any standard. For instance, Plato in his *Republic* described how an ideal state should be. It is called utopia.

Ideal of Reason : In Kant's philosophy it refers to reason's vain search for knowledge of totality of things, its conditions, structure, and possibilities. Kant calls this search the "transcendental illusion."

Ideal Speech Situation : This expression is used by Habermas to denote conditions of absolute freedom and equality which would have to be obtained in order for participants in discourse to reach rational agreement and thereby achieve a true (universally binding) consensus.

Idealism : It is an ontological thesis according to which ideas are primary and matter is secondary or derivative. Epistemological idealism maintains that our mind is not capable of receiving anything external to it. There are two fundamental forms of epistemological idealism: immanent idealism, and transcendental idealism. According to immanent idealism, human mind can possess or acquire knowledge of its own experiences. The chief exponent of this view is Berkeley. According to him, reality is mind-dependent. This doctrine is popularly known as subjective idealism. What is called a physical object is nothing but a complex of sensible qualities (ideas), whereas transcendental idealism holds that reality (phenomenon) is a sum total of appearances existing in space and enduring through time. Such a reality has no independent existence as it is necessarily dependent upon a priori forms of understanding (categories). Thus cognition is concerned with the constructions of thought which do not really exist. It is also called critical idealism. The chief advocate of such a thesis is Immanuel Kant. There is another form of idealism known as absolute or objective idealism. According to this thesis, the underlying reality of all existence is called "Absolute" or "Absolute Spirit." The well-known advocate of such a thesis is Hegel.

Idealization : It is an act of thought in the process of which the mind forms certain abstract objects that cannot be created or realized in practice. However, they serve as a means to provide scientific analysis of the real objects. For example, in physics we have a few idealized objects such as "absolute solid state", "ideal gas," "absolute black body." In mathematics, we have a few idealized objects like "point", "straight line," "actual infinity," etc.

Identity : It is the relation expressed in logic and mathematics by using the sign "=." For example, the total obtained by adding two numbers is identical with the addition of these two numbers (2+2=4). Numerical identity is the relation that expresses one and the same thing. For example, the President of India and the first citizen of India are identical. In other words, the things that share the same space and time are numerically identical.

Identity of Indiscernibles : This theory was advocated by Leibniz. According to this theory, if an object "A" has every property that the object "B" has, and the object 'B" has every property that A has, then the objects "A" and "B" have an indiscernible identity with each other.

Identity, Law of : It is one of the three laws of logic. According to the law of identity, a proposition is true if it is true (*A* is *A*).

Ideology : It is a set of ideas or notions and political norms that regulate a particular social and political action. Ideology is a backbone of any social system. However, ideology has become a key term in politics because the struggle between two opposite forces is fought on the ideological grounds. In its modern usage, it has a pejorative sense. According to Marxism, ideology is a false consciousness for it purports to justify material domination and inequality by appeal to illusions such as God, the people, the State, human nature, etc., which do not have any basis in real historical life. Such abstract ideas appeal to false notions of unchanging and eternal relationships.

Idols : Francis Bacon in his *Novum Organum* held that there are four impediments in the form of idols that prevent the proper use of the inductive method to obtain scientific knowledge. They are as follows: (1) *The Idols of the Tribe*: The anthropomorphic projection and wishful ways of thinking are inherent in the very nature of all human beings, all tribes, and all races. Therefore, their way of viewing things is regarded as the standard by which things really are. (2) *The Idols of the Den (cave)*: They are the private, unique personal prejudices. (3) *The Idols of the Market*: It is the failure to use language correctly and to define terms precisely. And (4) *The Idols of the Theatre:* It is the blind acceptance of tradition and authority without any rational scrutiny.

If : It is a term that is frequently used in our everyday language to express a condition. For example, "If he works hard, then he will win the prize" is a conditional statement. The conditional statement has the following truth-table:

p	q	$p \supset q$
T	T	T
T	F	F
F	T	T
F	F	T

Iff : It is an abbreviation of "if and only if." The presence of *iff* makes a statement a bi-conditional one. For example, "A statement is meaningful if and only if it is empirically verifiable." The bi-conditional statement has the following truth-table:

p	q	$p \equiv q$
T	T	T
T	F	F
F	T	F
F	F	T

Ignorance : It is a condition that denotes partial or complete absence of knowledge. In Advaita Vedānta, ignorance or nescience is technically known as *avidyā*. The antidote of ignorance is knowledge (*jñāna*).

Ignoratio Elenchi (L) : It is one of the non-verbal fallacies. This fallacy occurs when an argument is directed against the subject in question ignoring the real point at issue. There are many forms of irrelevancy. For example, a person may argue that he is entitled for a Degree of Doctor of Philosophy; in this connection it is irrelevant to state that he is the only son of his parents.

Illicit Conversion : It is a formal fallacy. This fallacy occurs when a conditional proposition, If p, then q is converted into If q, then *p*. For example, it is assumed that if it rains then the roads are wet, but this does not mean that if the roads are wet then it rains. See Consequent.

Illicit Major : It is a formal fallacy resulting from drawing a negative conclusion in a syllogism when the major term is not distributed in major premise.

Illocution : It is a form of speech act. For instance, while speaking one may say "be careful" to warn someone. By saying so he performed the act of warning. Similarly, there are many other illusionary acts that are performatory in their nature. They are "to promise," "to wish," "to warn," and so on. This term "illocution" was introduced by J.L. Austin. The theory of speech acts was further developed by John Searle in his *Speech Acts* (1969).

Illumination : It is nothing but intellectual or spiritual enlightenment usually described as a sudden flash of insight or understanding. Illumination is also a source of contemplation. In his doctrine of illumination St. Augustine holds that human mind possesses some sort of illumination in order to see eternal and necessary truths. The intelligible objects cannot be grasped without illumination. This illumination as an eternal reason comes from God just as light comes from the Sun.

Imagination : It is an act of mind that is free from the act of cognition or any rational process. The philosophers like Plato, Spinoza, and Locke rejected imagination as a valid source of knowledge. However, in the contemporary period imagination has become the focus of interest for existentialist philosophers.

Imitation : It is a popular theory in aesthetics according to which the creation of an artiste is primarily an imitation or revelatory process. In other words, the work of art is an imitation or representation of real Forms rather than physical objects. The work of art adequately represents the essence that the physical thing manifests inadequately.

Immanence : It is the inner or the inherent feature or the property or the characteristics of an object or a process. Immanent is often opposed to transcendental.

Immanent Critique : It is a form of critique whose standards are derived from the subject matter criticized. Normally the subject matter is some historically specific cultural ideal. External critique generally derives its standards from more universal (trans-historical and trans-cultural) conditions underlying speech, knowledge, and action.

Immaterialism : It is a doctrine that opposes matter as the ultimate reality. According to immaterialists, the reality is incorporeal, non-material, and spiritual One of the best exponents of immaterialism is Berkeley. According to him, the word "matter" is a misnomer.

Immediate Inference : It is an inference in which the conclusion follows from one premise alone. There are various types of immediate inference such as obversion, conversion, inversion and contraposition.

Immediate Knowledge : Knowledge that is obtained without any medium of senses is regarded as immediate knowledge. Intuition and revelation are considered to be the forms of immediate or direct knowledge that do not involve any process. Sometimes intuitive knowledge is also known as an a priori form of knowledge.

Immediate Perception : According to sense-datum philosophers, sense-data are immediately given in sense-experience. Hume envisaged that sense-impressions are the immediate objects of perception.

Immortality : It is a doctrine according to which the human soul survives the bodily death. The two important conceptions of immortality are: (1) *Temporal immortality* holds the view that mind continues to survive even after an individual's death. (2) *Eternality* is the view that soul ascends to the higher plane of timelessness. Strictly speaking, immortality is not only confined to post-existence (survival after death), but is also extended to the theory of transmigration of souls.

Immortalist : Any person who survives bodily death is called an immortalist.

Immutable : It is a state or quality of not being susceptible to any alteration. It is one of the attributes of God. According to Parmenides, the reality *per se* is immutable. Similarly, Advaita holds the view that *Brahman* as the Supreme Reality is immutable.

Imperative : It is the principal mood of a main verb in imperative sentences with which conduct-guiding, speech-acts are performed. These statements are of great interest to moral philosophers and logicians. According to Kant, all moral judgements involve imperatives. In other words, they "ought" to be performed.

Implication : It is a logical operation that forms a complex proposition from two independent propositions with the help of a logical connective. For example: If today is Tuesday, then tomorrow is Wednesday. It can be shown in the following way:

p	q	$p \supset q$
T	T	T
T	F	F
F	T	T
F	F	T

Impossible, Logically : Anything that is self-contradictory is logically impossible. It is a contradiction in terms to say that a triangle possesses only two angles.

Impression : It is an immediate and momentary conscious effect produced on us by the simulation of the sense-organs. According to Hume, the reality is made up of sense-impressions that are lively, vivid, and discrete entities. The ideas are the faint copies of these impressions. Hence, the philosophy of Hume is known as impressionism.

Improbabilism : It is a theory according to which empirical sciences cannot assign positive probability values to hypotheses or theories in order to show their degree of confirmation. They can only show the improbability and falsification of hypotheses or theories.

Inclination : It is a disposition or tendency or propensity to act in a particular manner. As moral agents we are disposed to act in certain ways.

Incoherence : It is illogical and incongruent way of thinking which ultimately results in fallacious conclusions.

Incompatible : The incompatibility of statements arises when two statements are not logically or conceptually related to each other. For example, the statement "God is benevolent and merciful" is incompatible with the statement "God punishes the sinners."

Incomplete Symbol : It is a symbol or expression that does not convey any meaning in isolation from the sentence or statement in which it occurs. For example, the logical connectives of the propositional calculus such as "or," "and," "if and then" and arithmetic operators such as the signs for addition, subtraction, multiplication and division do not convey any meaning on their own. According to Russell, even the definite descriptions such as "the so-and-so" are also incomplete symbols.

Inconceivability : It is a property that is unthinkable of a thing or an object or an event. For example, it is inconceivable that an object is both round and square.

Inconsistency : It is inconsistent to think of a set of propositional functions from which one can infer both p and $\sim p$.

Incontinence : It is an alternative vocabulary for a*c(k)rasia* or weakness of the will.

Incorrigible : A statement that is self-evidently true is called an incorrigible statement. For example, Descartes believed that "I think, therefore I am" is an incorrigible foundation of philosophy. Similarly, all a priori forms of knowledge are considered to be incorrigible as there is no experience to refute them.

Indefinite Reference : It is a reference made to something or other without specifying its particularity or specificity. For example, in the statement "I met a man," "a man" is an indefinite reference.

Indeterminism : It is a philosophical viewpoint that maintains that there is certain amount of loose-play in the processes of reality. It denies the necessary causal connection between one event and the other. See Freedom of Will.

Indian Philosophy : It is the philosophy that took birth in the Indian soil. In the Indian tradition, there are *ātmavādin*s and *anātma-vādin*s. For instance, Buddhists did not subscribe to the theory of the soul *(ātmavāda)*. Indian philosophy is classified into heterodox (*nāstika*) and orthodox (*āstika*) systems. The former (Cārvāka, Jainism, and Buddhism) do not believe in the authority of the Veda. The latter (Nyāya, Vaiśeṣika, Sāṁkhya, Yoga, Pūrva-Mīmāṁsā, and Uttara-Mīmāṁsā or Vedānta) believe in the authority of the Veda. By and large, Indian philosophy is *ātman*-centric. This is the reason why Indian philosophy is often characterized as essentially spiritualistic. Indian philosophy always emphasized the need of practical and direct realization of truth. The word *darśana* means "vision," and also the "instrument of vision." It stands for the direct, immediate and intuitive vision of reality, the actual perception of Truth, and also includes the means that lead to this realization. Annihilation of three kinds of pains, namely, *ādhyātmika* (physical and mental sufferings produced by natural and intra-organic causes); *ādhibhautika* (physical and mental sufferings produced by natural and extra-organic causes); and *ādhidaivika* (physical and mental sufferings produced by supernatural and extra-organic causes); and realization of supreme happiness is the end. *Śravaṇa* (hearing the truth), *manana* (intellectual conviction after critical analysis), and *nididhyāsana* (practical realization) are the means in almost all the schools of Indian philosophy, with an exception of Cārvāka, the ancient Indian materialist school. The Vedas are the oldest literary monuments of the Āryan mind. The origin of Indian philosophy, especially the orthodox systems, can be traced back to the Vedas. Indian philosophy as an autonomous system was not subjected to any external influences. One would not find the segregation between philosophy and theology in Indian philosophy. Similarly, metaphysics/ontology, epistemo-logy, logic and ethics are interdependent on each other in every system of Indian philosophy. However, one finds very sophisticated techniques of philosophizing in Indian philosophy. Each system of thought has its uniqueness in explaining the nature of reality in its own way. The development of Indian philosophy is largely attributed to the commentarial tradition followed in Indian philosophy. Every system before advancing its own standpoint highlights the standpoint of other systems (*pūrvapakṣa)*. Then it criticizes the standpoint of a particular system (*khaṇḍana*). Finally it advances its own standpoint (*siddhānta*).

Individual : An individual is an object that can be separated from other objects, and can be made a referent of the subject of a sentence. Sometimes, it is also understood as a particular.

Individualism : It is a political theory according to which the principal concern of the state is to protect the rights of the individuals. A state is a means through which the individuals attain their goals. Therefore, it is the state that exists for the sake of individuals, but not vice versa.

Individuate : It is a process by means of which one can separate, identify, and distinguish an individual among the others of a class or a species.

Individuation : It is a method of developing or abstracting an individual or particular thing from its corresponding universal.

Indra (S) : Indra is one of the Vedic gods. He was the greatest God of the Vedic Āryans. In the *Ṛgveda*, there are 250 hymns addressed to Indra. He was the greatest warrior. He helped the Vedic Āryans against their enemies who were rising in arms to destroy their culture and their political integrity. Lightning and thunder are the mighty weapons of Indra. He always carries a thunderbolt (*vajra*) that is made of iron.

Indriyas (S) : They are the senses that are the powers subservient to mind (*manas*). There are two types of *indriya*s, namely, *karmendriya*s and *jñānendriya*s. The functions of the former are speech, prehension, movement, excretion, and reproduction. The functions of the latter are sight, smell, taste, touch, and sound. According to Sāṁkhya, they are evolutes of *prakṛti*, the primordial substance.

Indubitable : A maxim or proposition is said to be indubitable when it does not require any proof for its validity.

Induction : It is one of the processes in logic. It proceeds from particular instances to generalizations. In induction, even if the premises are true the conclusions are mere probabilities.

Example: All the crows that I have hitherto seen are black; therefore, all the crows are black.

Still the conclusion of this inductive inference is contingent because our present experience of black crows cannot guarantee that there is not going to be any white crow in the future. This is also called the problem of induction. David Hume highlighted this problem. According to Hume, what guarantee do we have to assume that the instances which held good in the past are going to hold good in future? His answer to this question is negative. It is generally believed that sciences (natural sciences) follow inductive method to arrive at the desired results. One of the well-known exponents of the inductive method is John Stuart Mill. For details, see Mill's *Inductive Logic.*

Inevitability : It is a kind of logical necessity. For instance, if *q* necessarily follows from *p*, then it implies that it follows inevitably.

Inference : It is a process of reasoning in which a conclusion is deduced from one or two premises. If the conclusion is deduced from one premise, then such a conclusion is called enthymeme or immediate inference; whereas a mediate inference is one in which the conclusion is deduced from more than one premise.

Infinite and Finite : They are the categories denoting two diametrically opposed views with regard to the aspects of reality. Some philosophers consider that God being Absolute is infinite, while humans being mortals are only finite beings. The categories infinite and finite are also attached to space and time. According to some philosophers, space and time are infinite; others regarded space and time to be finite as we are concerned with the finite aspects of them, namely, the divisible units.

Innate Ideas : They are the ideas that are inborn. According to Descartes, who is a chief advocate of innatism, there are certain ideas in human mind that enter the body along with the soul. Such ideas are highly indubitable as they are very "clear and distinct" to human mind. Locke made a scathing attack on the doctrine of innate ideas in his *Essay Concerning Human Understanding*. According to him, mind is a blank sheet of paper (*tabula rasa*) in the beginning on which ideas are imprinted.

Instinct : In its broader sense of the term, instinct is opposed to a conscious activity. In other words, it is a kind of psychic activity that is characteristic of animals. The actions of animals are purely instinctual.

Instrumentalism : It is a theory developed by John Dewey, the American pragmatist. According to this doctrine, when a person faces any situation or predicament it is the human mind which acts as an instrument to produce ideas, concepts, and judgements which in turn help the individual to take a firm decision to overcome a situation or a predicament.

Intellect : It is the function of reason that makes ideas possible. It is a cognitive faculty that makes one understand and aware of what one intends to know.

Intension and Extension : The intension of a concept consists of the qualities or properties that make up the concept. The extension of a concept consists of the things that fall under the concept.

Intensive Quantity : In opposition to extensive quantity, intensive quantity does not require any known physical process of addition in order to produce greater quantity of the kind in question from a lesser quantity.

Intent : It is an act of directing mind towards an object of one's interest.

Intellectualism : It is a philosophical viewpoint that places intellect as the foreground for any cognitive activity, and also divorces cognition from sensory knowledge. Intellectualism was represented by Eleatics and Platonists in ancient Greece.

Intentionalism : It is a theory of mind and knowledge, according to which intentionality is the characteristic feature of mind in the sense that it is the basis for the cognitive and conative functions of mind.

Intentionality : According to Edmund Husserl, intentionality is the essential feature of consciousness in the sense that consciousness is always directed towards some object or the other. The intentional object need not be an object like chair or table or any other existing thing, but is merely that which the mental act is about. In fact, it was Brentano, the teacher of Husserl, who developed this notion in his intentional psychology.

Interactionism : It is a dualistic theory of mind-body relation advocated by Descartes. According to him, physical events cause mental events and vice versa. It is also known as psychophysical interactionism.

Internal Relations : According to this theory, the relations are dependent on their terms. Metaphysical absolutists hold the view that all the relations are internal to the absolute. All the relations of a thing are constitutive of its nature. Hegel and Bradley were the chief advocates of this position.

Inter-subjectivity : It is a view connected with the nature of language. Inter-subjectivity is one of the prerequisites for any language. Language being a social product is necessarily public. In other words, language is a medium through which man communicates his ideas to his fellow humans. Such a communication is impossible unless language is inter-subjective.

Intrinsic : The intrinsic value of a thing is a value in and of itself. For instance, adherence to truth has an intrinsic value. Any value that is not an instrument or a means to achieve something has intrinsic worth. In Indian ethics, *mokṣa* or liberation is an intrinsic value. It is an end in itself.

Introception : It is a form of personalism in which there is coalescence of the world of objective values with one's own substance by means of which a person attains reality.

Introspection : It is a way of knowing one's mind. In other words, it is a probe into one's inner feelings. There are two types of introspection. They are as follows: (1) One may resort to direct scrutiny of conscious states and processes at the time of their occurrence. (2) One may resort to the recovery of the past states and processes by a retrospective act. The modern equivalent of the term "introspection" is "reflection" or "inner sense." Gilbert Ryle in his *The Concept of Mind* held that introspection is a myth.

Introspectionism : It is a standpoint in psychology that advocates introspection as a method to analyse the psychological states of an individual. Introspection as a method is opposed to behaviourism. The latter relies on the overt or apparent behaviour of the individuals in analysing the psychological states of an individual.

Intutio : This term was introduced by Spinoza in a technical sense in his work *Ethics*. It is knowledge "of the third kind." Intuition of this kind is absolutely certain when compared to reason or *ratio*. It provides us with an adequate knowledge of the essence of things.

Intuition : It is an immediate and direct knowledge of anything. Such knowledge is supposed to be direct and impeccable. Intuitions occur to the mind like flashes. Thus intuition is not a process. As a source of knowledge, it has been accepted by Descartes, Spinoza, Locke, and others. It is also rated as the highest form of knowledge.

Intuitionism : This appellation is given to the school of mathematics founded by L.E.J. Brouwer. Intuitionists expressed their priority over logic and philosophy. All the proofs in mathematics are arrived at intuitively. Intuitionist school of mathematics rejects the methods and assumptions of classical mathematics. In ethics, ethical intuitionism was advocated by H.A. Prichard, E.F. Carrit, and W.D. Ross. According to ethical intuitionism, certain actions or kinds of action are known to be right or wrong by a direct intuition without any consideration of the value of their consequences. Thus ethical insight is something non-rational and unique.

Īśa Upaniṣad (S) : This Upaniṣad starts with a prayer that this and other world are full. Even if something is taken out from this full still it is full. This is known as the doctrine of infinite. The addition and subtraction make no difference to the infinite. As regards *Brahman*, the Upaniṣad says that it is One, and moves faster than mind. It is far yet near. It is outwards, yet inwards to us.

Islam : It is the name given to the religion founded by prophet Mohammad. Etymologically the term "Islam" means "to resign oneself." But it is not a fatalistic submission to the deity, but striving after righteousness, the practice of the law, obedience to rules, and formal performance of duties.

Isolationism : It is a trend in aesthetics that insists on the interpretation of art forms without considering their historical and cultural contexts.

Isomorphism : It is the relation that characterizes the correspondence between two different structures. Wittgenstein while advocating logical atomism in his *Tractatus* attempted to show that there is an isomorphic relation between the structure of language and that of reality by holding the view that language mirrors the reality.

Īśvara (S) : He is God, according to Advaita. He is also known as *Brahman* associated with the *māyā*. Thus He is *saguṇa Brahman*. Īśvara is not only the personal God, but also the creator of the universe.

Īśvarakṛṣṇa (c. second century CE) : He was a Sāṁkhya philosopher. He summarized the thought of Kapila's *Sāṁkhya-Sūtra* in about seventy verses which are called *Sāṁkhya-Kārikā*. Īśvarakṛṣṇa held that what can be known is dependent upon the means of cognition (*pramāṇa*).

J

Jacobi, Friedrich Henrich (1743 – 1819) : He was a German philosopher of "feeling." He refuted Kantian philosophy by reducing it to a system of absolute subjective idealism. According to him, the Kantian idealism could not grasp the ultimate reality. Jacobi was equally against the dogmatic rationalism of Spinoza. According to Jacobi, it is only by means of feeling and faith the truth is immediately revealed in consciousness. His important works include: *David Hume über den Glauben* (1787) and *Sendschreiben an Fichte* (1799).

Jaimini (c. second century BCE) : He was a great seer and sage who founded the Pūrva-Mīmāṁsā school. He is the author of the *Mīmāṁsā-Sūtra*. "Mīmāṁsā" literally means "revered thought." The other two prominent exponents of Mīmāṁsā are Kumārila Bhaṭṭa and his pupil Prabhākara.

Jainism : It is one of the heterodox systems of Indian philosophy. There is no difference between Jainism as a philosophy and as a religion. It is likely that it came into existence around fifth century BCE as a reaction to the Brāhmanism of the Vedas. Lord Mahāvīra was the twenty-fourth *tīrthaṅkara* of the Jaina order. Jainism is a form of pluralistic realism. It recognized two important categories in this world. They are: *jīva* or the soul and *ajīva* or non-soul. The *jīva* is the eternal substance whose essential nature is consciousness. The *jīva* animates the physical body in which it dwells. The *jīva* changes its magnitude according to the size of the body that it occupies. The *jīva*'s knowledge is imperfect and incomplete as long as it is embodied. Matter (*pudgaḷa*) is considered to be a mode of *ajīva* that possesses the properties like taste, smell, sound, colour, and so on. It is also atomistic. The other *ajīva*s are space (*ākāśa*), *dharma* or the principle of motion and *adharma*, the principle of non-motion. There is no single soul or Supreme God. There are many souls in the world which are either embodied or not in living creatures. Jainism classified knowledge into immediate (*aparokṣa*) and mediate (*parokṣa*). Immediate knowledge is further divided into *avadhi, manaḥparyāya* and *kevala*. Mediate knowledge is classified into *mati*, and *śruta*. According to Jainism, *pratyakṣa* or perceptual knowledge is only mediate. It is brought under *mati* along with inferential knowledge. *Śruta* includes verbal knowledge. *Avadhi* is clairvoyance, *manaḥparyāya* is telepathy, and *kevala* is omniscience. Further knowledge is divided into *pramāṇa* or knowledge of a thing, and *naya* or knowledge of a thing in its relation. Jaina logic is known as *syādvāda* or *saptabhaṅgīnaya* or the theory of the relativity of knowledge. It involves seven dialectical steps. They are: (1) *syādasti* or a thing is real; (2) *syānnāsti* or a thing is unreal; (3) *syādasti nāsti* or relatively, a thing is both real and unreal; (4) *syādavaktavyam* or relatively a thing is indescribable; (5) *syādasti ca avaktavyam* or a thing is real and is indescribable; (6) *syānnāsti ca avaktavyam* or relatively, a thing is unreal and is indescribable; and (7) *syādasti ca nāsti ca avaktavyam* or relatively, a thing is real, unreal, and indescribable. The Jaina metaphysics is realistic and relativistic pluralism and known as *anekāntavāda* or the doctrine of manyness of reality. As regards bondage, Jainism holds that *karma* is the link between soul and the body. Ignorance of truth and four passions — anger (*krodha*), greed (*lobha*), pride (*māna*), and delusion (*māyā*) are known as *kaṣāya*s or sticky substances where kārmic particles stick, attract the flow of kārmic matter towards the soul. The state when the kārmic particles actually begin to flow towards the soul to bind it is called *āśrava*. In ethics, Jainism preaches the five vows (*mahāvrata*). They are: (1) *ahiṁsā* or non-injury; (2) *satya* or truth in thought, word, and deed; (3) *asteya* or non-stealing in thought, word and action; (4) *brahmacarya* or abstention from self-indulgence of thought, speech or action; and (5) *aparigraha* or renunciation by thought, word and deed. Jainism is treated as a religion without God.

Jalpa (S) : It is one of the fallacious arguments known as wrangling. According to Nyāya, it is a kind of fallacious argument in which the parties involved in disputation try to win over the other by making use of not only the valid means of cognition, the negative modal or counter-factual conditional, but also false or improper analogies to establish the defects of the opponent's position.

Jamblicus (c. 270 – 330) : He was a Syrian neo-Platonist. His commentaries on Hellenic and Oriental theology were very popular. He transformed the teachings of Plotinus into a form of dogmatic theology that is akin to metaphysical pantheism.

James-Lang Theory : It is a theory of emotions advocated by William James in his *The Principles of Psychology.* According to this theory, certain subjective feelings are aroused in the subjects by bodily changes that follow the perception of some exciting fact. This theory is known as James-Lang theory.

James, William (1842 – 1910) : He was an American pragmatist and psychologist. He received his M.D. from Harvard Medical School in 1869. From medicine he moved to psychology and philosophy. As a pragmatist James held the view that utility is the criterion of truth. The whole function of philosophy, according to James, is to find out what difference does it make to one's own life, if this world-formula or that world-formula be the true one. He was chiefly concerned with the concrete concerns of life, facts, and action. As a radical empiricist James bitterly criticized the correspondence or copy-view theory of truth advocated by empiricists. According to him, the correspondence theory of truth relies on mere structural aspects of the objects without taking their functional aspects into consideration. Such a view of truth, claims James, does not have any "cash-value." He advocated that pragmatic theory of truth, unlike copy-view theory considers "cash-value" of the ideas. Thus truth, according to James, happens to an idea. James held that all formulations in science, theology and philosophy are only approximations. James was convinced that it is difficult to prove by any rational mode of argument that the will of man is either free or determined. However, by applying the pragmatic method one can judge what difference does it make to one's actual life to accept one or the other side of the dispute. His important works include: *The Principles of Psychology* (1890); *The Will to Believe* (1897); *The Varieties of Religious Experience* (1902); and *Pragmatism* (1907).

Jansenism : They are the teachings of Cornelius Jansen (1585 – 1638). According to Jansenism, the total corruption in human nature is attributed to the original sin. Man's inability to resist either concupiscence or grace is due to lack of freedom of will. Jansenism denied that Christ died for the sake of all men without exception. The doctrines of Jansenism were condemned by the Church.

Jaspers, Karl (1883 – 1969) : He was a German exponent of theistic existentialism. He started his career as a psychiatrist. To a great extent, Jaspers was influenced by Nietzsche and Kirkegaard. He analysed the possible attitude of man towards the world, and the decisions that an individual must take in the situations like death, struggle, change, guilt, and other similar situations. By deriving his motivation from the scientific method, Jaspers always looked for clarity and precision. According to Jaspers, the chief task of philosophy is to show that all conscious manifestations of man are based on the unconscious activity of existence. Jaspers believed that the real meaning of existence becomes clear to man only during the periods of deep shock. Jaspers recognized the importance of psychology and history in the domain of philosophy. His important works include: *Psychology der Weltanschauungen* (1919) and *Philosophie* (1932).

Jāti (S) : It means "birth," "class," "part," "generality." According to Buddhism, *jāti* is one of the links in the empirical wheel of existence. As universal, *jāti* represents the most essential or universal class character. Nyāya considers *jāti* as one of the sixteen categories. It is a fallacious argument that makes use of unessential, accidental similarities and dissimilarities to defeat the opponent. If one says "Man is an animal," the opponent argues that man cannot be animal because he does not share any colour of animals. Therefore, man cannot be treated as an animal.

Jayanta Bhaṭṭa (tenth century CE) : He was a Nyāya philosopher. As regards confirmatory knowledge (*phalajñāna*), Jayanta held that it does not require any evidence or support. One cannot doubt the veracity of confirmatory knowledge. For instance, my perception of water is confirmed if and only if it quenches my thirst. Similarly, Jayanta argued in favour of Āyurveda, the science of life. He held that the medical instructions of Āyurveda are valid because they are the instructions of a trustworthy person, and can also be verified. His important work is *Nyāyamañjarī*.

Jayarāśi (eighth century CE) : He was a sceptic and agnostic. In his work *Tattvopaplavasiṁha*, Jayarāśi writes that his work is intended to inform how wealth and power can be obtained. As a sceptic Jayarāśi did not construct any metaphysical system. He was critical of the *pramāṇa* method.

Jayatīrtha (fourteenth century CE) : He was a great dialectician of Dvaita Vedānta. His important works include: *Nyāyasudhā* and *Vādāvalī*.

Jehovah : This is the personal name of God or Supreme Being in Judaism. He is supposed to be the saviour of the humankind. See Judaism.

Jesuitism : It refers to the teachings and practices of the Jesuits. It is a religious order of the Roman Catholic Church mainly engaged in the missionary and educational activities. Originally it was known as the Company, but became the society of Jesus founded by Ignatius Loyola in 1534. Jesuits have special obedience to the Pope, who may send them on mission to any part of the globe. They largely depend upon alms and gifts for their support. The word "Jesuit" is used disparagingly in the sense of craftiness, deceit, duplicity, and equivocation.

Jīva (S) : It means "individual soul or self." Jainism holds that the individual soul is characterized by consciousness, life, immateriality, and extension in space. The size of an individual soul is the same as the size of the body in which it exists. According to Buddhism, there is nothing like an individual soul apart from a complex of changing constituents. Nyāya maintains that *jīva* is a non-composite, partless, eternal substance. According to Advaita, the *jīva* is a blend of the self (*ātman*) and the not-self (*anātman*) with a wrong interpretation of each as the other.

Jīvanmukta (S) : Advaita holds that the liberation is possible only when the *avidyā* or ignorance is completely destroyed. Thus the existence of the physical body is not an obstacle to achieve liberation. A person can achieve liberation while he is alive. Such a person is known as *jīvanmukta*.

Jīvanmukti (S) : This doctrine of liberation is advocated by Advaita Vedānta. According to this doctrine, a person is liberated from bondage while one is alive. His body continues to exist until his *prārabdha-karma* gets exhausted. One who attains *jīvanmukti* is called a *jīvanmukta*.

Jñāna (S) : It means "knowledge." According to Nyāya-Vaiśeṣika, knowledge is not only the knowledge of objects, but also about itself. Advaita maintains that the knowledge is a blend of *vṛtti* that is inspired by *sākṣī*. In this process of comprehension, *vṛtti* element is relative, while the element of consciousness is eternal. Thus knowledge is classified into *vṛtti-jñāna* and *sākṣi-jñāna*.

Jñāna-kāṇḍa (S) : Those parts of the Veda that deal with the knowledge of Brahman are known as *Jñāna-kāṇḍa*. They are: Āraṇyakas and Upaniṣads.

Jñāna-lakṣaṇa (S) : It is one of the types of extraordinary perception. The knowledge of an object is the relation characterized by the previous knowledge of the same object revived in memory. For instance, just by seeing the fire one can feel that it is very hot. It is possible for a person to tell, though the heat cannot be seen, that the fire is hot because of his previous experience.

Jñānendriyas (S) : They are the organs of knowledge. They are: the sense of sight (*cakṣu*), the sense of touch (*tvak*), the sense of hearing (*śrotra*), the sense of taste (*rasanā*), the sense of smell (*ghrāṇa*). However, Sāṁkhya considers mind (*manas*) as one of the organs of knowledge.

John of Salisbury (1115 – 80) : He was a great English prelate and humanist. He was tutored by Peter Abelard and Gilbert of Poitiers in Paris for dialectic and theology respectively. He advocated the absolute separation of church and state. In his *Metalogicus*, John made some changes in logic. He adopted practical attitude towards knowledge and rejected everything that is detrimental to pious way of life.

Judaism : It is the religion of the Jews who are supposed to be the descendents of the ancient Hebrews, "the chosen people." This religion is based on the revelation made to the prophet Moses on the Mount Sinai. Therefore, Judaism is not only a revealed religion, but also "the paradigm of a classical God-made religion." There is only one God, namely, Jehovah, according to the followers of Judaism. Messiah, the saviour, is yet to come. Judaism has three main pillars in the form of Jehovah, the God, Covenant, and the Torah (the Law). Jews believe in the Old Testament of the Bible and the *Talmad*. The Jewish God, besides having the metaphysical attributes of omnipotence, omniscience and benevolence, is pre-eminently imbued with such moral qualities as justice, mercy, kindness, love and holiness. In that sense Judaism is primarily an ethical religion giving out moral rules of conduct and a way of life of justice, mercy, humility, and modesty. God being the creator of the world created human beings in his own image. Therefore, the world is not treated as a place of scorn and lamentation, but as a working ground for righteousness and justice. Judaism believes in the immortality of the soul and consequently in a life after death. The Jewish place of worship is called Synagogue. It is the official religion of Israel.

Judgement : It is an expression of any idea or an opinion in the form of a declarative statement. Such statements are necessarily the assertions about the objects, relations, and situations. All judgements are propositions, but all propositions are not necessarily judgements, because judgements are not mere propositions. They are arrived at by the mind by a special procedure in the sense that they are not mere reportive definitions of our statements about the objects in question. According to Immanuel Kant, the mind with the help of the data supplied by sensations and the categories of understanding delivers a judgement about the status of an object in question. He classified judgements into analytic, synthetic and synthetic a priori. He defined an analytic judgement as a judgement in which the predicate term is already contained in the subject. Thus it does not give any new information, e.g. "All bodies have extension." On the contrary, a synthetic judgement is a judgement in which the predicate term is something new, e.g. "All bodies have specific gravity." In the case of a synthetic *a priori* judgement, Kant held that it is both necessary and informative, e.g. 7 + 5 = 12. All genuine knowledge, claimed Kant, constitutes synthetic a priori judgements. For more details see Kant's *Critique of Pure Reason.*

Judgement of Taste : The judgements of value are distinguished from the judgements of facts. The former, in a way, are the judgements of taste since they are highly subjective. The assertion that "The rose is beautiful or aesthetically pleasing" is a judgement of taste. In other words, it is the outcome of the interest that an object has aroused in making such an assertion.

Jung, Carl Gustuv (1875 – 1961) : He was a well-known Swiss psychiatrist and psychoanalyst, who advocated "analytical psychology" in the place of Freud's psychoneurosis. Jung made use of Freud's methods of free association and dream analysis, but stressed on his own method of word-association. He deviated from Freud's interpretation of psychoanalysis by minimizing the role of sex and stressed on the present conflict rather than childhood complexes in the explanation of neuroses. Jung is popularly known for his classification of human personality in terms of introverts and extroverts. He recognized four important operations of mental faculty. They are thinking, feeling, sensation, and intuition.

Justice : It is a normative concept of morality that concerns every political and social philosopher. The campaigns for justice are often the campaigns for social and economic equality. Distributive justice is concerned with who ought to get what things, whereas corrective justice deals with the nature of punishments. Retributive justice is a form of corrective justice whose motive is revenge or vindictiveness as expressed in the statement "An eye for an eye and a tooth for a tooth."

Justification : It is a form of logical or rational proof that provides sufficient grounds for an assertion or a claim or a statement or a conclusion. Scientific theories are acceptable only when they are rationally justified.

K

Kalā (S) : It means "art or limited ability." According to Kāśmīra Śaivism, *kalā* is one of the five principles that originate in *māyā*. These five principles along with *māyā* are called the six shackles (*ṣaṭkañcukas*). These six shackles constitute the mixed creation, which is the combination of purity and impurity.

Kāla (S) : It means "time." It is one of the substances (*dravyas*) according to Vaiśeṣika. The substances are of two types, namely, material and non-material. *Kāla* is a non-material substance. As a non-material substance *kāla* is one, imperceptible, indivisible, infinite, all-pervading and eternal. Its existence inferred from our cognition of temporal modes such as past, present and future. Therefore, it is regarded as a substratum of our temporal cognitions.

Kāma (S) : It refers to the enjoyment of the means. It is one of the four goals (*puruṣārthas*) of a human life. Since mere accumulation of wealth or property does not provide any satisfaction to an individual, *kāma* has been included as one of the basic goals of life as it promotes satisfaction, pleasure, and enjoyment. However, it should be within the purview of righteousness (*dharma*), which is a regulative principle.

Kaṇāda (S) : He was a great sage and seer who founded the Vaiśeṣika system. The term "Vaiśeṣika" is derived from *viśeṣa* means particularity. Kaṇāda is also known as Kaṇabhuk, Ulūka, and Kaśyapa. His system of thought is also called Aulūkya Darśana. It is believed that the name Kaṇāda was given to him as he used to lead a life of an ascetic by picking up grains from the fields. *Kaṇa* means particle. He authored the *Vaiśeṣika-Sūtra*.

Kant, Immanuel (1724 – 1804) : He was one of the most influential German Idealist philosophers and the advocate of transcendental idealism. His philosophy is known as transcendental philosophy or critical philosophy. Kant's problem in his *Critique of Pure Reason* is the problem of knowledge. Kant was completely dissatisfied with the explanations provided by rationalists and empiricists with regard to the origin and scope of knowledge. It was David Hume's theory of causation that made Kant woke up from his "dogmatic slumber." Contrary to Hume's view, Kant felt that it is true that the "idea of necessary connection" is not given in sense-experience, but it is known a priori. Thus he admitted the "necessary causal connection" between one event and the other. All genuine knowledge, according to Kant, is the knowledge resulting from *synthetic* a priori judgements. The propositions of mathematics serve as the best example of such a kind of knowledge. For example, "7 + 5 = 12" is a synthetic a priori judgement. It is synthetic because the number "12" is neither found in 7 nor in 5 nor in symbol "+." It is a priori because the total of 7 and 5 necessarily leads to 12. Further he made a distinction between analytic and synthetic judgements. The former consist of those judgements in which the predicate is already contained in the subject. For example, "All bodies have extension" is a clear case of analytic judgement, for a body ceases to be a body in the absence of "extension." In the case of synthetic judgements, the predicate is something new. For example, "All bodies have specific gravity." In this judgement, the predicate term "specific gravity" is something new. A body does not cease to be a body in the absence of "specific gravity." Kant observed that the pure perceptions without the thought and thoughts without perceptions are of no use in the quest for knowledge. The admixture of both will result in knowledge. Kant's Copernican revolution aims at proving that mind does not go in search of the objects to know what they are, rather the objects would conform to the operations of mind. In his structure of rational thought, Kant envisaged that there are twelve categories of understanding which are transcendental. Kant used the expression "transcendental" to mean a priori precondition for any possibility of knowledge. These categories are: (1) of quantity; (2) of quality; (3) of relation; and (4) of modality. Kant made a sharp distinction between *phenomenon* and *noumenon*. The senses along with the operations of mind (categories of understanding) will only reveal the nature of objects of phenomenal reality. But their noumenal reality or "thing-in-itself" is not known by any rational means. This clearly sets the limitation to human reason. In ethics, Kant felt that "good will" is the categorical imperative. Such a good will is inherent or intrinsic in every human individual. In his deontic ethics, Kant held that duty implies that we are under some moral obligation. Therefore, one must do duty for the sake of duty. The major works of Kant include: *Critique of Pure Reason* (1781); *Prolegomena to Any future Metaphysics* (1783); *Principle of the Metaphysics of Ethics* (1785); *Metaphysical First Principles of Natural Science* (1786); Revised edition of *Critique of Pure Reason* (1787); *Critique of Practical Reason* (1788); and *Critique of Judgement* (1790).

Kant-Laplace Hypothesis : It is a hypothesis formulated by Kant in his *Natural History and Theory of Heavens* (1755) and by Laplace in his *Exposition of the System of the World* (1756) concerning the origin of the solar system. According to this hypothesis, the solar system emerged from a rotating mass of incandescent gas that got gradually flattened at poles by throwing rings from its equator due to cooling and shrinking resulting in high velocity of spin. These rings became the planets and developed their own satellites by similar operation. Laplace believed that the rotating nebula is the primordial stuff by itself. But, Kant held that the nebula formed on its own was put into rotation by gravitational action on the original atoms. This resulted in the impact of atoms on one another that generated heat.

Kapila (S) : He was a great sage and seer who founded the Sāṁkhya system. This system is considered to be one of the oldest systems of Indian thought. Saṁkhya literally means number. Kapila is the author of *Sāṁkhya-Sūtra*. Sāṁkhya philosophy is also known as *Sāṁkhyapravacana*.

Karma (S) : It is one of the most important theories in classical Indian philosophy. According to this doctrine, an individual's birth is decided on the basis of his deeds and actions of his earlier birth. Every individual has to reap the fruits of his past deeds and actions. Thus this doctrine substantiates the view that there is rebirth. All the orthodox, and some heterodox systems such as Jainism and Buddhism accept this view. There are three types of *karma*. They are as follows: (1) *sañcita-karma* or the *karma* that is accumulated; (2) *prārabdha-karma* or the *karma* that is in motion; and (3) *āgāmi-karma* or the *karma* which is in store.

Karma-kāṇḍa (S) : The Vedas are classified into *karma-kāṇḍa* and *jñāna-kāṇḍa*. The former consists of *mantras* and Brāhmaṇas and the latter Āraṇyakas and Upaniṣads.

Karma Theory (S) : It means "action." According to the law of *karma*, every action, good or bad, produces its proper consequences in the life of an individual as a moral agent. Thus the law of *karma* is regarded as the conservation of virtues, merits, and demerits of actions. *Karma* in another sense is a force generated by an action that has potency of bearing a definite fruit. *Karma* in this sense is classified into the following kinds:

1. *Anārabdha-karma* or the action that is yet to bear fruits.
2. *Ārabdha-karma* or *prārabdha-karma* or the action which has begun to bear fruits like the present body and accompaniments.

Anārabdha-karma is further classified into the following kinds:

1. *Prākṭana* or *sañcita karma* or the *karma* which is accumulated from past lives.
2. *Kriyamāna* or *sañciyamāna karma* or the *karma* that is being gathered in this life.

Karma Mārga (S) : It is one of the ways of liberation according to the Vedāntic schools. However, Mīmāṁsā gives importance to only *karma* or action, which is called *dharma*.

Karmendriyas (S) : They are the powers of action such as reactive or muscular senses, and the sense-organs corresponding to the physiological capacities of expression or speech, seizing or handling, locomotion, excretion, and sexual activity.

Kaṭha Upaniṣad (S) : This Upaniṣad has its own philosophical significance. It teaches that knowledge of what happens to man after death is more valuable than anything that takes place in the world. It is none other than the knowledge of *ātman*, which is smaller than the smallest and greater than the greatest. The senses are higher than the objects; mind is higher than the senses; the individual's reason (*buddhi*) is higher than mind; the Cosmic Reason (*mahān ātma* or Logos) is higher than the individual's reason; the Unmanifest (*avyakta*), the same as the goddess Aditi of the Vedas, is higher than the Cosmic reason; and the *puruṣa* (*ātman*) is higher than the Unmanifest. There is nothing higher than the *puruṣa* (*ātman*). Everything else is a branch of the *ātman* and the *ātman* is their root. The whole is the *aśvattha* tree, whose roots are above and branches are below. That is the *ātman*.

Katharsis (Gk) : It means "purging." In Aristotle's *Poetics* we come across tragedy as an example of *katharsis*. The feelings or emotions such as pity and fear are purged or cleansed by means of aesthetic experience.

Kauṭilya (c. third century BCE) : He is the author of *Arthaśāstra* or the science of wealth. He explained in his work how the *artha*, one of the *puruṣārthas*, can be achieved. See *Arthaśāstra*.

Kena Upaniṣad (S) : This Upaniṣad raises the question: What is it that impels the senses and mind to perceive and understand? What is it that sustains all, but not sustained by anything? One who says that he knows it does not really know it, and one who says that he does not know it truly knows it. That is nothing but *ātman*. Without *ātman* the senses, the mind, even gods cannot do anything.

Kepler, Johannes (1571 – 1630) : He was a German mathematician, astronomer and natural philosopher. Based on Copernicus' heliocentric theory, Kepler provided a rational explanation for the spacing of the planets. Thus he deviated from the traditional theological explanation that was prevalent during his time. Kepler defended Tycho Brahe's astronomy against Nicolaus Ursus' criticism. Following the line of Copernicus, Kepler made use of mathematical principles in astronomical calculations, but modified Pythagorean theory of the uniform motion of planets in spherical objects. Kepler's three laws as illustrated by Newton suggest that: (1) the movement of planets in ellipses makes sun as one focus; (2) Their movement is not uniform; and (3) The revolution of planets around the sun is proportionate to their distance from the sun. His important works include: *Mysterium cosmographicum* (1596); *Apologia* (1600); *Astronomia nova* (1609); *Epitome astronomiae Copernicanae* (1612); and *Harmonia mundi* (1618).

Kevala (S) : It is one of the means of immediate knowledge accepted by Jainism. *Kevala* is the knowledge of everything in the universe. It is pure. One who attains *kevala jñāna* is known as *kevalī*.

Kevalānvayī (S) : Nyāya inference has been classified into *kevalānvayī, kevalavyatirekī,* and *anvayavyatirekī.* This classification is based on *vyāpti* and on the different methods of establishing it. The methods of induction by means of which universal causal relationship is established may be *anvaya, vyatireka* or both. *Kevalānvayī* is similar to Mill's "method of agreement." We have the *kevalānvayī* inference when the middle term is always positively related to the major term. The terms agree only in presence, since there is no negative instance of their agreement. See the following example.

All knowable objects are nameable.
The pot is a knowable object;
Therefore, the pot is nameable.

Kevalavyatirekī (S) : It is a kind of inference advocated by Nyāya. We have *kevalavyatirekī,* or unique correlation when the middle term is the diffrentium of the minor term and is always negatively related to the major term. The terms agree only in absence, for there is no positive instance of their agreement of presence. See the following example.

What is not different from other elements has no smell;
The earth has smell;
Therefore, the earth is different from other elements.

Keynes, John Maynard (1883 – 1946) : He was a famous British economist and the son of John Neville Keynes (1852 – 1949). Keynes was known for his contribution to the theory of probability. According to him, probability is most appropriate to propositions rather than to events. He argued that probability is objective in so far as a proposition has certain probability irrespective of our noticing it. However, he held that probabilities are assigned to propositions only in relation to other propositions or propositions taken as premises or evidence. In other words, we can talk of probability of *p,* given premise *q*; or probability of *p* given *r* and *s* as evidence. His important works include: *A Treatise on Probability* (1921) and *General Theory of Employment: Interest and Money* (1936).

Khaṇḍana (S) : It means "refutation." It is normally understood as the refutation of the opponent's view. The commentarial tradition in Indian philosophy proceeds by stating the view of the opponent (*pūrvapakṣa*), followed by refutation (*khaṇḍana*), and the statement of one's own position (*siddhānta*).

Kierkegaard, Søren Aabye (1813 – 55) : He was a Danish theistic existentialist philosopher who stressed on individual human concerns. Although he was trained in Hegelian philosophy, Kierkegaard was a bitter critic of Hegel. He said of Hegel: "If

Hegel had written the whole of his Logic and then said . . . that it was merely an experiment in thought, then he could certainly have been the greatest thinker who ever lived. As it is, he is mere comic." What made Kierkegaard to react so pungently against Hegelian idealism is that it is bereft of existence and moral institutions. According to him, an individual is lost in the crowd. For him, to think in existence means to recognize that one is faced with personal choices. Kierkegaard felt that Hegel's philosophy falsified man's understanding of reality by shifting its attention from the concrete individual to the concept of universals. He recognized that there are three important stages of human transition. They are: aesthetic stage, ethical stage, and religious stage. In the first stage an individual is attracted to all sensuous pleasures. In the second stage an individual is conditioned to certain moral obligations. And in the third stage the individual realizes the importance of faith in God. This stage is supposed to be the highest stage. The transition from ethical to religious stage is possible only by a leap of faith. Kierkegaard regarded truth as subjective. One need not exhibit what one believes as true in an objective manner. He was critical of such an account of truth. His important works include: *Either Or* (1843); *Philosophical Fragments* (1844); *Concluding Unscientific Postscript* (1846); *Works of Love* (1847); *Christian Discourses* ((1848); and *The Sickness unto Death* (1849).

Kind : It represents a type or class of entities that share a common character. Mill in his *System of Logic* uses this expression exclusively to refer to natural classes such as biological species in which the members of a class not only share a defining property, but also many other properties.

Kinesis (Gk) : It means "change" or "motion." Aristotle distinguishes three kinds of kinesis. They are: (1) change in quantity that is explained in terms of increase or decrease; (2) qualitative change; and (3) change in place. Apart from these changes, Aristotle also recognized substantial change in terms of generation, destruction and passing away.

Knower, The : The subject of knowledge as opposed to object is called the knower. The knower may be the perceiving mind, the transcendental subject, the pure ego, or an empirical self. A knowledge situation always presupposes the knower in the form of a subject and the known in the form of an object.

Knowledge : Knowledge is generally discussed under the head called epistemology. It is very difficult to define what knowledge is. Unlike belief, it is not a state of mind. Traditionally epistemology is regarded as a systematic investigation and exposition of the principles of the possibility of knowledge. Sophists' held that sense-experience is the only legitimate source of knowledge. Plato disregarded sense-experience as a valid source of knowledge, because all that we can form with the help of sense-experience is only opinion, but not knowledge. He distinguished knowledge from opinion, and belief. Aristotle classified knowledge into theoretical, practical and productive. The knowledge of First Principles (metaphysics) that is pursued for its own sake is theoretical knowledge. The knowledge that is pursued for the sake of actions, moral and political, is called practical knowledge. And the knowledge that is pursued for the sake of producing or creating something is productive knowledge. Modern philosophers like Descartes held that knowledge is certain and indubitable. He held that all knowledge is possible through reason alone. Thus deduction is the most important method to arrive at knowledge. John Locke attempted to define knowledge as "perception of the connection and agreement, or disagreement and repugnance of any of our ideas." According to him, all knowledge is possible through sense-experience. However, Locke recognized intuitive and demonstrative forms of knowledge. However, Locke while differentiating sensitive knowledge from intuitive and demonstrative types held the view that sensitive knowledge, in the strictest sense of the term "knowledge," is not knowledge at all, but it only passes under the title knowledge. Hume held that all genuine knowledge is obtained from sense-impressions. He made a distinction between knowledge obtained from relations of ideas (analytic) and knowledge obtained from matters of fact (synthetic). Kant made a distinction between a priori and a posteriori forms of knowledge. The former is the knowledge arrived at by means of reason alone, while the latter is the knowledge obtained by means of sense-experience. A priori knowledge is true in all possible worlds, but it is not the case with a posteriori knowledge. Kant further introduced knowledge that is synthetic a priori in its nature. The knowledge of mathematics is synthetic a priori for it provides us new information and also universal and necessary. Modern empiricists like Russell, Ayer and others recognized the Kantian distinction between a priori and a posteriori forms of knowledge, but they did not differentiate a priori from analytic and a posteriori from synthetic. Unlike Kant, following Hume, they held that knowledge of logic and mathematics is a priori and analytic, but not synthetic a priori. Further, modern epistemologists viewed that belief cannot be identified with knowledge, although knowledge presupposes belief. According to them, all knowledge is informative, but all information cannot be treated as knowledge. Philosophers like Russell argued that scientific knowledge alone can be characterized as knowledge in the real sense of the term "knowledge."

Knowledge by Acquaintance : Russell introduced this expression in his *The Problems of Philosophy* (1912). According to him, it is the knowledge of objects by direct perception. Russell held that the only objects of direct perception are hard-data (sense-data). For instance, when we perceive an object like chair, it is the hard-data of the chair that are directly given in perception. Therefore, one is directly acquainted with the hard-data of the chair, but not with the chair as a physical object.

Knowledge by Description : Unlike the knowledge by acquaintance, the knowledge by description provides us with indirect knowledge of objects. Russell claimed that we infer the existence of physical objects like chairs and tables only by means of knowledge by description. For instance, when we perceive an object like chair, it is the hard-data of the chair that are directly given in perception. From the hard-data of the chair, we infer the existence of the chair. Therefore, our knowledge of the chair is not direct but indirect. This indirect knowledge of the chair is the knowledge by description.

Knowledge de dicto and de re : Knowledge *de dicto* is diametrically opposed to knowledge *de re.* The former is knowledge of facts or propositions, while the latter is knowledge of a particular object or a group of objects that stand in some relation to each other.

Koffka, Kurt (1886 – 1941) : He was a co-founder of *Gestalt psychology* along with Wertheimer and Köhler. Although Koffka relied on Köhler's study of learning in apes that is explained in terms of trial and error method, he recognized the role of insight in the process of learning. His important work is *The Growth of the Mind* (1925).

Köhler, Wolfgang (1887 – 1967) : He was a German psychologist who developed Gestalt psychology along with Wertheimer and Koffka at Frankfurt. Later on he moved to United States of America as a Professor of psychology at Swarthmore College. He attempted to explain *Gestalt* psychology from the empirical and the theoretical points of view. He approached Gestalt psychology from the empirical point of view by studying the mentality of the apes. He felt that the animals do learn things by means of trial and error method. The trial and error behaviour of animals gradually leads them to success. On the theoretical level, Köhler introduced the concept of isomorphism. It is *Gestalt* psychology's theory of psychological representation. He advanced an identity theory of mind and body. His important works include: *Gestalt Psychology* (1929); *The Place of value in a World of Facts* (1938); and *Dynamics in Psychology* (1940).

Koran (Qoran) : It is the sacred scripture of the Muslims. This holy book consists of certain warnings, injunctions, assertions, arguments in support of certain doctrines, narratives, etc. that are intended to enforce a moral code. Koran stresses the ideal of the day of judgement and provides a realistic description of the sufferings of hell and the pleasures of paradise. Koran as a collection of commandments provides answers to special questions. In Koran one finds personal addresses by Allah to Mohammed. Thus it is treated as a diary of the prophet.

Kośa (S) : It means "sheath." According to the *Taittirīya Upaniṣad* and Vedāntins, the Self (*ātman*) is concealed by five *kośas*. They are: the sheath of food (*annamaya-kośa*), the sheath of vital air (*prāṇamaya-kośa*), the sheath of mind (*manomaya-kośa*), the sheath of intellect (*vijñānamaya-kośa*), and the sheath of bliss (*ānandamaya-kośa*). The first sheath constitutes the gross body (*sthūla śarīra*), the second, third and fourth constitute the subtle body (*sūkṣma śarīra*), and the fifth constitutes the causal body (*kāraṇa śarīra*).

Kratocracy : It is a form of government by those who are mighty enough to seize power by force or cunning methods.

Krause, Karl Christian Friedrich (1781 – 1832) : He was a German philosopher and a younger contemporary of Immanuel Kant. Krause tried to develop Kantian philosophy on the lines of pantheism and mysticism. He was greatly influenced by Fichte and Schelling while studying at Jena. Krause advocated panentheism according to which nature and human consciousness are part and parcel of God or Absolute Being. However, he felt that the Absolute can neither be reduced to nature nor to human consciousness. His important works include: *Grundl. d. Naturrechts* (1803) and *System d. Sittenlehre* (1810).

Kripke, Saul (1940 –) : He is an American philosopher and logician who has made some significant advances in the field of modal logic. His modal logic is based on the concepts of necessity and possibility. According to Kripke, the concept of necessity plays a vital role in the theory of direct reference. He is also of the view that necessity as analyticity has failed to understand the modal structures of language. Logical necessity has completely ignored the reference for it is concerned with the mere rules of language. In his famous work *Naming and Necessity* (1980), Kripke argued that only proper names have meanings in virtue of their reference, but not because they have descriptions. Kripke makes a distinction between the truths that are necessary because of formal relations in grammar, and truths that are necessary because of the grammar being the representation of language and reality. The latter are called "metaphysical truths." Thus Kripke recognized metaphysical necessity along with logical necessity. Kripke's semantics is often known as possible world semantics. His other important work is *Wittgenstein on Rules and Private language: An Elementary Exposition* (1982).

Krishnamurthy, Jiddu (1895 – 1990) : He is a well-known contemporary Indian philosopher. He was brought up by theosophists of India. But he came out of that order and propagated the philosophy of his own. According to Krishnamurthy, man is his own guide. He never accepted the concept of *guru*. He opposed all forms of theosophy and traditionalism. True spiritual quest for him is that which does not get itself associated with any school, idea, or dogma. Reality is pure life running its own course. The drive of evolution is to realize self-consciousness.

Kṣaṇikavāda (S) : It is a theory advocated by the Buddhists. It is popularly known as "the theory of momentariness." According to this theory, everything comes into existence in a moment, endures for a moment, and vanishes in a moment. Thus the existence of anything is momentary. Thus there is no permanent entity.

Kumārila Bhaṭṭa (eighth century CE) : He was one of the propagators of Mīmāṁsā philosophy and an older contemporary of Śaṅkara. He is the author of *Ślokavārttika* and *Tantravārttika.*

According to Kumārila, there are six valid sources (*pramāṇas*) of knowledge. They are: *pratyakṣa, anumāna, śabda, upamāna, arthāpatti,* and *anupalabdhi.* Advaita accepts all these six *pramāṇas.*

Kuo Hsiang (Kuo Tzü-hsüan) (c. CE 312) : He was the most influential Taoist thinker of medieval China. Kuo developed the notion of *li* or pattern that signifies the underlying structure of the cosmos. In this structure everything receives individual *fen* or attention. Thus all things are "one" in so far as they play their "natural" roles as parts of the very structure of the cosmos. Kuo wrote a commentary on *Chuang Tzú.*

Kūṭastha (S) : It is the name given to the consciousness or person that is present in the unity or knot of all the forces that constitute the Unconscious and that is stable and alive to everything which man does and experiences. The consciousness that is present in the unity of *buddhi, ahaṁkāra,* and *manas,* which together constitute the inner instrument *antaḥkaraṇa,* is called here as the group (*kūṭa*). It is also treated as a higher or deeper level of the Self (*ātman*).

L

Lacan, Jacques (1901 – 81) : He was a French psychoanalyst and practitioner. Influenced by Saussure's structural linguistics, Lacan transformed Freudian theory and practice of psychoanalysis. Lacan held that the unconscious is not an outcome of biological instincts and drives, but is a system of linguistic signifiers. He interpreted the Freudian processes of condensation and displacement as instances of metaphor and metonymy. Lacan's psycho-analytic method has had tremendous impact on literary theorists and on post-modern philosophers like Foucault, Derrida, and Deleuze.

Lachelier, J. (1831 – 1918) : He was a French philosopher who exerted a lot of influence on his students at Ecole Normale Superieure. He was Bergson's teacher. He followed Kantian idealism, but blended it with French spiritualism of Maine de Biran and Ravaisson.

Laissez-faire (F) : It means "allow things to proceed without interference." In other words, let people do or make whatever they want. It is a philosophy of governmental non-interference in the economic activities of the individuals. Also, it is a free enterprise founded on private ownership of goods, property, resources, and services. Man becomes more efficient and productive when allowed to seek his self-interest without governmental regulation or restriction. This philosophy is basically advocated by Adam Smith in his work the *Wealth of Nations* (1776).

Lamaism : It is an honourable title given to a Buddhist monk in Tibet. The religious beliefs and institutions of Tibet owe their allegiance to Mahāyāna Buddhism. It was introduced to the people of Tibet in the seventh century by the chieftain Srontaan-gampo. Lamaism was superimposed on the native Shamaistic Bon religion. It was mixed with Tāntric elements by the mythic Hindu Padmasambhava. The strong admixture of elements of the exorcismal, highly magically charged, and priest-ridden original Bon has given Buddhism a turn away from its philosophical foundations by producing Lamaism, which is a form that lays emphasis on *mantra*s. This form of worship is institutionalized. Lamaism believes in the double incarnation of the *bodhisattva* in the Dalai Lama, who is vested with political powers. Lamaism has been a link between the Indian and the Chinese traditions for centuries together.

Lambert, Johann Heinrich (1728 – 77) : He was a German philosopher, logician, mathematician, and one of the correspondents of Immanuel Kant. Lambert made significant contribution to the fields of physics and mathematics. He argued against the German rationalism and the British empiricism to advance a theory of phenomenalism that is akin to Kant and Tetens. He held that mind contains, as a repository, a number of basic concepts and principles that make knowledge possible. His important works include: *Neues Organon* (1764) and *Anlage zur Architectonic* (1771).

Lange, Friedrich Albert (1828 – 75) : He was a well-known German philosopher and social scientist. His celebrated work *History of Materialism* (1873 – 75) was based on Kantian point of view. Lange demonstrated the philosophical limitations of metaphysical materialism, and his appreciation of the value of materialism as a stimulus to critical thinking. He worked for a greater understanding of Kant's work and anticipated fictionalism. Lange advocated a restrictive positivist approach to interpretations of man and nature. He was a champion of democratic socialism.

Language : It is a system of communication through which humans exchange their ideas, feelings, etc. with fellow humans. Language is an inter-subjective phenomenon. Without language humans cannot advance in any field of scientific inquiry. Language consists of words, sentences, statements, and propositions. Words are supposed to be the smallest units. They are conventional signs. Sentences are formed out of words. A statement is considered to be the meaning of sentence. Every statement is a proposition provided it is significantly said to be either true or false. Language is a product of society. Thus, it is public. There are several natural languages. These languages are governed by the rules of syntax and semantics. Language and thought are inseparable from each other. Contrary to natural languages, formal languages are subjected to the rules of formation and transformation.

Language Game : The expression "language game" was first introduced by Wittgenstein in his *Philosophical Investigations* (1953) to highlight the multiple functions of language. He tries to draw a parallel between using language and playing games. He tells the reader not to ask for the common elements found among the various language games, but only to look for them. There are a number of crisscross relationships among the members of a family. Language game represents the form of life. Just as there are language games, there are forms of life. The rules of one language game do not have any validity in another language game.

Language, Object : It is the language that is used to talk about the things of which we are conscious. It is opposed to meta-language, which is used to talk about such a language or other languages. The expressions used in an object language have linguistic or syntactical reference, whereas the expressions of meta-language do not have. For example, "Sri Ram is intelligent" is a statement in object language. But the statement "Sri Ram is a proper name with six letters" is a meta-linguistic statement. The language that is being systematically analysed is called object language. The language that is being used in the analysis of this language is meta-language.

Lao Tzu (C. sixth century BCE) : He was a great Chinese philosopher believed to be the contemporary of Confucius and the author of the *Tao Te Ching* (Classic of tao and te). This work combines both paradoxical mysticism with hard-headed political advice and an appeal to return to a primitive utopia without corrupting the legacy of civilization that includes the ritual (*li*), luxury and writing.

Laplace, Pierre Simon De (1749 – 1827) : He was a French astronomer and mathematician who held the view that the solar system is stable, and consequently requires no periodical interference of a creator to restore its equilibrium. According to him, the solar system has its origin in primary nebula. He supported mechanistic form of determinism.

Law : A law is something that does not fail to occur under given conditions. There are natural and mechanical laws. The nature and its various processes are governed by natural laws. They are inherent in the nature. The discovery of such laws is the work of a scientist. On the other hand, mechanical laws are those laws that control the operations of mechanics. Such laws operate only in physical level. For example: the laws of thermodynamics.

Laws of Thought : According to traditional logic, there are three important laws of thought. They are: (1) Law of identity, according to which a proposition is true if it is true. (2) Law of non-contradiction, according to which a proposition cannot be both true and false at a time. (3) Law of excluded middle, according to which a proposition must be either true or false.

Leap : It is a radical change that takes place in an object or a phenomenon. According to Darwin, the transition from one stage to another stage is always explained in terms of a leap.

Legitimation Crisis : It is a crisis that results when the state is not in a position to procure the voluntary support and loyalty of its citizens. This occurs, for instance, when citizens no longer feel the laws of the state are morally just, because they are not implemented in a fair, impartial, and democratic way.

Leibniz, Gottfried Wilhelm (1646 – 1716) : He was a German rationalist philosopher and the inventor of differential calculus. According to Leibniz, reality consists of monads. These monads are miniature worlds by themselves. They have force. Thus he replaced extension with force. A monad is a point, not a mathematical or a physical point but a metaphysically existent point. Monads, claims Leibniz, come close to each other to form various objects in this world. Such a harmony among the monads is called "pre-established harmony." Monads do not have any causal relation. Monads are windowless. Every monad consists of *appetition* and *perception*. Essentially monads are logically prior to any corporeal substance. The highest monad is God. As regards the existence of God, Leibniz accepted for most part the proofs advanced for the existence of God. In theory of knowledge, Leibniz classified knowledge into necessary truths (truths of reason) and contingent truths (truths of fact). Necessary truths are those truths whose truth-value is conditioned by the "law of non-contradiction." On the contrary the truth-values of contingent truths are mere probabilities for they are conditioned by the "law of sufficient reason." Mathematical truths are the best examples for necessary truths, and empirical truths for contingent truths. As regards the existence of evil in this world, Leibniz held that God has given us the best of the possible worlds. For Leibniz, logic is the key to metaphysics. From the grammar of propositions he inferred the conclusions about the real world. His important works include: *Discourse on Metaphysics* (1686); *New Essays on Human Understanding* (1705); *New System of Nature and the Interaction of Substances* (1695-96); *Monadology* (1707); and *Theodicy* (1710).

Leibniz's Law : According to this law, if one object is identical with another object, then what is true of one object is also true of the other. For example, *X* has all the properties of *Y* then what is true of *X* must also be true of *Y*. It is also known as the law of "identity of indiscernibles."

Lemma : Anything that is taken for granted or assumed in logic is called lemma. The most common form of lemma in logic is the dilemma, which implies the need to choose between two alternatives. For example, either do this work or you come with us.

Lenin, Vladimir Ilyich (1870 – 1924) : He was a Russian Marxist philosopher and a statesman whose contribution to philosophy is his work *Materialism and Empirio Criticism* (1908). He attacked the subjective idealist philosophy of Berkeley. According to Lenin, ideas are copies of reality. Reality, for Lenin, consists of material objects whose processes are subjected to natural law. According to Lenin, Hegel's philosophy is the best base for proper understanding of the doctrines of Marx.

Leucippus (C. 450 – 420 BCE) : He was one of the ancient Greek atomists and contemporaries of Empedocles and Anaxagoras. Leucippus was the founder of the school of Abdera. He tried to explain the nature of reality in terms of atomic cosmology. According to him all qualitative differences in nature can be reduced to quantitative ones. Thus he opposed the homogeneous "Being" of Parmenides. Becoming, according to Leucippus, is essentially the result of the motion of atoms in space and their accidental coming together.

Liar Paradox : It is a paradox that often trades between truth and falsity. Liar paradox was first formulated by Eubulides of Miletus. He was a successor of Euclid. This paradox is also known as Megarian paradox. For example, the statement "All Cretons are liars" is followed by another statement "I am a Creton." If the statement "All Cretons are liars" is true, then the statement "I am a Creton" is false. Russell made use of this paradox to show that the grammatical meaning of a sentence does not reveal its logical meaning.

Libertarianism : It is a socio-political view that opposes all forms of social, economic, and political constraints on human freedom. Thus it allows freedom of will in performing any social action. In ethics, it is the view that humans have free will interpreted as an uncaused event. In metaphysics, it is the view that there are uncaused events in the universe.

Liberty : It is a right of a person to choose from among the available alternatives, or courses of action or goals without being restricted by authority of any kind. It is also a right of a person not to be interfered with in pursuit or possession of what he wills or values. It is also the right of individuals to express themselves whatever they wish, without constraint, and to employ the means they wish to obtain their interests. It is also viewed as a freedom or opportunity to act in accordance with one's choice.

Linguistic Philosophy : It is a branch of philosophy that deals with the usage of our day-to-day language. According to linguistic philosophers, all the problems of philosophy appear because of muddled thinking, and this muddled thinking is largely the product of improper use of language. Their chief focus is on the logical clarification of thought. Wittgenstein remarked that: "all the problems of philosophy appear and reappear when language goes on holiday." The emphasis of linguistic philosophers is more on semantics rather than on syntax. Although linguistic philosophy is treated as a part of analytic philosophy, there is a marked distinction between them. The former engages in the word analysis and the latter with the world analysis. John Searle in his work *Speech Acts* makes a distinction between linguistic philosophy and philosophy of language. According to him, linguistic philosophy is a name of a method, whereas philosophy of language is the name of a subject.

Locke, John (1632 – 1704) : He has been regarded as a pioneer of the British Empiricist movement, and a famous social and political philosopher who advocated the social contract theory. Locke, in his theory of knowledge, vehemently attacked the doctrine of innate ideas. He firmly believed that all genuine knowledge is possible through sense-experience alone. According to him, mind in the beginning is a blank sheet of paper void of everything. The ideas are imprinted on the mind with the help of sensation and reflection. These ideas are necessarily the copies of such ideas into: simple and complex ones. Locke recognized three levels of knowledge. They are: (1) intuitive knowledge, through which one knows one's immediate existence; (2) demonstrative knowledge, to establish the existence of God and to demonstrate certain mathematical truths; and (3) sensitive knowledge, which is the knowledge of the objects external to us. In political philosophy, Locke advocated social contract theory with a treatment of "the state of nature." According to Locke: "men living together according to reason, without a common superior on earth with authority to judge between them is properly the state of nature." He further held that men by nature are good. Locke advocated the doctrine of natural rights with correlative duties. Right to private property, according to Locke, precedes the civil law. The jurisdiction of private property is labour. His important works include: *An Essay Concerning Human Understanding* (1688); *Two Treatises of Civil Government* (1690); *The Reasonableness of Christianity as Delivered in the Scriptures* (1695); and *Vindications of the Reasonableness of Christianity* (1695 and 1697).

Locution : A locution is a meaningful assertion that abides by the rules of syntax. Contrary to an illocutionary act, locutionary act involves the use of a locution to express something more clearly and categorically.

Logic : It is a science of reasoning. Its basic concern is the validity of any argument rather than truth. In other words, the chief aim of logic is to make every argument consistent and coherent. There are two important types of logic. They are: inductive and deductive. Inductive logic proceeds from particulars to form general conclusion, while the deductive logic starts from generalizations to arrive at particular conclusions. Of late, the scope of logic has been amplified by the introduction of various forms of reasoning. For instance, formal logic deals with the forms of valid thinking and their structure. Many valued logic takes into account various meanings of propositions. Mathematical or symbolic logic is an application of formal methods of mathematics in the realm of logic. Modal logic deals with the structure of various propositions. The structure of any proposition includes the modalities such as "necessity," "reality," "possibility," "chance," and their negations. Deontic logic is concerned with the moral obligations of duty. Quantum logic is an outcome of modern theories of quantum physics. Dialectical logic is developed by dialectical materialists in accordance with the laws of dialectics.

Logical Atomism : It is a philosophy advocated by Russell and early Wittgenstein. Russell's *The Philosophy of Logical Atomism*, and early Wittgenstein's *Tractatus Logico-Philosophicus* developed the philosophy of logical atomism in detail. According to this doctrine, language mirrors the reality. Unlike physicists, claim logical atomists, they are not interested in physically breaking the atom into its components but are interested in breaking the atoms into their minute logical structures. Thus they arrive at what are called simples. By doing so certain complicated things can be made intelligible. These logical atoms are supposed to depict the reality in its simplest form possible. However, this doctrine was abandoned by both the writers due to its untenability.

Logical Constants : Logical constants are those through which one can identify the grammatical structure of a sentence. The most commonly employed logical constant are: "~," "&," "V," "⊃," "≡." One may even use additional logical constants if required.

Logical Construction : This expression was often used by Russell and John Wisdom to denote those entities that are problematic to philosophers. For instance, a material object is considered to be a "logical construct" out of actual and possible sense-data. The reason is that material objects are not directly given in sense-experience. What is immediately given in sense-experience are sense-data. The existence of material object is rather inferred from the given sense-data. Thus material objects are logical constructs. In other words, a logical construction has sense-data as its elements.

Logical Positivism : It is the name given to the ideas of the Vienna Circle. This school of thought was founded by a noted physicist Moritz Schlick in 1922. The chief objective of this school were: (1) to get rid of metaphysics from the sphere of philosophy in order to make philosophy a genuine branch of knowledge; and (2) to develop the taste for science and mathematics. According to logical positivists, the function of philosophy is the logical clarification of the language of day-to-day affairs and of science. One of the fundamental principles of logical positivism is the principle of verification. According to this principle, a statement is meaningful if and only if it is empirically verifiable. The chief exponents of logical positivism were Rudolf Carnap and A.J. Ayer. The logical positivist movement got disintegrated in the late 1930s due to the death of some of the leading members and also due to the Nazi aggression.

Logical Subject : It is the subject of a sentence expressed in a logically perfect language. For example, in the sentence "Wittgenstein is the author of *Tractaus Logico-Philosophicus*" "Wittgenstein" is the logical subject.

Logical Truth : It is a form of necessary truth held to owe truth to meaning of logical constants only.

Logically Perfect Language : It is a language in which grammatical and logical structures correspond with each other. Such a view is found in the writings of Russell and early Wittgenstein. For details see Russell's *The Philosophy of Logical Atomism* and Wittgenstein's *Tractatus Logico-Philosophicus*.

Logicism : It is a view advocated by Frege and Russell, according to which mathematics is considered to be the part of logic. The purpose of logicism is to ensure that the knowledge of mathematical truths will have the same status as the knowledge of logical truths. Logicism is opposed to psychologism.

Logistic Method : It is a method of studying a subject by formalizing it. For instance, the philosophers of science often analyse the theories of science into statements expressing their logical form. This is done with a view to clarify their interrelations.

Logos (Gk) : It can mean "discourse," "speech," "thought," "reason," "word," and "meaning." In Greek religion, *logos* is referred to as the divine word of god or gods that provides spiritual inspiration, wisdom, and guidance.

Lokācārya, Pillai (thirteenth century CE) : He was a Viśiṣṭādvaitin. He is also known as Vādakesari. He propagated the *Tengalai* sect of Vaiṣṇavism. According to Pillai Lokācārya, Tamil scriptures alone should be followed, as they are authentic sources of Vaiṣṇavism. As regards liberation, he claims that total surrender to God (*prapatti*) is the only way to liberation. God will take care of his worshippers.

Lokāyata (S) : It is a name given to the teachings of Cārvāka. The fundamental belief of the followers of Lokāyata is that there is no life after death. See Cārvāka.

Lottery Paradox : This paradox arises out of the principle that when a rational man believes each of the many propositions ought to believe their conjunction. This can be illustrated by the following example. There is a lottery with one thousand tickets starting with 1, 2, 3 . . . 1000. A rational man may claim that 1 will not win, 2 will not win, 3 will not win, and so on for each ticket. This amounts to saying that the belief in the conjunction of all these propositions is equivalent to saying that no ticket is going to win. But, this is not the case in reality. Out of 1000 tickets, one ticket is going to win. Therefore, the natural principle of combining all rational beliefs may lead to false consequences.

Love, Platonic : It is commonly understood as a spiritual comradeship or fellow love without the presence of sexual desire or sexual contact.

Lovejoy, Arthur Onken (1873 – 1962) : He was a great American philosopher and historian of ideas. He was a staunch defender of epistemological dualism, according to which the objects of reality are not identical with the ideas or images of those objects. According to him, the objects of reality and their ideas or images are spatially distinct. The idea or an image of a table is within us; whereas the actual table is external to us both spatially and temporally. For instance, when we perceive a distant star, by the time we have its image, the star may be extinct. As a historian of ideas, Lovejoy traces back the significance of the principle of plenitude from Plato onwards. According to him, this principle suggests to us how the real possibilities are realized by us in this world. His important works include: *The Revolt Against Dualism* (1930) and *The Great Chain of Being* (1936).

Lowenheim-Skolem Theorem : This theorem was first proved by Lowenheim in 1915. According to this theorem, if a formula of the pure functional calculus of first order containing no free individual variables, is satisfiable at all, it is satisfiable in a domain of individuals which is at most enumerable. Other simpler proofs of the theorem were advanced by Skolem afterwards. He arrived at a generalization that if an enumerable set of such formulae are simultaneously satisfiable, they are simultaneously satisfiable in a domain of individuals at most enumerable.

Lucretius, Carus (c. 98 – 54 BCE) : He was a Roman philosophical poet. His famous didactic poem was *De Natura Rerum*. In his *Six*

Books he gave a fine exposition of the philosophy of Epicurus. His books I and II deal with atomic theory, III deals with the morality of the soul, IV deals with sensation and thought, V deals with the origin and the development of the world, and VI with natural phenomena.

Lulliac Art : It was a science developed by Raymond Lully (1235-1315) that consists of the highest and most general principles, even above metaphysics and logic, which serve as the basic postulates of all sciences. From these principles Lully hoped to derive the fundamental assumptions about the sciences.

Lyceum : It was a public garden in Athens and its name was given to Aristotle's school of philosophy that was founded in 335 BCE.

Lyric : It is something to do with literary genre pertaining to the absolute uniqueness of the sensations of the poet. It is also regarded as an art that symbolizes the expression of sentiment. For more details see Croce.

M

Mach, Ernst (1838 – 1916) : He was an Austrian physicist and philosopher whose philosophy is considered to be radical empiricism or pure sensationalism. According to Mach, mind cannot go beyond its own sensations. Every scientific theory is based on the discovery of certain sort of sensations. Lenin vehemently criticized the philosophy of Mach in his *Materialism and Empirio-Criticism*. Logical positivists owe a lot to the sensationalism of Mach. His important works include: *The Science of Mechanics* (1893) and *The Analysis of Sensations* (1914).

Macrocosm : In general it is understood as a large complex or whole that is more than the sum total of its parts. It also refers to the universe in its totality.

Mādhava : He is one of the famous brothers of fourteenth century CE, namely, Mādhava and Sāyaṇa. He is responsible for establishment of a kingdom which was later known as Vijayanagara Empire, through the king Bukka Bhūpati. He was the Chief Minister to Bukka. In the later stages of life, he took *saṁnyāsa* and is known by the *āśrama* name as "Vidyāraṇya." After taking *saṁnyāsa*, he became the Śaṅkarācārya of Śṛṅgerīpīṭha in the tradition of Śaṅkara and continued to administer the state in the religious way. He wrote several monumental works alongside his many responsibilities. *Sarvadarśanasaṅgraha* was the first of its kind summarizing the Darśanas, both orthodox and heterodox. *Pañcadaśī* is another work elucidating the Advaita in a logical and experiential way. These two works are constantly studied ever since by the sincere students of Indian philosophy. Apart from these two he wrote

Mādhavīyadhatuvṛtti in Vyākaraṇa and *Jaiminīya Nyāyamālāvistāra* in Pūrvamīmāṁsādarśana. His other works include — *Daśopaniṣddīpīkā, Anubhūtiprakāśa,* commentaries on the *Manusmṛti* and the *Parāśarasmṛti* and *Śaṅkaradigvijaya,* a biographical account of Ādiśaṅkara. The introductory stanzas in the *Bhāṣya* of all the four Vedas including *Brāhmanas* proclaim the authorship of Mādhavācarya, and the *Vedabhāṣyas* are known as *Vidyāraṇyabhāṣyas* in the tradition. However, there is a view that these are actually written by the younger brother Sāyaṇa in the name of his elder brother Mādhava. Therefore, they are popularly called *Sāyaṇabhāṣyas*. They are huge in size and content and carry the distinction of being the first commentary written by a single author on all the four Vedas giving a uniform interpretation of ageless Vedas.

Madhva (C. CE 1238 – 1317) : Madhva is also known by other names such as Pūrṇaprajña, Ānandatīrtha, Nandītīrtha, and Vasudeva. He was the chief propagator of Dvaita, according to which world is as real as *Brahman*. Thus he advocated unqualified dualism. According to him the Reality admits fivefold differences. They are: between soul and God, between soul and soul, between soul and matter, between God and matter, and between matter and matter. His bias for difference is so great that he advocates difference of degrees in the possession of knowledge. It is unique to Madhva Vedānta. In epistemology, Madhva accepts, like Śrī Rāmānuja, only three sources of knowledge. They are: *pratyakṣa, anumāna,* and *śabda*. The God (Hari, Nārāyaṇa, Viṣṇu, Vāsudeva) is known only through scriptures. Like Rāmānuja, he holds that both Pūrva- and Uttara-Mīmāṁsā form into a single section. Liberation is possible only by realizing God. At least there are thirty-seven works written by Madhva. The important works of Madhva include: *Ṛg-Bhāṣya; Karma-Nirṇaya; Nṛsiṁha-Nakha-Stotra; Dvādaśa-Stotra;* and *Govindāṣṭaka-Ṭīkā*. The followers of Madhva philosophy were Jayatīrtha and Vsyāsatīrtha. The latter's work is *Nyāyāmṛta*.

Madhusūdana Sarasvati (sixteenth century CE) : He was an Advaitin. He refuted Vyāsatīrtha's arguments against monistic Vedānta in his illustrious work, *Advaita-Siddhi*. His other important works include: *Vedānta-Kalpa-Latikā*; *Advaita-Ratna-Rakṣaṇa*; *Ātma-Bodha-Ṭīkā*; and *Ānanda-Mandākinī*. Madhusūdana held the view that it is only the Vedāntic concept of liberation that appeals to men. The real nature of liberation is the freedom of the Self from *avidyā* or ignorance.

Mādhyamika (S) : It is another name for the *Śūnyavāda* Buddhist school. This school assumes its name because it follows the middle path (*madhyama*) between theories clinging to knowability of the noumenal and the sufficiency of the phenomenal. Nāgārjuna was one of the propagators and may be the first systematic exponent of *Śūnyavāda*, but not its founder. It is held that some of the *Mahāyāna-sūtra*s existed prior to Aśvaghoṣa. Śūnyavādins are the followers of middle path realized by the Buddha during his Enlightenment. This path avoids both the errors of existence and non-existence, affirmation and negation, eternalism and nihilism, also at once it transcends both the extremes. The word *śūnya* is misinterpreted and misunderstood by many scholars. The literal meaning of the word is "negation" or "void." Mādhyamikas use this word in its true philosophical sense. Śūnya essentially means indescribable as it is beyond the comprehension of reason and the categories of intellect. It is the Reality that ultimately transcends existence, non-existence, both and neither. Empirically it means relativity (*pratītyasamutpāda*). In its absolute sense, it is Reality (*tattva*) which is release from plurality (*nirvāṇa*). According to Aśvaghoṣa, the Reality is *tathatā*. As the ultimate Reality it is also known as *bhūta-tathatā*.

Mahābhārata (S) : It actually means "the great war of the Bharatas." It is a very important Hindu epic of 100,000 verses ascribed to Vyāsa. This great epic deals with a number of interesting topics that include philosophy, religion, polity, science, diplomacy and so on. The *Bhagavad-Gītā* is a part of this great epic.

Mahābhūta (S) : It means a "physical element." Indian tradition recognizes five *mahābhūta*s. They are earth, water, fire, air, and ether. Everything in this nature is made up of these *pañca-mahābhūta*s.

Mahat (S) : It means "great or mighty." It is the first product of *prakṛti,* according to Sāṁkhya.

Mahātmā (S) : It means "great soul." It is a term of respect prefixed to great personalities like M.K. Gandhi. In Indian philosophy, *mahātmā* generally refers to the super-individual or transcendental self or the Absolute.

Mahāvīra (549 – 477 BCE) : He is regarded as the twenty-fourth *tīrthaṅkara* or "Founders of the Faith of Jainism." According to Jainas, Ṛṣabhadeva was the founder of Jaina school of thought.

Mahāyāna Buddhism : It is a sect in Buddhism known as "Great vehicle." This sect of Budhism is popular in Tibet, China, Korea, and Japan. According to this sect, "Buddhahood" means devotion to the salvation of others. This devotion manifests itself in the worship of the Buddha and *bodhisattva*s. The philosophical schools such as Sūnyavāda and Vijñānavāda are part of Mahāyāna Buddhism.

Maieutic (Gk) : It means "one who acts like a midwife." Socratic method served as an intellectual midwife. The aim of this method is to inculcate ideas into pregnant minds. In fact, there are already ideas that are to be given birth, but they require someone to assist by asking the proper questions and prodding the intellect.

Maimon, Moses ben (1135 – 1204) : He was better known as Maimonaides (Abu Imran Musā Ibn Maimun Ibn Abdullah). He was a very famous Jewish philosopher of the Middle Ages who wrote a commentary on *Talmud.* His important work *Guide for the Perplexed* (*More nebukim* in Hebrew and *Dalalat al-hairin* in Arabic) contains a summary of the Jewish thought up to his time. This work was written in the Aristotelian spirit and was divided into three parts. The first part of the work deals with the problems of Biblical anthropomorphisms, Divine attributes, and exposition and criticism of the teachings of the *Kalam*. The second part deals with the proofs for the existence of God, matter and form, *creatio de novo*, and an exposition of prophecy. The third part deals with the nature of God, and the world including problems of providence, evil, presceience, freedom of will, teleology, and rationality of the precepts of the *Torah*. His writings influenced the great thinkers of the thirteenth century such as Albertus Magnus and Thomas Aquinas.

Maimon, Salomon (1754 – 1800) : He was a Jewish philosopher, writer and well-versed in Rabanical literature. In fact, Immanuel Kant acknowledged him as his most astute critical opponent. He wrote a number of historical works on philosophy and attempted to expound a system of symbolic logic. He developed a kind of speculative monism that influenced post-Kantian thinkers.

Maine de Biran, F.P. Gonthier (1766 – 1824) : He was a well-known French philosopher and psychologist. He vehemently opposed the dominant sensationalistic and materialistic psychology of Condillac and Cabanis. Under the influence of both Kant and Fichte he developed an idealistic and voluntaristic psychology. According to him, the mind directly experiences the activity of its will and at the same time the resistance offered by the *non-moi*. Based on this view, Maine de Biran advanced his theory of metaphysics that interprets the conceptions of force, substance, cause, etc., in terms of the directly experienced activity of the will. This system of psychology and metaphysics which came to be known as French spiritualism directly or indirectly influenced the thinkers like Cousin, Ravaisson, and Renouvier.

Major Premise : In any categorical syllogism the premise in which the major term occurs is called a major premise. For example, the syllogism consists of the following premisses:

All Men are Mortal.
Socrates is a man.
Therefore, Socrates is mortal.

In this syllogism, "mortal" is the major term (predicate of the conclusion). Then the premise "All men are mortal" is a major premise.

Major Term : In a categorical syllogism, one of the three terms that appears as a predicate of the conclusion is called major term. Aristotle called it by that name because of its significance in a syllogism. Major term is a term of greatest extension in the first or the perfect figure of syllogism. The middle term is also included in it, and the minor term comes under the middle term.

Malebranche, Nicolas (1638 – 1715) : He was a French theologian and philosopher who developed Cartesianism. Like Geulinex, he was interested in mind-body problem developed by Descartes and interpreted it from the point of view of occasionalism, according to which God finds an occasion to bring causal interaction between physical and mental states. He asserted that "we see all things in God." Therefore, God is the real cause of all events. He held that there is no possibility of interaction between mind and body. His important works include: *de la Recherche de la verite* (1674-75); *Conversations Chretiennes* (1676); and *Traite de Moral* (1683).

Malevolence : It is ill or evil will or disposition to do wrong or harm others. It is a vice opposed to the virtue of benevolence or good will.

Manas (S) : It means "mind." It is regarded as one of the functions of the internal organ or *antaḥkaraṇa*.

Maṇḍana Miśra (CE 680 – 750) : According to Vidyāraṇya, Maṇḍana later changed his name as Sureśvara. Before he became a disciple of Śaṅkara, Maṇḍana was a Mīmāṁsaka. He wrote *Brahmasiddhi*. Later on he was defeated by Śaṅkara and became an Advaitin. Then he wrote *Naiṣkarmyasiddhi* highlighting the basic teachings of Śaṅkara. However, it is hardly convincing to the critics. They hold that Maṇḍana and Sureśvara are two different persons. If we accept the identity as given in the *Śaṅkaradigvijaya* of Vidyāraṇya, then Maṇḍana @ Śureśvara wrote *Vidhiviveka*.

Māṇḍūkya Upaniṣad (S) : This Upaniṣad contains the gist of all other Upaniṣads. It teaches that the *ātman* has four states. They are: (1) the waking state (*jāgṛt*); (2) the dream state (*svapna*); (3) the state of dreamless sleep state (*suṣupti*); and (4) its original pure state (*turīya*). In the waking state the *ātman* is directed towards external objects through the mind and senses. In this state, the *ātman* is called vaiśvānara. In the dream state, the *ātman* is turned inwards towards the dream objects. In this state only mind functions. In this state the *ātman* is called *taijasa*. In dreamless sleep, the *ātman* sees nothing and desires nothing. All plurality becomes one in it. In this state the *ātman* is called *prājña*. The fourth state is the *ātman* in its purity. It is beyond thought and speech.

Manichaeanism : It was a religious movement started by the Babylonian prophet Mani (216 – 77), "the apostle of God." It is considered to be a religion independent of Christianity. In other words, it was revivalism of Buddhism and Zoroastrianism. As a dualistic religion, Manichaeanism believed that life is a struggle between two individual principles, good and evil.

Manifold of Sense : This term was frequently used by Kant in his *Critique of Pure Reason* to signify various and discrete elements of sense-experience. The manifold of sense-data is presented to the mind which organizes it with the help of concepts.

Mannheim, Karl (1893 – 1947) : He was a Hungarian-born German social scientist known for his sociology of knowledge. He worked at Frankfurt as a Professor of Sociology, and then left for UK in 1933 to become the first Professor of Sociology of Education at the University of London in 1943. He was trained in Hegelian lines and had sufficient background in the fields such as sociology of culture, of political ideologies, of social organization, of education, and of knowledge. According to Mannheim, sociology of knowledge attempts to investigate the social causes of beliefs (doxa) as opposed to reasons people have for them. Such an investigation, held Mannheim, proved the impossibility of "objective" knowledge of society. His important works include: *Man and Society in an Age of Reconstruction* (1940) and *Ideology and Utopia* (original German edition in 1929 and English edition in 1936).

Mansel, Henry Longueville (1820 – 71) : He was a British philosopher and clergyman who defended Scottish common sense philosophy. He was a Professor of Philosophy and Ecclectic History at Oxford. He derived his inspiration from the writings of Kant as interpreted by Sir William Hamilton. He defined logic as a science of laws of thought, and metaphysics as a study about ultimate nature of things that goes beyond the finite human faculties. According to Mansel, God is rationally inconceivable and the only possible conception of God is an analogical one derived from revelation. Therefore, the religious dogma is immune to rational criticism. This view of Mansel was criticized by Herbert Spencer, T.H. Huxley, and J.S. Mill. The important works of Mansel include: *Prolegomena Logica* (1851); *Metaphysics* (1860); and *The Limits of Religious Thought* (1858).

Mantra (S) : It is a pious thought couched in repeated prayerful utterances for meditation or charm. Also the *mantras* are the poetic portion of the Veda.

Many Questions : It is an informal fallacy known as the fallacy of many questions or the fallacy of a complex question. This fallacy consists in requiring a single answer to a question that either involves several questions that ought to be answered separately or contains an implicit assertion to which any unqualified answer gives assent. The classical case is the question, when did you stop smoking? No matter how the respondent answers, yes, or no the respondent concedes the presuppositions that: (1) he has a habit of smoking; and (2) he has stopped smoking now. Even if the respondent is a non-smoker, the way in which the question is asked makes him admit that he was a smoker.

Many-valued Logic : It is a logic that does not admit of the principle of bivalence, namely, every proposition is either true or false. But, it rejects the principle of bivalence in two ways: one the truth-functional mode (many-valued logic proper), where propositions may take many values beyond simple truth or falsity, values functionally determined by the values of their components. The other mode is called truth-value gap mode in which the only values are truth or falsity, but propositions may have neither. What value they do or do not have is not determined by the values or lack of values of their constituents. The origins of many-valued logic are attributed to the works of Lucksiewicz and Post around 1920 wherein they developed truth-tables and semantic methods. Lukasiewicz derived his inspiration for his three-valued logic from the propositions whose truth-value was open or possible. Such propositions are mainly the propositions of future. He felt that they might take a third value. For instance, let 1 represent truth, 0 falsity, and the third value we say.

Mao Tse-tung (1893 – 1976) : He was a very famous Chinese communist leader and the founder of People's Republic of China in 1949. He tried to apply Marxian ideology to China. Unlike orthodox Marxism which emphasized the role of workers in building up any socialist or communist society, Mao organized peasants in the villages. He applied the dialectical materialism of Marx to the traditional Chinese culture. Finally he started the Cultural Revolution in China in 1967 which had its evil repercussions on Chinese society. His important works include: *On Practice* (1937) and *On New Democracy* (1940).

Marburg School : It was one of the trends of Neo-Kantianism started by the thinkers like Cohen, Natorp, Cassirer and Stammuler. They mainly made use of the method of "transcendental logic" of Kant to pursue the studies in philosophy of science.

Marcel, Gabriel (1889 – 1973) : He was a French philosopher, writer and chief exponent of Catholic existentialism. He held the membership of the Academy of Political and Social Science of the Institute of France. Marcel authored thirty plays and many philosophical essays. According to Marcel, science is basically concerned with the world of objects; while philosophy is concerned with the existential experience through which one can comprehend God. Marcel made a distinction between problem and mystery. He evolved an existentialist approach that can reflectively explain the nature of mysteries by providing depth and meaningfulness to human life. In one of his celebrated essays entitled: "On the Ontological Mystery," Marcel poses the questions such as, Who am I? — Is Being empty or full? He mainly concentrated on I-Thou encounters that include the issues such as inter-subjectivity, transcendence, interpersonal relations, commitment and creative fidelity. Marcel's existentialist philosophy balanced despair and hope, infidelity and fidelity, self-deception and spirit of truth. He held that freedom and fundamental attitudes influence one's way of being and the interpretation of the meaning of life. He bitterly criticized undisciplined view of morality. His important works include: *Creative Fidelity* (1940); *Homo Viator* (1945); and *Les Hommes Contre l'humain* (1951).

Marcus Aurelius (121 – 80) : He was a Roman Emperor and well-known philosopher. He was the author of Meditations that appeared in twelve books. Marcus Aurelius was chiefly interested in the philosophy of Stoicism. Most of his works were written when he was on military campaigns. Marcus Aurelius believed, following in the footsteps of Posidonius, who was an eclectic, that it is the moral duty of every individual to take part in public affairs. As a stoic, Marcus did not believe in the immortality of the soul, but held the view that happiness lies in patient acceptance of the will of the panentheistic Stoic God who is the material soul of a material universe. One of the important sayings of Marcus is, "It is a privilege of a human being to love even those who stumble."

Maritain, Jacques (1882 – 1973) : He was a French Catholic philosopher and a prominent neo-Thomist who gave a novel interpretation of Aquinas' philosophy. In fact, it was Henri Bergson's metaphysical despair that saved him from committing suicide. Later on he found the philosophy of Aquinas more convenient and rejected Bergson's philosophy to arrive at a realistic account of the concept and a unified theory of knowledge that incorporates the empirical sciences with the philosophy of nature, metaphysics, theology and mysticism. Maritain opposed both skepticism and idealism that separated mind from sensibility. His important works include: *Art and Scholasticism* (1920); *Distinguish to Unite or The Degrees of Knowledge* (1932); *Integral Humanism* (1936); and *Man and the State* (1961).

Marx, Karl (1818 – 83) : He was a German philosopher and a social theorist who advocated the philosophy of dialectical materialism. He was educated at the Universities of Bonn and Berlin. He received his doctoral degree in philosophy from the University of Berlin in 1841 for his thesis on *The Difference Between the Democritean and Epicurean Natural Philosophy*. Marx owes so much to Hegel and Feurbach. He applied the Hegelian dialectics to Feurbach's materialism to advocate a new philosophy that gives the socio-historical account of man, man's place in nature, and his interaction with nature to mould nature for his benefits. Young Marx attacked the religiously and politically conservative philosophy of Hegel which accommodated the very notions of private property and alienation. According to Marx, alienation or estrangement is of three types, namely, (1) the alienation among the individuals; (2) the alienation from their own labour; and (3) the alienation from the product of their own labour. In one of his principal works entitled *Das Kapital* (1867) Marx tried to provide a historical account of how economic and social conditions determined the various stages of human history. He held that these stages of social development ultimately culminate in communism which anticipates the withering away of the state. His important works include: *The German Ideology* (1846); *Communist Manifesto* (1848); and *Das Kapital* (1867).

Marxist-Leninism : It is a variant of Marxism associated with the thought of V.I. Lenin. One of the important precepts of this philosophy is that the masses must be led by a select cadre of highly disciplined revolutionaries (vanguards).

Mass Noun : It is a term that refers to an uncountable thing or an object. For instance, there are cans of oil in that room. The cans that contain oil can be counted, but oil cannot be counted. Here "oil" is a mass noun.

Material Cause : In Aristotle's theory of causation, material cause is considered to be a factor in the explanation of the thing being as it is.

Materialism : It is an ontological view according to which matter is primary and thought or spirit is secondary or derivative. One of the most ancient forms of materialism in the form of atomism was advocated by Leucippus and Democritus. According to them, the natural processes can be explained in terms of arrangement and rearrangement of atoms that are supposed to be the minute particles of matter. There are various forms of materialism. Vulgar materialism is a simplified doctrine. The advocates of this doctrine claim that thought is a material secretion of the brain. Mechanistic materialism tries to interpret natural phenomena in terms of mechanical motion of elementary particles called atoms. Dialectical materialism explains the natural processes in terms of laws of dialectics such as unity and diversity of opposite forces, the transformation of quantity into quality, and the law of negation of negation.

Materialism, Reductive : According to this thesis, everything in this universe can ultimately be explained, including consciousness, in terms of matter in motion.

Materialization : Sometimes it is also known as concretization, individuation, particularization, and actualization. This expression refers to the process of the individuation of prime matter into a particular form.

Materially : In scholasticism, a predicate is said to belong to a subject materially when it belongs to it by reason of its matter or subject, but formally when it belongs to it by reason of its form. For example, fire is materially destructive, but formally warm.

Material Mode of Speech : This expression was first introduced by Rudolf Carnap based upon his distinction between "object sentence" and "syntactical sentences." A sentence is syntactical if it can be translated into another sentence of the same language that refers to signs or formal properties and relations between signs. All non-syntactical sentences are said to be object sentences. In a natural language such as English, the formal properties of a sentence may indicate that it is an object-sentence when it is in fact syntactical. Such a sentence is expressed in the material mode of speech.

Mathematics : The traditional meaning of the subject is that it is "the science of quantity" or "the science of discrete and continuous magnitude." But, modern mathematicians do not subscribe to this definition as mathematics is a single connected whole which includes a number of branches. According to a view, which is widely held by mathematicians, it is characteristic of mathematics as a branch of knowledge that it starts with a set of undefined elements, properties, functions, and relations; and a set of unproved or indubitable propositions called axioms. From these axioms are derived theorems by using the methods of formal logic. Also, it is viewed that mathematics can be reduced to logic. The doctrine that the concepts of mathematics are empirical in nature, and its postulates are elementary experimental truths is held by the philosophers like J.S. Mill, H. Helmholtz, M. Pasch, and others. However, the contemporary mathematicians hold that the propositions of mathematics do not say anything about empirical reality. Thus, they are tautologies. Ludwig Wittgenstein characterized the propositions of mathematics as the scaffoldings of reality in his *Tractatus Logico-Philosophicus*. Kant held that the judgements of mathematics are synthetic a priori. They are the most genuine of all the judgements.

Mathesis Universalis (L) : It means "universal mathematics." One major objective of Leibniz's programme for logic was to develop universal mathematics or universal calculus for manipulating the universal language by means of deductions. Leibniz thought that the universal language could be constructed on the basis of relatively few simpler terms. Such language would be of immense value to scientists and philosophers in reasoning as well as in communication. The development of symbolic logic can be traced back to Leibniz's conception of universal mathematics.

Matter : It is something that is traditionally contrasted either with spirit or form. In the philosophy of Plato, matter and form are two different things. But Aristotle rectified this mistake of Plato by holding that matterless form or formless matter is an absurdity. Coming to Descartes, he separated matter from mind. According to him, matter can exist independent of mind, while mind can exist independent of matter. Modern scientists conceived that matter is the primordial stuff from which everything has ultimately emerged. What we call atoms are the smallest particles of matter. One of the chief attributes of matter is extension.

Matter, Prime : It is the matter in its pure potentiality devoid of any properties or characteristics. If at all it has any property means it is not having any property.

Maxim, Ethical : An ethical maxim is any rule of conduct that ought to be followed by any individual as a moral agent as a good guide for action. For instance, Descartes' maxim is to try always to conquer himself rather than fortune. According to Kant, every voluntary act proceeds according to a maxim or "subjective principle of action."

Māyā (S) : It means "illusion or cosmic illusion." According to Advaita Vedānta, *māyā* is *anādi* because we do not know when it came into existence, and *anirvacanīya* because it is neither real nor unreal. It is *sadasat-vilakṣaṇa*. It is a *bhāva-padārtha*. *Māyā* has two important powers. They are the power of concealment (*āvaraṇa-śakti*), and power of projection (*vikṣepa-śakti*). With its power of concealment it conceals the very nature of *Brahman*, and with its power of projection it projects *Brahman* as something other than what it is. Īśvara or God or *saguṇa Brahman* is the projection of *Brahman* in association with *māyā*. The latter is only an appearance, while the former is the reality. Radhakrishnan interpreted the term *māyā* in the following manner. (1) *Māyā* represents the phenomenal character of the world of forms. The world of forms is not self-explanatory. Therefore, it is phenomenal in its nature. (2) The inexplicable relation between the world of forms and *Brahman* is the result of *māyā*, for the world of forms and *Brahman* are heterogeneous in their nature and every attempt to explain the relation between them would be an absurdity. (3) *Brahman* is treated as the cause or the creator of the world only in the sense that *Brahman* is the ground for everything. Therefore, the world is grounded in *Brahman*, but it does not affect the very nature of *Brahman*. The world grounded in *Brahman* is called *māyā*. (4) The appearance of *Brahman* as the world is also explained in terms of *māyā*. (5) The employment of the dialectical logic to prove the self-contradictory nature of the world of forms leads us to the conception of a perfect personality, Īśvara, who is capable of self-expression. The capacity or power of self-expression is called *māyā*. (6) The energy of Īśvara transforms into various adjuncts (*upādhis*) from which all existence comes forth. This energy is the unmanifested matter (*avyakta prakṛti*). It is called *māyā*.

McTaggart, John McTaggart Ellis (1866 – 1925) : He was a British idealist philosopher who held the view that the time is unreal. According to him, reality is essentially spiritual. He was influenced by Hegelian idealism. He denied the existence of God. According to McTaggart, matter, space, and time are mere appearances. However, he defended the theory of individual immortality. His important works include: *Studies in Hegelian Dialictic* (1896); *Studies in Hegelian Cosmology* (1901); *A Commentary on Hegel's Logic* (1910); and *The Nature of Existence* (2 vols., 1921 & 1927).

Mead, George Herbert (1863 – 1931) : He was a Professor of philosophy at Chicago University. He was recognized as one of the leading followers of John Dewey. Mead was often referred to as a social behaviourist, for he employed the categories of stimulus and response in order to explain human behaviour. He examined the nature of self-consciousness whose development is reflected in mind, self, and society. His important posthumous works include: *Philosophy of the Present* (1932); *Mind, Self, and Society* (1934); *Movements of Thought in Nineteenth Century* (1936); and *The Philosophy of the Act* (1938).

Mean, the Golden : This expression is used by Aristotle. It is an ethical principle according to which virtue consists in following a course of action somewhere between the extreme of too much (excess), and the extreme of too little (defect). The mean is not absolute centre point, but can be shifted and adjusted.

Meaning : There are various theories of meaning whose main aim is to explore the various possibilities of understanding of words, concepts, sentences, statements, etc. According to verification theory of meaning, a sentence is meaningful if and only if it is empirically verifiable. This theory was advocated by logical positivists. Use theory of meaning maintains that the meaning of a word is the context in which it is actually used. This is the theory advocated by later Wittgenstein. Picture theory of meaning advocated by early Wittgenstein maintains that the meaning of a word is derived from what is pictured in reality. Meaning is often concerned with the semantic notions such as reference and truth. We talk of word meaning and sentence meaning.

Meaning, Cognitive : It refers to those statements that give information and claim that information as true or false.

Meaning as Naming : According to this view, the meaning of a statement is the object named by it. Both Russell and early Wittgenstein subscribed to this theory.

Meaning as Usage : According to this theory, the meaning of any expression consists in the way in which the language is used by a speaker in a particular context. Also, it partly depends upon the behaviour of the speaker in that context. Later Wittgenstein expounded this theory in his Philosophical Investigations (1953).

Mechanism : It is a philosophical point of view popularized by Descartes. He chose to call his science mechanics on the ground that his science takes into account the sizes, shapes, and motions to explain any physical process. Thus he ignores the real qualities of the objects. According to Descartes, there is no matter in corporeal bodies other than the aspects required for quantitative analysis. In the process of identifying quantifiables in corporeal bodies, mechanism refutes Aristotle's conception that "final causes" as the purpose or the end does not find any place in scientific investigation. Mechanism maintains that a genuine scientific endeavour aims at the search for mechanical models.

Mediation : It is a term used by Hegel to designate a dialectical unity between mutually interdependent and opposed terms.

Meinong, Alexius Von (1853 – 1920) : He was an Austrian philosopher, logician and psychologist studied under Franz Brentano. Meinong held the view that the thinking consists of three important aspects, namely, mental act, its content, and its object. According to Meinong, objects have two types of existence. Some have objective existence like chairs, tables, and some have mere subjective existence like gold mountains, winged-horses. Such objects are called ideal objects. Thus there are two types of existence. The *sein* of material objects and the *sosein* of ideal objects. As a matter of fact, Meinong's object theory is based on Brentano's version of immanent intentionality thesis, according to which every psychological state contains an intended object towards which the mental act or event is semantically directed. Meinong's idea of ideal or non-existent objects has been attacked by Russell in his celebrated article "On Denoting" published in 1905. The important works of Meinong include: *On Assumptions* (1902) and *Uber Annahmen* (1907).

Meliorism : It is the view that the world is neither completely evil nor completely good, but there is a scope for changing the relative amounts of good and evil. Human effort is capable of improving the living conditions of the humans in this world. This term was first introduced by George Eliot and later on advocated by William James in his philosophy of pragmatism.

Melissus of Samos (C. 450 BCE) : He was the one who advanced a positive proof of the Eleatic doctrine of being as one and eternal, motionless and without change. According to him, the senses are untrustworthy as they often deceive us.

Memory : It is a process of recapitulation by which certain events or incidents of the past or immediate past can be brought to the notice of mind. Often memory serves as a source of knowledge, though epistemologists do not rely on memory as every claim to knowledge by means of memory needs to be justified. Skeptics outrightly reject the claims of memory. From the viewpoint of biology, memory is a sum total of mental models constructed by human mind. It is connected with the process of thinking. Thus memory serves as a feedback for a definite mental activity. In artificial intelligence, memory of a system plays a key role.

Mencius (C. 371 – 289 BCE) : He was also known as Meng-tzu, Meng K'O. He was a native of Tsao in present Shatung. He studied under Tzu Ssu, the grandson of Confucius. Mencius is regarded as the greatest Confucian in Chinese history. He held that human nature is basically good. Perhaps what he meant by that is that human nature is good if only the natural development of humans is unimpeded. According to him every human being has four hearts or sprouts. They are: (1) benevolence (*jen*); (2) righteousness (*yi*); (3) ritual propriety (*li*); and (4) wisdom (*chih*). He believed that although humans can cultivate themselves, there is possibility of environmental effect on their moral development. This effect may be positive or negative. He always suggested to the rulers to create such social conditions that would promote social virtue.

Mentalism : It is a metaphysical theory according to which minds and their subjective states alone are real. This theory is akin to idealist theories. The subjective-idealism of Berkeley comes under this category.

Merleau-Ponty, Maurice (1908 – 1961) : He was a French philosopher who tried to establish some relationship between the consciousness and the world in which we live by rejecting the dualistic conception of mind and body. He conceived that the objects of one's own experience are enigmatic. His existential phenomenology is opposed to the dualism of Descartes. He rejected Sartre's existential dualism between being-in-itself and being-for-itself which is akin to the dualism between matter and mind. All our enquiries, according to Merleau-Ponty, must be based on a descriptive account of our perceptual experiences. Thus he tried to set aside the distinction between "inner" and "outer." In his *magnum opus, The Phenomenology of Perception* (1945), he developed a kind of psychology of perception that highlights the role of the body in perceptual experience. He was a bitter critic of sense-datum theory.

Mesmerism : It is a term coined from the name of F. Mesmer (1734 – 1815) to refer to hypnotic phenomena.

Meta-ethics : It is the study of the characteristics (nature of) ethics in general. This study includes the analysis of the methods, language, logical structure, and reasoning used to arrive at and justify moral decisions and knowledge.

Meta-language : It is the language that is used in the description of object language and its concepts. For example; the discussion on the rules of any language is possible only through meta-language. The rules of the language in question become object language and the language used to describe such rules is called meta-language. In formal logic, any uninterrupted formal language is considered to be object language. Sometimes it so happens that both object language and meta-language are the same natural language. In such a situation, one must be circumspect enough to distinguish the words of meta-language from those of object language. Let us say that "Four is a number word." Here the word "four" is considered to be the word of object language, and the "number word" is a meta-linguistic expression.

Meta-logical : Anything that is based on logic is called meta-logical. The meta-logical truths are the laws of thought, the formal conditions of thinking in reason.

Metaphor : Metaphors consist of primary and secondary terms. The primary term of a metaphor refers to the thing that is described; while the secondary term is the description given to the thing being described.

Metaphysics : The term "metaphysics" is derived from the Greek term "meta-ta-phusica," meaning "beyond physical existence." This term was first introduced by Aristotle to philosophy. According to him, it is a science of "first principles." Thus it is also known as "First Philosophy." Its main task is to investigate the first principles of whatever exists. But in the modern period, metaphysics is treated as a science or a doctrine that deals with the ultimate status of reality. However, some contemporary philosophers have gone a step forward to say that metaphysics deals with supersensible reality. There are two important types of metaphysics, namely, transcendental and immanent. Transcendentalists believe that ultimate reality transcends the limits of all empirical experience, while immanent metaphysician holds that ultimate reality is an all-pervading principle. It is omnipresent. Some philosophers hold that ontology is part and parcel of metaphysics. If metaphysics deals with the abstract principles, ontology deals with the relation of those principles to the material world. Anti-metaphysicians do not consider metaphysics as a genuine branch of philosophy. See Comte, and Logical Positivism.

Metempsychosis : It is a view that is prevalent in oriental religions that our souls lived in other bodies earlier. It is also known as the transmigration of soul. According to the deeds of an individual, the soul transmigrates into a human or a non-human body.

Method : It can be explained in the following ways. (1) It is a procedure employed to attain certain end. (2) It is a process of employing knowing techniques to acquire the knowledge of a given subject matter. And (3) It is a science that formulates the rules of any procedure.

Methodic Doubt : It was employed by Descartes to arrive at the foundation of philosophy, namely, *cogito-ergo-sum*. It can also be interpreted as the suspension of judgement with regard to possible truths until they are demonstrated to be either true or false.

Method of Concomitant Variation : It is one of the logical methods advocated by J.S. Mill. A phenomenon may vary in any manner whenever another phenomenon varies in a specified manner. Then the phenomenon that varies under a specific manner or a circumstance may be regarded as a cause or an effect, or it is somehow linked up with the phenomenon that varies in any manner through some fact of causation.

Method of Simple Enumeration : It is an inductive process by means of which the initial probability of a generalization is increased by more instances exactly the same as those previously observed.

Method of Trial and Error : It is a method of solving a problem by putting any given hypothesis to direct test in actuality rather than by considering them imaginatively in terms of foreseen consequences.

Methodology : It is a study of methods. The chief objective of methodology is to elucidate merits and demerits of various methods, and their applications to different disciplines. Without a proper theoretical foundation of methods, sciences cannot progress.

Middle Term : It is one of the three terms in a categorical syllogism. Since this term appears in both the premisses, Aristotle called it middle term. See the following example:

All men are mortal.

Socrates is a man.

Therefore, Socrates is mortal.

In the above-mentioned syllogism, the term "man" appeared in both the premisses; hence it is the middle term.

Mill, James (1773 – 1836) : He was the father of John Stuart Mill, and a very close associate of Jeremy Bentham as a member of utilitarian school. He was a philosophical radical. James Mill contributed a great lot to psychology in the form of associationism. His important works include: *Elements of Political Economy* (1821) and *Analysis of the Phenomena of the Human Mind* (1929).

Mill, John Stuart (1806 – 73) : He was a British philosopher, moralist, and an empiricist who is considered to be the champion of inductivism. Mill in his *System of Logic* (1843) has made a sharp distinction between general and singular terms, between concrete and abstract terms, and between connotation and denotation. According to Mill, general terms are those refer to a group of things (e.g. crow). Singular terms are those which refer to a particular individual or an object (e.g. Plato). On the other hand concrete terms are those that refer to the most general objects (e.g. man, white). Abstract terms are those refer to abstract qualities like "humanity," "cowness," etc. In ethics, Mill advocated utilitarianism. But unlike Bentham, Mill stressed on the qualitative aspect of the pleasure. His important works include: *Principles of Political Economy* (1848); *On Liberty* (1859); and *On Utilitarianism* (1863).

Millet Seed Paradox : It is a paradox highlighted by Zeno of Elea. It is also known as heap. According to him, when a single millet seed does not make any sound when it is dropped on the ground, how come 1000 millet seeds make sound when they are dropped together on the ground? Zeno feels that it is highly nonsensical to think that 1000 nothings make sound.

Mīmāṁsā (S) : Originally Mīmāṁsā means "investigation" or "inquiry." This school was founded by the great seer and sage Jaimini, who was the author of *Mīmāṁsā-Sūtra*. This school of thought is also known as Pūrva-Mīmāṁsā or Karma-Mīmāṁsā. The objective of Mīmāṁsā school is to establish the authority of the Veda. It is essentially a book of principles of textual interpretation to establish the purport of the Vedas which is, according to Jaimini, ritualistic. Śabarasvāmin wrote a commentary on Jaimini's *Mīmāṁsā-Sūtra*. This commentary has been further explained by Kumārila and Prabhākara. Kumārila's work is divided into three important parts, namely, *Ślokavārttika*, *Tantravārttika*, and *Ṭupṭīkā*. Prbhākara's commentary is known as *Bṛhati*. As regards the sources of knowledge, Kumārila admits six sources (*pramāṇa*s). They are: (1) *pratyakṣa*, (2) *anumāna*, (3) *śabda*, (4) *upamāna*, (5) *arthāpatti*, and (6) *anupalabdhi*. Both Kumārila and Prabhākara hold that knowledge by itself is a *pramāṇa*. Of the above six *pramāṇa*s, Prabhākara admits the first five. Negation cannot be treated as independent *pramāṇa* for it is dependent on *pratyakṣa* or *anumāna*. Kumārila's theory of error is called *viparīta khyāti*, and Prabhākara's *akhyāti*. According to Mīmāṁsā, *dharma* is *karma*. *Adharma* is demerit or non-performance of action. It is the supreme duty, the "ought" or "categorical imperative." Action being the final import of the Veda, every individual must plunge into action. There are three important *karma*s recognized by Mīmāṁsā. They are: (1) Obligatory actions are those that have to be performed by every individual. Their performance supports man, society, and the universe. The non-performance of these actions is called *adharma* or demerit. (2) Occasional actions which are to be performed on account of some specific occasion such as eclipse. These are also obligatory in nature, while performing these there is no gain of merit but not doing so invites demerit. (3) These actions are only optional. The injunctions regarding these actions are concerned with particular aims of the agent. If one wants to be the king of heaven, he has to perform a certain type of sacrifice. The *karma*s or actions associated with the black magic are discouraged by Mīmāṁsā. The reality of *ātman* is accepted by Mīmāṁsā as distinct from mind (*manas*), senses and physical body.

Mind : This term is understood in two different senses. (1) The individual mind is the self or subject which perceives, remembers, thinks, wills, feels, reasons, etc. and which is functionally related to an individual bodily organism. (2) Mind is considered to be a spiritual or metaphysical substance that pervades all individual minds and is often contrasted with material substance. See Descartes.

Mind-body Problem : An incisive analysis of mind-body problem was first given by René Descartes. According to Descartes, the mind can exist independent of the body, and the body can exist independent of the mind. The important attribute of mind is consciousness, whereas the important attribute of body is extension. Descartes felt that there is interaction between mind and body. Such an interaction between mind and body is possible in the pineal gland of the human body. However, critics questioned Descartes for holding such a view. They argued as to how an extended thing can interact with a non-extended thing (mind)? The alternative suggested to this mind-body problem by Spinoza is psychophysical parallelism. According to this theory, the nature of an object is expressed in two different languages, namely, physical and mental. Thus there is a kind of parallelism between mind and body. Opposing these two views, philosophers like Malebranche introduced occasionalism. This theory holds that God finds an occasion to bring some kind of causal connection between mind and body. Modern philosophers do not agree with the Cartesian dualism. They argue that a person is a combination of both mind and body. See Strawson, and Wittgenstein.

Mind, Disembodied : It is the mind that continues to possess mental qualities such as feeling, thinking, perceiving, and willing without being in a body.

Mind-dust Theory : It is a theory that individual minds result from the combination of the particles of mind that have existed in association with material atoms. Its rival thesis is known as emergent evolution that assumes that mind is a novel emergent in the process of biological evolution.

Mind-stuff Theory : It is a theory according to which the individual minds are constituted of psychic particles analogous to physical atoms. This theory differs from mind-dust theory in its emphasis on the constitution rather than the genesis of mind.

Minor Arts : These arts are empirically distinguished from sculpture and painting. They are: jewellery, miniature, textiles, pottery, etc.

Minor Premise : In a categorical syllogism the premise in which the minor term occurs is called a minor premise. For example: the syllogism consists of the following premisses.

All men are mortal.

Socrates is a man.

Therefore, Socrates is mortal.

In this syllogism, "Socrates" (subject of the conclusion) is a minor term. Then the premise "Socrates is a man" is a minor premise.

Minor Term : The subject term that occurs in the conclusion of a categorical syllogism is called a minor term. For instance, the syllogism consists of the following premisses and conclusion:

> All men are mortal.
>
> Socrates is a man.
>
> Therefore, Socrates is mortal.

In this syllogism, the conclusion "Socrates is mortal" consists of the subject term "Socrates." This subject term is called minor term.

Miracle : It is a term popularly used in religious language. Miracle often discredits a belief. A miracle in this sense is inexplicable. Religious beliefs are often strengthened by miracles.

Miraculous Doctor : It is the traditional nickname given to Roger Bacon.

Misology : It is an expression used to refer to any contempt for logic.

Mnemonics : It is an arbitrary framework or device for assisting the memory. It is opposed to logically valid moods and figures of a syllogism.

Modalism : It is a theological doctrine of the second and the third centuries CE that affirms the unity of substance and personality in God. The Son and the Holy Spirit are but "modes" of God the father. It is also known as monarchism. The adherents of this position are Patripassians.

Modality : Modality is a way in which a sentence characterizes another related sentence or proposition as true. Modal logic is basically concerned with logical modalities. For example: the *de dicto* claim is attached to a thing as a whole. In this sense, it is a necessity concerning its metaphysical aspects, while *de re* claim is concerned with a property of a thing. In this sense, it is an ontological necessity.

Mode : This term is derived from the Latin term "modus." It was John Locke who distinguished simple modes from mixed modes. The simple mode of an idea is a simple way of thinking of an idea, for example: "red," "hot," etc. Mixed modes are those basically required in a moral discourse. They are conglomeration of various simple ideas arranged at the pleasure of the mind. For example, murder, glory, etc.

Mode, Formal : The formal mode statements are those statements that are concerned with the words themselves. For example, "Man is a noun," "Man is a three-letter word," and so on.

Mode, Material : The material mode statements are those statements that are concerned with things. For example, "Fish live in water," "Chairs are meant for sitting," and so on.

Modus Intelligibilis (L) : It means "intelligible world." It refers to Plato's world of Forms or Ideas which serve as the models for the imperfect existence in the world of becoming.

Modus Ponens (L) : It means "the mood that affirms something." For example: if p then q. In other words, q therefore p. It is shown in the following way:

$$\begin{array}{l} p \supset q \\ p \\ \hline \therefore q \\ \hline \end{array}$$

Modus Tollens (L) : It means "the mood that denies something." For example: if p, then q. But *not-q*, therefore *not-p*. This is shown in the following way:

$$\begin{array}{r} p \supset q \\ \sim q \\ \hline \therefore \sim p \\ \hline \end{array}$$

Moha (S) : It is a kind of attachment to the phenomenal things that results in detraction, perplexity, delusion, and beclouding of the mind.

Monad : In Greek monad means "number one." In fact, it was Bruno who named his metaphysical units monads to distinguish them from the Democritean atoms. He held that they are the centres of the world life. Later on the term "monad" was used by Leibniz to denote those metaphysical (spiritual) entities that constitute reality. Most probably, he borrowed this expression from Augustine or Bruno or protestant Scholastics. According to Leibniz, monads do not have any extension. In the place of extension they have force. They are windowless. Each monad by itself is a tiny universe. Monads have *appetition* and *perception*. There are higher, lower and bare monads. God is the highest monad who is responsible for the pre-established harmony among the monads. See Leibniz.

Monism : It is a metaphysical theory, according to which there is only one substance. For example; materialists believe that matter is the only reality. Similarly, idealists believe that idea or spirit is the only reality. In that sense both materialists and idealists are monists. There is another peculiar system called type monism. For example, in the philosophy of Leibniz, monads are supposed to be the ultimate constituents of reality. Though there are innumerable monads, they all belong to one category in the sense that they share essential features. Thus Leibniz's metaphysics is an example for type monism. Similar is the case with David Hume. The ultimate constituents of reality are sense-impressions. But all of them belong to one type.

Monism, Neutral : According to this doctrine, the ultimate stuff from which the world is constituted is neither mental nor material. It is called neutral stuff. For instance, Hume regarded his sense-impressions neutral stuff.

Monotheism : It is a religious doctrine, according to which there is only one God. For example, there is only one God in Heaven for Christians; and Allah is the only God for Muslims.

Montaigne, Michel De (1533 – 92) : He was a French humanist and novelist. His essays are famous for his tolerant study of himself and through himself of mankind as a whole. He doubted the possibility of certain knowledge and recommended a return to nature and revelation. He was a keen observer of human frailities. His sceptical philosophy was first set out in his essay, "Apologie de Raimond Sebon" (1580).

Montesquieu, Charles De Secondat (1689 – 1755) : He was a well-known French historian, jurist, and writer. In his celebrated work *De l'esprit deslois* (1748) he classified the various forms of government not on the basis of the location of the power but on that of the "animating principle." He held that virtue is the principle of republics, honour of monarchies, and fear of despotism. He suggested that the legislative, executive, and judicial powers should be given to independently acting bodies. This theory of separation helped the founding fathers of the American Republic.

Mood : A mode is one of the various ways in which valid syllogisms can be constructed within the four figures of categorical syllogism. The valid syllogisms in each figure are called moods of that figure.

Moore, George Edward (1873 – 1958) : He was a well-known British analytical philosopher who advocated sense-datum theory. Though Moore accepted the existence of physical objects independent of a perceiver's mind, he held the view that all that we perceive in sense-experience are sense-data but not material objects. Moore was very critical of Berkeley's subjective idealism in his famous essay "The Refutation of Idealism" (1903). Moore's analysis is known as realism and analysis. According to Moore, philosophy must analyse our talk about the world. Thus he comes under the category of world analysts. Like Russell, he too was influenced by Platonic realism at one time, but he abandoned it for it could not fit into his philosophy of common sense. In ethics, he highlighted a fallacy called "naturalistic fallacy." According to this fallacy, we tend to ascribe certain qualities as natural to the objects. For example, good is not a natural property of anything. He conceived that "good" is indefinable inasmuch as it is unanalysable. But "the good" is definable. His important works include: *Principia Ethica* (1903); *Ethics* (1912); *Philosophical Studies* (1922); *Some Main Problems of Philosophy* (1953), etc.

Moral : It is a term opposed to immoral or amoral. Ethics is a branch of study that deals with moral concepts. Of late, it has become a convention to use the expression "moral" for individual morality, and the expression "ethics" to social morality.

Moral Law : According to Kant, it is the formula that expresses the necessity of an action done from duty in terms of one's own reflection.

Mortalist : A mortalist is a person who believes that when one dies that is the end of it. There is no question of survival.

Motion : It is a chief attribute and a mode of existence of all matter. Motion denotes change in reality. The motion of matter is absolute, whereas the rest is relative. In one sense, we are under constant motion as the earth moves round the sun.

Mukti (S) : It means "liberation" or "salvation." There are two types of *mukti*, namely, *jīvan-mukti* and *videha-mukti*. In the case of the former, a person gets liberated while he is alive; whereas in the case of the latter a person gets liberated only after his death. Advaita Vedānta subsribes to the concept of *jīvan-mukti*.

Multiplicity, Doctrine of : According to this doctrine, the universe consists of a variety of things that can never be reduced to a Unity or a One.

Mundus Intelligibilis (L) : According to Plato, the world of intelligible realities refers to the world of Forms or Ideas or Concepts that are eternal.

Mundus Sensibilis (L) : It means "the world of sensibles." This expression refers to the objects perceived by our senses that are the imperfect copies of the realm of perfect Forms. For details see Plato.

Muṇḍaka Upaniṣad (S) : This Upaniṣad distinguishes higher knowledge from the lower. The former is the knowledge of *Brahman*, while the latter is the knowledge of empirical sciences, arts, the Vedas and their subsidiaries. The *ātman* (*puruṣa*) throws out the world out of itself and withdraws it again into itself. The life of action belongs to the world of ignorance. The *ātman* cannot be known by study or intellect. It can be grasped only by him who is chosen by it.

Muni (S) : It means a "sage." A *muni* is one who remains in a constant state of contemplation on reality.

Mystical Experience : It is a state of union with higher reality that can never be expressed in terms of language. The mystic experience can also be a state of pure overwhelming feeling.

Mysticism : It is a religious viewpoint, according to which certain experiences are mystical in the sense that they cannot be described. Mysticism denies any possibility of approaching the ineffable, transcendental reality by any rational means. The knowledge of such a reality is possible only through some special, non-rational means, and such knowledge is incommunicable.

Myth of the Er : In the concluding chapter of Plato's *Republic* there is some discussion devoted to the study of the fate of the souls after death, and the choices available for them before reincarnation. This is known as the myth of the Er.

Mythical Thinking : It is a kind of pre-rational thinking. In this state human mind casts its perceptions of reality in the form of artistic intuition and imagery.

Mythology : It is a view of reality that is often characterized as primitive. Myths were narratives born in the early stages of history when there was not much scientific explanation for certain happenings in this reality. Of late, myth is used as a term that denotes a kind of unwarranted belief in something.

N

Nagel, Ernest (1901 – 85) : He was a Czech-born American philosopher, who was chiefly interested in logic and philosophy of science. Nagel shared with Russell and the philosophers of Vienna Circle the issues related to mathematics, logic, and probability theory. He was committed to contextualist naturalism. His contextualism is reflected in his contention that ideas of determinism, probability, explanation, and reduction can be discussed only in the light of a given theory or formulation, but on the basis of their subject matter. His important works include: *An Introduction of Logic and Scientific Method* (1934) co-authored with his teacher M.R. Cohen, *Principles of the Theory of Probability* (1939); and *The Structure of Science* (1960).

Naïve Realism : It is called by Wilfred Sellars "direct realism." According to this doctrine, we can perceive the features of objects directly. Like any other realist, a naïve realist believes in the existence of eternal world and the ability to know it. Sense-datum philosophers such as Russell, Price, and Ayer attacked this position in their theories of perception.

Nāma and Rūpa (S) : According to Advaita Vedānta, only the empirical objects have name and form. *Nāma* and *rūpa* are necessary for the identification of empirical objects.

Name : It is a linguistic expression that denotes a particular object or a quality. Proper names are the names given to the objects, qualities, persons, etc. For example, Ram, Ganga, etc. are the names of persons.

Nāstika (S) : A system is called *nāstika* or unorthodox in Indian tradition when it does not accept the authority of the Veda. They are Cārvāka, Jainism, and Buddhism.

Nativism : It is a thesis according to which mind has certain elements of knowledge that are not derived from sense-experience. This view is akin to the common sense view advocated by Thomas Reid (1710 – 96).

Natura naturans (L) : It is the active creative nature that is responsible for all that exists. For Spinoza, *Natura naturans* is a causal agent of modes and attributes.

Natura naturata (L) : This expression was used by Benedict Spinoza to refer to the things created in nature. In other words, it is the reality created by *Natura naturans*.

Natural Language : The languages such as English, Hindi, Russian, etc., are called natural languages. They are different from the artificial languages like Esperanto and Ido.

Natural Theology : It is an attempt to prove the existence of God, and human immortality by means of observation of ordinary course of nature.

Naturalism : It has different connotations in philosophy. One interpretation of naturalism is that it is a view that naturalism desists from any reference to supernatural principle while explaining the processes of reality in terms of natural processes, which in turn can be explained in terms of scientifically verifiable concepts. In another sense, naturalism denies all possible differences between human and animal behaviour. According to this view, human conduct and social institutions are more complex patterns of behaviour than that of lower organisms. Naturalism does not believe in immortality, reincarnation and, transmigration. The universe has its own structure and originates in its own structure. There are no unnatural causes responsible for its existence.

Naturalism, Critical : It is one of the forms of naturalism according to which mere mechanical or materialistic interpretations of reality are not sufficient to understand reality. Mind, life, and values are other factors that form part of reality, and they cannot be interpreted in terms of matter in motion.

Naturalism, Ethical : According to this doctrine, there is no watertight distinction between facts about the world and judgements about the world, and how humans ought to act in it. Moral evaluations contain facts about natural phenomena.

Naturalistic Fallacy : It is a fallacy often committed by ascribing natural status to certain properties. It was G.E. Moore who highlighted this fallacy in his work *Principia Ethica* (1903). According to him, the properties like good, bad, ugly, etc. are not considered to be natural properties of the objects.

Nature : It is the phenomenal world in which humans are part and parcel of the endless diversity of its manifestations. Nature is considered to be the objective reality existing independent of perceiving mind. According to some interpretations, nature is God's creation. But some interpretations say that nature has no beginning. Some interpretations try to show that nature is the product of evolution, and is governed by certain inherent laws.

Necessary Condition : In opposition to sufficient condition, a necessary condition is one of the conditions of the cause of a given phenomenon or event. For example, soil, sunlight, water, air, and manure are all necessary conditions for a proper growth of a tree. None of them by itself becomes a sufficient condition.

Necessitarianism : It is a theory according to which all events in the universe are determined by causes, and these causes are necessitated to happen. This expression is used as a synonym to pre-determinism.

Necessity and Chance : These are two important philosophical categories. They reflect the essence and the manifestations of the phenomena. Necessity operates through laws, while chance may or may not occur. A chance may take any form. In logic, necessity represents universality and certainty.

Negation : It is a form of logical operation with the help of which a new proposition is deduced from a given proposition. If a given proposition is true, then its negation is false and vice versa.

Negation of the Negation, law of : It is one of the laws of dialectics, according to which a particular theory or a paradigm is not completely annihilated or negated by a new one, but some of the essential features of an old theory or a paradigm are assimilated into the new.

Neo-Freudianism : It is a viewpoint in philosophy that studies man, his place and role in the structure of social institutions by means of psychoanalysis advocated by Freud. Neo-Freudianism attacks the modern Western society where man loses his uniqueness, and alienates from the external world and from himself. The remedy for such forms of human alienation is psychoanalysis which arouses critical elements in man's consciousness and transforms his life, values and ideals for a better future.

Neo-Hegelianism : This school of thought flourished under the patronage of T.H. Green, F.H. Bradley, J. Royce, and M. McTaggart. Neo-Hegelianism limits its application to the consciousness alone. Its main objective is to defend religion and speculative philosophy.

Neo-Kantianism : It is a philosophical trend that reproduces and develops the idealist and metaphysical elements in the philosophy of Immanuel Kant. It completely ignores the dialectical and materialist elements in Kant's philosophy. The "thing-in-itself" is either discarded completely or reinterpreted according to idealist notions. The Marburg school philosophers like Cohen and Cassirer. have applied Kant's doctrine of "transcendental analytic" to various concepts of philosophy of science. Neo-Kantianism has exerted considerable influence on the trends of axiology.

Neologist : A person who introduces a new word or a meaning into a language or discipline is called a neologist. In theology, a neologist is one who introduces a new doctrine that is contrary to an established one.

Neo-Platonism : According to neo-Platonism, matter is the lowest link in the hierarchy of the universe. Neo-Platonic school was founded by Plotinus. The idealistic doctrines of Plato have been transformed into theosophy. As such Neo-Platonism was against Christianity. It incorporated numerous elements of Oriental magic and mythology. It was also considered to be a link between ancient and medieval thought.

Neo-positivism : It is one of the twentieth century trends in philosophy that claims that the sole function of philosophy is the logical analysis of language. Logical positivism is the most influential form of neo-Positivism. Its main objectives are to eliminate metaphysics from philosophy in order to make philosophy a genuine branch of knowledge, and to analyse the concepts of everyday language and of science. According to neo-Positivists, ethical pronouncements are mere exhortations to moral virtue. Strictly speaking, they do not convey any meaning.

Neo-Protestantism : It is a trend in modern theology that vehemently opposed the liberal Christianity and counter-posed the Absolute Supreme God to man, limited in his potentialities. God is considered to be a subject who can freely exercise His Will.

Neo-Pythagoreanism : It is a mixture of the philosophies of Pythagoras, Plato, Stoics, and Peripatetic school. Number symbolism, mysticism, and astrology are the characteristic features of this school of thought.

Neo-realism : It is a twentieth-century philosophical trend represented by the philosophers like G.E. Moore and Russell.

Neo-Realist theory of knowledge is based on the view that cognizable thing can directly enter the mind. It recognizes the existence of particulars only.

Neti, neti (S) : It means "not this, not this." This expression is found in the *Bṛhadāraṇyaka Upaniṣad* (2.3.6.). The indescribable, quality-less *Brahman* is explained by means of this *neti, neti* method.

Neurath, Otto (1882 – 1945) : He was one of the leading members of logical positivism who developed the thesis of physicalism. According to physicalism, all empirical statements can ultimately be reducible to physicalistic language. This enables us to gain the inter-subjective understanding of language. Neurath held the view that verification consists in comparing one set of statements with another set of statements rather than dealing directly with any form of experience.

Newton, (Sir) Isaac (1642 – 1727) : He was a famous British physicist and mathematician who developed Galilean mechanics. In contrast to Descartes' method, Newton's method is empirical and inductive. He advocated mechanistic materialism in explaining the nature of reality. According to Newton, the processes in reality can be explained in terms of mechanical motion of atoms. This motion is not inherent in them. It is purely an external force. He recognized the objective significance of three-dimensional space, and uni-dimensional nature of time. He is also regarded as the inventor of differential calculus.

Nicolai, Friedrich (1733 – 1811) : He was one of the followers of Leibniz-Wolffian school that developed an eclectic reconciliation of rationalism and empiricism in a popular form which served as a base for Kant's critical philosophy.

Nicomachus (second century CE) : He was a Neo-Pythagorean philosopher. It is believed that original Nicomachus was the son of Aristotle after whom Aristotle named his ethics known as Nicomachian ethics.

Nietzsche, Friedrich (1844 – 1900) : He was a German philosopher and writer who bitterly criticized Christian and utilitarian ethics. His epistemological relativism led to reassessment of all the values and culminated in the opposition of "slave" morality to "master" morality. He claimed that for all practical purposes "God is dead on the earth." He believed that one motive force in human affairs is the will to power. Such a will to power is in an "overman" or "superman" (Ubermensch). Nietzsche wrote philosophy in a manner calculated more to provoke serious thought than to give formal answers. He developed no formal system because system building, according to Nietzsche, assumes that one has at hand certain self-evident truths upon which to build. Nietzsche held that philosophy must be less pretentious, pay more attention to questions concerning human values than to abstract systems. Although Nietzsche was an atheist by temperament he contemplated the "death of God" with mixed reactions. He wondered at the consequences that would follow once everyone had become fully aware of all the implications of the death of God, a cultural event that is not yet become apparent to modern man. In his search for new foundations for values in a day when God could no longer be the goal and sanction of human conduct, Nietzsche turned to aesthetic dimension of human nature as the most promising alternative to religion. Greek tragedy, for Nietzsche, is a great work of art. It represents the conquest of Dionysus by Apollo. The former was the symbol of the dynamic stream of life, which knows no restraints or barriers and defies all limitations. In the worship of Dionysus, the individual would lapse into a drunken frenzy and thereby lose his own identity. Apollo, on the other hand, was the symbol of order and restraint, and provided beauty to art. Thus Dionysus symbolized man's unity with life where his own individuality is lost or absorbed in the larger reality of life force, whereas Apollo was the symbol of the "principle of individuation," that power that controls and restrains the dynamic processes of life in order to create a formed work of art or a controlled personal character. Nietzsche rejected that there is universal and absolute system of morality that everyone must equally obey. He bitterly attacked Christian values for inculcating slave morality among men. Thus he recommended the trans-valuation of values to overcome this mentality. His imprint works include: *The Birth of the Tragedy from the Spirit of Music* (1872); *Thus Spake Zarathustra* (1883-91); *Beyond Good and Evil* (1886); and *Geneology of Morals* (1887).

Nihilism : It is a philosophical viewpoint that denies every positive ideal or goal. This term was first introduced by Jacobi. According to nihilism, all knowledge is illusory, worthless, meaningless, relative, and insignificant. In metaphysics, nihilism claims that the universe is meaningless and without purpose.

Nihilism, Ethical : This doctrine denies the very possibility of ethical philosophy by denying the validity of all ethical distinctions. Therefore this position is not seriously taken by ethical philosophers.

Nimbārka (c. twelfth century CE) : He is also known as Nimbāditya or Niyamānanda. His philosophy is known as Dvaitādvita or Bhedā-bhedasanakasampradāya of Vaiṣṇavism. He revived the philosophy of *bhedābhedavādins* like Aśmarathya, Bhartṛprapañca, Bhāskara, and Yādava. His philosophy resembles that of Rāmānuja in many respects. He admits three realities: God, souls and matter. However, souls and matter are dependent on God. The individual soul is essentially of the nature of knowledge (*jñāna svarūpa*). But it is also the substratum of knowledge. The soul is controlled by God. There are many souls. The souls are atomic in size, and eternal, yet the souls suffer from births and deaths due to *karma* and *avidyā*. His important works include: *Vedāntapārijātakaustubha*; *Daśaślokī*; and *Madhvamukhamardana*.

Nirguṇa (S) : It means "qualityless." *Brahman per se* is called *nirguṇa* as it is devoid of all qualities according to the Upaniṣads. In the Vedāntic systems of philosophy, Advaita subscribes to that view.

Nirvāṇa (S) : This expression is used by the Buddhists to refer to that state of attainment wherein all pain, suffering, mental anguish and above all, bondage from *saṁsāra* cease to exist. In other words, it is a state of liberation.

Nisus : It is the creative principle of emergent evolution.

Nityavāda (S) : According to the Vedāntic systems the Supreme Reality, *Brahman*, is immutable (*nitya*).

Niyama (S) : It is one of the eightfold disciplines of Yoga. *Niyama* should be imposed on oneself of good and kind habits, including bathing, eating hygienic food, controlling the body, contentedness, cheerfulness, study and piety.

Noema (Gr) : In Husserl's phenomenology, noema is the objective sense of the noesis, together with the character of the sense as posited in a certain manner. For every dimension of the noesis there is a corresponding dimension of the noema.

Noesis (Gr) : It means "intelligence," "thought," "understanding," "mind," etc. In Greek philosophy, noesis is the knowledge that results from the operation of nous, the mind, reason, intellectual faculty. In Husserls' phenomenology, noesis represents that current in the stream of consciousness that is intrinsically intentional in that it points to an object as beyond itself.

Noetic : It is the apprehension of something by means of reason without any involvement of sense-experience.

Nolition : It is a state or act of negative volition.

Nomic : Any explanation that is subjected to the laws of nature is called nomic.

Nominalism : It is a view that particulars alone exist, and that universals are mere names representing the particulars. Universals do not have independent existence but have observable likeness among the particulars of sense-experience. William of Ockham was a leading nominalist. Even Locke is considered to be a nominalist because of his assertion that particulars alone are nameable and are also given in sense-experience.

Non-being : This expression refers to non-existence. It is often used to designate anything that is unreal. In Hegel's dialectic, non-being is the anti-thesis of being. It also means the absence of determinateness.

Non-contradiction, Principle of : According to this principle, proposition cannot be both true and false. For instance, the proposition *p* is true. If *p* is true, then *not-p* is false.

Non-Euclidean Geometry : The Geometry that does not accept the parallel postulates of Euclid. Euclidean geometry provides certain postulates from which all the theorems can be deduced.

Non-naturalistic Ethics : It is an ethical theory that advocates the view that ethical properties or relations are non-natural. G.E. Moore's ethical intuitionism can be characterized as non-naturalism.

Non-rigid Designator : A non-rigid designator does not designate the same thing in every possible world.

Non sequitur (L) : It means "it does not follow." This expression is applicable only for drawing conclusions irrespective of their validity.

Noology : It is a field of mental science in which the will does not function in the production of mental events. According to Hamilton, it is the science of the noetic.

No-ownership Theory : It is a metaphysical theory about self advocated by P.F. Strawson. This particular theory is the outcome of Cartesian mind-body problem. It holds that the conscious experiences that are associated with the subject are not the part of that consciousness. In other words, they are not owned by the subject of experience.

Normative : It is a normative principle that sets to establish a standard of correctness by prescribing certain rules. Normative ethics deals with the standardization of moral concepts.

Norms : They are a set of standard rules that serve as criteria to judge something. To maintain proper regularity and discipline in various fields, norms are essential. They are different from rules. Norms are not flexible.

Nothing : It literally means "not a thing." According to Kant, nothing represents emptiness of a concept, or an object or an intuition. Hegel viewed it as the immediate, indeterminate notion of being. For Peirce, nothing is that which possesses contrary attributes.

Notion : It is a technical term used by Hegel to designate the essence or the nature of object on one side, and true thought of that essence or nature on the other side. These two aspects of notion are discussed in the third chapter of his *Logic*.

Noumenon : This term is introduced by Immanuel Kant in his *Critique of Pure Reason* to denote "thing-in-itself." According to Kant, neither reason (categories of understanding) nor sense-experience can ever provide us with the knowledge of "thing-in-itself." The world of God, Freedom, and Immortality belong to the realm of noumena.

Noun : A noun is that which serves as a proper or common name in any natural language. In the sentence "Ram is intelligent," the subject "Ram" is a noun.

Nous (Gk) : It means "mind." For Plato, nous represents the rational part of the soul. For Aristotle, it represents the intellect that is further divided into active and passive reason. According to him, the active reason is immortal.

Null Set : It is a set or class that consists of no individuals within it.

Number : The notion of number is closely associated with mathematics, especially with quantification. According to Plato, numbers are abstract entities that exist independent of human consciousness. They are timeless and non-spatial entities. Contrary to this view, intuitionists consider numbers to be the products of processes. Later on it is conceived that numbers are sets.

Numerical Identity : It is the same in the sense of one and the same thing.

Nyāya (S) : It is one of the orthodox systems of Indian thought founded by the great sage and seer Akṣapāda Gautama. The philosophy of Nyāya is best illustrated in the *Nyāya-Sūtra* of Gautama. This work is further commented by Vātsyāyana in his *Nyāya-Bhāṣya*. Udyotakara is the *vārttikakāra*. This school of thought is primarily concerned with logic and epistemology. It is also known as *āṇvīkṣikī* and *tarka*. Its philosophy is called the philosophy of logical realism. Nyāya-Vaiśeṣika are allied systems. Both the systems agree that bondage is due to ignorance. Liberation is possible only through the right knowledge of reality. Nyāya recognizes sixteen important categories. It accepts four *pramāṇas*, namely, *pratykṣa* or perception, *anumāna* or inference, *upamāna* or comparison, and *śabda* or verbal testimony. Gautama felt that salvation (*niḥśreyas*) can be obtained only if the right effort is made. Our effort can be right only if it is in accordance with reality. But we have to know what reality is. Our knowledge has to be right and logically valid. Therefore, Gautama enunciated sixteen categories of logic, epistemology, and argumentation as means to salvation. They are as follows: (1) the valid means of cognition (*pramāṇa*); (2) the knowable (*prameya*); (3) doubt (*saṁśaya*); (4) purpose (*prayojana*); (5) example (*dṛṣṭānta*); (6) established doctrine (*siddhānta*); (7) members of syllogism (*avayava*); (8) the negative modal or counterfactual conditional (*tarka*); (9) ascertainment (*nirṇaya*); (10) controversy (*vāda*); (11) wrangling (*jalpa*); (12) destructive dialectic (*vitaṇḍa*); (13) fallacies of syllogism (*hetvābhāsas*); (14) quibbling (*chala*); (15) futile argument (*jāti*); and (16) grounds of defeat (*nigraha sthānas*).

O

Object : It is an entity towards which our consciousness is directed. The cognitive or epistemological object of mind is anything perceived, imagined, conceived, or thought about. The conative object is anything desired, willed, or avoided.

Objective : This term is used in many senses. Anything that is not subjective is called objective, in other words, anything that is public and non-subjective.

Object Language : It is different from meta-language. According to Alfred Tarsky, every statement in any language(s) is a statement about object language. For example, the statement "snow is white" is true if and only if snow is white. It is a statement about snow and its property "whiteness." In other words, it is the language that speaks of non-linguistic subjects.

Obligation : It is a duty that has to be performed by an individual under certain moral constraints. Obligations are many and varied. Every moral obligation is an "ought."

Oblivescence : It is a state wherein the gradual obliteration of memory takes place.

Observation : It is a purposive perception of the objective reality that provides us with the primary data for various claims to knowledge. Observation may be simple or complex, or direct or indirect. It is regarded as one of the postulates of scientific investigation.

Obversion : It is a form of immediate inference. It is a process of changing the quality of the proposition without changing the meaning. The given proposition is called the obvertend and the inferred proposition is called obverse and the process is called obversion. The obverted form of the original statement is logically possible by negating the predicate term and changing the statement from negative to affirmative to negative. For example; the statement "All logicians are scrupulous" can be obverted into "No logician is non-scrupulous."

Occasion : It is an external circumstance that provides an impulse for other events. Occasion may give rise to one or other phenomenon. The occasion of anything is its antecedent reference; whereas the cause is its logical reference.

Occasionalism : It is a philosophical viewpoint concerned with the mind-body relationship advocated by Malebranche. In opposition to psychophysical interactionism advocated by Descartes, occasionalists hold the view that the interaction between mind and body is possible because of divine intervention. God being supreme Reality finds an occasion to fuse them together.

Occultism : It is the doctrine that admits the existence of supernatural forces beyond scientific investigation.

Ockham, William of (1285 – 1349) : He was a medieval British theologian and scholastic philosopher who advocated nominalism. He introduced a principle of ontological economy which holds: "do not multiply entities beyond necessity." Such a principle is popularly known as Ockham's razor. In episemology, Ockham held that universality cannot be attributed merely to terms or propositions, but also to things that exist apart from discourse. In theology, Ockham argued that the so-called proofs for the existence of God, or immortality of the soul cannot be established demonstratively. Therefore the religious doctrines rest on pure faith.

Oedipus Effect : This term was first introduced by Karl Popper to denote certain predicative statements about human behaviour. The predications about human affairs may have a tendency to bring about either their verification or falsification.

Ontological Argument : It is one of the proofs for the existence of God advanced by St. Anselm. According to this proof, God being perfect cannot be deprived of existence. Thus God is a "Being" who exists. Kant attacked this proof by holding the view that existence cannot be a predicate. To ascribe any predicate to any subject, first of all its existence is guaranteed.

Ontology : It is a branch of philosophy that deals with the existence of Being. Ontologists are basically concerned with the essences of things. Some ontologists are monists, some are pluralists, and some are dualists. For example, Hegel's ontology is monistic as it is the "Absolute Idea" which is ontologically real for him. For Leibniz, monads are ontologically real. Although his system is pluralistic, for he accepted plurality of monads, it can be called type monism. Similarly, Hume advocated that reality is nothing but a stream of sense-impressions. Thus, what is ontologically real for Hume consists of atomistic sense-impressions. His ontology becomes a pluralistic one. However, since all the sense-impressions are of the same nature, his doctrine can also be called type monism. Descartes advocated dualistic ontology by admitting the existence of two independent substances, mind and body.

Open Class : It is a class of things that could always permit more members.

Open Question Argument : It is an argument introduced by G.E. Moore to show that "good" is indefinable. He argued that if "X" is "Y" is a definition, then the question "is *Y X* ? cannot be substantial. But all the questions of the form "Is *X* good?" are open questions.

Open Texture : It is an expression introduced by Waismann to explain that any statement about a material object in which various terms are used are non-exhaustive in the sense that we cannot foresee the conditions in which it is true as there are many possible conditions for its being true.

Operationalism : It is a popular theory in philosophy of science that tries to explain the physical entities, properties, and processes in terms of a set of operations and experiments by which they are understood.

Optimism and Pessimism : They are two contrasting viewpoints concerning the good and evil in this world. According to optimism, there is an element of hope that good always prevails over evil, so that something good is always expected or hoped. Contrary to the above view, pessimism is a view that evil prevails over good, so that something bad is always expected or hoped. Leibniz was a champion of optimism, while Schopenhauer and Nietzsche advocated pessimism.

Or (Disjunction) : It is a logical connective that can be used in its exclusive sense or in its inclusive sense. In its exclusive sense, it takes the following form: He is either insane or pretending to be insane. In its inclusive sense, it takes the following form: "He is either mad or lazy or both." The former is symbolized as "^" and the latter as *v*. They have two different truth tables. They are as follows:

p	q	$p \wedge q$	p	q	$p \vee q$
T	T	F	T	T	T
T	F	T	T	F	T
T	T	T	F	T	T
F	F	F	F	F	T

Ordinary Language : Any non-technical language is called ordinary language. The words of ordinary language will have standard use. The philosophers of ordinary language are of the opinion that by analysing the concepts of ordinary language one can better understand the nature of reality. The well-known ordinary language philosophers are J.L. Austin, later Wittgenstein, Gilbert Ryle, and John Wisdom.

Organon (Gk) : It means "instrument." It is the name given to Aristotle's six treatises on logic. They are Categories, Deinterpretatione, Prior Analytics, Posterior Analytics, Topics and Sophistical Refutations.

Origen (c. 185 – 254) : He was one of the famous Christian theologians who attempted to reconcile the Christianity with the Greek philosophy through speculative and allegorical interpretation of Biblical texts. His major critical work on the *Old Testament* is *Hexapla.*

Original Sin : According to Christian tradition, every human being inherits the sin that was brought into the world through the disobedience of Adam and Eve. Only by means of Divine grace every human individual can be rescued from such a state. Many theologians interpret that sin originates in human pride by disobeying the decree of God.

Orphic Literature : They were the mystic writings of mythical Orpheus (sixth century BCE), who was supposed to be the founder of a Greek religious-philosophical movement. The Orphic literature combines mythology and rational thinking in explaining the mysteries related to cosmogony, theogony, man's original creation and his destiny after death. The ancient Greek philosophers such as Pythagoras, Empedocles, and Plato were influenced by the views advocated by Orpheus.

Ortega Y Gasset, Jose (1883 – 1955) : He was a Spanish philosopher and essayist who advocated epistemological perspectivism. He believed that the reality can be interpreted by alternative systems of concepts and every interpretation is unique and true. The only ultimate reality is the experience of each individual's life. His important works include: *Meditaciones del Quijote* (1914), translated as *Meditations on quixote* (1961); *The Revolt of the Masses* (1931); and *The Modern Theme* (1933).

Other Minds : It is an epistemological problem concerning the knowledge of other minds. Some epistemologists conceive that the experiences of each individual are private to one's own self. Then there is no possibility, even in principle, to know what is going on in other's minds. Though the epistemologists have suggested various ways of knowing what is happening in other minds, skeptics always question the veracity of the truth about the statements about other minds. The philosophers like J.L. Austin, Ryle and Wittgenstein ridiculed the position of skeptics and held that there are various possibilities of having the knowledge of other minds.

Orthodoxy : It refers to certain beliefs that are declared by a group to be true and normative. Heresy is a departure from such beliefs of any orthodoxy.

Ousia (Gk) : It means "substance." It is one of the ten categories listed by Aristotle. It is also understood as reality.

P

Pacifism : It is a doctrine that opposes all forms of war on moral and religious grounds. It is also opposed to all forms of killing and violence. Nuclear pacifism opposes wars that employ nuclear material for destructive purposes. A pacifist is one who actively promotes peace and justice among people. Although violence in any form is highly condemnable, at times it is not opposed for the purpose of self-defence. Absolute pacifism does not approve of war under any circumstances.

Pāda (S) : It means "part," "chapter," "foot." According to *Māṇḍūkya Upaniṣad* the Self (*ātman*) has four *pāda*s. They are *vaiśvānara, taijasa, prājña, turīya*. The first three are parts and the fourth is the whole.

Padārtha (S) : It means "category." Jainism recognized two *padārtha*s. They are individual self (*jīva*), and non-soul (*ajīva*). Individual soul is an extended, conscious, immaterial substance. The non-soul is divided into time (*kāla*), space (*ākāśa*), medium of motion (*dharma*), medium of rest (*adharma*), and matter (*pudgaḷa*). Excepting time, all other substances are extended, and non-conscious. Nyāya recognized sixteen categories. They are: the sources of knowledge (*pramāṇa*), objects of knowledge (*prameya*), doubt (*saṁśaya*), purpose (*prayojana*), instances (*dṛṣṭānta*), established conclusion (*siddhānta*), members of a syllogism (*avayava*), *reductio ad absurdum* (*tarka*), argument (*jalpa*), decisive knowledge (*nirṇaya*), argument for truth (*vāda*), mere destructive argument (*vitaṇḍa*), fallacious reasons (*hetvābhāsa*), quibbling (*chala*), specious and unavailing objections (*jāti*), and vulnerable points (*nigraha sthāna*). Vaiśeṣika recognized seven *padārthas*. They are: substance (*dravya*), quality (*guṇa*), action (*karma*), generality (*sāmānya*), particularity (*viśeṣa*), inherence (*samavāya*), and non-existence (*abhāva*).

Padmāsana (S) : It is the lotus throne on which Brahmā, Viṣṇu, and Lakṣmī are portrayed as seated. It is one of the *yogāsanas* practised by sitting cross-legged with feet resting on the opposite thighs and the soles turned upwards. It is the position recommended for meditation.

Paine, Thomas (1737 – 1809) : He was a British-born American political philosopher who held the view that the government and the society are two different things. His attack on Christianity brought him the fame as an atheist. His uncompromising egalitarianism brought him fame. He defended French Revolution as he opposed the concentration of power in any one individual. According to him, sovereignty resides in human beings. He opposed all forms of slavery and remained as a supporter of universal male suffrage. His important works include: *Common Sense* (1776); *Reflections on the Revolution in France* (1790); *The Rights of Man* (1791-2); and *The Age of Reason* (1794 and 1796).

Pallavas (250 – 750) : It was a south Indian dynasty that ruled the southern part of India. Their capital was Canjeevaram (Kāñcīpuram), which is regarded as one of the sacred places of Hinduism. Pallavas built a very big Kailaśanātha temple and the complex of Māmallapuram (Mahābalipuram).

Pañcamukhaliṅga (S) : It is a conic shaped five-faced *Śivaliṅga* representing the various aspects of Śiva. The fifth face is not visible, because it indicates Śiva's unmanifest nature.

Pāñcarātra (S) : It is a sect of Viṣṇu worshippers originated in Kashmir in the first or second century CE. According to this tradition, Viṣṇu manifests himself in this world with his full essential nature through emanations. This is known as the theory of *vyūhas*. This doctrine is different from the incarnations (*avatāras*) of Lord Viṣṇu. According to this sect, an *avatāra* is a lesser manifestation of God. This sect reached its peak during the tenth century CE and later it became a part of Tāntrism. Viśiṣṭādvaita has its roots in Pāñcarātrāgama.

Panentheism : Unlike pantheism, according to which God is the world and the world is God, panentheism holds that the world is in God. In other words, God is much more than the world. According to the doctrine of panentheism, God is both immanent and transcendent.

Pāṇini (fifth century BCE) : He was the author of the earliest Sanskrit grammar of very high standard. He used analytical approach to present a perfect phonetics as well as a logical alphabetical system. He is treated as a *ṛṣi* in Indian tradition. His important work is *Aṣṭādhyāyī*.

Panlogism : It is a philosophical view that advocates that all the development in nature and society is the realization of the logical activity of the universal mind. It conceives that the laws of logic are the only driving forces of all development. Hegel is considered to be an advocate of panlogism.

Pan-objectivism : It is an extreme form of realism that attributes real objectivity to all objects of knowledge irrespective of their veridical or non-veridical nature.

Pan-psychism : It is a form of animism that holds that all the things in nature possess life and psychics. In other words, physical world is basically sentient and psychical. The chief advocates of pan-psychism are A.N. Whitehead, K.G. Jung, Ch. Strong, Hartshorne, and Sprigge. The modern versions of pan-psychism are partly akin to hylozoism, according to which matter is intrinsically alive.

Pan-Satanism : It is a vague and widespread belief that the world is somehow identified with the devil or Satan. Schopenhaur's philosophy is regarded as a kind of Pan-Satanism.

Pantheism : It is a philosophical viewpoint that maintains that God as an impersonal principle does not exist outside nature, but very much part and parcel of nature. Pantheism identifies God with nature so as to eliminate supernatural element. This term was first introduced by Toland. However, pantheism is an official doctrine of Bruno and Spinoza.

Pantheistic Personalism : According to this doctrine, reality consists of a Supreme Personality of which the world of persons are parts. The divine personality has no separate existence from its creation.

Paracelsus, Theophrastus Bombastus von Hohenheim (1493 – 1541) : He was a Swiss physicist and chemist who wanted to use philosophy as one of the pillars of medical science. His philosophy is a combination of neo-Platonism, experimentalism, and superstitious magic. He rejected the traditional theories of Galen and Arab physicists.

Paradigm : This term is popularized by Thomas Kuhn through his *The Structure of Scientific Revolutions* (1962). According to Kuhn, a well-established scientific theory in any field of scientific research is called a paradigm. What is called normal science is the stage of science where there are paradigms in every field of esoteric research. In other words, a paradigm is an accepted model that is successfully employed to arrive at certain desired results.

Paradigm Case Argument : This argument intends to disprove skeptical contentions by holding that a word is taught by reference to clear cases. Every word that we use must have an objective reference. When someone says that it is not a real diamond, he must be in a position to identify a real one.

Paradox : It is a conclusion arrived at by a valid deductive reasoning that contradicts the generally accepted beliefs. A paradox is something that goes "beyond belief." Paradoxes can appear in scientific theory as well as in ordinary discourse. For example, Zeno's paradoxes are set against motion and divisibility of space and time.

Parallelism : It is a view advocated by Spinoza that the relation between mind and body can be explained in terms of psychophysical parallelism. According to this doctrine, the language of mind and the language of body are parallel to each other. In other words, what is expressed in mental language can also be expressed in physical language. For instance, the object "table" is a physical state, while the "idea of that table" is a mental state.

Paralogism : It is a fallacious syllogism or an error in reasoning. In Kant's philosophy, paralogisms are arguments alleging to prove all substantivity, simplicity and eternality of the soul or pure ego.

Paramāṇu (S) : In Indian philosophy it refers to an infinitely small or absolutely magnitudeless particle, or discrete physical entity.

Pāramārthika (S) : In Advaita Vedānta, *pāramārthika* or trans-empirical refers to the absolute reality *Brahman* which is *nirguṇa, niravayava.* In opposition to *vyāvahārika* or empirical, *pāramārthika* is not bound by any language, relation, reason or logic.

Parapsychology : It is a branch of psychology that is concerned with the forms of sensuality which cannot be explained by means of sense-organs. In other words, it deals with the extra-sensory perception (ESP).

Pariṇāmavāda (S) : According to Sāṁkhya theory of evolution, world is the resultant effect of the *pariṇāma* or change of the *prakṛti* or the primordial matter which is constituted by three *guṇa*s or qualities, namely, *sattva, rajas,* and *tamas.* The evolution takes place when the equilibrium among these three *guṇa*s is disturbed because of the *prakṛti*'s proximity with the *puruṣa.*

Parmenides (c. 515 – 440 BCE) : He was an ancient Greek philosopher who advocated that reality is one, eternal, immobile, indivisible and free from all contradictions. He vigorously attacked the "doctrine of truth" in support of "doctrine of opinion." In the "doctrine of opinion," Parmenides expounded his astronomical, physical, and physiological hypotheses. Thus he advocated monism. In his poem *On Nature*, Parmenides distinguishes three types of enquiry. The first one is about the truth. It is defined as "that it is, and can be." The second is about ignorance. It is defined as "that it is not, and must necessarily not be." The third type is "what is this 'it'?" If we observe the objection to the second type, "it is whatever is for thinking and saying," that is the object of thought or knowledge. Martin Heidegger was influenced by Parmenides.

Parsing : It is a process of determining the syntactic structure of a sentence according to the rules of a given grammar. The grammar of natural languages differs from language to language.

Parsimony, the Law of : This is also known as economy principle or Ockham's razor. According to law, one should not multiply the entities beyond necessity. This law is attributed to William of Ockham.

Parsons, Talcott (1902 – 79) : He was a well-known American sociologist who founded the functional school. He introduced structural-functional analysis to construct a model of social system the basic elements of which is the interaction between the individuals.

Pārśvanātha (S) : He was the twenty-third *tīrthaṅkara* of the Jain order who lived, according to the Jaina tradition, 250 years before Vardhamāna Mahāvīra, the twenty-fourth *tīrthaṅkara*.

Particular : It is a member of a class or a set as opposed to the property that defines a class or a set. It is an individual opposed to universal. Individual objects are called particulars. Strawson calls them "basic particulars."

Particular Proposition : In traditional logic, propositions "I" and "O" are called particular propositions. The former are called particular affirmative and the latter particular negative.

Pascal, Blaise (1623 – 62) : He was a French mathematician, philosopher, and a physicist who founded the theory of probability. He oscillated between rationalism and skepticism; and maintained the superiority of faith over reason. At this stage of his thought theology becomes central to his philosophy. His *18 Letters Provinciales* (1656-57) are directed against Jesuits.

Passive Empiricism : It is a doctrine according to which knowledge arises by way of experience with the emphasis upon the negative character of the mind. The mind can only act on the stimulus of contact with the world outside itself. Locke is considered to be a passive empiricist.

Past : It is one of the aspects of time that refers to the events that have already taken place. Time is unidimentional and is continuous. It has three divisions, namely, past, present, and future.

Patañjali (S) : He is a great seer and sage who is the founder of Yoga system. He authored the *Yoga-Sūtra*. According to Patañjali, spiritual realization is the only way to be free from all limitations of body, the senses and the mind. See Yoga.

Pathetic Fallacy : Strictly speaking it is not a fallacy, but a mistaken assumption that inanimate things have feelings, emotions, dispositions, and so on like animate things.

Patripassianism : It is a teaching according to which even god is not exempted from suffering. In Christian thought this view was held by Sabellius in connection with the sufferings of Jesus.

Peano's Postulates : Giuseppe Peano (1858 – 1932) advanced five postulates from which the entire arithmetic is derived. The following are the postulates:

1. 0 is a number.
2. The successor of any number is a number.
3. No two numbers have the same successor.
4. 0 is not the successor of any natural number.
5. If predicate *P* is true of 0, then it is also true of any number.

Pearson, Karl (1857 – 1936) : He is a British philosopher and mathematician who maintained that the task of science is to classify and describe facts. As a true follower of Mach, he believed that material objects are nothing but a bundle of sensations.

Peirce, Charles Sanders (1839 – 1914) : He is the pioneer of American pragmatic movement. According to Peirce, words derive their meanings from actions. Philosophers must follow the scientific method. No philosophical propositions should be accepted without any proof. He was chiefly influenced by logic and scientific method. His works on semiotics have considerably influenced mathematical logic and positivism. Peirce also worked on the theory of probability and the logic of relations. For him, scientific knowledge alone can be branded as knowledge in its real sense of the term. His writings were published under the title: *Collected Papers* (1931 – 58).

Peirce's Law : It is a theorem in propositional calculus, $[\{p \supset q\} \supset p] \supset p$.

Pelagianism : It is a heresy propagated by a British monk Pelagius, according to which there is no original sin, and man can attain eternal life with his own free will without God's intervention. Pelagius was notably influenced by Stoic doctrines. He and his followers revolted against the decrees of the Church.

Perception : It is one of the most important sources of knowledge. According to empiricists, all genuine knowledge is possible through sense-perception alone. Such sense-perception is classified into the perception of sensation and the perception of reflection. Hume classified sense-perception into impressions, and ideas. Impressions are more vivid and lively atomic units; while the ideas are philosophers who denied perception as an authentic source of knowledge. Plato asserted that perceptual knowledge is not knowledge, but it is mere opinion. Similarly, Descartes doubted the very testimony of senses to refute perceptual knowledge as a valid source. Unlike Plato and

Descartes, Kant did not deny the role of perception in the acquisition of knowledge. He held the view that "concepts without percepts are empty and percepts without concepts are blind." In its broader sense, the term "perception" involves mental as well as sense-perception. Even reason can be termed as the perception of mind in this sense. According to Sophists and Cārvāka, perception is the only genuine source of knowledge. Plato, Descartes and other rationalists did not accord much importance to perception as a source of knowledge as it is capable of misleading. Empiricists hold the view that perception is the only genuine source of knowledge as against reason. In Indian philosophy, every system accepted perception (*pratyakṣa*) as a source of knowledge although the theories of perception differ from system to system. In fact, it is regarded as the *jyeṣṭha pramāṇa*.

Perception, non-Sensory : This experience lacks any sensory content. According to Montague, space and time have this characteristic when experienced by man.

Perception, Pure : It is an experience wherein an object is perceived as it is. Such perception of an object is devoid of any categories of understanding. For example, the *nirvikalpaka-pratyakṣa* in Indian epistemology can be termed as pure perception. According to the Buddhists, *nirvikalapa pratyakṣa* is pure and genuine form of perception devoid of error.

Perfectionism : It is an ethical theory according to which every one ought to aim at perfection as it is the sole virtue. It is also the cultivation of one's own endowments as talents.

Perfection, Principle of : It is a principle postulated by Leibniz, according to which God created the best of the possible worlds so that maximum perfection is achieved.

Performative Utterance : It is a term introduced by J.L. Austin, according to which utterances such as "I promise," "I warn," "I wish" are acts of performance, but not descriptions of any act. They are also known as illocutionary acts.

Per genus et differentiam (L) : It means "by kind and difference." Aristotle's logic is based on this principle to define various things. Man as "a rational animal" belongs to a particular species, but this species is a class of the much wider class called genus.

Peripety (Gk) : According to Aristotle, what is essential in a plot of a tragedy is the sudden reversal of conditions or fortunes. Such a condition is called peripety.

Perlocution : This term is frequently used by J.L. Austin for any utterance with perlocutionary effects. When utterance is made it must have some psychological impact on the hearer. For example, "I will shoot you." This utterance may cause some behavioural change in the hearer.

Persenotum (L) : It means "known through itself." St. Thomas Aquinas used this term to anything that is self-evident.

Persistence : It is a condition of enduring in time with or without change.

Person : The term "person" has been used by philosophers in different ways. According to Boethius, a person is an individual substance with rationality. John Locke writes in his *Essay*, a person is "a thinking intelligent being that has reason and reflection and can consider itself as itself, the same thinking thing, in different times and places; which it does only by that consciousness which is inseparable from thinking." Locke tried to distinguish a person from a man. He conceived that a person is one who is intelligent to promote law, happiness and misery. Thus the term "person" is a forensic term for Locke. According to Kant, a person is one whose actions are capable of imputation. He strongly believed that since persons are capable of imposing laws themselves they deserve respect. As against dualist conception of person, a non-dualist holds that a person has both body and consciousness. P.F. Strawson in his *Individuals* defines a person as "the concept of a type of entity such that both predicates ascribing states of consciousness and predicates ascribing corporeal characteristics, a physical situation, etc., are equally applicable to a single individual of that single type." Not only that, the concept of person is logically a primitive concept for Strawson.

Personal Idealism : It is the affirmation of reality in the person and the personal nature of the World-Ground. It is similar to Absolutistic Personalism.

Personal Identity : It is a philosopher's view concerning the identity of a person. The term "identity" is at least used in two senses, namely, to pick out and to recognize. When it is used in the sense of "to pick out," identification may be called "individuation." In the second sense, it necessitates a judgement that two individuations belong to the same person. The philosophical problem is that on what principle do we make assertions about personal identity. Both Reid and Hume refuted the view that memory can be the base for personal identity.

Personalism : It is a philosophical view according to which the existence of a person is ontologically prior to all philosophical inquiry. Personalism maintains that every philosophical inquiry must be based on the concept of person. This theory believes that God is the manifestation of personality. In fact, the doctrine of person reached its culmination in Greek philosophy, especially in Socrates (499 – 399 BCE). According to him, the soul or the self is the centre from which all the actions of a man spring.

Perspectivism : According to this view, external reality must be interpreted through different systems of concepts, beliefs, and predilections. There is no one universally accepted criterion to determine the superiority or validity of one interpretation over the other. Every perspective has its own rationality behind its view. Nietzsche and Ortega Y Gasset are the champions of such a view. Even W.V. Quine subscribes to this view.

Pessimism : It is a kind of negative attitude gained by reflection on life, man and the world. Such an attitude is the result of neurotic or physiological conditions of an individual. The pessimistic attitude makes individuals gloomy, despondent, and magnifies sorrow and evil in this world. The philosophies advocated by the Buddhism and Shopenhauer are the best examples for pessimism.

Petitio Principii (L) : It is a non-verbal fallacy called "begging the question." This fallacy occurs when a desired conclusion is drawn from a premise or a general proposition whose validity is in question. For example, it is argued that it is wrong to tax the industrialists as they promote trade in the country. It amounts to saying that "The taxes levied on industrialists is wrong." But this assumption needs adequate justification.

Phala (S) : It means "fruit." According to Indian philosophy, every *karma* or action results in some *phala*. This may be good or bad. The *phala* of a *karma* depends upon the deeds of the individuals. This is what is technically called *karmaphala*.

Phantasm : This term was used by Thomas Hobbes to refer to an image or representation directly given to the precepient.

Phantasy : In Scholasticism, it represents the internal sense which perceives objects even when they are absent.

Phenomenalism : It is an extreme form of subjective idealism. It reduces all reality to sensations or to sense-impressions. Berkeley reduced the entire reality to mental faculty by claiming that "to be is to be perceived." Hume reduced reality to discrete, unconnected, atomic sensory units called impressions. These impressions are neither mental nor material. Linguistic phenomenalism tries to reduce the statements about material objects to the statements about sense-data without any residue. Many modern empiricists subscribe to this view.

Phenomenal World : The world of objects or external world or empirical world is known as phenomenal world. According to Plato, phenomenal world represents the process of becoming a world of things that are temporal and the replica of the ideal world that is eternal. In Kant's philosophy, phenomenal world is the world that can be known as opposed to the world in-itself (noumenal world).

Phenomenology : It is a philosophy introduced by Edmund Husserl. It is a study of the essence of the intuitive processes. Thus it is an a priori method seeking knowledge by abstracting objects (epoch or bracketing out the reality) from their experiential context. Phenomenology as a rigorous science claims that the essential feature of consciousness is intentionality. Consciousness is always directed towards some object or the other. The process of phenomenological reduction leaves us with bare consciousness. The phenomena arrived at by means of phenomenological reduction are non-empirical. Heidegger used phenomenology as a method. See Husserl.

Phenomenon : A phenomenon is an object or occurrence that is perceived by senses in contrast to reason. According to Kant, phenomenon is an object interpreted by categories of understanding that is opposed to noumenon.

Philo of Alexandria (c. 20 BCE – CE 50) : He was a Jewish theologian and neo-Platonic philosopher who attempted to synthesize the Greek and the Jewish thought.

Philosopher King : This term was coined by Plato and used frequently in his *Republic* to justify the view that philosophers alone are fit to be the rulers for the philosophers possess highest knowledge (wisdom). According to Plato, those who have the knowledge of the world of Forms are supposed to have been endowed with wisdom.

Philosophers' Stone : It is a hypothetical substance needed by alchemists for changing base metals into gold.

Philosophes : It is a field of wisdom that is often distinguished from mere fields of learning and pleasure. Sometimes it is also referred to the eighteenth-century French philosophers like Condercet, Condillac, Rousseau, and Voltaire.

Philosophical Radicals : The followers of Jeremy Bentham who exerted considerable practical influence on certain moral principles are known as philosophical radicals. Bentham advocated utilitarian ethics. See Bentham.

Philosophy : Etymologically the term "philosophy" is derived from the Greek term *fileosophia*, which means "love of wisdom." If we abide by this interpretation, all those who are interested in having concrete knowledge of reality are called philosophers as they are seeking wisdom in their respective fields. This makes us to identify philosophy with science. What is called "science" now was known as "natural philosophy" at one time. However, there are many interpretations of philosophy. Some interpret philosophy as world outlook, for some philosophy is a universal science. Some philosophers tried to make a sharp distinction between science and philosophy by asserting that philosophy aims at understanding, whereas science aims at explanation. Philosophy of science, a new branch in philosophy, claims that philosophy in order to understand the nature of reality has to depend upon the results of science. On the other hand, analytical philosophy is concerned with the logical clarification of concepts used in science and in everyday language. There are several branches of philosophy.

Philosophy of Change : According to this doctrine, change is the only enduring principle and therefore the fundamental reality. This view was advocated by Heraclitus, and in modern times by Henri Bergson.

Phrastic and Neustic : It was R.M. Hare who introduced this distinction between the *phrastic* and *neustic* elements among the sentences. For example, the sentences "please put on the light" (indicative sentence), "put on the light," (imperative sentence), "Has he put on the light?" (Interrogative sentence), have something in common, that is "put on the light." The phrastic element refers to this common element, whereas the neustic element refers to the element of difference among the sentences.

Phronesis (Gk) : According to Aristotle, it is practical knowledge or wisdom of the proper ends of conduct and of the means of attaining them. It is distinguished from theoretical knowledge or science or technical skill.

Physicalism : It is a theory advocated by neo-positivists that holds that all the statements are cognitively meaningful in so far as they are expressed in physicalist language. In other words, every statement is expressed as a proposition designating publicly observable properties. This doctrine was developed by the thinkers like Rudolf Carnap and J.J.C. Smart.

Pistology : It is a noun derived from the Greek root *pistis* meaning "faith." It is a science of faith or religious belief. Pistology is a part of theology concerned with faith and its scope as opposed to reason.

Pity : It is a kind of condescending feeling for other living creatures in their suffering. This word is often used as a synonym for the word "mercy." According to Hinduism, pity (*daya*) is regarded as an ethical impulse.

Plato (c. 428/427 – 348/347 BCE) : He was an ancient Greek philosopher, and a disciple of Socrates whose philosophy is known as objective idealism. For Plato, reality is eternal, immutable, and consists of Forms. Such a reality is the world of Forms. The phenomenal world is a replica of the world of Forms. It is only a transient world. Plato believed in the existence and reality of universals. According to him, Form is completely separated from matter or material existents. Authentic knowledge is the knowledge of Forms. Plato maintained that the source of knowledge is the immortal human soul's recollection of the world of Forms. All information that is obtained through sense-experience is mere opinion. It cannot be, held Plato, considered knowledge at all. In ethics, Plato advocated the view that every human soul consists of two parts, rational and irrational. If the rational part controls the irrational part, then that man is a just man. If the irrational part controls the rational part, then that man is an unjust man. In politics, Plato held the view that democracy is the worst form of government. His important dialogues include: *Sophist*; *Parmenides*; *Theaetetus*; *Republic*; *Meno*; *Crito*; *Euthyphro*; *Cratylus*; *Phaedo*; *Timaeus*, etc.

Pleasure and Pain : They are the two most important terms that we come across in ethical discourse. Philosophers have given various accounts of pleasure and pain. According to Aristotle, pleasure is a perfection supervening on certain activities, while the pain is its opposite. Spinoza defined pleasure as the feeling with which one passes from lesser state of perfection to a greater, and the pain as the feeling with which one makes the reverse transition. Bentham in his utilitarian ethics tried to make a quantitative distinction between pleasure and pain.

Plentitude, Principle of : It is a term coined by Lovejoy to explain the view that we can realize all possibilities in the world. The created Universe does not have any gaps. In other words, it is treated as a continuum.

Plenum : In opposition to vacuum, the space is filled with matter. The term is widely used by the Greek cosmologists.

Pluralative Logic : It is generally associated with Sir William Hamilton. According to him, "most" is a quantifier like "all," "some," "no," etc. if most As are Bs, and most Bs are Cs.

Pluralism : Any system in metaphysics is considered to be pluralistic in which the reality is composed of independent, discrete, unconnected elements that cannot be reduced to one another. In Leibniz's metaphysics, reality consists of many independent, discrete entitles called monads. Each monad is a tiny universe by itself. Similarly, for Hume, reality is a stream of sense impression. Thus Hume's metaphysics is a pluralistic one.

Pneuma (Gk) : It means "breath of life." Stoics and Epicureans believed that *pneuma* is the vital force in man. Even *New Testament* recognized *pneuma* as the spirit of man that is contrasted with psyche or soul.

Pneumatology : It is a branch of metaphysics that deals with the theory and science of spiritual beings such as God, human soul, angels, etc. In the course of eighteenth century this term was chiefly used to denote the study of the human soul.

Poincare, Jules Henri (1854 – 1912) : He was a famous French mathematician and philosopher who advocated a special theory of relativity. He asserted that laws of science are not related to the real world. He was influenced by both positivism and pragmatism. Poincare opposed the logistic method in the foundations of mathematics, especially that of Russell and Lousis Couturat.

Point-event : This term was used by A.N. Whitehead to signify an event with all its dimensions ideally restricted.

Polar Concepts : They are the concepts that oppose each other, for example, certainly and uncertainly (doubt), finite and infinite, determinism and indeterminism, etc. According to the polar concept argument, the meaning of any concept is derived from its opposite. This argument is used to discredit the claim of the skeptic, according to which there is no possibility of knowledge since certainty is not possible. Later Wittgenstein freely makes use of this argument.

Polysyllogism : It is a complex syllogism that includes many syllogisms in which the conclusion of each syllogism forms a premise for the other syllogism. In other words, the conclusion of the preceding syllogism forms a premise in the consequent one. This also is known as sorites.

Polytheism : It is a religious doctrine, according to which there are many gods. For example, Hinduism believes in the existence of many gods and goddesses.

Popper, (Sir) Karl Raymond (1902 – 98) : He was an Austrian-born British philosopher of science who advocated the theory of falsification according to which a theory is scientific in so far as it is falsifiable. What he meant by that is that every theory to be scientific must give scope for its negation. The principle of falsification of Popper mainly serves in demarcating science from pseudo-science. In his epistemology Popper claimed that knowledge undergoes evolution through critical examination. He recognized three important realms in his later thought. They are: material objects, mental processes, and organic activity that is primarily responsible for cultural growth. In his social and political theory, Popper attacked Plato, Hegel and Marx, and labelled them enemies of the open society. He also attacked historicism. His main works include: *The Logic of Scientific Discovery* (1935); *The Open Society and its Enemies* (1945); *The Poverty of Historicism* (1957); *Conjectures and Refutations* (1963); *Objective Knowledge* (1972).

Porphyry (C. 232 – 304) : He was a disciple of Plotinus. He applied Aristotelian logic to neo-platonic philosophy. His method of classification by means of dichotomy is known as the "Tree of Porphyry."

Port Royal : It is a name given to the logic developed by Arnauld, Nicole, and Pascal. According to Port Royal logic, a careful definition of various terms and concepts is an essential part of logic. What is called modern linguistic analysis has its foundations is Port Royal logic.

Posidonius of Rhodes (C. 135 – 50 BCE) : He was an eclectic philosopher of the Stoic school. He incorporated the doctrines of Plato and Aristotle into his philosophy.

Positivism : It is a school of thought that believes in the positive facts, thus aims at blanket rejection of metaphysics. The chief architect of positivism was the French philosopher and sociologist Auguste Comte. According to Comte, there are three important stages of human knowledge. They are: theological, metaphysical, and positive stages. The spirit of Comte's positivism is seen in the writings of neo-positivists of Vienna

Circle who claimed to stand for "logical and scientific foundations" of philosophy. Their chief motto is to eliminate all speculative doctrines from the sphere of philosophy.

Possessive : Any quality that is appertaining to someone or something is said to be possessive. For example, "my," "your," "its," "his," etc.

Possibility : Every probability is a possibility. There are types of possibilities. For instances, there are logical possibilities, empirical possibilities, and technical possibilities. What is logically possible may be empirically impossible and vice versa. It is also the case that what is possible usually happens, but does not have to happen.

Pythogoras (fifth century BCE) : He was an ancient Greek mathematician who tried to interpret the nature of reality in terms of numbers. He recognized ten pairs of opposites whose relationships constitute the basis of all reality. They are as follows:

One	Plurality
Limited	Unlimited
Right	Left
Odd	Even
Male	Female
At rest	Motion
Straight	Crooked
Light	Darkness
Good	Bad
Square	Oblong

Q

Quadrivium (L) : During the Middle Ages, the University courses consisted of astronomy, geometry, arithmetic, and music as high order subjects. The lower order subjects were known as *trivium*. They are: grammar, rhetoric, and logic.

Quaestio (L) : It means "question." During the Middle Ages, a form of philosophical writing originated from the practice of oral debate in the universities. It was known as quaestio.

Qualia (L) : It means "quality," "property," "nature," "state," "kind," "condition." Quale is the Latin singular for "of what kind or property" a thing has.

Qualitative Identity : It is the same in the sense of having same qualities. For example, if *X* has all the properties that *Y* has, then *X* is qualitatively identical with *Y*.

Quality : It is one of the categories of understanding listed by Kant. This category consists of the sub-categories such as reality, negation, and limitation. In traditional logic, quality refers to whether a categorical statement is affirmative or negative. A quality can be a property of a thing or an entity. For example, Berkeley and Hume regarded colours, tastes, smells, sounds, and the feelings of touch as sensible qualities. This is the view of modern empiricists too.

Quantification Suppressed : It is an ambiguity that arises in ordinary conversation where we do not know whether the statement refers to all members of a class or not. For example, "Children like icecream." It is not clear whether "All children like icecream" or "only some children like icecream." The generalization is only a sweeping assertion. This is known as the suppression of quantification.

Quantifier : A quantifier is a word or a symbol or a sign in logic that denotes "all," or "some" or "no." Sir William Hamilton has included even "most" in the list of quantifiers. His logic is known as pluralative logic.

Quantifier Shift Fallacy : Any argument or a fallacy that involves confusing universal and particular quantities is called quantifier shift fallacy. For example, "Children like icecream." It is not clear whether "All children like icecream" or "Some children like icecream."

Quantity : It is one of the categories of understanding listed by Kant. This category includes three sub-categories, namely, unity, plurality, and totality. Quantity also represents mass or weight.

Quantum : It is an indivisible unit or atom, of any physical quantity. Quantum mechanics is based on the existence of quanta of energy.

Quantum Mechanics : It is a branch of quantum physics that deals with the sub-atomic particles. It is the most important physical theory, and a modification of classical mechanics. Quantum mechanics has been developed on the basis of the study of sub-atomic structures and phenomena of emission and absorption of light by matter. The prominent theories that come under quantum theory are the wave mechanics of Schrödinger, particle mechanics of Heisenberg, and the transformation theory of Jordan and Dirac. The wave mechanics introduced a distinction between waves and particles, according to which an electron, or a photon (quantum of light) is to be considered in some of its aspects as wave, in others as particle.

Quiddity (L) : The question "quid est ?" (what is it ?) can be answered by explaining the nature of a thing. Thus it serves as an essential distinguishing feature of a thing in its definition. Otherwise the term *quiddity* means "that-which-is-to-be." Of late the term *quiddity* is used in its trivial or pejorative sense.

Quine, Willard Van Orman (1908 – 2000) : He was an American philosopher-logician who followed Carnap and has been the most influential philosopher of language in America. One of his famous papers "Two Dogmas of Empiricism" (1950) is chiefly directed against the "analyticity and reductionism" practised by empiricists. According to him, these two dogmas of empiricism are logically ill-founded. In the same paper Quine attacks the supposed cleavage between "analytic and synthetic." According to him, all knowledge is man-made fabric. There is nothing ready-made. In his essay "On What There Is" Quine talks about our ontological priorities. For him, to say "to be" means to be a value of a variable. His important works include: *Mathematical Logic* (1940); *From a Logical Point of View* (1953); *Word and Object* (1960); *The Ways of Paradox* (1966); *Ontological Relativity and Other Essays* (1969); *Philosophy of Logic* (1970); and *The Roots of Reference* (1973).

Quintessence (L) : It is a pure fifth element that is supposed to be the essence of heavenly bodies in Aristotle's physics. It is separated from other four elements, namely, earth, air, fire, and water. According to alchemists, it is supposed to be the *prima materia* from which everything evolved. This term is also used by the scholars to refer to the highest and nearest essence of anything.

R

Radhakrishnan, Sarvepalli (1880 – 1975) : He has been one of the most influential twentieth-century Indian philosophers and statesmen. His greatest contribution to philosophy is that he interpreted the philosophy of the East to the West and vice versa. He was the first philosopher who gave a lot of importance to comparative philosophy. He firmly believed that intuition is the basis for all other forms of cognition. Radhakrishnan held the view that the spirit in man is as real as his body. Without the realization of the spirit there is no humanity. Consequently, there cannot be freedom, democracy, morality and religion. His important works include: *Idealist View of Life* (1932); *Eastern Religions and Western Thought* (1940); *Contemporary Indian Philosophy* (1952); and *Indian Philosophy* (1962).

Rajas (S) : Sāṁkhya holds that *rajas* is one of the *guṇa*s of *prakṛti*. It is a tendency that promotes motion and action. It also represents courage or chivalry.

Ramakrishna (1836 – 86) : His original name was Gadadhar. Ramakrishna is regarded as one of the great spiritual giants, and a mystic of modern India. Being an extraordinary man, he contributed a lot to the upliftment of humanity, towards religion, precious religious harmony, unity and peace. According to him, religion is nothing but a way of life that influences man to a great extent in every aspect of life. He believed in Goddess Kāli and considered the idol of Kāli at Dakshineswar as the symbol of God. Ramakrishna is also considered to be a synthesizer of the world religions. He had admiration for all the religions as he believed that every religion has something unique to offer from its own standpoint. Swami Vivekananda is a well-known disciple of Ramakrishna who spread his message throughout the world.

Ramaṇa Maharṣi (1879 – 1950) : He was one of the first Hindu *yogīs* who had spiritual experience at the age of sixteen. He spent his whole life in Tiruvannamalai near the foot of the Arunachala hill. He always preached a method of inquiry into one's own inner self. Following the tradition of Advaita he believed that the realization of inner self leads to liberation.

Rāmānuja, Śrī (1017 – 1137) : He was the chief propagator of Viśiṣṭādvaita. The school of Rāmānuja has its origin in Pāñcarātra religious thought. Rāmānuja holds that the forerunners of his thought are: Bodhāyana, Ṭaṅka, Dramiḍa, Guhadeva, and Kapardin. Rāmānuja did not agree with his teacher Yādavaprakāśa, who held that *Brahman*, the individual souls (*jīva*s), and the world are all real; yet they are both identical with, and different from, one another. He could not see that logical contradiction in holding the view that the same relation cannot be both identity and difference. In fact, Rāmānuja was indebted to Yāmunācārya, whom he never met. He was influenced by Yāmuna's *Siddhitrayī*. According to Rāmānuja, there is a soul-body relationship (*apṛthak-siddhi*). In other words, the relation between *Brahman* and souls and matter is inseparable. The body may undergo change, but the spirit remains the same. The only way to liberation, according to Rāmānuja, is the path of devotion (*bhakti mārga*) and complete self-surrender (*prapatti*). The important works of Rāmānuja include: *Śrībhāṣya; Vedāntasāra; Vedāntadīpa; Vedārthasaṁgraha;* and a commentary on the *Bhagavad-Gītā*.

Ramsey, Frank Plumpton (1903 – 30) : He was a British mathematician and philosopher who held the view that when one utters a true statement one need not add "It is true" as a prefix to it. For example, in the statement "It is true that Delhi is the capital of India," "it is true" is redundant because whether one adds "it is true" or not the statement "Delhi is the capital of India" is true. His only posthumous publication is *Foundations of Mathematics and other Logical Essays.*

Random : Anything that happens without a definite direction, purpose, order, system, method is at random. For example, it is on the basis of random sampling we decide whether the water in a particular area is contaminated or not.

Ratio (L) : It means "reason." According to Spinoza, *ratio* is one of the forms of definite knowledge. It always leads to a common sense view of the world.

Rationale : The explanation offered for accepting certain basic principles in support of an idea or a view is the rationale behind it.

Rationalism : It is an epistemological doctrine that claims that all genuine knowledge is possible through reason alone. The Continental rationalists Descartes, Spinoza, and Leibniz were chiefly influenced by geometrical method. They firmly believed that the ideas constitute knowledge. Such ideas have their source in reason. Descartes and Leibniz believed in the doctrine of innate ideas. According to this doctrine, certain ideas are inborn and are highly indubitable. The ideas that are produced by intuition or reason are also true as they are "clear and distinct" to human mind. Rationalists did not attach much value to the ideas obtained through sense-experience that give us knowledge; it cannot be certain and necessary, and universal. They admitted all forms of a priori knowledge. They subscribe to coherence theory of truth.

Rawls, John (1921 – 2002) : He was an American philosopher who reviewed the social contract theory advocated by Hobbes, Rousseau, and Locke. He argued that no group as a matter of justice should be better off than any other group. He applied the principle of fairness to have a just society. His theory of justice goes very close to Kantian "Categorical Imperative." His views go against the principles of utilitarianism. His theory of justice places general good above individual interests. His important work is *A Theory of Justice* (1971).

Real : Anything that can exist independent of one's perception or consciousness is treated as real.

Realism : It is a philosophical viewpoint according to which reality exists independent of human consciousness. Opposing the views of nominalists, realists claim that universals have real existence rather than the particulars of sense-experience. Contrary to the view of idealists, realists assert that reality is not mind dependent but exists independent of the knowing subject. Naïve realists, also known as direct realists, hold that in perception the surfaces of the objects are given in sense-experience.

Recollection : According to Plato, all knowledge is possible through recollection. He conceived that every individual soul being a part of Universal Soul has the knowledge of highest Forms. It is only through recollection that individual soul comes to know of it. He advocated this view in his famous dialogue *Meno*.

Recursive : This term is used in formal logic to refer to a procedure that can go on without any stop unless something is specified to terminate it.

Reductio ad absurdum (L) : It means "reduction to absurdity." It is a way of arguing in which a statement is proved to be true because its falsity leads to absurdity.

Reductionism or Reductivism : It is a view according to which the reality can be reduced to one's own sensations. Linguistic phenomenalists attempted to reduce the statements about material objects to the statements about sense-data without any residue. In psychology, reductionism tries to reduce the human behaviour to that of animal behaviour. The two chief exponents of this view are Pavalov and Skinner. All those who hold phenomenalism as a theory of perception are reductionists.

Reductive Fallacy : It is also known as "nothing but" fallacy. This fallacy occurs when a whole is reduced to its parts. It is true that a whole is composed of its parts. This does not mean that by knowing the nature of each part of the whole one can know the whole.

Referent : It can be a thing or an object or a quality or a situation to which something is referred.

Reflection : According to John Locke, reflection is a form of experience. In this sense, it is purely internal. The ideas that are produced by reflection are the ideas such as love, hatred, pain, pleasure, etc. Sometimes it is also interpreted as introspection.

Refutation : It is a formal disproof of an argument or an assertion showing its falsity or error.

Reid, Thomas (1710 – 96) : He was a Scottish philosopher who advocated a common sense viewpoint. According to him, sensations are capable of giving us immediate knowledge of mind-independent reality. Reid held that those philosophers who advocated the theory of ideas have gone against ordinary language that is rooted in common sense. His important works include: *Inquiry into the Human Mind on the Principles of Common Sense* (1764); *Essays on the Intellectual Powers of Man* (1785); and *Essays on the Active Powers of Man* (1788).

Reification or Reism : It is a view that regards abstractions as real and prior to their referents. For example, the noun beauty is an abstraction that is attributed to a referent. In this sense, beauty is considered as an actual existent that is prior to the object to which it is attributed. It is also known as the fallacy of concretism.

Reincarnation : This term is popularly used in theology to denote the reappearance of God or some supernatural spirit in a different form altogether. It is also considered to be a synonym for "metempsychosis."

Relation : It is one of the categories of understanding postulated by Immanuel Kant. It includes substance, causality, and community.

Relational : A proposition or a statement that has more than one subject, affirming or denying a relation between them.

Relations, External : The relationship between two objects is said to be an external relationship only when it does not affect the nature of the objects. For example, "The book of Philosophy is on the table." The relationship between the book of philosophy and the table is purely an external relation. The book on the table is not only distinguishable from the table, but also separable from it. G.E. Moore advocated that there are only external relations. In Indian tradition such a relation is postulated by Vaiśeṣika in the name of *saṁyoga*.

Relations, Internal : The internal relations are those that directly affect the nature of the object in question. For example, "Man is a rational being." Bradley held that relations are only internal. In Indian tradition Vaiśeṣika postulated such a relation in the name of inherence (*samavāya*). Here the relationship between two entities is distinguishable, but not separable.

Relativism : It is the view that maintains that our judgements with regard to any knowledge claim are relative. We cannot have absolute knowledge of any phenomena. Any attempt to arrive at absolute truth, claim relativists, is an absurdity.

Relativity Theory : The theory of relativity was propounded by Albert Einstein. According to this theory, the spatio-temporal framework of the world is essentially derived from the process of observing it. Thus the classical notions of space and time are refuted by the theory of relativity.

Religion : It is a strong faith in some supernatural Spirit or God. Religion and reason cannot go together. The postulates of religious experience cannot be established by means of any investigation. They are accepted as a matter of faith. Every religion has its own ideals. For example, Hinduism believes in *mokṣa*. Some say that where reason ends, there faith begins.

Religion, Philosophy of : It is a branch of philosophy that is concerned with the proofs for the existence of God, the transmigration of soul, the problem of immortality, the nature of good and evil, etc. It is mainly concerned with the philosophy behind any religious practice.

Renaissance : It refers to the period of cultural revivalism which took place at the end of Medieval times. This movement started in Italy in fourteenth century and spread to France and England in fifteenth and sixteenth centuries respectively. This movement undermined the Christian supremacy and did not accept any prescriptions from clerical authority. This movement ushered in humanitarianism.

Representationalism : It is a theory that holds that the ideas being copies of objects external to us are nothing but representations of objects. Such a theory of perception was advocated by John Locke. Thus, all that mind comes into contact with is a set of ideas, but not with the objects.

Retrospection : It is the ability to reflect on the past operations of consciousness, or past events.

Rhetoric : It is the art of articulation through which one can impress and persuade others.

Right : It is a privilege sanctioned to individuals by state. For instance, the Constitution of India has guaranteed certain rights to its citizens. John Locke held that every individual possesses certain natural rights. It is the responsibility of the government to protect the natural rights of the individuals.

Romanticism : It is a movement started in Germany in the late eighteenth and in early nineteenth centuries against rationalism and empiricism. The seeds of romanticism are seen in the writings of idealist thinkers like Rousseau, Kant and Emerson. As an artistic method romanticism tries to explain the relation between self and phenomenal world, and at the same time it brings out the power of imagination of human will.

Rorty, Richard Mackay (1931 –) : He is one of the leading contemporary American philosophers. He is known for his critique of epistemology. He held that modern philosophy that emerged out of the womb of seventeenth-century notions of knowledge and mind, has become stale, insipid and out of place in the "conversation of mankind." According to Rorty, the self-image exhibited by most of the analytical philosophers is an act of self-deception and a grand illusion. The important issues with which the contemporary analytic philosophers are occupied are the problem of mind-body identity, justification of the claims to knowledge, reference and meaning. Taking the cue from later Wittgenstein, although Rorty owes his allegiance to pragmatism advanced by James and Dewey, he holds that these problems cannot be solved, but can be deconstructed. The influence of pragmatism on Rorty is evident from his approach to the problems of philosophy. He shares the views of the great pragmatists against Kant, Husserl, Russell, and C.L. Lewis for their attempt to convert philosophy into a foundational discipline. Rorty's admiration for Wittgenstein, Heidegger and Dewey is the result of their efforts to make philosophy therapeutic rather than constructive, edifying rather than systematic. His most important works include: *The Linguistic Turn: Recent Essays in Philosophical Method* (1967); *Philosophy and the Mirror of Nature* (1979); *Consequences of Pragmatism* (1982); *Contingency, Irony and Solidarity* (1989); and *Objectivity, Relativism and Truth* (1991).

Ross, William David (1877 – 1971) : He was a British Aristotelian scholar and moral philosopher. As a moral intuitionist, Ross advocated the view that "right" and "good" are empirically indefinable to signify objective properties, the presence of which is known intuitively to the persons who are mature and educated. This view of Ross evoked much controversy in the

English-speaking world. His important works include: *The Right and the Good* (1930) and *Foundations of Ethics* (1939).

Rousseau, Jean-Jacques (1712 – 78) : He was a French political and social philosopher who advocated the social contract theory. According to him, it is the general will, which is important than social contract. For the sake of collective general will every individual has to contribute. He believed that the supremacy in the state must be with the people who have the power to vote on any legislative proposal. According to him, state is the higher entity than any individual. Man is by nature free, but there must be legal sanctions in the civilized state. This is for the benefit of every individual. His important works are: *Du Contract Social* (1762) and *Emile* (1762).

Royce, Josiah (1855 – 1916) : He was an American philosopher who was influenced by Hegel. Royce held the view that to have an idea that there is something called continuous world, it is necessary that there is an "Absolute experience to which all facts are known and for which all the facts are subject to universal law." His important works include: *Religious Aspects of Philosophy* (1885) and *The World and the Individual* (1900 – 01).

Russell, Bertrand Arthur William (1872 – 1970) : He was a British mathematician and philosopher who is rated as one of the outstanding philosophers in the twentieth century. Along with A.N. Whitehead, Russell wrote *Principia Mathematica*. He firmly believed that mathematics can be reduced to logic. According to him, "logic is the boyhood of mathematics and mathematics is the manhood of logic." He was an ardent idealist in the beginning. He broke away from that tradition because of his friend G.E. Moore, and became a realist. As an analytical philosopher, especially an advocate of logical atomism, Russell held the views that language mirrors the reality. He claimed that logical atomism is a species of realism. The only function of philosophy is the logical clarification of language. As an empiricist, Russell maintained that what is immediately given in sense-experience is the sense-datum, which he called the knowledge by acquaintance, but not material objects. He asserted that all the material objects are nothing but "logical constructions" out of actual and possible sense-data. As a social philosopher he was active in leading a campaign against nuclear armament. He won the Nobel Prize in 1950 for his contribution to literature. He did not believe in the existence of God and immortality of the soul. He held that those beliefs are mere logical possibilities without any ground to support them. To a great extent Russell supported the views of Hume as regards causation and induction. He presented the same Humean philosophy in a different linguistic garb. Russell wrote a large number of books. The important among them are *The Philosophy of Leibniz* (1900); *The Principles of Mathematics* (1903); *Principia Mathematica* (1910-13) in 3 volumes; *The Problems of Philosophy* (1912); *Our Knowledge of the External World* (1914); *The Analysis of Mind* (1921); *The Analysis of Matter* (1927); *An Enquiry into Meaning and Truth* (1940); *History of Western Philosophy* (1946); *Human Knowledge: Its Scope and Limits* (1948), etc.

Ryle, Gilbert (1900 – 76) : He was a British analytical philosopher and the follower of ordinary language philosophy. His book *The Concept of Mind* (1949) is basically concerned with the logical geography of mental concepts. In that work, Ryle criticizes Descartes' myth, namely, the dualism between mind and body. This dualism is based on a category mistake, according to which it is a mistake to think that two entities belonging to two different categories are reduced to one logical category. He also labelled the doctrine of Descartes "an official doctrine." He also criticized the Cartesian conception of man by dubbing it "the dogma of the Ghost in the Machine." The other important work of Ryle is *Dilemmas* (1953).

S

Śabda (S) : *Śabda* is one of the valid means of knowledge. It is the knowledge obtained by means of verbal testimony. Nyāya-Vaiśeṣika, Mīmāṁsā, and Advaita admitted that *śabda* or *āgama* is a valid means of knowledge. It is the statement of a trustworthy person (*āptavākya*) and consists in understanding its meaning. *Śabda* is of two types, namely, scriptural (*vaidika*) and secular (*laukika*). The *vaidika śabda* is perfect and infallible because the Vedas are *apauruṣeya*. The *laukika śabda* being the testimony of human beings is not infallible. A word is a potent symbol that signifies an object. Sentences are made out of words. But a sentence in order to be intelligible must fulfil the following conditions. They are *ākāṅkṣā, yogyatā, sannidhi*, and *tātparya*. Cārvāka does not admit *śabda pramāṇa*.

Saint-Simon Claude-Henri de Rouvroy, Comte de (1760 – 1825) : He was a French sociologist who emphasized that any political vision must have its base in social and historical conditions. According to him, all the members of working class are *industriels*. He was associated with the historian Thierry and positivist Comte.

Sākṣin (S) : It is the self that witnesses all the human actions. According to Advaita, the *sākṣin* is neutral. It is always associated with internal organ (*antaḥkaraṇa*).

Salva Veritate (L) : It means "the truth being preserved." It was first introduced by Leibniz to explain the nature of synonymity. According to him, two terms are synonymous to each other in so far as they are mutually interchangeable in a sentence without changing its meaning. For instance, the term "bachelor" is synonymous to the term "unmarried man." In that sense, they are interchangeable.

Samādhi (S) : It means "concentration." It is one of the eight disciplines prescribed by the Yoga system. It is the final step in the practice of Yoga. In this state, mind is so deeply absorbed in the object of contemplation that it loses itself in the object. Thus it has no awareness of itself.

Sāṁkhya : It is one of the oldest six orthodox systems of Indian philosophy. It is founded by the great sage and seer Kapila. He might have lived before Buddha and authored the famous *Sāṁkhya-sūtra*. Īśvarakṛṣṇa (c. fifth century CE) is the summariser of the Sāṁkhya tradition. The word "Sāṁkhya" is derived from the word "Saṁkhyā" meaning right knowledge and also number. According to Sāṁkhya, there are two prime categories, *prakṛti* and *puruṣa*; the former is dynamic and possesses three important *guṇas*, namely, *sattva*, *rajas*, and *tamas*, and the latter is static and is of the nature of consciousness. Sāṁkhya and Yoga are considered to be the twin systems. Sāṁkhya is an uncompromising dualism blended with pluralistic spiritualism and atheistic realism. As regards causation Sāṁkhya believes in *satkāryavāda*, according to which effect pre-exists in cause. Sāṁkhya advocates a theory of evolution according to which the entire world is the resultant effect of the proximity of *prakṛti* and *puruṣa*. The proximity between these two ultimate realities disturbs the state of equilibrium that exists among the *guṇas* of *prakṛti* and gives rise to evolution. The evolution is teleological. There are twenty-four evolutes. The first evolute is *mahat*. It is followed by *ahaṁkāra*, *manas*, five sensory organs, five motor organs, five *tanmātras*, five *mahābhūtas*, and the *puruṣa*. In epistemology, Sāṁkhya accepts *pratyakṣa*, *anumāna*, and *śabda*. Sāṁkhya believes that bondage and liberation are only phenomenal. It is only the ego, the product of *prakṛti*, which is bound. Consequently, it is the ego that is liberated. The original Sāṁkhya was monistic and theistic. But the classical Sāṁkhya is atheistic.

Sanction : A sanction is that which serves as an obligation for an individual to act or not to act in accordance with a rule or a maxim.

Śaṅkara, Ādi (788 – 820) : He is regarded as one of the legendary figures of Indian tradition, and is also regarded as the chief propagator of Advaita Vedānta. He is also considered to be one of the greatest dialecticians of the tradition. According to Śaṅkara, *Brahman* is identical with *ātman*. There is no Reality other than *Brahman*. His *magnum opus* is *Brahma-Sūtra-Bhāṣya*. Śaṅkara's main works being commentaries, it is difficult to say how many kinds of means of valid cognition (*pramāṇa*s) were accepted by him. However, it is held that he admitted six *pramāṇa*s, namely, *pratyakṣa, anumāna, śabda, upamāna, arthāpatti,* and *anupalabdhi*. According to Śaṅkara, *māyā* or *avidyā* is not pure illusion. It is not only absence of knowledge. Śaṅkara held that from the phenomenal (*vyāvahārika*) point of view the world is real. It is not an illusion. It is empirically real. He distinguished the dream state from waking state. Things experienced in the dream appear to be true so long as the dream lasts. But one comes to know that it is a dream only when one is in the waking state. Thus the objects of dream experience are contradicted by the objects of waking experience. Similar is the case with our *vyāvahārika* world. It is public and is the creation of Īśvara or *saguṇa Brahman*. The world of plurality is real until one is completely freed from *avidyā*. The transition from *vyāvahārika* to *pāramārthika* makes us realize that the world of plurality is only a *mithyā*. In soteriology, Śaṅkara advocated *jīvanmukti,* according to which an individual gets liberated while he is alive. His body continues to exist till the *prārabdha-karma* gets exhausted. Śaṅkara wrote many commentaries, minor and major works. He wrote commentaries on ten major Upaniṣads, and on the *Bhagavad-Gītā*.

Santayana, George (1863 – 1952) : He was a Spanish-born American philosopher and writer who expressed the view that all rational processes are the expressions of the animal compulsion to believe in certain things or phenomena. For instance, the belief in the existence of matter is one among those things or phenomena. He viewed that the real grasp of essences of things or phenomena enables the mind to retain the changing data of experience. He was a naturalist. He commented that America is a young nation with old mentality. His important works include: *The Life of Reason* (1905-06); *Scepticism and Animal Faith* (1923); *The Realm of Essence* (1927); *The Realm of Matter* (1930), *The Realm of Truth* (1938); and *The Realm of Spirit* (1940).

Sartre, Jean Paul (1905 – 80) : He was a French atheistic existentialist and a novelist who recognized two types of being. They are: *en-soi* (being-in-itself), and *pour-soi* (being-for-itself). "Being-in-itself" represents the existence of inert, insentient objects; while the "being-for-itself" represents the conscious existence of a human individual. According to Sartre, human individual is condemned to be free. He has to opt for his own course of action among the choices available to him. Sartre is a champion of freedom. His notion of freedom is akin to that of Fichte. He always considered "the other" as hell. In his plays and novels he tried to show that man is the architect of his own life and character. He refused to accept the Nobel Prize awarded to him in 1964 for his contribution to literature. His important works are *Naucea* (1938); *Being and Nothingness* (1943); *The Flies* (1943); *The Age of Reason* (1945); *Existentialism is a Humanism* (1946); *The Reprieve* (1947); *Iron in the Soul* (1949); *Critique of Dialectical Reason* (1960).

Satire : It is a form of artistic expression that belittles a particular idea or an opinion or a view.

Satisfaction : It is a technical term used in formal semantics when an object or a sequence of objects satisfies the attribution of a predicate to the object or a sequence of objects in question. For example, "Bombay is a very big city." This expression is true of Bombay. Hence the attribution "very big city" fulfils the condition of satisfaction.

Satkāryavāda (S) : It is a theory of causation, according to which the effect pre-exists in its cause prior to its manifestation. This theory is propounded by Sāṁkhya school. According to Sāṁkhya, the world is an evolution of *prakṛti*. It is also known as *pariṇāmavāda*.

Sattva (S) : According to Sāṁkhya, it is one of the three *guṇa*s of *prakṛti*. It is the quality that is responsible for the self-manifestation and self-maintenance of *prakṛti*. It also represents light or knowledge.

Sautrāntika : It is one of the realistic schools of Buddhism. According to this school, both mental and non-mental are real. All the objects existing external to the mind are real. Our perception of objects depends upon the objects existing outside the mind. Such a view is called representationalism (*bāhyānumeyavāda*).

Sc(k)epticism : This term has its origin in the Greek term *skepsis* meaning doubt. It is one of the popular theories in epistemology. A skeptic is one who doubts the possibility of every epistemological claim to knowledge. However, the Greek skeptics like Pyrrho (c. 365 – 175 BCE) and Sextus Empiricus (c. 150 – 210) introduced skepticism as a method to arrive at certainty. In fact, they recommended the suspension of judgement. Even René Descartes in modern period had introduced "doubting method" to arrive at certainty. These skeptics are called methodical or methodological skeptics. The skepticism advocated by David Hume is called psychological skepticism, which corrodes all forms of certainty. This form of skepticism is more prevalent in the epistemological doctrines of the majority of modern thinkers.

Schelling, Friedrich Witheim Joseph Von (1775 – 1854) : He was a German idealist philosopher whose transcendental idealism is akin to that of Kant. His transcendental idealism is an attempt to modify the views of Kant with regard to the self and its relation to the world of things. According to Schelling, consciousness is the only immediate object of knowledge. The knowledge of objective world only arises as a limiting condition in the process by which consciousness is aware of it. He was also a champion of romanticism. His important work is *The System of Transcendental Idealism* (1800).

Schema : In traditional logic, the figure of a syllogism is called schema.

Schiller, Ferdinand Canning Scott (1865 – 1937) : He was a British philosopher who claimed to be the follower of the Greek philosopher Protagoras. According to him, truth and reality are mere human constructions. He held the view that there is an objective world given independently of us. In this sense, he is a realist. He distinguished humanism from pragmatism only to show that the former has broader application than the latter. He opposed Bradley's rigid Hegelian absolutism. His important work is *Humanism* (1903).

Schism : It is a division in belief about a thing which leads to group factions and divisions. For example, there is a schism as regards the approach of Wittgenstein to language, namely, early Wittgenstein and later Wittgenstein.

Schlick, Moritz (1882 – 1936) : He was an Austrian physicist and a philosopher who founded the Vienna Circle. He was a Professor of Philosophy of the Inductive Sciences. According to Schlick, the function of philosophy is the logical clarification of thought. The chief aim of the "Vienna Circle" is to eliminate metaphysics from the sphere of philosophy to make philosophy a genuine branch of knowledge. In order to distinguish meaningful statements from meaningless assertions, Schlick introduced the principle of verification. According to this principle, "the meaning of a statement is the method of its verification." He accepted the strong form of the verification principle which not only excluded metaphysics, but also theoretical science. He called the statements of ethics as nonsense because they cannot be verified. His important work is *The Problems of Ethics* (1939).

Scholasticism : It is a kind of philosophical method practised during the Medieval period. By derivation it is a method of disputation engineered by Peter Abelard (1017 – 1142). Scholastics believe that for any contemplation on the ultimate reasons for the existence of things and phenomena what is required is leisure. Scholasticism sometimes leads to endless and meaningless discussions. The supposed "Golden age" of scholasticism was the thirteenth century. St. Thomas Aquinas was an accomplished scholastic of his time.

Schopenhauer, Arthur (1788 – 1860) : He was a German idealist philosopher who admitted Kant's classification of the world into phenomenal and noumenal. According to the phenomenal aspect, the self is that which appears as the object of perception and the self as a *Ding-an-Sich* (*noumenon*) is the manifestation of the will. Thus the ultimate driving force of the reality is the will. It seems that he was influenced by both Buddhism and Vedānta. He firmly believed that the evil and the pain in the world are due to the exercise of the will. His important work is *The World as Will and Idea* (1819).

Science : It is a systematic effort to obtain the knowledge of nature, society, and thought. In this sense science is nothing but man's systematic understanding of the various phenomena (natural and social). Science is always persuasive and necessarily based on evidence or proof. There are exact sciences, natural sciences and social sciences.

Science, Philosophy of : It is a branch of philosophy that is basically concerned with the methods and approaches adopted by various empirical sciences in the quest for knowledge of the reality. On the basis of the results of the empirical sciences, the philosophers of science evaluate the rationality behind every method and approach for a better understanding of the reality. The noted philosophers of science are Sir Karl Popper, Thomas Kuhn, Feyerband, and Lakotas.

Scientism : It is the belief that the methods of natural sciences can successfully be applied to human sciences. In another sense, every practice is claimed to be scientific whether it is or not.

Scotism : It is the philosophy of Duns Scotus and his followers.

Self : It is the unity that lasts throughout the changes and that which is aware of such an unity. It is often referred to as "I" or "Pure ego" or "Subject." According to Hume, there is no continuous self. He conceived that self is a bundle of impressions. Even the followers of Hume, the modern empiricists, dismissed the notion of self as something irrational. Similar view is advocated by the Buddhists. Therefore, they are known as *anātmavādin*s.

Self-alienation : It is a condition of the self in which it is aware of its estrangement from itself, and also from other objects or individuals. It is one of the forms of alienation recognized by the Marxists.

Self-evident : A statement or an entity or an explanation that does not require any proof to establish itself is called self-evident. For example, Descartes' statement "I think, therefore I am" is self-evident.

Self-existence : In Spinoza's philosophy, substance is regarded as self-existent. Even Descartes held such a view about substance. In that sense, anything that does not depend on any other thing for its existence is self-existent. *Brahman* is self-existent according to Advaita. The world for its existence is dependent on *Brahman*. In Heidegger's philosophy Being is self-existent. All the beings are grounded in Being for their existence.

Semantics : It is a branch of linguistics that deals with the theories of meaning. This branch is of immense importance to the branches like linguistics, philosophy of language, and logic. It is in the field of semantics that a distinction is made between surface and depth semantics (grammar). Also, to a great extent it is concerned with the question whether words independent of sentences in which they occur have meanings or not. Thus both "word meaning" and "sentence meaning" come under the study of semantics.

Semesiology : It has its origin in the Greek word *semasia*. It is the study of the meanings of the words.

Semiosis : It is a state of understanding that results from the usage of a symbol. A symbol can be a sign, linguistic expression, and speech form.

Semiotics : It is the study of the nature and kinds of various signs. It is also concerned with how signs produce the intended meaning or effect when they are used in communication.

Sensation : It is a kind of psychical state occurring as a result of direct influence of the objects on the sense-organs. Such an experience is private to one's own self. Sensation is of two types, external and internal. External sensation is caused by any one of the five senses, namely, sense of sight, sense of touch, sense of taste, sense of sound, and sense of smell. Internal sensation is caused by reflections or psychical acts of the mind.

Sensationalism : It is a doctrine in epistemology, according to which sensations are the sole source of knowledge. For example, Berkeley and Hume are called pure sensationalists. Both these philosophers reduced reality to sensible qualities and sense-impressions respectively. The ontology of sensationalism is that there is nothing except sensations. Ultimately everything is explained in terms of sensations.

Sense-data : This term was first introduced by G.E. Moore to denote those objects that are immediately given in sense-experience. Subsequently, the term has been used more freely by H.H. Price, A.J. Ayer and other analytical philosophers. According to these philosophers, what is immediately given in sense-experience is called "sense-datum." They also held the view that the so-called material objects are nothing but the "logical constructions" out of actual and possible sense-data.

Sensibilia : This term is introduced by Bertrand Russell to denote the unsensed sense-data. In his *The Problems of Philosophy*, Russell used this expression.

Sensible World : It is the world that is presented to the senses. It is also referred to as phenomenal, or the world of things or objects. According to Kant, sensible world is known as phenomena.

Sensor : A sense-organ of a living being that receives stimuli is called sensor. In some cases the entire organism may function as a sensor.

Sensorium : This term was put into use by Newton to denote the seat in the brain of sensation and perception.

Set : A set is a collection of objects or members that become or form the members of that set.

Sextus Empiricus (c. second century CE) : He was a well-known Greek physician and skeptic who started the empirical school of medicine. He made use of Pyrrhonic skepticism to arrive at certainty. He believed that by suspending all forms of judgement one can arrive at the state of ataraxia or the tranquillity of mind. His important works are: *Hypotyposes and Adversus Mathematicos; Outlines of Pyrrohonism*; and *Against the Logicians, Physicists, and Ethicists.*

Shaftesbury, Anthony Ashley Cooper (1671 – 1713) : He was a British moral philosopher and a writer who was chiefly influenced by John Locke. In opposition to Hobbes' view, Shaftesbury held that man is naturally moral as he has inherent affection for virtue. His important work is *Characteristics of Men, Manners, Opinions, Times.*

Siddhānta or Uttarapakṣa (S) : It means conclusion. It is the position or the view of the philosopher along with the proof. In other words, it is known as the subsequent view.

Sidgwick, Henry (1838 – 1900) : He was a British moral philosopher who advocated utilitarian ethics. According to

Sidgwick, the obligation to promote general happiness is realized only when it is regarded as moral intuition. One of his important works is *Methods of Ethics* (1874).

Sign and Symbol : A satisfactory definition for these terms is not possible. For instance, words are supposed to be the conventional signs; while language is considered to be a kind of symbolism. In that sense, language consists of signs. A twister in the sky is said to be a natural sign. In a sense a sign is something that stands for anything. A symbol is a sign by which one knows or infers a thing. Sometimes it is stated that the meaning of a symbol is restricted to a conventional sign.

Simple Enumeration : It is a form of inductive procedure by means of which a property of a class or things or objects is decided on the basis of random sampling. For example, this vessel consists of coffee seeds. To know whether they are good quality seeds or not, one must randomly check a few seeds. If those randomly selected seeds are good, then all those seeds in that vessel are good quality seeds. This method was introduced by J.S. Mill.

Sin : This term frequently occurs in theology. According to theology, sin is a kind of offence against God. Sinners are those who go against the commands of God.

Smith, Adam (1723 – 90) : He was a Scottish economist and a philosopher, who is well-known for his work *The Wealth of Nations* (1776). His political economy is based on the simple system of natural liberty. He held that the general welfare of humanity is perpetuated only when an individual's own interest is promoted. His other important work is *Theory of Moral Sentiments* (1759). In this work he tried to show that our moral judgements are the outcome of our concern for fellow beings. Thus they have more impartial status.

Social Contract : It is an agreement or a covenant that takes place between individuals, or between individuals and the Government for the betterment of the society. In the process of social contract, some individuals have to sacrifice their liberties for the development of state as a whole. Hobbes, Locke, and Rousseau, were the champions of social contract theory. However, each one differs form the other in the interpretation of it.

Socrates (C. 470 – 399 BCE) : He was an ancient Greek philosopher and teacher of Plato. He never believed in writing. He used to give discourses in public places. According to him, all knowledge is conceptual. The logic of disputation was the method adopted by Socrates to arrive at certain conclusions. It is believed that Socrates believed in the immortality of the soul. He was charged with impiety and corrupting the youth by his Government. He was put to death by forcing him to drink hemlock.

Solipsism : The theory that "I" and my own self alone exist. All others' existence is reduced to my own existence. In fact, every subjective idealist doctrine ultimately boils down to solipsism. According to Wittgenstein, solipsism is inconsistent because the question of "I" does not arise unless there are others.

Some : In logic, it is considered as a quantifier. "Some" denotes at least one. It can also mean everyone except one.

Sophists : They were supposed to be wise and learned. They taught several things to the people by selling their ideas. They were the intellectual warehouses. Their teachings were known through Plato's criticism against them. Like Cārvāka of Indian tradition, Sophists believed that sense-experience is the only legitimate source of knowledge. According to Hegel, Sophists were subjective idealists. Unlike pre-Socratic philosophers, who gave importance to reality (*physis*), Sophists believed in what is held to be right (*nomos*).

Sorel, Georges (1847 – 1922) : He was a French philosopher who was chiefly influenced by Nietzsche, Marx, and Bergson. He emphasized the creative role of violence in history. According to him, compromise and mediation are the characteristic features of a decadent social system. His important work is *Reflexions sur la violence* (1908).

Sorites : It is an argument that consists of many premisses and terms but satisfies the criteria for syllogisms. The conclusion of each syllogism becomes the premise of its succeeding syllogism. It is also called polysyllogism.

Sortal Universal : It is a general term that supplies a principle for counting what falls under it.

Soul : Sometimes it is also used as a synonym for self. In religion, soul is considered to be an incorporeal, immortal, and immaterial force capable of existing independently of body in the other world. According to Plato, soul is an eternal idea; while Hegel regarded it as the lowest sensory manifestation of the spirit in its relation with matter.

Specious Present : It is the time gap that is almost negligible between two events. Because of such least temporal gap between one event and the other we may say that they are co-present or contemporaneous.

Speech Acts : They are the acts that are performed while speaking. This term was introduced by J.L. Austin. According to Austin, speech acts can be classified into locutionary, illocutionary, and perlocutionary acts. A locutionary act is one in which a statement is uttered with a definite reference. For example, "This is red." An illocutionary act is one in which the statement uttered implies the act in question. For Example, "I promise that I will definitely come." It is not only an utterance but also the performance of an act. A perlocutionary act is one in which a statement uttered will have some specific effects upon the feelings, thoughts, or behaviour of an individual. For example, "You are a wicked person" is a perlocutionary utterance.

Spencer, Herbert (1820 – 1903) : He was a British philosopher who advocated a social theory of evolution. His theory of evolution sets out to show that there is a progress from indefinite incoherent homogeneity to a definite coherent heterogeneity. His important books are *First Principles* (1862); and *Principles of Ethics* (1879 – 83).

Spengler, Oswald (1880 – 1936) : He was a German philosopher who was chiefly interested in history. According to him, every system of thought or value is determined on the basis of existing social culture. Therefore, it cannot have universal validity. He was a thoroughgoing relativist. His important work is *Der Untergang des Abendlandes* (1918 and 1922), 2 vols.

Spinoza, Benedictus (1632 – 77) : He was a continental rationalist who reduced the Cartesian dual substances into one. If there are two infinite substances, each one tries to limit the other. According to Spinoza, there is only one substance with two important knowable attributes, namely, thought and extension. He was expelled from his Jewish community for his radical views on God. Spinoza considered that Substance, God, and Nature are one. He conceived that substance is that "which is in itself and is conceived through itself." Substance is self-caused (*Causa sui*). He advocated psycho-physical parallelism. His important works include: Descartes' *Principles of Philosophy* (1663); *Treatise on Theology and Politics* (1670); and *Ethics* (1677).

Śravaṇa (S) : It is one of the spiritual stages prescribed by Advaita for the attainment of liberation (*mukti*). It consists in listening to the scriptural instructions about the Self (*ātman*).

Śruti (S) : Śruti is the Veda or the scriptural authority. It also means anything that is orally transmitted.

Stagirite, the : It is a nickname given to Aristotle as he was born in Stagira.

Stratonion Presumption : It is a view according to which whosoever wants to postulate the existence of God must give sufficient reasons for such a postulation.

Strawson, (Sir) Peter Frederick (1919 – 2006) : He was a British analytic philosopher who posited material objects as basic particulars in his work *Individuals* (1959). In logic, Strawson tries to show the relationship between ordinary language and formal logic. Also, he holds that in making statements we presuppose the existence of the subject class. He attacked Russell's notion of the theory of descriptions in his famous article "On Referring" (1950). According to Strawson, Russell confused reference with descriptions. Strawson opposed the correspondence theory of truth. He states that the statements, when they are true, do not really correspond with facts but only state them. His other important work is *An Introduction to Logical Theory* (1952).

Stream of Consciousness : It is a term coined by American pragmatist and psychologist, William James, to denote the continuity of thought process.

Structuralism : It is a scientific point of view basically concerned with the structures of the objects. As a reaction to positivism, structuralism was developed by sociologists and linguists in the twentieth century. It makes use of structural methods of research developed by mathematics, physics, and other natural sciences. The characteristic feature of structuralism is to investigate into the intrinsic, timeless properties of objects, and to establish relations of elements of the system under consideration. Structuralism resembles the Aristotelian notion of form as against content. Levi Strauss is a popular exponent of structuralism.

Subaltern : It is a term that is used in the traditional square of opposition that is popular in scholastic logic. In this traditional square, the universal affirmative propositions and the particular affirmative propositions stand subaltern to each other. For example, "All men are mortal" (A) is a subaltern of "Some men are mortal" (I).

Sub-contraries : In a traditional square of opposition, particular affirmative propositions and particular negative propositions are sub-contraries to each other. For example, "Some crows are black" (I) and "Some crows are not black" (O) are sub-contraries.

Subjectivism : In its general sense, it is a viewpoint that reduces every situation to one's own mental attitude. Moral subjectivists claim that all moral virtues are the tastes of respective individuals. What is claimed as a value by one individual may not be a value for another. Extreme form of subjectivism leads to emotivism. Subjectivism is opposed to objectivism.

Sublime, the : Anything that is beyond comparison and considered to be of highest value and greatness is sublime. For instance, the truth of God is a sublime truth.

Subsistence : It is a mode of being that is distinguished from the three-dimensional existence of the objects. According to Meinong and others, subsistence is a monochrome and insubstantial analogue which does not exist in space and time, but is real such as relation, number, universal spirit, soul, etc. It is also said that qualities being dependent on the substance for their existence, they cannot have independent existence apart from the substance. In other words, they subsist in the substance.

Substance : It is something that exists on its own, and can be conceived through itself. Spinoza called it *causa sui*. In another sense, a substance is that which constitutes the essential nature of a thing that makes a thing what it is. There are two types of substance, namely, spiritual and material. The chief attribute of a spiritual substance is non-extension, while the important attribute of material substance is extension.

Substratum : Anything that acts as a locus or a base for a set of qualities, modes, accidents, and changes is called substratum. Sometimes a substance is also called substratum.

Subtle Doctor : It was the nickname given to the scholastic philosopher Duns Scotus.

Sufficient Condition : *A* is a sufficient condition of *B*. If whenever there is *A*, then there is *B*.

Summum bonum (L) : It means "the highest good." It was Aristotle who introduced this term into ethics to denote the greatest good that is sought by every human individual.

Supervenient Features or Characteristics or Qualities : The qualities or properties that are dependent upon some other qualities or properties are called supervenient characteristics.

Supposition : In medieval logic, a noun or a substantive that stands for a thing or things is called supposition. For example, "bat" in "Bat is a mammal" is a supposition.

Syllogism : It is a valid deductive argument with two premisses and a conclusion that follows from the premisses. It is of two kinds, namely, inductive and deductive. The conclusion of an inductive syllogism is only probable if its premisses are true. On the contrary, the conclusion of a deductive syllogism is true if its premisses are true.

Symptom : In the work of later Wittgenstein, symptom is contrasted with criterion. According to him, a symptom serves as evidence rather than a criterion. For example, whenever there is *A*, it is invariably followed by *B*. In that sense, *A* is a symptom of *B*.

Syncategorematic : In traditional logic, there are certain words that cannot be stated on their own, in the sense that they do not convey any meaning unless they are joined with a categorematic term to form a categorical statement. For example, the words such as "all," "an," "some," etc., are syncategorematic words.

Syntax : It is the study of rules of structure of language. In logic, syntax deals with the formal arrangement of symbols.

Synthesis : It is a process of bringing all the simple elements together to form a complex whole. The method of synthesis is advanced by many philosophers. In Hegel's philosophy, synthesis is nothing but the fusion of two diametrically opposite ideas known as thesis and antithesis. Synthetic approach to philosophy is diametrically opposite to analytic approach.

Synthetic Judgement : According to Kant, a synthetic judgement is a judgement in which the predicate is something new. Hence it gives new information about the world. For example, the judgement "All bodies have specific gravity" is a synthetic judgement. See Analytic and Synthetic.

T

Tables of Investigation, the Three : According to Francis Bacon, there are three important tables of investigation. They are: (1) *The table of Affirmation* or *The rule of Presence*: This rule emphasizes the enumeration and examination of all the varied positive examples of the phenomena under investigation that possess the same qualities. For instance, fire, human body, the sun, light, friction, etc., possess heat. (2) *The table of Negation* or *The rule of Counter-example*: This rule maintains that one must state all the negative instances where a particular quality does not present, but where one might think it should be. And (3) *The table of Comparison* or *The rule of Differing Degrees*: According to this principle, all the differences among the phenomena must be examined in order to find any correlations that exist among them.

Tabula rasa (L) : It means "a blank sheet or tablet." According to Locke, mind in the beginning is a blank sheet of paper on which later on the impressions (ideas) are imprinted. Thus Locke vehemently criticized the doctrine of innate ideas.

Tādātmya (S) : It means "identity of being" or "self-sameness." According to Advaita Vedānta, the identity between *Brahman* and *ātman* is *tādātmya.*

Taittirīya Upaniṣad (S) : This Upaniṣad gives details about the five kinds of union, namely, the union of physical elements like earth, water, air and so on; the union of shining beings like sun, fire, and lightning; the union of knowledge like that in the teacher, student, and discourses; the union of creative beings like father, mother, and creation; and the union of physiological parts like the upper jaw, the lower jaw, and speech. This Upaniṣad also analyses the nature of internal world by giving the structure of five sheaths (*pañcakośas*), namely, *annamaya-kośa*, *prāṇamaya-kośa*, *manomaya-kośa*, *vijñānamaya-kośa*, and *ānandamaya-kośa*, that envelop the Self (*ātman*). According to this Upaniṣad, *Brahman* is the Truth, Consciousness, and the Infinite.

Tamas (S) : It is one of the three *guṇas* of *prakṛti*, according to Sāṁkhya. It is the principle responsible for inertia (*jaḍatva*). *Tamas* is of an indifferent nature. It represents darkness or dullness. It serves to restrain certain activities or actions.

Ṭaṅka (S) : He is a pre-Rāmānuja Viśiṣṭādvaitin. Ṭaṅka's name was mentioned in Rāmānuja's *Śrī Bhāṣya*.

Tanmātras (S) : There are five important elements (*pañca mahābhūtas*). They are: ether, air, fire, water, and earth. These five elements are derived from the *tanmātras* such as sound, touch, sight, taste, smell respectively.

Taoism : It was a Chinese philosophical school of thought as old as Confucianism. Its known founder is Lao-tze (C. 604 BCE). Tao means "a way of life." The basic teachings of Taoism rest on the principle of not doing anything and not resisting anything. The Tao way of life can be achieved by virtue, by compassion, humility, and non-violence.

Tarka (S) : It means "reasoning." It is one of the sixteen categories of Nyāya School. It consists in seeking reasons for supporting a statement or an argument.

Tarski, Alfred (1902 – 83) : He was a Polish-American logician and mathematician who advocated semantic theory of truth. According to this theory, any attempt to define truth in natural language will fall foul of liar paradox. His theory of truth served as a good basis for theory of meaning. Tarski distinguishes between first-order language and second-order language (meta-language). For instance the statement, "Snow is white is true *iff* and only if snow is white" has two components. As a statement it is about snow and its qualities. This statement is true provided "whiteness" is the quality of snow. Thus "is true" and "is false," according to Tarski belong to meta-language. Tarski's theory is an advanced version of correspondence theory. His important work is "The Concept of Truth in Formalized Languages," in *Logic, Semantics and Mathematics* (1956).

Taste : It is one of the five senses. It is also a personal preference.

Taṭastha-Lakṣaṇa (S) : It means "accidental or adventitious qualities." *Brahman*, according to Advaita, can be interpreted from two standpoints, namely, relative (*vyāvahārika*) and absolute (*pāramārthika*). From the relative point of view, *Brahman* is *saguṇātmaka*. Therefore, it has qualities. These qualities are only accidental qualities which are superimposed on *Brahman*. From the absolute point of view, there is nothing other than *Brahman*.

Tat-tvam-asi (S) : It means "that-thou-art." It is a *mahāvākya* that appears in *Chāndogya Upaniṣad*. According to this *mahāvākya*, the *jīva* is essentially *Brahman*. This is the view of Advaita Vedānta.

Tautology : It is a proposition that does not give any new information except analysing what is already given in an explicit form. In that sense, the propositions of exact sciences like logic and mathematics are mere tautologies. For example, the statements "all circles are round," "2+2=4" are tautologies.

Techne (Gk) : It means "skill or craft." In Aristotle's philosophy, the term *techne* denotes that which is created by humans in contrast to natural things or phenomena. The products of science can be called *techne* as they are the artefacts of mankind.

Teilhard, de Chardin, Pierre (1881 – 1955) : He was a French natural philosopher and geologist whose main interest was to show why there is no further development into species after *Homo-sapiens*. He firmly believed that there are two fundamental principles of evolution of organic matter. They are: non-finality and complexification. However, contends Teilhard, *Homo-sapiens* is a unique species that could resist the further division of species. In his works he tried to prove the transcendental existence of God. His important works include: *La Phenomene humain* (1938-40) and *Le Milieu divin* (1957).

Teleological Argument : It is one of the proofs for the existence of God. It is an argument based on the view that there is order and purpose in this world; such an order and purpose is the design of an intelligent creator (God).

Telepathy : It is a form of extra sensory perception through which one can introspect the minds of others. It is one of the possibilities of establishing the knowledge of other minds. However, telepathy has its own defects in establishing the knowledge of other minds in the sense that it is restricted to two persons, namely, the subject and the one who practices telepathy.

Telos (Gk) : It means "the fulfilment of an activity." It can also be interpreted as "goal," "purpose," "aim," "result," and "the end."

Temperament : It represents the bodily, mental, and pre-dispositional character of an individual. There are four types of temperament. They are: sanguine, phlegmatic, bilious, and melancholic.

Temporal : Anything that is transient and worldly as opposed to supernatural, which is eternal is temporal. In Plato's philosophy, the world of Forms is an eternal non-temporal reality, while the world of things is transient and temporal.

Term : A term is something that can be applied to something. In logic, there can be subject and predicate terms. For instance, the sentence "Sriram is tall" has both subject and predicate terms. "Sriram" is the subject term, while "Tall" is the predicate term. See Minor Term, Major Term.

Term, Distributed : A term is said to be distributed when it is preceded by a universal quantifier. For example, "all" is a quantifier and refers to all the items that it can mean. Thus the term in question is distributed.

Tertiary Quality : It is opposed to primary and secondary qualities. Unlike primary and secondary qualities, tertiary quality is imposed on the object in question by the percipient. For example, beauty, good, bad and ugly are tertiary qualities. They are not the natural properties of anything.

Thales of Miletus (c. 624 – 546 BCE) : He was the first Greek philosopher who made an inquiry into the nature of things as a whole. He is also regarded as the father of philosophy. According to Thales, water is the primordial stuff from which everything has emerged. He was first to predict the solar eclipse in 585 BCE. He was one of the seven wise men of the Greek tradition. He put all his mathematical and astronomical knowledge for good use. He always looked for an explanation of natural things within nature.

Thanatism : It is a belief that death results in the cessation and annihilation of consciousness.

Thanatology : It is a study of various aspects of death and dying.

Theaetetus (c. 414 – 369 BCE) : He was an ancient Greek mathematician who joined Plato in establishing the Academy of Athens. The works of Theaetatus were used by Euclid. Plato's dialogue *Theaetatus* was mainly concerned with the definition of knowledge, and it is believed that it is named after Theaetatus.

Theism : It is a belief in divine things. Belief in one God is called monotheism, while the belief in many gods is called polytheism.

Theist : One who believes in the existence of God or in some supernatural power is a theist.

Theodicy : It is a religious-philosophical view advocated by Leibniz. According to this view, the goodness of the God can be justified in view of the evil in the world. It is also held by Leibniz that God is so benevolent that he has given us the best of the possible worlds.

Theology : It is the study of the relationship between the divine (eternal and perfect) world and the physical world.

Theology, Negative : It is a view that since human knowledge is finite, it is not possible to know the Infinite (God) in its proper sense. Whatever interpretations we present about God are only partial and incomplete.

Theophrastus (c. 370 – 288 BCE) : He was an ancient Greek mathematician and also a pupil of Aristotle. He succeeded Aristotle as a head of Lyceum, the school started by the former.

Theorem : A theorem is anything that is established as maxim, a rule or a principle. From a theorem one can deduce many valid conclusions. Theorems can be proved, unlike maxims.

Theoretical : Anything that is not practical and abstract is theoretical. It is also concerned with the general issues or principles about things.

Theoria (Gk) : It means "viewing." According to Plato, *theoria* means contemplation or the intuitive grasp of the Being (world of Forms).

Theory : A theory is a system of generally accepted authentic knowledge which provides a comprehensive picture of the essential regularities in reality. Though a theory is considered to be antithetical to practice, theory and practice cannot be separated from each other. However, theories are flexible in the sense that a more fundamental and vital theory may replace the earlier theory. For example, at one time it was theoretically conceived by the physicists that the earth was flat, but this theory of earth was replaced by another theory, namely, the earth is round. This is the reason why Diogenes of Sinope, the founder of the cynic sect, held the view that theories are highly pretentious.

Theory of Types : It is a theory advocated by Bertrand Russell and A.N. Whitehead in their *Pricipia Mathematica*. The main aim of this theory is to avoid certain logical contradictions or paradoxes on the basis that "Whatever involves all of a collection must not be one of the collection." For example, a class of classes cannot be a member of that class.

Thinking : According to Descartes, thinking is a mental activity which is the chief attribute of mind or mental faculty. Descartes went on to prove that it is because "I think, therefore I exist." With the help of thinking a person makes use of various concepts acquired in the process of learning something.

Thought Experiment : It is basically a technique of testing a hypothesis or assumption by imagining a situation and what could be said about it. This technique is commonly used by philosophers to argue either in favour of a hypothesis or against it.

Thrasymachus (c. 427 BCE) : He was an ancient Greek Sophist known through Plato's *The Republic*. He was a great teacher and author of treatises on rhetoric. His "middle-style" of rhetoric was novel and innovative. As a foil to Socrates, Thrasymachus' view on justice was represented in the following manner. Justice is that which benefits the stronger, mainly the rulers. The ruled always feel that justice is always for someone else.

Tillich, Paul (1886 – 1965) : He was a German theologian, whose approach to religion is the combination of existentialism, depth psychology, and neo-Scholastic ontology. He is well known as a crypto-atheist. According to Tillich, it is the systematic theology that advanced fresh Christian answers to the deeper existential questions posed by individuals and cultures. According to him, every age has its distinctive "crisis" or "fullness of time." Such a situation leads to creative thought and action. His important works include: *The Protestant Era* (1948) and *Systematic Theology* (1951-65, 3 volumes).

Time : It is one of the fundamental categories of physical sciences. Philosophers and scientists have interpreted it in several ways. British metaphysician McTaggart held the view that time is unreal. According to Kant, time is a form of intuition, and is absolute. Scientists like Newton and Einstein held the view that time is unidimensional. According to Newton, time is objective, though absolute, and can exist independent of the perceiving subject. All change in space takes place in time. Einstein radically departed from Newton in holding the view that time is a relative concept, and is the fourth dimension of space. Thus space and time are inseparable from each other.

Timocracy (Gk) : It means "control." According to Plato, it is a form of state in which the love of honour, glory, and esteem are considered to be the highest ideals. As regards timocracy, Aristotle held that it is a state where honour is distributed according to the economic status.

Timology (Gk) : It means "worth." It is basically concerned with what makes a thing or an object valuable or worthy. It is also viewed as a belief that all the values are intrinsically valuable.

Tīrthaṅkara (Pr.) : The prophets of Jainism are known as *tīrthaṅkara*s. All of them are supposed to have attained *kaivalya* after their death.

Token : Any sign such as a word or an utterance or gesture can be called a token. For instance, when we give a telegram, each word that we include in the message is counted as a token though some words are repeated.

Transcendental : It is something like going beyond the ordinary level of experience. According to Scholastics, unity, good, truth, etc. are considered to be transcendental categories. In Kant's philosophy these are all called transcendent objects, whereas the term "transcendental" signifies the a priori condition for all possible knowledge. Thus Kant's method is called transcendental method.

Transmigration : At the time of death the soul or the spirit transmigrates into another body. It is a prevalent view of Hindu religious doctrines.

Trāsa (S) : According to Jainism, the *jīva*s are of two types, namely, *trāsa* and *baddha*. All those *jīva*s who have movement are called *trāsa jīva*s. Under this category we can include humans, animals, gods, devils, etc.

Tripuṭi (S) : It means "triple form." In the process of cognition there are three things involved. They are the cognizer, the object of cognition, and the means of cognition. They are called *tripuṭi*. The knowledge that results from this process is called *tripuṭi-jñāna*.

Triratna (S) : It means "three jewels." Jainism considers that the right knowledge (*samyag-jñāna*), the right vision (*samyag-darśana*), and the right conduct (*samyag-caritra*) are the three jewels or virtues. According to Buddhism, Buddha, *Dharma*, and *Saṁgha* are considered to be the three jewels. Viśiṣṭādvaita recognized *mantraratna (dvaya)*, *purāṇaratna* (*Viṣnu Purāṇa*), and *stotraratna* (a work of Yāmuna) as three jewels.

Truth : The principal concern of the epistemologists is to find out the relation between knowledge and truth, for the former necessarily involves the latter. Aristotle defined truth in the following manner. He held that: "to say of something that it is when it is not is false; and to say of something that it is when it is, is true. Epistemologically speaking, there is no universally accepted definition of truth. According to Alfred Tarski, any attempt to define truth in natural languages falls foul of a liar paradox. There are only interpretations of truth. Each interpretation sets certain conditions under which a proposition is true or false. A lexicographer might define truth as something that corresponds to facts. The most prominent theories of truth can be classified under classical theories and modern theories. The former are: (1) the correspondence theory; (2) the coherence theory; and (3) pragmatic theory. The latter includes: (1) the semantic theory of truth and (2) the redundant theory of truth. The classical theories of truth claim respectively that the criteria of truth are correspondence with facts, coherence with other propositions of judgements, and success or usefulness in practice. But none of these theories defines what truth is. The theory of redundance was advocated by P.F. Ramsey. According to him, when it is said: "It is true that New Delhi is the capital of India" amounts to saying that: "New Delhi is the capital of India." In this statement the prefix "It is true" is redundant. Similarly, Tarski advanced semantic theory of truth that is akin to Ramsey's. This theory of truth intends to avoid the liar paradox by distinguishing between object language and meta-language. See the following statement: "The statement "Snow is white is true if and only if Snow is white." The meta-linguistic expression "snow is white is true" is dependent upon the object language statement "Snow is white" for its truth-value. However, both the modern theories of truth are the recent versions of correspondence. See coherence theory, correspondence theory, and pragmatic theory.

Tuccham (S) : Anything that is unreal such as "sky-lotus," is called *tuccham*. According to Advaita, *māyā* is unreal to an enlightened person.

Tyche : It is a Greek term for "luck." Anything that happens suddenly without being necessitated to happen. It serves as a base to achieve some desired goal. According to Plato, tyche (chance) is one of the three causes of events. The other two causes are: nature (PHYSICS) and human purposiveness (TECHNE). Aristotle distinguished an accident from tyche (chance).

Tychism : This term is introduced by Charles Saunders Pierce, the pioneer of pragmatism. According to tychism, the absolute chance is a characteristic feature of the events of this objective world. This theory holds that there are many theories that do not have causes at all in order to explain the biological processes of nature. In other words, they are tychistic in character.

Type : A class of things belongs to one particular set or type. For example, all the words can be classified under one type irrespective of their meanings.

U

Ubicatio (L) : It means "whereness" or the condition of being located in space.

Udāharaṇa (S) : It means "illustration." *Udāharaṇa* is one of the five limbs of a syllogism that is essential for establishing the validity of an argument. For example, wherever there is smoke, there is fire "as in the kitchen."

Udayana (c. tenth century CE) : He was one of the philosophers who wrote a commentary called *Kiraṇāvalī* on Praśastapāda's commentary on *Vaiśeṣika-Sūtra*. In fact, he commented on both Nyāya and Vaiśeṣika. Another important commentary of Udayana is *Nyāyatātparyaṭīkā-Pariśuddhi*.

Udgītha (S) : He is one who sings the hymns in sweet musical tunes to entertain and propitiate the gods.

Udyotakara (c. seventh century CE) : He wrote a commentary called *Nyāyavārttika* on Gautama's *Nyāya-Sūtra*. He wrote another commentary called *Bhāṣyavārttika* in which he attacked Diṅnāga's position on Nyāya.

Ugly, Paradox of the : In our day-to-day experience, anything that is distasteful and unappealing is regarded as ugly. However, there are certain circumstances in which the ugly has an appealing aesthetic fascination and some kind of pleasure associated with it. This is called the paradox of ugly.

Ulūka (S) : He was the father of Kaṇāda, the founder of Vaiśeṣika *darśana*.

Umāsvāti (c. CE 85) : He was a Jaina philosopher, who wrote a commentary called *Tattvārthādhigama-Sūtra* on Jaina philosophy.

Uncaused Cause : It is a cause that does not have any cause to cause it. It is a cause that causes things to happen but it is not caused by anything. The term is generally applied to eternal God.

Uncertainty, Principle of : According to this principle, in subatomic level it is not possible to locate the position, and also the motion or velocity of an electron at a time. At a given movement either the position can be located or the velocity is known. Heisenberg and other physicists have applied this principle to explain the nature of uncaused events. This principle is also known as the theory of indeterminacy.

Understanding : Understanding is generally considered to be a faculty of mind which has the ability to comprehend, discern, judge, interpret, and explain. According to Descartes, it is the work of the faculty of understanding to have "clarity and distinction." Wittgenstein attacked this view of Descartes. According to him, understanding is not a mental phenomenon.

Understanding, Categories of : Kant postulated twelve categories of understanding that serve as the formal material in the acquisition of the knowledge of phenomena. They are also known as the pure concepts of understanding. They are classified under four major heads. They are as follows:

		Quantity
Universal	All S/is/P	Unity
Particular Some	S/is/P	Plurality
Singular This	S/is/P	Totality

		Quality
Affirmative	S is P	Reality
Negative	S/is not/P	Negation
Infinite	S/is/not-P	Limitation

		Relation
Categorical	S is P	Substance-Accident
Hypothetical	If S, then P	Cause-effect
Disjunctive	S is either P or Q	Reciprocity or Action-reaction

		Modality
Problematic	S may be P	Possibility-Impossibility
Assertor	S is P	Existence-Non-existence
Necessary	S must be P	Necessity-Contingency

Undetermined : It is nothing but the inability to judge the correctness or the truth of a given statement or a situation or an event.

Undistributed Middle : It is a formal fallacy that occurs when a middle term is not distributed in a syllogism. For example:

> All Danes are Scandinavians.
>
> Some Scandinavians are Norwegians.
>
> Therefore, some Scandinavians are not Danes.

In this syllogism, the middle term "Scandinavians" is not distributed even once. Hence it is a fallacious syllogism.

Unextended : In Descartes' philosophy Mind is regarded as an unextended substance. In other words, it does not occupy spatio-temporal relations.

Uniformity of Nature, Principle of the : According to this principle, the events that held good in the past are also going to hold good in the future. Under given conditions an event does not fail to occur. This keeps on happening whenever such conditions are present. This theory was attacked by David Hume. According to him, what guarantee do we have to say that the events that happened earlier are going to happen, under given conditions, in future? He says that there is no such guarantee.

Unity, Organic : According to Aristotle, the organic unity represents the fulfilment of a primary activity by the parts as an integral whole. No part of an organic whole acts independently. The parts of an organic whole act in relation to other parts in the same whole. Any change occurring in one part necessarily affects the other parts. For instance, human body is considered to be an organic whole.

Universal : Any universal is an abstract general idea which is apprehended by mind rather than by sense-experience. Mind forms abstract general ideas by abstracting certain essential features from many other features. Thus the reality of universal is independent of any exemplification in space and time. For example, "chair," "man," "tree," etc. are universal concepts.

Universal Proposition : It is a proposition that ascribes or denies a property to a specified class of individuals. For example, the proposition "All crows are black" is an universal proposition or generalization.

Universalia ante res (L) : It means "universals independent of thing." According to Plato, Universals have independent existence apart from particular things.

Universalia in rebus (L) : It means "universals existing within particulars." According to Aristotle, universals cannot exist apart from particulars. Every object possesses essential and accidental features. The essential features of an object form universal, whereas the accidental features form particular.

Universalia post res (L) : It means that "universals are derived from particulars." According to nominalists and conceptualists, universals are abstracted from particular existents.

Utility, Principle of : It is also known as pleasure principle. According to this doctrine, all human beings desire pleasure and the absence of pain. Each individual tries to seek his own pleasure.

Upamāna (S) : It means "similarity," "comparison." Nyāya, Mīmāṁsā, and Advaita admit *upamāna* as a valid means of knowledge. The resultant knowledge of *upamāna* is called *upamiti*. According to Nyāya, it is the cognition of similarity between two objects which gives rise to the knowledge of relation of a name and the object referred to by it. Unlike Nyāya, Mīmāṁsā and Advaita interpret *upamāna* as the cognition of similarity between one's own cow and hitherto unknown wild cow. The resultant knowledge of the cognition is in the form of realizing that one's cow is similar to the wild cow that is being seen at present.

Upaniṣads (S) : They are ancient Hindu sacred literary works that discuss the theories of creation, the nature of supreme Reality, *Brahman*, by knowing which everything is known. The four *mahāvākyas*, namely, consciousness is *Brahman* (*prajñānam brahma*), I am *Brahman* (*aham brahmāsmi*), That thou art (*tat tvam asi*), and This *ātman* is *Brahman* (*ayamātmā brahma*) are taken from the *Aitareya*, the *Bṛhadāraṇyaka*, the *Chāndogya*, and the *Māṇḍūkya* Upaniṣads respectively are the concluding portions of the Vedas (Vedānta). They are also known as Śruti. There are at least one hundred and eight Upaniṣads. There may be many more. The chief among them are:*Īśa*, *Kena*, *Kaṭha*, *Praśna*, *Muṇḍaka*, *Māṇḍūkya*, *Taittirīya*, *Aitareya*, *Chāndogya*, *Bṛhadāraṇyaka*, and *Śvetāśvatara*.

Utilitarianism : It is one of the theories of ethics. This theory emphasizes the greatest happiness to the greatest number. Jeremy Bentham and John Stuart Mill are the chief advocates of this theory. Bentham stressed on the quantitative aspect of utilitarian theory, while Mill stressed on the qualitative aspect of utilitarianism. The utilitarian standard, according to Mill, "is not the agent's own greatest happiness, but the greatest amount of happiness altogether." Further a distinction is made between act utilitarianism and rule utilitarianism. In the case of the former, the moral worth of an act is judged according to the consequences (good or bad) which are generated by each individual act judged in itself. In other words, it amounts to saying that at any given moment you should act in such a way that your act will contribute to the greatest good of the greatest number. In the case of the latter, the moral worth of an act is judged according to the consequences (good or bad) which ensue from following a general rule of conduct. In other words, it amounts to saying that you should obey those moral rules that generate the greatest happiness to the greatest number of people.

Utopianism : Thomas More in his work *Utopia* (1516) refers to perfect or ideal human conditions which cannot be realized at all. In this sense utopia is an imaginary social structure that embodies an arbitrary self-imposed social ideal as the goal of the society. A utopian ideal is impracticable and scientifically unfounded. Some philosophers termed Plato's *Republic*, Marx's communist society, and Gandhi's *rāmarājya* as utopia.

V

Vācaspati Miśra : He is one of the most important philosophers and commentators of the tenth century CE. He hails from Mithila. He is also called "Ṣaḍdarśana-vācaspati" as he wrote very important and exhaustive commentaries on cardinal texts of all the six systems of Indian philosophy. His last *magnum opus* is *Bhāmati* which is a commentary on Śaṅkara's *Brahmasūtrabhāṣya*. It is believed that he named it after his wife in recognition of her services throughout his life. The impact of *Bhāmati* is so great that it gave rise to a new tradition called "Bhāmati prasthāna" within the fold of Śaṅkara's Advaita. His other works are: *Nyāyasūcīnibandha* and *Nyāyavārttikatātparyatīkā* in Nyāya Darśana, *Tattvakaumudī* on *Sāṁkhya-kārikā* in Sāṁkhya Darśana, *Tattvavaisāradī* on *Vyāsabhāṣya* in Yoga Darśana, *Tattvabindu* and *Nyāyakaṇikā*, a commentary on *Vidhiviveka* in Pūrvamīmāṁsā Darśana. It is known that he wrote a commentary on the *Brahmasiddhi* called *Brahmatattvasamīkṣā* which is not available. He is known for his ability to uphold the position of the concerned school of philosophy in the matters of contention while commenting on each and every Darśana in a logically unassailable way.

Vacuous Statement : In logic, a vacuous statement is true because its subject term has no denotation or because its antecedent is false. For example, a conditional (if *p* then *q*) is true only when its consequent *q* is true or when its antecedent *p* is false. So "if men can fly then arsenic is poisonous" is vacuously true.

Vāda (S) : It means "debate or argument." It is one of the sixteen categories recognized by Nyāya. It is held between two people who are interested in knowing the truth and reality.

Vadakalai (T) : It is the one of the sects of Vaiṣṇavites known as the northern sect. The followers of this sect adhere to the teachings of Veṅkaṭanātha, who is popularly known as Vedāntadeśika. They respect Tamil (*divya*) *Prabandham* along with traditional Sanskrit texts.

Vagueness : Anything (a word, or an idea, or a statement, or a concept) that is not clearly defined is called vague. Vagueness cannot be confused with ambiguity. In the case of ambiguity, there may be two or more meanings for a word that are precise and definite. But in the case of vagueness, a decision cannot be reached as to whether or not to apply a word to a specific person. For example, the word "bald" does not specify the number of hairs one must have to be called bald.

Vāg-Yoga (S) : It is nothing but the sensation of *karma* particles through the medium of speech. The Jains believe that *vāg-yoga* is a type of *āśrava*.

Vaibhāṣika : It is one of the realistic schools of Buddhism belonging to Hīnayāna tradition. According to this school, both internal and external objects are real. But this school differs from Sautrāntika as regards the way in which external objects are known. They are directly perceived, but not inferred from their ideas or representations in the mind. This view may be called direct realism (*bāhya-pratyakṣa-vāda*).

Vaidika (S) : Anything that is related to the Veda is called Vaidika.

Vaikārika (S) : It refers to the *sāttvika* component of the ego. *Vaikārika* is the first development of the *buddhi* (intellect), according to the Sāṁkhya theory of evolution.

Vaikhānasa (S) : They are the Āgama texts that originated from Lord Brahmā. Vaikhānasa are the valid source books for the Viśiṣṭādvaitins and Dvaitins. Also, Vaikhānasa is a sect of Viśiṣṭādvatins and Dvaitins who follow the teachings of the sage Vikhānasa.

Vairāgya (S) : It means the "sense of detachment" or "world-weariness." A spiritual aspirant must develop this attitude towards the sensuous pleasures in order to realize *Brahman*, the Supreme Reality.

Vaiśeṣika (S) : It is one of the six orthodox systems of Indian philosophy founded by Kaṇāda. This school is closely associated with Nyāya. Etymologically the term *viśeṣa* means distinction. This system is called thus because of its unique doctrine of "particularity." The chief commentator of Kaṇāda's *Vaiśeṣika-Sūtra* is Praśastapāda. Udayana is another important commentator of this school. He wrote a commentary called *Kiraṇāvalī* on Praśastapāda's commentary. Another important commentary on Praśastapāda's work is Śrīdhara's *Nyāyakandai*. Vaiśeṣika accepted seven categories (*padārthas*). They are: substance (*dravya*), quality (*guṇa*), activity (*karma*), universal (*sāmānya*), particular (*viśeṣa*), inherence (*samavāya*), and non-existence (*abhāva*). According to this school, the valid *pramāṇas* are perception or *pratyakṣa*, inference or *anumāna*, and verbal testimony or *śabda*.

Vaiśvānara (S) : The Self (*ātman*) in the waking state is called *vaiśvānara*. It is responsible for all the creatures' diverse ways of enjoyment of various objects. According to Advaita, *vaiśvānara* is the cosmic Self (*samiṣṭi*) in the state of waking, whereas *viśva* is the waking individual self (*vyaṣṭi*).

Vākovākya (S) : It is the science of logic. In the *Chāndogya Upaniṣad*, Nyāya system is referred to as *vākovākya*.

Validity : In any system of formal logic, an argument or a proposition is said to be valid in so far as it is deduced or derived from a set of accepted premisses. Thus validity is attached to an argument or a proposition that abides by the above-said conditions. Validity cannot guarantee truth.

Vallabha (1481 – 1533) : His philosophy is known as Śuddhādvaita or pure non-dualism. According to the tradition he has developed the views of Viṣṇusvāmī. Vallabha held that *Brahman* is the independent reality and is identified with Śrī Kṛṣṇa. His essence is existence (*sat*), knowledge (*cit*), and bliss (*ānanda*). Souls and matter are His real manifestations. They are His parts. *Māyā* or *avidyā* is His power through which He manifests Himself as many. But this manifestation is neither an error nor an illusion. Therefore, Vallabha's view is neither *vivarta* nor *pariṇāma*. It is something in between the two. It is known as *avikṛtapariṇāmavāda*. The universe is not a *vivarta* for it is a real manifestation. It is also not a *pariṇāma* for this manifestation does not involve any change or transformation. The universe is a natural emanation from God. In epistemology, Vallabha opposes *samavāya* as a relation and treats it as mere *tādātmya*. Vallabha's important commentaries are *Aṇubhāṣya*, a commentary on *Brahma-Sūtra*, and *Subodhinī*, a commentary on *Bhāgavata*.

Values : They are socially accepted norms to evaluate objects, persons, and situations that form part and parcel of society. Value system is the backbone of a civilized society. Values may change from one society to another society and also from time to time. There are both material and non-material values. For example, every society abides by certain moral values which form part of non-material values.

Variable : In logic, a variable is a symbol or a sign that is substituted for a statement, or a predicate, or an object, or a term, or a meaning. For example, the variable *p* may stand for a statement such as "Sriram is courageous."

Varṇa (S) : It means "caste," "colour," and "letter." According to the traditional Hindu society, there are four main classes. They are (1) brāhmaṇas, who study and teach the Veda; (2) kṣatriyas, who are courageous people and rulers; (3) vaiśyas, who are traders; and (4) śūdras, who are supposed to serve others. This division is based on the functional division of the society.

Vasubandhu (CE 420 – 500) : He was a Buddhist philosopher who belongs to the camp of Sarvāstivādins, who hold the view that everything exists. They are the realists of an extreme type. His important work on Vaibhāṣika, which is a realist school, is *Abhidharmakoṣa*. Vasubandhu held that everything is a *dharma*, and *dharma* is explained in terms of an object or a category. There are two types of objects, namely, compounded and uncompounded. The former comprises matter (*rūpa*), mind (*citta*), the mental (*caitta*), and the non-mental (*cittaviprayukta*). The latter comprises space (*ākāśa*), which is eternal and omnipresent substance; the cessation of existence that is not observed by mind (*apratisaṁkhyānirodha*) and the cessation of existence which is attained by the knowledge of ultimate truth (*pratisaṁkhyānirodha*).

Vātsyāyana (S) : He is regarded as one of the most important commentators on the *Nyāya-Sūtra* of Gautama. He is the *bhāṣyakāra* of Nyāya School. According to Vātsyāyana, there is a distinction between Nyāya and *Āṇvīkṣikī*. The former combines logic with metaphysics, while the latter is only the science of logic. But most of the interpreters of Nyāya do not make this subtle distinction.

Vedānta (S) : The expression "Vedānta (Veda+anta)" signifies the end portions of the Veda (Upaniṣads), and also the essence of the Veda. There are around 108 Upaniṣads. Śaṅkara wrote commentaries on ten major Upaniṣads.

Vedas (S) : The word "Veda" is derived from the Sanskrit root *vid* meaning knowledge or wisdom. The Vedas are the most sacred teachings of Hinduism. They are orally transmitted to the students by the teachers in *āśrama*s. According to the Hindu tradition, the Vedas are eternal, uncreated by humans, and nothing could have preceded them. They are four in number. They are the *Ṛgveda*, the *Yajurveda*, the *Sāmaveda*, and the *Atharvaveda*. The Vedas are classified into the *mantra*s or the Saṁhitās, the Brāhmaṇas, the Āraṇyakas, and the Upaniṣads. A *mantra* is a sacred passage to be recited, whereas a *saṁhitā* is the conglomeration of *mantra*s. The Brāhmaṇas deal with the ritualistic aspects of the original texts, whereas the Āraṇyakas, which are part of the Brāhmaṇas, deal with certain meditations to be observed, and the kinds of rituals to be performed outside home. The Upaniṣads are the end portions of the Vedas. They contain the reflections about the ultimate reality. The *mantras*, and the Brāhmaṇas form *karma-kāṇḍa*, while the Āraṇyakas form the *upāsanā-kāṇḍa* and the Upaniṣads form the *jñāna-kāṇḍa*.

Verbal Dispute : It is often contrasted with a real dispute. A verbal dispute is caused by the meanings of the words or the concepts that are applied in a particular usage.

Veridical : In contrast to non-veridical experiences such as hallucinations, illusions, delusions, mirages, etc. a veridical experience is always characterized by truth. This expression is commonly used in the "argument from illusion" to distinguish veridical experiences from non-veridical ones. For details see Perception.

Verification or Verifiability : It is one of the epistemological principles introduced by logical positivists to demarcate meaningful assertions from meaningless ones. According to Moritz Schlick, the pioneer of logical positivist movement, the meaning of a statement is the method of its verification. According to A.J. Ayer, another important logical positivist, a statement is meaningful only if it is empirically verifiable. For example, the statement "God is omnipotent" is a metaphysical assertion because it cannot be verified by sense-experience, hence nonsensical. The logical positivists dismissed all those statements that cannot be verified by empirical experience. Thus the statements about ethics, aesthetics, and religion are treated as nonsensical. The only consolation given to the statements of ethics is that they are called pseudo-statements. The advocates of this principle dub the ethical pronouncements as mere emotions of the speaker. For details see Emotivism.

Verity : The quality of being true or genuine is called verity. It is also regarded as the conformity of a statement with the fact or reality.

Vidyā (S) : According to the Upaniṣads, there are thirty-two types of meditations for achieving liberation. Kauṭilya recognized four important branches of knowledge (*vidyā*). They are *āṇvīkṣikī* or logic and philosophy, *trayī* or the Vedic religion, *vārtā* or economic science and philosophy of wealth, and *daṇḍanīti* or the science of polity.

Vidyāraṇya (sixteenth century CE) : Vidyāraṇya was the founder of the great Vijayanagara Empire. He was an Advaitin. His important work is *Pañcadaśī*. The work is so named because it consists of fifteen chapters (*pañcadaśa-prakaraṇa*). The fifteen chapters are grouped into three parts: *viveka-pañcaka* (dealing with the discrimination of the real from the non-real); *dīpa-pañcaka* (expounding the nature of the Self as pure consciousness); and *ānanda-pañcaka* (dwelling on the bliss nature of *Brahman*). In fact, each part deals with the three aspects of *Brahman*, namely, *sat*, *cit*, and *ānanda*. The essential doctrines of the Vedānta are dealt with in every chapter. Vidyāraṇya analyses the three states of experience, namely, waking, dream, and deep sleep to show the reality of the self.

Vienna Circle : It is a philosophical movement started by Moritz Schlick and his associates who shared a common interest. Logical positivism is the label given to the ideas of Vienna Circle (1922). The chief objectives of the Circle are to eliminate metaphysics from the sphere of philosophy, to make philosophy a genuine branch of knowledge, and to promote a powerful "logical technique" to solve the problems of philosophy. According to the members of the Vienna Circle, the sole function of philosophy is the "logical clarification of our thought and the concepts of science." The other members of the Circle were Rudolf Carnap, Hans Hahn, Otto Neurath, Victor Kraft, Carl Menger, Kurt Godel, Friderich Waismann, and Carl Hempel.

Vijātīya-bheda (S) : It is the difference that exists between two things belonging to two different universals (*jāti*). For example, a cow is different from a table.

Vijñāna (S) : According to the Buddhist doctrine of the dependent origination (*pratītyasamputpāda*), *vijñāna* is considered to be one of the links in the causal chain of existence.

Vijñānamaya-kośa (S) : It is known as intellectual sheath. It is the fourth of the five sheaths discussed in the *Taittirīya Upaniṣad*. The aim of this discussion is to analyse the nature of the internal world. *Vijñānamaya-kośa* is located within mental sheath (*manomaya-kośa*). The subtle body consists of *vijñānamaya-kośa*, *manomaya-kośa*, and *prāṇamaya-kośa*.

Vindication : It is a way of justification of induction that tries to show that though it is uncertain whether induction will work or not, it is reasonable to apply induction as a method like any other method. The argument goes like this: If there is no regularity in the universe, then all the methods along with induction fail. When there is no such irregularity, then induction works.

Viparīta-khyāti (S) : This theory of error advocated by Kumārila is known as misapprehension. According to this theory, error occurs only when the object appears other than what it is. The object of error is held to be real, but it is the identity of its appearance with its basis that is unreal. There is a logical distinction between truth and error. In fact, error is the result of misapprehension, but not mere non-apprehension. In other words, it is the result of both omission and commission.

Viśeṣa (S) : It means particularity. It is one of the categories in Vaiśeṣika metaphysics. This is the category that distinguishes one particular from the other. These *viśeṣa*s are eternal, innumerable, and partless. The pluralism of Vaiśeṣika is the outcome of this category.

Viśiṣṭādvaita (S) : It is also known as qualified monism. Viśiṣṭādvaita is one of the three schools of Vedānta. One of the chief propagators of this school of thought is Śrī Rāmānuja. In fact, Viśiṣṭādvaita represents the Śrīvaiṣṇava system of thought. The term "Śrīvaiṣṇavism" (Śrī + Viṣṇu) implies that the Supreme

Lord of this school of thought is Śrī Viṣṇu. The appellation "Viśiṣṭādvaita " is given to this school of thought only after Rāmānuja (eleventh century CE). In fact, Rāmānuja himself used the appellation "Viśiṣṭadravyaikya." The appellation "Viśiṣṭādvita" was given by Sudarśanasūri (thirteenth century CE) who wrote his commentary *Śrutaprakāśikā* on Rāmānuja's *Śrībhāṣya*. Another important figure of this school is Veṅkaṭanātha (Vedāntadeśika). According to this school of thought, there are three ultimate realities. They are: Īśvara (God), *cit* (mind), and *acit* (non-mind). These three realities form an organic unity. This is the reason why it is called Viśiṣṭādvita. The *Brahman* (God) is *saguṇa*. The Lord has all the good qualities in Him. According to this school, liberation is possible through *bhakti-mārga*. Both action (*karma*) and knowledge (*jñāna*) are subservient to *bhakti*. Another important concept of this school is self-surrender (*prapatti*).

Viṣṇu (S) : He is the Supreme Lord. According to Viśiṣṭādvaita, He is the sole Reality, and the only means to liberation. He is always consorted with *Śrī* (Lakṣmī).

Vitalism : According to vitalism, all the living beings are endowed with an active principle called life or life force. In the language of Aristotle, it is called *entelechy*, whereas Bergson calls it *élan vital*. Such a vital force cannot be reduced to physical or chemical processes.

Vitaṇḍavāda (S) : It means "destructive argument." It is one of the sixteen categories accepted by Nyāya. The aim of *vitaṇḍa-vāda* is to demolish the doctrine of the opponent without offering any alternative one.

Vitarka (S) : It is a state of *samādhi*. It is of two types, *savitarka* and *nirvitarka*. In *savitarka samādhi*, the mind concentrates on the objects by remembering their names and qualities, whereas in *nirvitarka samādhi*, the mind concentrates on the objects without remembering their names and qualities.

Vivartavāda (S) : It is also known as the theory of apparent change. This theory is advocated by Advaita, according to which things appear other than what they are. According to Advaita theory of causation, the world is an illusory appearance superimposed on *Brahman* by *māyā/avidyā* (ignorance). Vivartavāda is best explained by means of rope-snake analogy. Sometimes a rope appears to be a snake. At that time the cognition of the snake is accepted as true. But only in the subsequent cognition we come to realize that it is only a rope. Thus the rope appearing as snake is only a case of transfiguration. As a matter of fact, there is no change in the form of transformation of rope into snake.

Vivekananda, Swami (1863 – 1902) : His original name was Narendra Nath Dutta. He was an Indian social reformer and a pupil of Sri Ramakrishna. Vivekananda tried to bring the ideas of Advaita Vedānta closer to the scientific principles of his day. He advocated a single religion based on the teachings of Advaita, which he called "universal religion."

Void : The Greek atomists admitted the notion of void as an empty space or Vacuum. It is also known as "not-being" as opposed to "being." The void is devoid of all qualities. It does not have power, potentiality, and existence. It is regarded as a pure space that is absolute nothing. It is the belief of the atomists that atoms occupied the void before they moved to some other place. However, the void will be occupied by other atoms. The atomists' defence of void is based on the following arguments. (1) Unless there is void between the objects and the atoms that constitute objects, there cannot be movement of objects and atoms. (2) Every object consists of void within itself. This is the reason why certain objects can be compressed and some objects absorb liquids. When objects are compressed atoms occupy void that exists between them.

Volition : It is the act of willing that is inherent in human individual. In that sense every physical act is preceded by a volition. This particular theory was bitterly criticized by Gilbert

Ryle in his *The Concept of Mind*. According to Ryle, if volition is a voluntary mental act, then it must originate in some other volition. Then that volition as a mental act must originate in some other volition. Thus it leads to *ad infinitum*.

Voltaire (1694 – 1778) : It was the pen-name of Francois Marie Arouet. He was a very famous French essayist, historian, and philosopher who is considered to be a major figure of the English enlightenment. He was exiled and imprisoned for his writings. He was a champion of the spirit of tolerance during the time of enlightenment. His views on religion and ethics are based on natural law. He opposed all forms of dogmatic religion. His chief philosophical works include: *Lettres Philosophiques* (1734); *Candide* (1759); and *Dictionnaire Philosophique* (1764).

Voluntarism : It is a thesis according to which the will or the volition is more fundamental than intellect, reason or passion in the description of reality. The two prominent advocates of such a theory are Schopenhauer and William James.

Vortex Theory : This theory was advocated by Cartesians and Occasionalists. According to this theory, empty spaces and vacuums do not exist. A subtle matter occupies the space. It is also known as "ether." There is no unoccupied space. The notion of unoccupied space is an illusion or false.

Vr̥tti (S) : It is a modification of the internal organ. *Vr̥tti* is what makes knowledge of empirical reality possible. It acts as a connection between the knowing subject and the object known. It is a modification of *antaḥkaraṇa* that pervades the object.

Vr̥tti-jñāna (S) : It means empirical knowledge. The knowledge of empirical objects, according to Advaita, is possible through the modifications of *antaḥkaraṇa*, and the reflection of consciousness therein. *Vr̥tti-jñāna* is of two types, namely, *aparokṣa* (immediate) and *parokṣa* (mediate).

Vyākaraṇa (S) : It means grammar. *Vyākaraṇa* is considered to be one of the important limbs of the Vedas.

Vyakti (S) : This term refers to individual. It is opposed to the term universal (*jāti*).

Vyāpti (S) : It means invariable concomitance. It is one of the most important aspects in inference (*anumāna*). An inferential cognition is based on *vyāpti*. The correlation between the two terms, the one which is pervaded, and the term that is the pervader, is called *vyāpti*. The reason (*hetu*) is pervaded and the subject (*sādhya*) is the pervader. It is the relation of co-existence of the *hetu* and *sādhya*. In an inference, "wherever smoke exists there exists the fire." This is the statement of *vyāpti*.

Vyāsa (S) : He is also known as Veda-Vyāsa. He was the one who classified the Veda into four main Vedas. The final fixation of the *R̥gveda* might have taken place sometime in 1000 BCE. The fixation of *Sāmaveda* and *Yajurveda* might have been done around 800-700 BCE. The *Atharvaveda* was arranged in the course of the Brāhmanization around 600 BCE. The expression "Vyāsa" came to be regarded as the personal name. Vyāsa is supposed to be the mythical compiler of many important works of Hinduism such as *Mahābhārata*, Purāṇas, and some commentaries. He is called Kr̥ṣṇa Dvaipāyana in the *Mahābhārata*. He derived this name from the colour of his skin, which is dark (Kr̥ṣṇa), and the island (*dvīpa*), where he was born on the banks of the Yamunā.

Vyatireka-vyāpti (S) : It means negative pervasion. It is one of the forms of inference in which only the agreement of absence of the middle term and the major term is observed. For example, where there is no object, there is no shadow of that object.

Vyāvahārika-satya (S) : This expression refers to empirical reality, which has mere relative existence.

Vyavasāya-jñāna (S) : It means original cognition. It is a view of Nyāya, according to which any determinate cognition that provides only cognition of an object, but not the awareness of such a cognition by the cognizer, is known as *vyavasāya-jñāna*.

W

Waismann, Freidrich (1896 – 1959) : He was an Austrian-born philosopher closely associated with the Vienna Circle. According to Waismann, the human choice of conventions is key to mathematical conventionalism. He strongly believed that our linguistic conventions influence our world-view. The open texture of concepts rules over a strict verifiability by observation. His important works include: *An Introduction to Mathematical Thinking* (1936 in German and 1951 in English); *The Principles of Linguistic Philosophy* (1965); and *How I See Philosophy* (1968).

Wai wang (C) : Mencius used this expression that refers to an individual who through his virtues and abilities gains the necessary qualifications of a ruler.

Wang Chung (c. 27 – 100) : He was an independent thinker, although his writings bear the mark of Taoistic naturalism. He was an ardent critic of all erroneous beliefs.

Wang Yang-Ming (1473 – 1529) : He was a Neo-Confucian philosopher. He was well known for his doctrines of the unity of knowledge and action (*chih-hsing ho-I*) and innate knowledge of the good (*liang-chih*). Wang was also branded as a metaphysical idealist for he belived in the quasi-identity of mind and *li* (principle reason). Wang was basically concerned with the question, how can an individual become a Confucian sage (*sheng*)? This question can be answered, according to Wang, only by those who have understanding and commitment to the Confucian vision of *jen* (ideal of the universe as a moral community).

Ward, James (1843 – 1925) : He was a British philosopher and psychologist who came under the influence of Lotze, Herbert, and Brentano. Ward was critical of the associationism advocated by Bain and its allied discipline known as reductive naturalism that was popular in the nineteenth century. Ward's psychology disapproved the sensationalism advocated by associationists that regarded mind as passive and capable of only receptivity. According to Ward, mind's inherent activity reveals that there is a prior existence of ego or subject capable of feeling and of conation. Such a subject shapes both experience and behaviour of an individual by the willful exercise of attention. His important work is "Psychology" written for the *Encyclopedia of Britannica* (1886, 9th edition).

Warranted Assertibility : This expression is associated with John Dewey's instrumentalism. According to him, the abstract knowledge that is obtained by strict use of the methods of logic and science may be confused and unarticulated, but it can be ordered and unified in our experience.

Watson, J.B. (1878 – 1958) : He was the first self-styled psychological behaviourist who held that human behaviour must be explained in terms of "stimulus" and "response." He studied and served as an instructor at the University of Chicago. According to Watson, the psychologist himself can provide the stimulus to control the human activity. The programme for a behaviouristic psychology employed the objective methods of the biological sciences and excluded the introspective method of earlier psychology. One of the most important works of Watson is *An Introduction to Comparative Psychology* (1914).

Wayward Causal Chain : It is a causal chain that takes an unexpected direction in the process of analysing any key concept. Sometimes causal analysis is hampered by a deviant causal chain. This is possible in two ways: (1) those cases of causal analysis in which the accepted causal route is adhered to, but the desired or anticipated event does not occur; and (2) those cases of causal

actual entities or events are related to each other and how these entities are further related to other entities. He held that consciousness and mind are not entities apart from events. Every event is an item of experience, with two poles, one mental and the other physical, between which it fluctuates. Consciousness is an ordering and unifying aspect of events, such that the whole appears as more than the aggregate of its parts and as a new unit of occurrence. He viewed self-consciousness as a best example of an actual occasion. Whitehead viewed reality as an infinite capacity and potentiality for the occurrence of event-experiences. It is also an indefinite actualization of this capacity in a world of realized experiences and occurrences. His important works include, *Treatise on Universal Algebra* (1903); *Mathematical Concepts of the Material World* (1905); *Principia Mathematica* (1910-13 in 3 volumes), co-authored with Bertrand Russell; *Principles of Natural Knowledge* (1919); *The Concept of Nature* (1920); *Science and the Modern World* (1925); *Process and Reality* (1929); and *Adventures of Ideas* (1933).

Whole : It is a unity or a system as in an organic whole. It also refers to something that has parts. The term "whole" is frequently used in the disciplines like biology, psychology, and sociology. But, most of the applications of the term "whole" explicitly refer to the principle that asserts that a whole is more than the sum total of its parts. According to empiricist methodology, the meanings of the terms "whole," "part," "sum," and "more" are far from clear. But, it is interpreted by many that in the part-whole relationship, the whole is an object whose parts are mutually interdependent in the sense that a change affecting one of its parts will bring about changes in all other parts; and because of this interdependence the "whole" is said to be more than the sum total of its parts. Such a whole is known as organic or biological whole. If the whole is identified with the sum total of its parts, such a whole is technically called mechanistic whole.

Wholeness : A totality of integral parts of an organism and their interconnections viewed as a whole. Thus a whole is not a mere sum total of its integral parts, but more than that. Such a whole is known as biological or organic whole.

Whole-part, Principle of : The nature of a whole cannot be apprehended just by analysing its constituent parts. A proper explanation of the nature of a whole is possible only when the interrelationships that exist among its constituent parts are understood.

Will : It is an individual's conscious determination to perform certain action or actions. Idealist philosophers are of the view that will power is purely intrinsic. It cannot be influenced by external factors. On the other hand, objectivists and materialists conceive that will power is generated in the human individual by virtue of his participation in a social process. Thus it is objective, and is necessarily influenced by certain factors in the society.

Will : It is the power to control and determine our actions in the context of our desires and intentions.

Will and the Understanding : Benedict Spinoza made no distinction between the understanding and the will. According to him, once the understanding is clear and distinct, then there is no chance for the will to reject it. Spinoza believed that the perception of truth is identical with having knowledge of that perception, and accepting it.

Will, Autonomy of the : According to Immanuel Kant, the condition of the pure rational will, in which the will is guided to choose, is unaffected by such things as consequences, results, ulterior ends, happiness, compulsion, fame, pleasure for oneself or for the other. It is affected by an obligation to rational and universal principles.

Will to Believe : William James used this expression. According to him, the will to believe in the absence of evidence is a reasonable and creative aspect of the human mind. This will lead to further possibilities for discovery and commitment.

Will to Power : This expression is used by Nietzsche. According to him, all human actions are ultimately motivated by power and aim at control over others. The means and values used in this process are determined by the individual wishes and the creative standards of the Superman.

William of Ockham (1285 – 1349) : He was a British philosopher known for his principle of economy called "Ockham's razor." According to this principle, one should not multiply the things or entities beyond necessity. As a radical empiricist he maintained that the particular objects of sense-experience are the only reality. In his theory of knowledge, he distinguished intuitive knowledge from abstractive knowledge. The former, claimed Ockham, is immediate and direct, while the latter is derived from intuitive knowledge. It is not the knowledge of facts, but of propositions.

Wisdom : The highest kind of knowledge is called wisdom. It also refers to our prudent judgement as to how to use knowledge in our day-to-day life. According to Plato, the knowledge of the Forms alone is characterized as wisdom.

Wisdom, Arthur John Terence Dibben (1904 – 93) : He is a British analytical philosopher who was chiefly influenced by Ludwig Wittgenstein. He supported Russell and Wittgenstein in holding the view that certain entitles are no more than "logical constructions" out of more fundamental entitles (for example, sense-impressions). The statements of the "logical constructs" can be translated into the statements about the sense-data. His chief works include: *Other Minds* (1952); *Philosophy and Psychoanalysis* (1953); and *Paradox and Discovery* (1965).

Wittgenstein, Ludwig (1889 – 1951) : He is an Austrian-born British linguistic philosopher who advocated logical atomism in his very famous work *Tractatus Logico-Philosophicus* (1919).

The Wittgenstein of *Tractatus* is known as early Wittgenstein. The early Wittgenstein maintained that language mirrors the reality. He tried to construct a kind of ideal or logically perfect language to analyse the nature of reality. Thus he advocated formalism. The only function of philosophy, according to Wittgenstein, is the logical clarification of thought. In order to show that there is one to one correspondence between language and reality he introduced picture theory of meaning. The Wittgenstein of *Philosophical Investigations* (1953) is known as later Wittgenstein. Later Wittgenstein attacked his earlier position only to show that formalism which he advocated to show the isomorphic relation between language and reality is not a tenable one. Instead, he advocated informalism to show that language has many functions. In the place of picture theory of meaning he advocated use theory, according to which the meaning of a word is derived from the context in which it is used. In fact, he tried to solve the problem of meaning by introducing the notion of "use." The other important works of Wittgenstein, some of them are posthumous publications, include: *Notebooks* (1914 – 16); *Remarks on the Foundations of Mathematics* (1956); *The Blue and Brown Books* (1958); *Zettle* (1967); and *On Certainty* (1969).

Wolf, Christian (1679 – 1754) : He was a German rationalist philosopher who has provided a systematic approach to philosophy. As an ideal follower of Leibniz, he felt that philosophy is basically concerned with the study of essence rather than existence. All philosophical maxims can be deduced, claimed Wolf, from Leibniz's principle of sufficient reason and identity. One of the notable works of Wolf is *Philosophia Prima Sive Ontologia* (1729).

Word : It is a conventional sign, and is treated as an independent unit of communication. A word is a systematic arrangement of alphabets. It can be a noun, verb, adverb, adjective, preposition, conjunction, etc.

World-event : It is an event conceived in four dimensions including its duration. The three dimensions of space are length, width and height. Duration is the dimension of time.

World Ground : It is the source, cause, essence, or sustaining power within or behind the world.

World-line : It is a line conceived in four dimensions. It can also be a line that cuts across space-time.

World-point : It is a four-dimensional point. It can also be a geometrical point that is durationless.

World Soul : It is an analogue of human soul. Since world is produced out of life and animation it is regarded as animate. Since it is animate, world as a whole consists of a soul. Such a view was advocated by Plato, Stoics, neo-Platonists, and Bruno.

World-View : In German it is expressed as *weltanschauung*. It is an expression that denotes the system of beliefs that globally informs a given culture's outlook on life, namely, its basic way of perceiving reality and organizing society.

Wundt, Wilhelm Max (1832 – 1920) : He was a famous German physiologist, psychologist, and philosopher. He was a Professor of Philosophy at Leipzig and there he founded the first psychological laboratory in 1879. Wundt's psychological approach combines exact physical and physiological measurement to stimulus and response along with an introspective analysis of the internal experience that supervenes between stimulus and response. He affirmed exact parallelism between the physiological and psychological series. On its introspective side, Wundt's psychology classified sensations with respect to modality, intensity, duration, extension, and so on. It also classified feelings into pleasant and unpleasant, tense or relaxed, excited or depressed. One of the most important works of Wundt is *Principles of Physiological Psychology* (1873-74).

X

Xenophanes of Colophon (c. 570 – 475 BCE) : He was an ancient Greek poet-philosopher who founded the Elatic school. He opposed the doctrines of both Thales and Pythagoras. He attacked the Pythagorean doctrine of the transmigration of souls in one of his poems. He was a well-known critic of anthropomorphism and mythology. He openly declared that people create gods only in their own image. According to him, there is only one God who is different from mortal beings. In his epistemology, Xenophanes proved that sense-experience cannot give us complete knowledge of reality. He made a distinction between knowledge and opinion. The latter is the result of sense-experience.

Xenophon (c. 430 – 350 BCE) : He was a Greek soldier and historian. He authored a number of Socratic dialogues. His important works cover history, education, politics, etc. His interest in philosophy as a social thinker made him write Socratic dialogues. These dialogues provide us with valuable information about Socrates and his followers. As a matter of fact, these dialogues are the only ones to survive intact apart from those of Plato. Some of the important Socratic dialogues of Xenophon include: *Memorabilia, Apology of Socrates*; *Symposium*; and *Oeconomicus*.

Y

Yādavaprakāśa (tenth century CE) : He was the teacher of Śrī Rāmānuja. According to Yādavaprakāśa, *Brahman*, individual souls, and the world of matter are all real, and yet they are both identical with, and different from, one another. He did not realize that the same relation could not be both identity and difference. He argued that it was natural and that our theory should accord with facts, but not facts with theory. He advocated *brahmapariṇāmavāda*. Although *Brahman* transforms itself into the world, it can remain pure and perfect. Śrī Rāmānuja did not agree with this view of Yādavaprakāśa.

Yajña (S) : It is a ritual sacrifice performed by the Hindus to propitiate the gods for obtaining what is desired by them. This is known as *daiva-yajña*. This *yajña* is distinguished from *brahma-yajña* in which one dedicates oneself to *Brahman*, the Supreme Reality. There are other kinds of *yajña*. They are: *dravya-yajña* is performed with actual materials of libation, *tapo-yajña* is performed for asceticism or self-control, *yoga-yajña* is performed for union or communion, *svādhyāya-yajña* is performed for scriptural studies, and *jñāna-yajña* is performed for knowledge or wisdom.

Yājñavalkya (S) : He was a great Upaniṣadic sage and seer who taught his wife Maitreyī about the nature of *Brahman/ātman*. In the *Bṛhadāraṇyaka Upaniṣad* there is a reference to Yājñavalkya. He held that nobody wants an object of pleasure just for the object's sake, but for the sake of *ātman*. Therefore one should know what *ātman* is. By knowing *ātman* everything is known. When it is realized that everything is *ātman*, then there is no difference between the knower and the known. In other words, this *ātman* is *Brahman* (*ayam ātma brahma*). In the famous debate between Yājñavalkya and a number of enquirers about the truth, the former tells Ārtabhāga that after death the senses and mind of an individual become one with their deities, who are their sources. But the actions (*karmas*), merits or demerits, of the individual accompany them and lead them to another life. To Cakrayāna he tells that *ātman* lives through the life-principle and works through all life functions. Thus none can see the seer, none can hear the hearer, none can know the knower. To Uddālaka he tells that *ātman* is present inwardly in everything (*antaryāmin*) and knows everything, but nothing knows it. It is the ultimate seer, hearer, thinker, and knower. To his second wife Gārgī he tells that *ātman* is neither subtle nor gross; it is neither the senses nor the life-principle. It is neither inwards nor outwards. It is imperishable. At its command the sun and the moon move, the elements and time perform their functions; everything is founded in it. It is the same as *Brahman*, the *Brahman* is knowledge and bliss (*vijñānam ānandam brahma*). To the king Janaka, Yājñavalkya teaches that the *ātman* is the guiding light of man. It is true that the light of the sun, the moon, the fire, and speech guide a man. But in the absence of all these, it is the light of the *ātman* that guides a man. For example, in dream we act and see things. What is the light that guides us during dream state? It is the light of the *ātman*. This light is imperishable.

Yajurveda (S) : It is one of the four Vedas. It mainly consists of prose formulae and explanatory passages. This Veda is available in two major recensions called dark (*kṛṣṇa*) and white (*śukla*) *Yajurveda*. This Veda contains passages to be recited at the sacrifices, mainly those addressed to the various objects that are utilized in the sacrifices and at other rituals. There are various explanations and interpretations, different theories and postulations, narrations of stories. All these are connected to the rituals or elements connected with the rituals. In the dark *Yajurveda* the text and the interpretations are mixed together, but in the white *Yajurveda* there are only the original texts. The dark *Yajurveda* is also known as the *Taittirīya* branch and the white is known as Vājasaneyī branch. The former contains three more branches, namely, Kāṭhaka, Kapisthala, and Maitrāyaṇī, and the latter contains two more sub-recensions, namely, Mādhyandina and Kaṇva.

Yama (S) : **1.** He was a Vedic god and the son of Vivaśvat. He was supposed to be mortal who for the first time saw the path to the region beyond, and he went over there and became a king of that region of joy beyond. He was known in the Hindu tradition as the god of death. **2.** It is one of the eight limbs of *aṣṭāṅga yoga* propounded by Patañjali. It means abstention from injury through thought, word, or deed (*ahiṁsā*), from falsehood (*asatya*), from stealing (*asteya*), from passions and lust (*brahmacarya*), and from avarice (*aparigṛha*). In fact, *yama* is one of the five external aids to *yoga*.

Yāmunācārya (tenth century CE) : He was one of the distinguished teachers of the Viśiṣṭādvaita tradition. Śrī Rāmānuja was indebted to Yāmuna, although he did not meet him while he was alive. It appears that Śrī Rāmānuja was influenced by Yāmuna's *Siddhitrayī*. Following the tradition of *Pāñcarātrāgama*, another name for the Vaiṣṇava tradition, Yāmuna held that the *Brahman* is the same as the personal God (Īśvara), and the individual souls and the world are real. This view is accepted by both Yāmuna and Śrī Rāmānuja. But, they did not accept the view that the relation between God and the world, and the individual souls is both identity and difference. See Viśiṣṭādvaita.

Yāska (eighth century BCE) : He was the author of *Nirukta* or etymology, the first lexicon of the Āryans. Yāska developed a distinct philosophy of language that emphasized the significance of the meaning of the grammatical predicate and the verb.

Yathārtha-khyāti (S) : It is also known as the theory of the apprehension of the real. This theory of error is advocated by

Rāmānuja. According to him, error is one of omission only, but not commission. Since all knowledge is intrinsically valid, there is no scope for error. Knowledge always corresponds to its object. *Sat-khyāti* or *yathārtha-khyāti* means that in knowledge it is the existent real that is cognized. In other words, there is real object corresponding to its content. The theory of quintuplication suggests that some particles of silver are actually present in the shell. Therefore, when the shell is mistaken for silver, it (silver) is partially presented to consciousness. Hence there is no ideal or subjective element in error. It is only partial knowledge and there is no watertight distinction between knowledge and error.

Yatirāja : It is one of the names of Śri Rāmānuja.

Yin and Yang (C) : These are the two basic concepts in ancient Chinese philosophy. In the *Book of Changes* these two expressions are used as opposites. It is also held that everything in this world is produced out of the interaction between *yin* and *yang*. They are opposed to each other like light and darkness, cold and warm, being and non-being and so on. According to Lao Tzu, *yin* and *yang* out of their own nature would not have produced themselves or interacted with each other. The thing that provided basis and context for their interaction is *Tao*. It is the source of both being and non-being. It is regarded as the first principle of existence.

Yoga (S) : It means "practice," "contemplation," "union." It is one of the six orthodox systems of Indian philosophy founded by the sage Patañjali. It is an allied system of Sāṁkhya. According to Patañjali, Yoga is a spiritual path to attain perfection through the control of the body, senses and the mind. As an allied system of Sāṁkhya, Yoga, by and large, accepts the metaphysics and epistemology of the former. Yoga believes in God as the highest Self distinct from other selves. Hence it is called *seśvara* or theistic Sāṁkhya. The classical Sāṁkhya is *nirīśvara* or atheistic. The *Yoga-Sūtra* of Patañjali is classified into four parts. They are: (1)

samādhipāda that deals with the nature and aim of concentration; (2) *sādhanapāda* that discusses the means to realize this end; (3) *vibhūtipāda* that deals with the supra-normal powers which can be obtained by means of Yoga; and (4) *kaivalyapāda* that deals with the nature of liberation and the reality of transcendental self. Yoga aims at the perfection of the body, the senses and the mind. It believes that a sound mind needs a sound body. The sensual passions often distract both body and mind. In order to conquer sensual passions, Yoga suggests the eightfold path (*aṣṭāṅga yoga*). The eightfold path of Yoga consists of the following aspects. (1) *Yama* means *ahiṁsā* or abstention from injury by means of thought, word and deed, *satya* or abstention from falsehood, *asteya* or abstention from stealing, *brahmacarya* or abstention from passions and lust, and *aparigraha* or abstention from avarice. (2) *Niyama* means self-culture that includes *śauca* or external and internal purification, *santoṣa* or contentment, *tapas* or austerity, *svādhyāya* or self-study, and *Īśvarapraṇidhāna* or devotion to God. (3) *Āsana* means steady and comfortable posture that disciplines the body for proper meditation. There are various kinds of postures. (4) *Prāṇāyāma* means control of breath by regulating inhalation, retention, and exhalation. Such an act is highly conducive to the concentration of mind. (5) *Pratyāhāra* is the control of the senses and consists in withdrawing the senses from their objects. These five aids are the external aids (*bahiraṅga sādhanā*) to Yoga. There are three internal aids (*aṅtaraṅga sādhanā*). They are: (1) *Dhāraṇā* or fixing of the mind on the object of meditation like the tip of the nose or the mid-point of the eyebrows or the lotus of the heart or the image of one's favourite deity. The mind must be steadfast like an unflickering flame of a lamp. (2) *Dhyāna* or meditation consists in the undisturbed flow of thought of the object of meditation (*pratyayaikatānatā*). (3) *Samādhi* or concentration is the final stage in Yoga. In this stage the mind is completely absorbed in the object of meditation. In *dhyāna* the act of meditation and the object of meditation remain separate, but they become one in *samādhi*. It is the ecstatic state in which the link with the external world is completely cut-off. *Samādhi* is of two kinds. They are: (i) *Samprajñāta* or conscious *samādhi;* and (ii) *Asaṁprajñāta* or supra-conscious *samādhi*. In the case of the former the object of concentration persists (*ekāgra*), and in the latter it is transcended (*niruddha*).

Yogācāra (S) : It is one of the idealistic schools of Buddhism also known as *Vijñānavāda*. This school derives its name from its emphasis on critical inquiry (*yoga*), and exemplary conduct (*ācāra*). It is believed that this school was founded by Asaṅga. The distinguishing feature of this school is that it admits the reality of pure consciousness (*ālayavijñāna*) alone. Consequently, external objects are unreal. They are mere mental projections. Yogācāra accepts the Doctrine of Dependent Origination (*pratītyasamutpāda*). According to this school, consciousness is an ever-changing stream. Everything is ultimately reduced to the ideas of mind. In other words, no object can ever be experienced apart from consciousness. Hence consciousness and its objects are one and the same.

Yogaja (S) : It is one of the three kinds of extra-sensory perception (*alaukika pratyakṣa*) recognized by the Nyāya School. This is the intuitive and immediate apprehension of all existence, past, present and future, and of all objects, the infinitesimal as well as the infinite. This perception is possessed by the *yogins* through the power of meditation. It is akin to the *kevala jñāna* of the Jains, and the *bodhi* of the Buddhists, the *kaivalya* of the Sāṁkhya-Yoga, and *Aparokṣānubhūti* of the Vedāntins.

Yogāṅgas (S) : They are the eight limbs of *Yoga* prescribed by Patañjali. They are: *yama, niyama, āsana, prāṇāyāma, pratyāhāra, dhāraṇā, dhyāna*, and *samādhi*. See Yoga.

Yukti (S) : It means "reasoning." It is not treated as a separate *pramāṇa* by any Indian philosophical system. According to Caraka, *yukti* invoves a series of reasonings to arrive at a logical conclusion. For example, the forecasting of good or bad harvest from the conditions of the ground, the estimated amount of rains, climatic conditions and the like come under *yukti*. Thus it is only a logical aid to a *pramāṇa*, but cannot be treated as an independent *pramāṇa*.

Yuga (S) : It means "age or period." According to the Hindu mythology, there are four important *yugas*. They are: (1) *Kṛta yuga*, the golden period, was the period in which the *dharma* walked with its four legs so as to respect the righteousness. (2) *Tretā yuga* was the period in which Śrī Rāma was born as the Yugapuruṣa to protect *dharma*, which was walking with three legs. (3) *Dvāpara yuga* was the period in which Śrī Kṛṣṇa was born as the Yugapuruṣa to protect *dharma* against *adharma* that crippled righteousness and made it walk with two legs. (4) *Kali yuga* is the present age or period in which Kalki will be born as Yugapuruṣa to protect *dharma* against *adharma*. The latter made the former walk with its lone leg. Even that single leg is not in proper form.

Z

Zabarella, Jacopo (1532 – 89) : He was an Italian Aristotelian scholar. He wrote a number of commentaries on Aristotle's *Physics* and *On the soul*. Also, he discussed the views of other interpreters like Averroes. Zabarella's most distinguished work in the field of logic is his *Opera Logica* (1578). According to him, logic is the preliminary inquiry that provides us with the necessary tools for any proper philosophical analysis. He recognized order and method as two important tools of philosophical analysis. Order helps us in organizing the content of any given discipline in order to approach and apprehend it easily. Method helps us in drawing syllogistic inferences. Zabarella classified the orders and methods adopted by other interpreters into compositive and resolutive orders and methods. The compositive order is applicable to theoretical disciplines wherein it proceeds from the first principles to their consequences. The resolutive order is applicable to practical disciplines wherein it proceeds from the desired ends to appropriate means. A compositive method, according to Zabarella, arrives at particular instances from general principles by means of inference. The resolutive method arrives at general principles from particular instances like in inductive reasoning.

Zaddik, Joseph Ibn (1080 – 1149) : He was a judge at Cordova and a well-known Jewish philosopher. His important philosophical work written in Arabic is the *Microcosm* (Heb. Olam Katon).

Zarathustra (Zoroaster) (c. 628 – 551 BCE) : He was the Persian prophet and the founder of the Iranian religion called

Zoroastrianism and Zend Avesta, the basic sacred text. Zoroaster was a married man with children before he received the revelatory message from God at the age of thirty. The angel Vohu Mana told Zoroaster that there is only one God Ahura Mazda and he must serve as His prophet. Zoroaster was murdered at the age of seventy-seven.

Zen Buddhism : It is a variety of Buddhism originated in China in sixth century CE, and became very popular in Japan through the writings of D.T. Suzuki. One of the heroes of Zen is the fierce looking Indian monk Bodhidharma who brought Buddhism to China. Unlike the other Buddhist schools, Zen Buddhism postulates one essence of the Buddha. It preaches "sudden awakening," the comprehension of truth. Zen as a way of life is neither a philosophy nor a religion. As such it incorporates certain aims, prescribes certain practices and rests upon certain presuppositions. Zen as a way of life is not a matter of beliefs, but of doing. The aim of Zen is to arrive at a state of experience wherein there is no distinction between subject and object. Such an experience allows one to see directly the fullness of one's self without the mediation of intellect. The three basic features of Zen are practice, enlightenment and teachings. Of these three, practice is accorded the highest importance. *Zagen* is the chief discipline of Zen practice and enlightenment. It aims at achieving the required conditions for seeing one's self directly in its purity and fullness. The discipline of *zagen* can be practised by bringing one's hands, feet, arms, trunk, and head under one's control. It is followed by certain special forms of concentration to bring the activities of mind under control. Thus *zagen* involves an idea of *yoga* that has a history of more than four thousand years.

Zend Avesta : It is a commentary on the basic text composed by the followers of Zarathustra. This commentary is used as a sacred scripture by the Parsis although it is unintelligible due to its archaic language.

Zeno of Elea (c. 490 – 430 BC) : He was an ideal disciple of Parmenides, and is well known for his logical paradoxes.

Following the line of Parmenides, Zeno argued against the notion of divisibility of space and time, and motion. His views can be summed up in the following way:

(1) It is logically impossible to conceive plurality of things as divisibility is an absurdity.

(2) The idea of motion leads to an unwarranted contradiction. This he tried to show with a well-known paradox called "moving arrow" paradox. As reported by Aristotle, Zeno's arguments involve the concept of infinity. According to the bisection argument advanced by Zeno, there is no motion because that which moves must traverse the half of the distance at every stage before it arrives at the goal. This leads to *ad infinitum*. Therefore, there is no possibility of motion. The Achilles argument is also advanced to show the impossibility of motion. According to this argument, the fleet-footed Achilles and a slow moving tortoise run a race. The tortoise is given a head start, and it is expected that Achilles can quickly overtake it. But, by the time Achilles reached the tortoise's starting point, the latter has moved some distance. Thus it gained a new start. In the process Achilles lags behind as he can never cover the distance moved by the tortoise.

Zeno the Stoic (C. 330 – 260 BCE) : He is also known as the Zeno of Cytium. He was the founder of stoicism. He was a pupil of the Cynic philosopher Crates. Although the complete works of Zeno are not available, it appears that he laid down the general principles of the Stoic school. One of the fundamental tenets of this school is that the end of man is to live in harmony with nature.

Zero : It is the greatest contribution of Indian mathematicians to the field of mathematics. As per the available records, zero was invented by the Indians in CE 595. Some hold the view that zero is the outcome of the "potent void" or *śūnyatā* or *śūnya*. Or it might have been the other way round. Though there appears to be some similarity between these two unlike "void," zero has the potential to upgrade the value of other numerals when it is placed after them. It is also believed that whosoever has invented zero is treated second to Buddha in his greatness.

Zetetic (Gk) : It is an expression for "an enquiry," "an investigation," "a search for something." It refers to the inquisitiveness of the seeker of the truth.

Zodiac : It is a sign used by the Indian astrologers in the early centuries of our time. Perhaps they were influenced by the Greeks. However, both the Greek and the Indian astrologers have their own significance. The Indian astrology is based on the movement of planets or *graha*s.

Zoroastrianism : It is an ancient Iranian religion. Its origin is attributed to the mythical prophet Zarathustra, also known as Zoroaster. Its main teachings are based on the view that good is a personification of the God of light and evil is the personification of the God of darkness. Zoroastrianism is a monotheistic religion according to which Ahura Mazda is the only Supreme God, although there is an internal dualism in Godhead. The supreme God is all-powerful, all-wise, and all-good. He is the creator and also the ruler of the world. The three important ethical commandments of Zoroastrianism are: good thoughts, good words and good deeds. Zoroastrianism believes in the life after death, and the law of retribution. Fire is treated as very pure and treated as a symbol of divine purity by Zoroastrians like the Hindus. The eschatological doctrines of Zoroastrianism maintain that at the end of the world there will be resurrection of the dead and a future saviour will be born to a virgin. These views of Zoroastrianism certainly influenced Judaism and Christianity.

Zwingliism : This appellation is given to the theological thought of Huldreich Zwingli (1481-1531), the early Protestant reformer, of Zurich, Switzerland. Zwingli's theology focused on the all-pervading nature of God. He accepted St. Augustine's doctrine of man's original sin and sinfulness with some modifications. In the famous Marburg Colloquy, he differed with Luther and his followers on the interpretation of Lord's Supper.

Important Foreign Phrases

Addendum (L)	: an appendix, thing or things added.
Ad hoc (L)	: for this purpose or work. An *ad hoc* Hypothesis.
Ad homenium (L)	: to the man, personal.
Ad infinitum (L)	: to infinity, and so on to its logical conclusion.
Ad interim (L)	: for the time being.
Ad nauseam (L)	: to the point of disgust.
A fortiori (L)	: with stronger reason.
Alias (L)	: otherwise; normally applied to second name.
Alibi (L)	: elsewhere, it is used as a legal term.
Alma mater (L)	: fostering mother, the institute where one studied or trained.
Apologia (Gk)	: a written justification of one's conduct and actions.
A posteriori (L)	: from effect to cause, by induction.
A priori (L)	: from cause to effect, by deduction.
Apropos (F)	: to the point.
Argumentum ad hominem (L):	rejecting someone's arguments by making use of his own principles.
Bona fide (L)	: in good faith.

Bonhomie (F)	:	good nature.
Bourgeois (F)	:	member of the middle-class, homely.
Bourgeoisie (F)	:	the middle-class (in Marxist use: the capitalist classes).
Campo santo (It)	:	graveyard.
Canard (F)	:	a rumour.
Causa sui (L)	:	self-caused.
Cogito ergo sum (L)	:	I think, therefore I am.
Corrigendum (L)	:	correction(s).
Cul-de-sac (F)	:	dead end or blind alley.
Cum grano salis (L)	:	with some skepticism.
Cum privilegio (L)	:	with privilege.
De facto (L)	:	from the fact, in reality.
Dei gratia (L)	:	by the grace of God.
De jure (L)	:	in law, rightful.
De novo (L)	:	anew, fresh.
Detour (F)	:	round about, not direct.
Divide et impera (L)	:	divide and rule.
Double enendre (F)	:	double meaning.
Elan (F)	:	dash or spirit.
Elite (F)	:	the best, the pick.
Emeritus (L)	:	from merit.
En attendant (F)	:	in the meantime.
En bloc (F)	:	in a lump.
En effect (F)	:	in effect.
Enfant terrible (F)	:	a child who causes disturbance.

En masse (F) : in a body.
Ergo (L) : therefore.
Eureka (Gk) : I got it!
Ex gratia (L) : as an act of grace.
Ex hypothesi (L) : from the hypothesis.
Ex nihilio nihil fit (L) : nothing comes out of nothing.
Ex officio (L) : by virtue of his office.
Ex parte (L) : from one side, from a partisan.
Ex post facto (L) : after the event.
Ex tempore (L) : without any preparation.
Ex voto (L) : something made because of a vow.

Facsimile (L) : do the like, exact copy.
Factotum (L) : a man of all work.
Fait accompli (F) : a feat that is already accomplished.
Faux pas (F) : a false step.

Genius loci (L) : a genius of the place.
Gratis (L) : free of charge, for nothing.

Helluo librorum (L) : a devourer of books, a bookworm.
Honoris causa (L) : for the sake of honour.

Ibidem (*ibid*) (L) : in the same place.
Ignoratio elanchi (L) : ignoring the point at issue.
Impedimenta (L) : things that obstruct progress.
In camera (L) : in secret.
In esse (L) : in being, in fact.
In posse (L) : in potential existence.
In situ (L) : in its original place.

Inter alia (L)	:	among other things.
In toto (L)	:	in total.
In vacuo (L)	:	in empty space.
Ipso facto (L)	:	in the fact itself.
Ipso jure (L)	:	by the law itself.
Jacta est alea (L)	:	the die is cast.
Jus divinium (L)	:	by the divine law.
Jus gentium (L)	:	by the law of nations.
Kalendao Graecae (Gk)	:	the Greek calendar.
Kitsch (G)	:	counterfiet.
Lacuna (L)	:	a gap.
Laisser-aller (F)	:	freedom from restraint.
Laissez-faire (F)	:	non-interference, allowing things to find their own level.
Lex non scripta (L)	:	the unwritten law.
Lex scripta (L)	:	the statute law.
Lingua franca (It)	:	the mother tongue.
Locus standi (L)	:	a place for standing.
Mandamus (L)	:	we command.
Mea culpa (L)	:	by my own fault.
Mean monde (F)	:	beautiful or fashionable world.
Me judice (L)	:	in my opinion.
Modus operandi (L)	:	the way of working.
Modus vivandi (L)	:	the mode of living.
Mutatis mutandis (L)	:	after making the necessary changes.

Nihil ad rem (L)	:	nothing to the point.
Non sequitur (L)	:	a false conclusion, it does not follow from this.
Nous (Gk)	:	mind, intelligence.
Obiter dictum (L)	:	a thing said by the way.
Odium theologicum (L)	:	the hatred of theologians.
Onus probandi (L)	:	the burden of proof.
Pace (L)	:	not to give offence to.
Par excellence (F)	:	pre-eminently.
Par example (F)	:	for example.
Pari passu (L)	:	side by side.
Pas (L)	:	precedence.
Passim (L)	:	everywhere.
Persona non grata (L)	:	non acceptable person.
Post hoc ergo propter hoc (L)	:	after this, therefore, on account of this.
Prima donna (It)	:	first lady.
Prima facie (L)	:	at first view, on the face of it.
Pro forma (L)	:	for the sake of form.
Pro rata (L)	:	according to rate or proportion.
Protege (F)	:	one under the protection of another.
Quid pro quo (L)	:	something in return.
Quo ad hoc (L)	:	to this extent.
Raconteur (F)	:	a teller of stories.
Raison d'être (F)	:	the reason for a thing's existence.
Reductio ad absurdum (L)	:	a reduction to the absurdity.

Recontre (F)	:	an encounter, a hostile meeting.
Résumé (F)	:	a summary, synopsis.
Sanctum sanctorum (L)	:	holy of holies.
Sic passim (L)	:	so everywhere.
Sine cura (L)	:	without charge or care.
Sine die (L)	:	without a day being appointed.
Status quo (L)	:	the stage in which, the existing condition.
Sub judice (L)	:	under consideration.
Sui generis (L)	:	of its own peculiar kind.
Summom bonum (L)	:	the chief good.
Tableau vivant (F)	:	a living picture.
Tabula rasa (L)	:	a blank sheet.
Tertium quid (L)	:	a third something.
Ut infra (L)	:	as below.
Ut supra (L)	:	as above.
Verbatim et literatim (L)	:	word for word and letter for letter.
Vice versa (L)	:	conversely.
Vis-à-vis (F)	:	face to face.
Viva voce (L)	:	by the living voice.
Wanderlust (Gr)	:	passion for travelling.
Weltanschauung (Gr)	:	world-view, conception.
Zeitgeist (Gr)	:	time-spirit.
Zum Beispiel (Gr)	:	for example.